W9-CXN-030

CHEF SAUCES
OVER 1300 SAUCES

By Matthew and Mary Ann Fazio

Published by Fazio Publication
Affiliated with Dennis Alfonso

To order additional books, send a check or money order for $29.95*
(FREE SHIPPING) to:

CHEF SAUCES
3931 E. Cholla Canyon Drive
Phoenix, AZ 85044
(800) 411-9899 / (602) 604-1542
Arizona residents please add 8% for sales tax

OR

Visit our web site www.chefsauces.com

All rights reserved. No part of this book may be reproduced or transmitted in any form
or by any means, electronic or mechanical, including photocopying, recording or by any
information storage and retrieval system without written permission from the author,
except for the inclusion of brief quotations in a review.

Copyright 1992	Txu 517 229	CHEF SAUCES Over 1300 Sauces	$29.95
First printing	March 1994		
Copyright 2000		CHEF SAUCES Over 300 Hot! Hot! Hot! Sauces	$19.95

Disclaimer

This book was created for research purpose for sauce making for all types of foods. Sold for the understanding that the
author has suggested these ingredients for the purpose of their taste. The amount of sauce we suggest is good for between
2 and 8 servings. Every effort has been taken to make this book mistake free in the recipe of ingredients. We are not
responsible for typographical error in ingredient content. This book was designed for use as a general suggestion in sauce
making. We feel that this book is for educational and entertainment purposes.

We as writer and owners of the CHEF SAUCES have tried the sauces in our book on foods we preferred. The degree of
hot flavor is what we found hot to our taste. Any chile peppers can be substituted in these recipes.

The authors and Fazio Publishing shall have neither liability nor responsibility to any person or entity with respect to any
loss or damage caused, or alleged to be caused, directly or indirectly by the information contained in this book.

The Chef Sauces Tree of Life Sauce
Take four beautiful people.

Philomena DiGiovanna
&
Charles Fazio

GiaGiananti
&
Daniel Tedesco

Put them together.

Joseph Fazio
Matthew Fazio
Louis Fazio

Mary Ann Tedesco
Patricia Tedesco
Daniel Tedesco

Blend gently.

Matthew Fazio & Mary Ann Tedesco

made

Deborah Ann
Charles Anthony
Daniel Matthew

Deborah Ann Fazio & Christopher Stueben	Charles Anthony Fazio (& Anita Guardi)	Daniel Matthew Fazio & Kathleen Rae
Nicole Brittany	Danielle Nicole	Mark Daniel
James Matthew	Charles Joseph	Alyssa Deanna
Tara Michelle		

Charles Anthony Fazio & Angela Dulin
David

Joseph Fazio	Louis & Regina (Santeramo)	FazioPatricia (Tedesco) & John Morgan	Daniel & Barbara (Kaiser) Tedesco
Joseph	Dana	Donna Ann	Daniel
James	Alicia & Richard	Doreen	David
		Patricia	

Donna & Frank Deperino (Gina & Christa)
Doreen & Joe Winkhart (John, Nicholas & Baby)
Tricia & Kevin McGuire (Vincent & Dillon)

Blended with additional Love
Chris, Erica, Stefanie & Dennis Alfonso

A LA KING SAUCE

½ cup all purpose flour
¼ lb. mushrooms, sliced
1 egg yolk, lightly beaten
2 tbsp. dry sherry (optional)

¼ green bell pepper
¼ tsp. white pepper
1 egg yolk, beaten

¼ red bell pepper
¼ cup butter
2 cups milk

Melt the butter in a saucepan, over medium heat. Add green and red pepper strips and sauté 1 to 2 minutes. Add the mushrooms; sauté over low heat until the peppers are soft. Add flour, salt and pepper, and then blend. Warm milk and pour into saucepan all at once, using a whisk to produce a smooth sauce. Bring sauce to a boil. Stir a little of the hot sauce into the egg yolk. Lower the heat and stir in egg yolk. Add sherry, if desired.
*Good over poultry or shrimp.

****

ACAPULCO SAUCE

½ tsp. ground ginger
1 tbsp. garlic powder
6 oz. Mandarin orange
½ cup chopped green Jalapin peppers

6 oz. pineapples
1 tbsp. lemon juice
1 tbsp. cornstarch

2 tbsp. butter
½ cup Kaklina
1 tbsp. water

Mix all ingredients together in a bowl, until well blended.
*Use to marinate poultry overnight.

****

ADOBO SAUCE

1 tbsp. chopped ginger
½ tsp. black pepper
½ cup limejuice

6 cloves garlic
1 tsp. cumin seed

1 ½ tsp. salt
1 sliced onion

Coarsely chop the garlic and ginger. Place in a mortar and pestle with the salt and mash to a smooth paste. Work in cumin, pepper and lime juice (or sour orange juice) to taste.
*Use to marinate pork loin or chicken overnight.

****

ABRUZZESE SAUCE

12 garlic cloves, pressed
1 tbsp. red pepper flakes
6 oz. Parmesan and Romano cheese

1-cup olive oil
2 tbsp. parsley

1-cup mushrooms
1-cup chicken broth

Crush pepper flakes, then julienne mushrooms. Heat oil in a saucepan; add all ingredients, except broth, cook for 5 minutes. Add broth and simmer 10 minutes.
*Use over pasta.

AIOLI GRAND SAUCE

1 ½ slices white bread
1 tbsp. red wine vinegar
⅛ tsp. cayenne pepper

6 cloves garlic
½ cup mayonnaise
1 ¼ cup olive oil

¼ cup milk
salt

Place garlic and bread in a food processor for 10 seconds. Add milk, mayonnaise, wine, cayenne pepper and salt and blend a few second. Add oil a little at a time.
*Good over poultry.

****

AIOLI SAUCE

6 med. garlic cloves
½ cup olive oil

2 egg yolks
2 tsp. lemon juice

Salt
Pepper

Press the garlic cloves through a garlic press into a medium bowl. Add egg yolks, one at a time, and beat until combined. Slowly drip in oil, beating constantly. When sauce begins to thicken, stir in lemon juice or vinegar, and continue to add oil, gradually increasing to a steady trickle. Enough oil has been added when sauce becomes really thick. Add pepper; stir well.
*Good over poultry and vegetables.

****

ALBERT SAUCE

2 tbsp. English mustard
1 tbsp. vinegar

⅛ cup Horseradish
2 tbsp. sugar

1 tbsp. butter

Heat butter and mustard in a saucepan, then add remainder of ingredients. Continue to heat for 2 minutes.
*Good over fish or ham.

****

ALFREDO SAUCE I

1-cup heavy cream
1 lg. egg yolk

1 cup Parmesan cheese
1 tbsp. lemon juice

½ cup butter
3 oz. pine nuts

Heat butter and cream in a saucepan until boiling, whisk in cheese, lemon juice, egg yolk and pepper. Heat for 3 minutes and sprinkle in pine nuts.
*Good over poultry.

ALFREDO SAUCE II

1 ½ cup heavy cream
¾ cup grated Parmesan

1 tsp. coarse pepper
½ tsp. salt

¼ cup butter

Melt butter in a saucepan; and add cream, heat for 2 minutes. Add salt, nutmeg, cheese and pepper, heat for 2 minutes more.
*Good over poultry.

****

ALL DAY ALL NIGHT CHILI SAUCE

2 lbs. ground beef
1 lg. red bell pepper
2 28-oz. cans plum tomatoes
1 24-oz. can vegetable juice
2 15-oz. cans red kidney beans

3 tbsp. olive oil
1 lg. green pepper
2 tbsp. chili powder
4 garlic cloves

1 lg. onion
1 tbsp. oregano
½ tsp. sugar
¼ tsp. cumin

Cook ground beef in large saucepan over high heat, crumbling with fork until browned; pour off drippings. Heat oil in a medium skillet over medium high heat. Add onion and bell peppers, stirring occasionally; cook until soft, about 10 minutes. Add peppers and onion mixture to ground beef. Then add the 2 cans of tomatoes to meat mixture. Add remaining ingredients, except the kidney beans. Simmer until thick, stirring occasionally, 3 hours, add kidney beans and cook for a few minutes more.
*Good over rice.

****

ALLSPICE LIQUEUR SAUCE

2 tsp. Allspice liqueur

1 pkg. soup mix

8 oz. sour cream

Use onion or mushroom soup mix. Blend all ingredients together in a bowl, until well blended. Chill.
*Good over poultry or as a dip.

****

ALMOND CHOCOLATE BAR SAUCE

4 - 1.45 oz. almond chocolate bars

¼ cup hot water

Melt the four chocolate bars in the top of a double boiler, and then add hot water. Stir until smooth.
*Good over ice cream and desserts.

ALMOND LIQUEUR SAUCE I

½ tsp. almond extract   ½ cup sugar syrup   1 ½ cup vodka

Place all the ingredients together in a bottle; shake well. Mature for 5 days.
*Good over duck, poultry, desserts or ice cream.

****

ALMOND LIQUEUR SAUCE II

3 oz. chopped almonds   Pinch of cinnamon   1 ½ cups vodka
½ cup sugar syrup

Combine all ingredients in a bottle, shake well; let mixture stand about 2 weeks. Strain and sweeten. Mature a few more weeks.
*Good over duck, poultry, desserts or ice cream.

****

ALMOND SAUCE

½ tsp. garlic puree   1 chopped onion   2 tbsp. butter
½ cup minced parsley   2 cups tomato puree   1 tbsp. oil
½ cup almonds   ½ tsp. sugar   Salt to taste
Freshly ground pepper

Heat butter and oil in a saucepan; sauté onion and garlic puree but do not brown, about 5 minutes. Stir in tomato puree and parsley; season with salt and pepper. Stir in sugar and almonds and simmer for 10 minutes more.
*Good over poultry.

****

ALMOND-RUM FUDGE SAUCE

½ cup chocolate syrup   2 tbsp. dark rum   1 tbsp. butter
2 tbsp. toasted slivered almonds

In a small saucepan, heat chocolate syrup and butter. Stir over low heat until smooth, thick and shiny, about 4 minutes. Add rum and almond.
*Good over ice cream, sliced pears or bananas.

ALSATIAN ONION SAUCE

3 lg. sweet onions, sliced
3 cups veal stock
salt and pepper

2 tbsp. sherry vinegar
1 cup heavy cream
⅛ tsp. nutmeg

6 tbsp. butter
½ tsp. sugar

Melt butter and onions in a saucepan, cook for 10 minutes on a low heat. Slowly add sugar and cook 10 minutes. Add 1 ½ cups of stock and cook another 10 minutes over medium heat. Add ½ cup cream and cook an additional 5 minutes. Pour into blender or food processor and puree, adding sherry vinegar and the remaining cream and stock. Heat an additional 5 minutes.
*Good over veal or meat.

****

AMARETTO BAR SAUCE

1 clove garlic, minced
¼ tsp. ground cinnamon
¼ tsp. fennel

¼ cup soy sauce
¼ tsp. cloves
Dash cayenne pepper

¼ cup Amaretto
¼ tsp. anise

Place all ingredients together in a saucepan and heat until well blended, about 2 minutes.
*Use over meat and poultry.

****

AMARETTO DUCK SAUCE

1 cup light brown sugar
½ cup honey or butter

½ cup orange juice

⅓ cup Amaretto

Place all ingredients in a saucepan and heat until dissolved.
*Use over duck.

****

AMARETTO RASPBERRY SAUCE

10 oz. frozen raspberries
 2 tbsp. Amaretto

1 tsp. cornstarch

1 tbsp. water

Place raspberries into a blender; add cornstarch and water. Pour mixture into a small saucepan and heat until thickened. Stir Amaretto into mixture.
*Good over poultry.

AMERICAN CREOLE SAUCE

½ lg. green bell pepper   4 med. sliced mushrooms   ¼ cup butter
4 fresh parsley, chopped   ¼ red bell pepper   1 med. onion
2 cups Espagnole Sauce   Red (cayenne) pepper   Salt and pepper

Melt butter in a saucepan over low heat. Add mushrooms, onion, green and red peppers and parsley.
Cook 9 to 10 minutes until peppers are soft. In a separate saucepan, warm Espagnole Sauce. Add salt,
pepper and red pepper, to vegetables, according to taste. Bring just to a boil; reduce heat and simmer,
covered, 45 to 50 minutes. Transfer to a gravy boat and serve hot.
*Good over pork.

****

AMERICAN-STYLE LIGHT MARINADE SAUCE

1 tsp. chili pepper   ½ cup olive oil   2 lg. onions
½ cup Worcestershire sauce   ¼ cup molasses   2 lg. tomatoes

Seed tomatoes, and then coarsely chop tomatoes and onions. Combine all ingredients, except the oil, and
blend in food processor or blender. Gradually add olive oil until smooth.
*Good to marinade beef.

****

ANCHOVY SAUCE I

¼ cup strips of ham   2 anchovy fillets   1 tbsp. olive oil
¼ cup cucumber   1 tbsp. lemon juice   ⅓ tsp. chervil
Dash of flour   1 tbsp. butter

Marinate cucumber in oil. Heat all ingredients in a saucepan, for 15 minutes.
*Good over veal.

****

ANCHOVY SAUCE II

6 - 8 anchovies, chopped   2 cloves garlic   ¼ cup olive oil
2 cups tomatoes, chopped   ½ cup Italian olives   ¼ tsp. salt
½ cup parsley, minced   ¼ tsp. black pepper

Heat olive oil in skillet; add garlic. Drain oil from anchovies, chop and add to skillet, mash until almost a
paste. Add tomatoes and olives; simmer 5 minutes, until mixture thickens, add parsley, salt and pepper.
Simmer 8 to 10 minutes.
*Good over pasta.

ANCHOVY TOMATO SAUCE

3 tbsp. olive oil	1 lg. onion	2 lbs. ripe tomatoes
1 tsp. sugar	2 whole cloves	1 bay leaf
1 garlic clove	2 tsp. vinegar	Salt and pepper
2 oz. can anchovies or ½ tube anchovy paste		

Pour oil in a saucepan, add onion and cook until translucent. Add peeled, chopped tomatoes and remaining ingredients. Simmer uncovered 20 minutes.
*Good over pasta.

****

ANDALOUSE SAUCE

½ cup tomato sauce	2 cups of mayonnaise	½ sweet red pepper
1 tsp. tarragon or chives		

Combine very thick tomato sauce with mayonnaise in a medium bowl. Fold in red pepper, seeded and chopped fine, along with 1 teaspoon of tarragon or chives, or a mixture of the two. Mix well.
*Good over poultry or pasta.

****

ANDALUSIAN SAUCE

1 cup Veloute Sauce	1 red bell pepper	2 tbsp. tomato paste
1 tbsp. chopped parsley	1 tsp. lemon juice	1 tbsp. chopped pimento

Char pepper under broiler until black all over. Set-aside until cool; peel off skin. Cut pepper into lengthwise strips, then dice. Combine all ingredients in a bowl.
*Good over pasta.

****

ANGELICA SAUCE

½ oz. angelica root or stems	1 ½ cups vodka	½ cup sugar syrup
½ oz. chopped almonds or almond extract		

Soak the cut up angelica and almond extract in vodka for 5 days. Strain; then add sugar syrup or honey. Mature 2 months.

Optional flavorings: pinch of nutmeg, mace, cinnamon, 1 clove garlic, yellow food coloring optional.
*Good over desserts or ice cream.

ANISE SEED SAUCE

⅔ tbsp. anise seed   ½ tsp. fennel seed   1 ½ cups vodka
½ tsp. coriander seed   ½ cup sugar syrup

Grind the seeds and soak in vodka for 1 week. Shake frequently. Add sugar syrup.
*Good over desserts or ice cream.

****

APPLE CIDER CHEESE SAUCE

3 tbsp. apple juice   1 tsp. lemon juice   ½ tsp. dry mustard
1-cup apple cider   1 tbsp. cornstarch   Dash white pepper
3 cups (12 oz.) shredded Cheddar cheese

Pour cider and lemon juice in a saucepan and cook over medium heat until bubbly. Lower heat and gradually stir in cheese. Continue to heat until cheese melts. In a small bowl, blend mustard and cornstarch with apple juice. Blend into cheese mixture and continue to cook, stirring 2 to 3 minutes or until mixture is thick and creamy. Season with white pepper.
*Good over pork.

****

APPLE GLAZE SAUCE

1-cup apple juice   2 tbsp. minced onion   3 tbsp. butter
2 tbsp. cider vinegar   1 tsp. brown sugar

Heat butter with onion for 1 minute in a saucepan. Add apple juice, cider vinegar and brown sugar. Heat for another 2 minutes.
*Good over pork.

****

APPLE RAISIN SAUCE

1 ¼ cups apple juice   ¼ cup ketchup   4 slices onion
1 tbsp. brown mustard   1-cup beef broth   2 tbsp. oil
1 cup cooked chopped pork   ½ cup raisins   1 tbsp. cornstarch

Heat oil in skillet, stir in onion and sauté until transparent. Add 1-cup apple juice, ketchup, mustard and beef broth; mix well. Add raisins and pork chops, cover and simmer 45 minutes or until tender.
*Good over pork chops or pasta.

APPLE SAUCE

2 tbsp. lemon juice	1 lb. apples	3 tbsp. butter
Pinch of ground cinnamon	1 whole clove	Sugar to taste

Place the peeled, cored, sliced apples in a medium saucepan. Add butter, lemon juice, clove and sugar. Cover and cook over very low heat until apples are soft. Remove the clove. Use a fork to beat the mixture gently until it is fluffy. Add a pinch of cinnamon.
*Good over pork.

****

APPLE SCOTCH SAUCE

1 cup dark brown sugar	2 egg yolks	3 tbsp. flour
½ tsp. grated nutmeg	1 cup whole milk	¼ tsp. salt
½ cup applesauce	¼ cup cream	1 tbsp. vanilla

Put egg yolks, brown sugar, flour, salt, milk, and cream in a saucepan; beat together with whisk. Cook over medium heat, stirring until thick and smooth. Stir in vanilla. Mix applesauce with nutmeg and add to mixture.
*Good over desserts or ice cream.

****

APPLE-ROSEMARY SAUCE

1 cup dry white wine	2 shallots, chopped	2 cloves garlic
1 pint heavy cream	2 lg. apples, chopped	2 sprigs rosemary
1 tbsp. Dijon mustard	2 tbsp. coarse mustard	

Heat wine in a saucepan; add shallot and garlic. Reduce heat and add cream and simmer 20 minutes. Add apples; continue to simmer for 20 minutes. Add mustard and rosemary, simmering another 15 minutes. Remove rosemary and puree sauce.
*Good for lamb.

APPLEJACK CREAM SAUCE

1 cup applejack brandy
3 tbsp. unsalted butter
¼ lb. shiitake mushrooms

2 cups whipping cream
1 med. shallot, minced
2 oz. smoked ham, julienne

3 garlic cloves
½ med. apple

Combine applejack, apple, garlic and shallot in a medium saucepan and simmer until mixture is almost dry, stirring occasionally, about 10 minutes. Add cream and cook until slightly thickened, about 20 minutes. Strain sauce through fine sieve; keep warm. Melt butter in heavy large skillet over low heat. Add mushrooms and sauté 2 minutes. Add ham and sauté 2 minutes. Remove from heat.
*Good over pasta.

****

APPLESAUCE-MAYONNAISE-MINT SAUCE

¼ cup cider or white wine
1 tsp. Dijon mustard
Freshly ground pepper

1 cup applesauce
½ cup mayonnaise
2 tsp. freshly grated horseradish

2 sprigs mint
Salt to taste

Put applesauce into saucepan with cider or wine and mint. Simmer for 15 minutes until slightly reduced. Remove mint and cool. Stir in horseradish, mayonnaise, and seasonings. Chill
*Good over pork.

****

APRICOT SAUCE I

1 ⅓ cups apple cider
½ tsp. ground allspice

8 oz. dried apricots
¼ tsp. ground cloves

6 tbsp. brown sugar

Pour apple cider over dried apricots in a bowl. Cover and refrigerate overnight. Purée apricot mixture in a blender. Stir in brown sugar, cinnamon, allspice and ground cloves. Place mixture in a saucepan and heat until well blended.
*Good over ham.

****

APRICOT SAUCE II

⅓ cup apricot nectar

⅓ cup chicken broth

2 tbsp. cornstarch

Place all ingredients in a saucepan and heat until thickened.
*Good over ice cream, desserts and poultry.

APRICOT & COGNAC SAUCE

⅔ cup dried apricots
1 tsp. cornstarch

1 ½ to 2 tbsp. sugar
¼ cup Cognac

1 cup water
2 tsp. water

Cook apricots with 1 cup water and sugar, in a saucepan, 5 to 7 minutes or until they are soft; the liquid will reduce slightly. Using a slotted spoon, remove apricots. Set aside. Mix cornstarch with the 2 teaspoons water; add to apricot liquid and cook over medium heat, stirring, until the liquid thickens and clears. Transfer to a food processor or blender. Add reserved apricots and process to a puree. Return apricot puree to saucepan. Add Cognac and heat without boiling. Serve hot.
*Good over pork.

****

APRICOT BUTTER SAUCE

2 ½ cups dried apricots
½ cup granulated sugar

3 ¼ cups water
1 tbsp. apricot brandy

2 tbsp. lemon juice

Put water, apricots and sugar in 2-quart saucepan over medium-high heat; bring to a boil. Reduce heat to low; simmer uncovered 10 to 15 minutes, stirring occasionally, until apricots are tender and about 1 cup water is left. Remove from heat; stir in lemon juice and brandy. Process in food processor or blender until smooth and thick.
*Good on toast, muffins, in custard or in tarts.

****

APRICOT GLAZED SAUCE

⅛ tsp. ground cloves
1 ½ tbsp. lemon juice

1 tbsp. cornstarch
1 cup apricot nectar

⅓ cup sugar

Mix sugar, cloves and cornstarch in a saucepan. Stir in apricot nectar and lemon juice; cook until thickened.
*Good over ham or chicken.

****

APRICOT PRESERVE SAUCE

12 oz. apricot preserve
½ tsp. curry powder
¼ cup sweet vermouth

1 can apricot halves
2 tbsp. prepared mustard
2 green onions, minced

1 tbsp. cornstarch
1 tsp. salt
pepper

Coarsely chop apricot halves and set aside. Place in a saucepan, salt, curry, pepper, preserve, and mustard. In a cup mix cornstarch with vermouth. Stir into the curry mixture. Boil 1 minute or until clear. Add apricots and minced onions into mixture and heat 2 minutes.
*Good over Brisket.

APRICOT-GINGER SAUCE

| 16-oz. apricot halves | ¼ tsp. ground ginger | 1 tbsp. sugar |
| ½ reserved syrup | 2 tsp. cornstarch | 2 tbsp. water |

Puree apricot. Place them in a saucepan with all the remaining ingredients and mix together; heat for 2 minutes.
*Good over shrimp.

****

APRICOT-MINT SAUCE

| 16-oz. can apricot halves | 1 tsp. fresh mint | ⅛ tsp. mace |
| ¼ cup vanilla low-fat yogurt | | |

Drain the light syrup from the apricots. Combine all ingredients in a blender, cover and process until smooth. Pour into a bowl; cover and chill.
*Good with sliced melon or mixed fruit salad.

****

APRICOT-YOGURT DIP SAUCE

| 8 oz. whole dried apricots | 2 tbsp. Amaretto liqueur | 1 ¼ cups water |
| ⅔ cup plain low-fat yogurt | | |

Soak apricots in water 2 to 3 hours. Drain apricots and place in a blender or food processor with Amaretto and yogurt; blend until smooth. If mixture is too thick, add a small amount of the liquid in which the apricots were soaked. Spoon apricot mixture into saucepan and heat for 2 minutes on the stove.
*Good over desserts or ice cream.

****

ARTICHOKE PARMESAN SAUCE

4-oz. can artichoke hearts	¼ cup sour cream	¼ tsp. cayenne
1 ½ tbsp. lemon juice	⅓ cup dill leaves	2 egg yolks
½ cup Parmesan cheese	¼ lb. butter	

Drain artichoke hearts, place in a food processor. Add cayenne, sour cream and dill; mix well. In top of double boiler whisk in egg yolks and lemon juice, then add butter. Whisk until butter has melted. If curdling starts, whisk in ice water. When thick, add cheese and mix well adding artichoke puree and mix well.
*Good over pasta.

ASPARAGUS CHEESE SAUCE

11 oz. cheddar cheese soup   10 oz. asparagus   ½ cup water

Mix soup and water in a saucepan. Stir in chopped asparagus; heat to boiling, reduce heat and simmer 5 minutes.
*Good over pasta.

****

ASPARAGUS TIPS SAUCE

1-cup asparagus tips   ¼ cup breadcrumbs   4 oz. butter
½ cup Gruyere cheese   1-cup heavy cream   salt and pepper
¼ cup chicken stock

Melt butter in a saucepan; add breadcrumbs and heat for 2 minutes. Add cheese, cream, stock and asparagus tips, cook for an additional 5 minutes. Add salt and pepper to taste.
*Good over pasta.

****

AVIGNON SAUCE

1 clove garlic, crushed   1-cup white sauce   Pinch parsley
¼ cup grated Parmesan   1 egg yolk

Place all ingredients together in a saucepan and heat for 2 minutes.
*Good for pasta.

****

AVOCADO SAUCE I

⅓ cup whipping cream   ⅓ cup water   2 avocados
4 tsp. whipping cream   juice of 1 lemon   Salt and pepper
½ tsp. finely grated lemon peel

Cut avocados in half, peel, remove pits and cut into pieces. Place in a food processor. Add all ingredients, except 4 teaspoons whipping cream and puree. Transfer to a small saucepan over medium heat and bring to a boil. Reduce heat and simmer gently until sauce reduces to about 1 cup. Remove from heat and cool slightly. Fold in remaining cream.
*Good over vegetables.

AVOCADO SAUCE II

½ cup whipped cream	¼ cup sour cream	salt and pepper
1 ½ tsp. lemon juice	1 cup chicken stock	1 ripe avocado
½ tbsp. chopped chives	paprika	

Heat all ingredients except cream, in a small saucepan; mix until well blended. Then add cream and heat for 5 minutes.
*Good over pasta.

****

AVOCADO SAUCE III

2 ripe avocados, mashed	¼ cup minced onion	1 tomato
2 tbsp. chopped cilantro	½ cup sour cream	salt & pepper
1 tbsp. Tequila		

Mix all ingredients together in a bowl, until well blended, then refrigerate.
*Good over vegetables.

****

AZTEC CHILI SAUCE

2 tbsp. chili powder	5 oz. tomato sauce	2 tsp. sugar
1 sm. green pepper, diced	6 oz. tomato paste	1 cup water
8 oz. whole kernel corn	10 oz. kidney beans	1 tsp. salt
2 tbsp. oil		

Heat oil in saucepan; add all remaining ingredients. Heat about 15 minutes.
*Good over poultry, all meats or pasta.

****

BABA RUM SAUCE

½ cup pineapple and syrup   ¼ cup butter   1 oz. rum
¼ cup baking soda

Place butter and baking soda in a saucepan and heat. Add pineapple, syrup and rum, stirring until well blended.
*Good over desserts or ice cream.

****

BABY BACK RIB SAUCE

(dry rub)	5 tsp. chili powder	10 tbsp. paprika
10 tbsp. black pepper	5 tbsp. garlic powder	2 tbsp. celery salt
1 tbsp. dry mustard	5 tsp. red pepper	

(wet rub)	1 tbsp. white pepper	32 oz. ketchup
1 cup apple cider vinegar	1 cup apple juice	1 apple, grated
½ cup Worcestershire	1 tbsp. garlic powder	1 cup soy sauce
1 med. onion, grated	¼ cup green pepper, grated	

Mix all dry ingredients together, rub into meat. Let stand 8 to 10 hours. Combine ketchup, soy sauce, Worcestershire sauce, garlic powder, vinegar, apple juice and white pepper in a saucepan and bring to a light boil. Add onion, apple and green pepper; cook about 30 minutes, or desired thickness.
*Good over pork or poultry.

****

BACON AND HONEY MUSTARD SAUCE

3 slices bacon   2 tsp. Dijon mustard   3 tbsp. honey

Cook bacon until crisp. Remove fat from pan, then add honey and mustard and mix well.
*Use over chicken, pork or fish.

****

BACON HORSERADISH SAUCE

¼ cup real bacon bits   1 cup mayonnaise   1 cup sour cream
¼ cup prepared horseradish

Stir all ingredients in a bowl, until well blended. Cover; chill.
*Good over baked potato.

BACON SAUCE

½ lb. slab bacon, diced
1 clove garlic, bruised

2 tbsp. olive oil
1 cup tomato puree

2 tbsp. butter
salt and pepper

Pour olive oil in a saucepan; sauté diced bacon and garlic until golden brown. Discard garlic. Add tomato puree and butter; simmer, covered. Add season with salt and pepper to taste.
*Good over pasta.

****

BACON, TOMATO AND CHEESE SAUCE

¼ pound Canadian bacon
1 cup cheddar cheese

2 cups tomatoes
2 tbsp. parsley

1 tbsp. olive oil
Salt and pepper

In a skillet, heat olive oil and bacon strips for 3 minutes. Add tomatoes, cheese and parsley and toss gently.
*Good over pasta.

****

BAGNA CAUDA SAUCE I

¼ cup vegetable oil
2-oz. can anchovy fillets

3 tsp. garlic puree
½ cup walnuts

½ cup butter

Mince anchovy fillets and finely chop walnuts. In a saucepan, cook butter, oil and garlic puree over a very low heat for 10 minutes. Do not let garlic brown. Stir in anchovy fillets and cook until they dissolve. Stir in walnuts. Keep warm.
*Good over pasta.

****

BAGNA CAUDA SAUCE II

6 flat canned anchovy fillets
3 lg. garlic cloves, chopped

¼ cup olive oil
6 tbsp. butter

Salt
Pepper

Crush anchovy fillets and garlic in a mortar and pestle until they form a paste. Heat oil and butter in a small saucepan and add the anchovy garlic mixture, stirring well to combine. Add pepper and transfer to heatproof serving disk or fondue and serve hot.
*Good over pasta.

BAKLAVA SAUCE

2 cups honey
2 whole cloves

2 cups sugar
1-stick cinnamon

3 cups water
½ cup walnuts

First heat cinnamon stick for 2 minutes in a saucepan. Then mix all ingredients together for 5 minutes, until well blended. Remove the cloves and cinnamon stick. Add walnuts.
*Good over ice cream or desserts.

****

BALSAMIC VINAIGRETTE SAUCE

⅓ cup balsamic vinegar
½ cup peanut oil

½ cup olive oil
½ tsp. ground pepper

1 tsp. salt

Place vinegar in a small bowl, gradually whisk in oils in a steady stream. Add salt and pepper.
*Good over salad.

****

BANANA KETCHUP SAUCE

½ cup seedless raisins
½ tsp. cayenne pepper
½ tsp. grated nutmeg
½ tsp. ground cinnamon
2 tsp. ground allspice
¼ tsp. ground cloves

½ cup chopped onion
1 cup cider vinegar
1 cup tomato paste
½ cup brown sugar
¼ cup corn syrup
1 lg. garlic clove

¼ cup rum
2 lg. bananas
3 cups water
½ tbsp. salt
½ tsp. pepper

Combine raisins, onions, garlic and tomato paste in a saucepan. Blend in a little vinegar. Place bananas in a blender, adding a little vinegar; add to saucepan, then add remaining vinegar, water, brown sugar and cayenne pepper. Bring to a boil and cook for a ½ hour; add corn syrup, allspice, cinnamon, nutmeg, pepper and cloves and continue to cook for 15 minutes.
*Good for roast pork, ham and poultry.

****

BANANA LIQUEUR SAUCE

2 bananas, mashed
3 cups vodka

1 cup sugar syrup

1 tsp. vanilla

Mash bananas, vanilla, sugar syrup and vodka in a bowl. Cover bowl and shake gently. Strain. Keep cold for 1 week.
*Good over ice cream.

BANANA SAUCE

1 cup confectioners' sugar	1 tsp. dark rum	2 egg yolks
1 cup whipping cream	1 tsp. vanilla	salt
2 med. ripe bananas	½ tsp. nutmeg	

Beat egg yolks, sugar, rum, vanilla and salt in a small bowl with mixer for 2 minutes. Beat cream in a bowl, until soft peaks; fold in yolks mixture and bananas.
*Good over desserts.

****

BARBECUE CREAM OF COCONUT SAUCE

½ cup Cream of Coconut	½ cup tomato sauce	3 tbsp. oil
4 tbsp. white vinegar	½ tsp. onion powder	1 tsp. salt
½ tsp. ground ginger	2 crushed garlic cloves	

Mix all ingredients together in a bowl, until well blended. Keep refrigerated.
*Good for ribs and chicken.

****

BARBECUE MUSTARD SAUCE

¼ cup sherry or dry wine	1 lg. diced onion	1 tbsp. flour
1 tbsp. dry mustard	¼ tsp. dried thyme	1 tbsp. butter
1 cup prepared mustard		

Blend all ingredients for 2 seconds, in a blender. Pour contents into saucepan and stir about 5 minutes over low heat.
*Good for ribs, meat and poultry.

****

BARBECUE SAUCE I

1 med. onion, chopped	1 garlic clove, crushed	½ cup butter
¼ cup dry red wine	½ tsp. brown sugar	1 tsp. salt
½ tsp. ground pepper	½ tsp. chili powder	1 cup water
2 tbsp. Worcestershire sauce	4 drops hot pepper sauce	2 tbsp. ketchup

In a medium saucepan, melt butter over low heat; add onion and garlic and cook until soft, but not brown. Add all remaining ingredients; stir well. Bring to a boil, reduce heat and simmer for about 15 minutes.
*Good for ribs, meat and poultry.

BARBECUE SAUCE II

1 tbsp. red wine vinegar
1 tbsp. Worcestershire sauce
½ cup orange juice

1 tbsp. tomato paste
1 ¼ cups chicken broth
2 tsp. dry mustard

2 tbsp. honey
2 tbsp. cornstarch

Put tomato paste, vinegar honey, dry mustard, Worcestershire sauce and broth in a small saucepan and simmer 10 minutes. Blend cornstarch with orange juice; stir into sauce and simmer 1 minute.
*Good for ribs, meat and poultry.

****

BARBECUE SAUCE III

1 32-oz. bottle ketchup
1 ½ tbsp. Tabasco sauce
3 tbsp. white vinegar
1 tsp. garlic powder
¼ cup Worcestershire sauce

1 cup dark molasses
2 ½ tbsp. dry mustard
1 lg. green pepper
¼ cup liquid smoke

1 ½ med. onion
½ cup lemon juice
½ cup water
¾ cup brown sugar

Chop onions and pepper, then combine all ingredients except water in a large pot. Pour water into empty ketchup bottle and swirl around. Pour into pot and bring mixture to a boil, stirring occasionally. Simmer for 2 hours.
*Good for ribs, meat and poultry.

****

BARBECUE SAUCE IV

¼ cup brown sugar
1 cup tomato sauce
¼ cup Worcestershire sauce

1 tsp. chili powder
¼ cup vinegar
1 tsp. celery seed

1 tsp. salt
1 chopped onion
2 cups water

Mix all ingredients together, in a saucepan, until well blended, simmer slowly ½ hour.
*Good with any meat or poultry.

****

BARBECUE SAUCE V

¼ cup brown sugar
1-cup tomato sauce
¼ cup Worcestershire

1 tsp. Chili powder
¼ cup vinegar
1 tsp. celery seed

1 tsp. salt
2 cups water
1 onion, chopped

Combine all ingredients in a saucepan; simmer slowly for ½ hour.
*Good for ribs, beef and poultry.

BARBECUE SAUCE VI

2 cups cider vinegar
1 tbsp. lemon juice

2 sticks margarine or butter
¼ tsp. dried red pepper flakes

1 tsp. salt

Combine vinegar, butter and salt in a saucepan. Heat until butter is melted, then add lemon juice and pepper flakes.
*Good over chicken, ribs or beef.

****

BARBECUE SAUCE VII

1 tbsp. Worcestershire sauce
1 lg. chopped onion
⅓ cup red wine vinegar
½ cup cola beverage

½ garlic cloves
14 oz. ketchup
2 tbsp. brown sugar
¼ tsp. pepper

1 cup water
½ cup butter
¼ tsp. salt

Melt butter in saucepan. Add chopped onion and crushed garlic; cook over low heat about 5 minutes. Add remaining ingredients, except cola; simmer about 20 minutes. Remove from heat; add cola.
*Good for meats and poultry.

****

BARBECUE SAUCE VIII

½ cup lemon juice
¼ tsp. garlic salt
1 med. chopped onion
1 tbsp. Worcestershire sauce

½ tsp. pepper
1 cup ketchup
½ cup water

1 tbsp. paprika
1 tbsp. sugar
1 tsp. salt

Mix garlic salt, pepper, paprika, sugar and salt. Add onion, ketchup, water, lemon juice or vinegar and Worcestershire sauce. Heat mixture in a saucepan and bring to a boil with occasional stirring.
*Good for ribs, meat and poultry.

****

BARBECUE SAUCE IX

½ cup chopped celery
¾ cup red wine vinegar
1 tbsp. Worcestershire
1 tsp. ground pepper

1 sm. green pepper
¾ cup brown sugar
2 tsp. dry mustard

⅓ cup salad oil
2 tbsp. chives
2 tsp. salt

Heat oil, celery and green pepper in a saucepan, simmer, covered, about 10 minutes, until vegetables are soft. Puree in blender. Add remaining ingredients; mix thoroughly.
*Good over pork or chicken.

BARBECUE SAUCE X

½ cup chopped onions
2 tbsp. wine vinegar
1 cup chili sauce
1 tsp. French-style mustard

1 tbsp. bacon drippings
¼ cup lemon juice
1 tsp. ground pepper

½ cup apple juice
¼ cup molasses
¼ cup ketchup

Sauté onions in the drippings or vegetable oil, in a saucepan, until brown. Add the rest of the ingredients and bring to a boil. Reduce heat and simmer for 20 minutes.
*Good for meats or chickens.

****

BARBECUE SAUCE XI

¼ cup brown sugar
1 cup tomato sauce
¼ cup Worcestershire
1 cup orange juice

1 tsp. Chili powder
¼ cup vinegar
1 tsp. celery seed

1 tsp. salt
2 cups water
1 onion, chopped

Combine all ingredients in a saucepan; simmer slowly for a ½ hour.
*Good over any meat.

****

BARBECUE SAUCE XII

1 qt. apple cider vinegar
¼ tsp. liquid smoke
1 tbsp. red pepper flakes

¾ tbsp. red pepper
1 tbsp. brown sugar

½ cup salt
½ cup ginger ale

Mix vinegar and salt in a saucepan. Bring to a boil and remove from heat. Mix in remaining ingredients; allow to cool.
*Good for ribs and poultry.

****

BARBECUE SAUCE XIII

1 green pepper, diced
¼ cup raspberry vinegar
2 tbsp. Worcestershire
1 tbsp. prepared mustard

1 tbsp. honey mustard
¼ cup lemon juice
2 tbsp. brown sugar
1 lg. red bell pepper

2 chopped onions
3 tbsp. butter
3 tbsp. ketchup
Dash of Tabasco

Seed and dice bell peppers. Sauté onion and green pepper in butter in a saucepan until tender. Stir in ketchup, vinegar, lemon juice, Worcestershire sauce, brown sugar, mustard, Tabasco and diced red bell peppers. Bring to a boil, reduce heat and simmer for 30 minutes, stirring occasionally.
*Good over chicken, ribs or beef.

BARBECUE SAUCE XIV

½ cup brown sugar
2 cups tomato sauce
1 tsp. dry mustard

¼ cup vinegar
2 cups ketchup
Salt and pepper

½ cup water
1 tbsp. molasses

Place brown sugar, water and vinegar in a saucepan; bring to a boil. Reduce heat and simmer for 5 minutes. Add tomato sauce, ketchup, molasses and dry mustard. Bring to a boil, stirring constantly. Reduce heat and simmer for 15 minutes. Add salt and pepper to taste.
*Good over ribs, chops or beef.

****

BARBECUE SAUCE XV

3 tbsp. light corn syrup
1 tbsp. hot pepper sauce
1 tsp. grated lemon peel

¼ cup Dijon mustard
2 tbsp. white vinegar
3 tbsp. hoisin sauce

2 cups ketchup
2 garlic cloves
3 tbsp. lemon juice

Mix all ingredients in a bowl, until well blended. Refrigerate.
*Good over poultry and ribs.

****

BARBECUED WALNUT SAUCE

2 tbsp. melted butter
¼ cup Worcestershire

Dash Tabasco sauce
4 cups walnuts

1 tbsp. ketchup
salt

In a baking dish, mix butter, Worcestershire sauce, ketchup, Tabasco sauce and walnuts together. Place in a 375° oven for 15 minutes. Stir every 5 minutes. Remove from oven, then add salt to taste.
*Good over chicken.

****

BASIC BARBECUE SAUCE

½ cup chopped onion
¼ tsp. cayenne pepper
¼ cup light brown sugar
2 tbsp. Worcestershire sauce

2 tbsp. minced garlic
1 tsp. ground cumin
½ cup malt vinegar

2 tbsp. corn oil
1 cup ketchup
¼ cup soy sauce

Pour oil in a saucepan over low heat. Add onion, garlic, cumin and cayenne. Cook for 5 minutes stirring occasionally. Add remaining ingredients. Simmer for 10 minutes, stirring often, until slightly thickened.
*Good for ribs and poultry.

BASIC CHANTILLY CREAM SAUCE

2 tbsp. confectioners' sugar   1 cup whipping cream   1 egg white
1 tsp. apricot or peach brandy

Whip cream with electric mixer until stiff peaks form. Add confectioners' sugar, 1 tablespoon at a time, beating in gently. Add brandy, a small amount at a time. Fold in egg white gently; beat thoroughly.
*Good over desserts.

****

BASIC FRESCA SAUCE

1 med. red onion   1 chopped cilantro   3 lg. tomatoes
1 minced garlic clove   ½ jalapeno pepper   1 tbsp. limejuice
Salt and pepper

Cut out core of tomatoes; dice but do not peel or remove seeds. Dice onion and combine with tomatoes. Add cilantro, garlic, jalapeno pepper, limejuice, salt and pepper to taste. Allow to stand for 30 minutes to blend.
*Good with fish, meat or chicken.

****

BASIC GRAVY SAUCE

¼ cup un-sifted flour   ¼ cup butter   2 cups water
2 tsp. instant bouillon

Use beef or chicken flavor instant bouillon. Use pan drippings or butter. In a medium skillet, stir flour into butter (pan drippings), cooking until flour is dark brown. Stir in water and bouillon; cook and stir until thickened and bouillon dissolves.
*Good over all meats.

****

BASIC MOLASSES BARBECUE SAUCE

2 cups cooking oil   4 cups lemon juice   ¼ cup cornstarch
12 oz. jar molasses   1 tbsp. black pepper   6 bay leaves
¼ cup salt   3 cloves garlic, minced

Combine cornstarch and lemon juice in a saucepan. Cook and stir over low heat until mixture bubbles and thickens. Cool. Using a beater, add remaining ingredients until thoroughly blended and thickened. Store in refrigerator until needed.
*Good for ribs, pork or poultry.

BASIL AND PROSCIUTTO SAUCE

2 garlic cloves
½ cup prosciutto
Pinch hot pepper

⅓ cup olive oil
Salt and pepper

1 cup basil
¼ Parmesan

Cook minced garlic in olive oil, in a skillet, over low heat until soft. Add fresh basil leaves, julienned prosciutto. Season to taste with salt, pepper and a pinch of hot pepper. Add grated Parmesan before serving.
*Good over pasta.

****

BASIL AND SUN DRIED TOMATO SAUCE

1 lg. green roasted pepper
2 tbsp. sun-dried tomatoes
1 lg. red roasted pepper

2 tbsp. garlic
1 cup fresh basil
3 tbsp. olive oil

1 tbsp. butter
3 tbsp. parsley

Heat all ingredients together, in a saucepan, for 3 to 5 minutes.
*Good over pasta.

****

BASIL CREAM BALSAMIC VINEGAR SAUCE

2 oz. Muenster cheese
2 tbsp. Balsamic vinegar
⅔ cup whipping cream

½ cup fresh basil
1 med. garlic clove

2 tbsp. olive oil
salt and pepper

Mince cheese. Place basil, garlic, oil and salt in a blender for 5 seconds. Pour contents of blender into a skillet; add cheese and heat for 2 minutes.
*Good over fish.

****

BASIL TARTAR SAUCE

½ cup basil leaves
1 tsp. lemon juice
Dash ground red pepper

½ cup mayonnaise
1 tsp. minced garlic
Dash red pepper sauce

1 tbsp. sour cream
⅛ tsp. salt

Rinse basil under very hot water; pat dry. In a food processor puree all ingredients until smooth.
*Good over fish or shrimp.

BEAN SAUCE

1 cup cooked beans
1 clove garlic
1 sm. chili pepper
¼ cup Parmesan cheese

4 tbsp. olive oil
¼ cup parsley
⅛ tsp. Rosemary

¼ cup ham
⅛ tsp. sugar
salt and pepper

Heat ham, garlic, parsley, sage and rosemary in oil, in a saucepan for 3 minutes. Add beans and chilies and cook 5 minutes longer.
*Good over pasta.

****

BEAN NEAPOLITAN SAUCE

1 cup cooked beans
8 oz. plum tomatoes
¼ cup celery

1 clove garlic
1 tbsp. tomato paste
¼ cup water

1 tbsp. sugar
4 tbsp. olive oil

Heat oil and garlic in saucepan; add celery, tomatoes, tomato paste, water and sugar. Cook 5 minutes. Add beans and cook 2 minutes longer.
*Good for pasta.

****

BÉARNAISE SAUCE I

Juice of ½ lemon
1 tsp. dried tarragon

4 egg yolks
½ cup butter

1 tbsp. water

In a medium size glass bowl, combine egg yolks, lemon juice and water, beat until the consistency of heavy cream. In another glass dish, place butter and microwave at high speed 1 ½ to 2 minutes, until melted, stir in tarragon. Gradually pour butter mixture into egg mixture, beating constantly. Microwave on high 10 to 15 seconds; beat 5 seconds. Repeat microwaving and beating until sauce is smooth and creamy.
*Good over ham.

****

BÉARNAISE SAUCE II

1 tsp. Worcestershire sauce
3 tbsp. Tarragon vinegar
1 sm. diced onion

4 egg yolks
¼ cup butter

¼ cup water
½ tsp. salt

Blend all ingredients for 5 seconds in a blender. Pour into saucepan and cook over low heat. Stir constantly until thick.
*Good with roast beef, fish or vegetables.

BÉARNAISE SAUCE III

2 tbsp. dry white wine
1 tbsp. chopped parsley

2 tbsp. tarragon vinegar
2 cups Hollandaise sauce

⅓ cup shallots
1 tbsp. tarragon

Combine white wine, vinegar, chopped shallots and parsley in a saucepan. Heat until all but about a tablespoon of the liquid has evaporated. Stir into the hollandaise along with 1 tablespoon of finely chopped fresh tarragon.
*Good over pork, beef, fish or vegetables.

****

BÉCHAMEL SAUCE I

2 tbsp. grated onion
2 sprigs fresh parsley
Pinch of freshly grated nutmeg

⅓ cup all purpose flour
6 black peppercorns
Salt

3 cups milk
⅓ cup butter

Warm milk in a saucepan over a very low heat. Melt butter in another saucepan; add onion and sauté until golden, do not burn them. Stir in flour and cook over low heat for 3 minutes or until bubbly. Gradually add milk, whisking constantly. Cook until sauce thickens, then add parsley, nutmeg, peppercorns, and salt. Keep heat very low and continue cooking 20 to 25 minutes, stirring frequently. Thin with a little milk, if desired. Strain through a fine sieve.
*Good over pasta.

****

BÉCHAMEL SAUCE II

½ cup cream
½ cup chicken broth
1 tbsp. minced onion

2 tbsp. butter
½ tsp. salt

2 tbsp. flour
⅛ tsp. pepper

Heat butter in a saucepan; blend in flour, salt, and pepper, stir until bubbly. Gradually add the cream, chicken broth and onion, stirring until smooth. Bring to a boil; cook and stir 1 to 2 minutes longer.
*Good over pasta.

****

BEEF AND MOZZARELLA SAUCE

¼ lb. lean ground beef
2 cups canned tomatoes

¼ cup olive oil
½ lb. mozzarella

2 tbsp. minced onion
salt and pepper

Dice mozzarella. Pour olive oil in a saucepan; sauté ground beef until well broken up and lightly browned about 5 minutes. Add onion and sauté briefly. Add tomatoes and bring to a boil, breaking them up. Simmer, uncovered until reduced to sauce like consistency. Season to taste with salt and pepper. Last minute add mozzarella.
*Good over pasta.

BEEF MARINADE SAUCE

1 cup Burgundy
2 sprigs tarragon (or ⅛ tsp. dried)

½ cup olive oil
2 sprigs thyme

2 stalks parsley
1 bay leaf

Combine all ingredients in small container with lid; cover and shake well.
*Marinade the beef for ½ hour, then cook.

****

BEEF-BURGUNDY SAUCE

3 beef bouillon cubes
3 tbsp. flour

½ cup Burgundy wine

2 cups water

Heat 1-cup water in saucepan to dissolve bouillon. Meanwhile mix flour, remaining cup of water and the wine; stir into bouillon. Stir over medium heat until thickened, 3 to 4 minutes.
*Good on beef.

****

BEER AND TOMATOES CASSEROLE SAUCE

2 cloves garlic
2 ginger root
1 lb. pot roast, chopped

1 can Plum tomatoes
1 bottle beer

2 med. onions
2 apples

Mix all ingredients in a bowl, except meat, until well blended. Pour over meat in a casserole dish and cook 1 ½ hours at 425° degrees.
*Good over pasta.

****

BEER CHEESE SAUCE

4 cups Lancashire cheese
1 sm. onion, chopped

1 cup light ale
5 tbsp. half and half

1 tbsp. butter
4 tsp. cornstarch

One pound or 4 cups of Monterey Jack cheese can be used in place of Lancashire cheese. Melt butter in a large saucepan and cook onion until soft. Pour in ale and heat until bubbly. Over low heat, stir in cheese. Continue to heat until cheese has melted. Blend cornstarch with half and half in a small bowl. Add to cheese mixture and cook, stirring 2 to 3 minutes or until smooth and thickened.
*Good over chicken.

BEER SAUCE I

1 med. grated carrot	1 cup cooked bacon	1 ½ cup beer
4 tbsp. cranberry sauce	1 tsp. ground cumin	6 tbsp. butter
3 tbsp. all purpose flour	½ cup beef stock	3 tbsp. water
1 lg. green apple, chopped	½ cup grated onion	salt and pepper

Heat 3 tablespoons butter in a saucepan; cook carrots, bacon, and onion until softened about 10 minutes. Mix in cumin, beer and stock, bring to a boil and cook for 15 minutes. Mix flour and water together and add to sauce. Bring to a boil. Melt 3 tablespoons butter in another saucepan with apples; cook for 7 minutes or until tender. Add apple mixture and cranberries to sauce.
*Good over pork.

****

BEER SAUCE II

3 cups cheddar cheese	¼ tsp. paprika	½ cup beer
1 tsp. dry mustard		

Mix cheese, paprika, pepper and mustard. Cook beer in a saucepan, until reduced by half, then add cheese mixture and cook for 5 minutes.
*Good over poultry.

****

BERCY SAUCE

½ cup dry white wine	½ cup dry white wine	½ tbsp. butter
½ cup Fish Veloute Sauce	2 tsp. finely chopped fresh parsley	

In a small saucepan, melt butter. Sauté green onion in butter until soft. Add wine and simmer over medium heat until the liquid is reduced by half. Add Fish Veloute Sauce and simmer, stirring often. Mix in parsley and serve hot.
*Good over fish.

BÉARNAISE SAUCE

2 tbsp. dry white wine
2 sprigs fresh chervil
2 tbsp. white wine vinegar
2 tsp. chopped fresh tarragon

¾ cup firm butter
1 sm. chopped green onion
Red (cayenne) pepper

4 black peppercorns
3 egg yolks
salt

Combine onion, chervil, tarragon, crushed peppercorns, vinegar and wine in a saucepan. Cook over medium heat until liquid is reduced by half. Place egg yolks in top of a double boiler over simmering water. Strain onion mixture through a fine sieve into egg yolks; whisk until blended. Do not allow water to boil. Slowly add pieces of butter, whisking constantly. Make sure each piece is melted and absorbed before adding the next piece, then add seasoning. Sauce should be smooth.
*Good over beef, fish or vegetables.

****

BÉARNAISE SAUCE

¼ cup tarragon vinegar
6 black peppercorns, crushed
⅛ tsp. cayenne pepper
1 ½ cups butter

2 chopped shallots
2 tbsp. dry white wine
4 tsp. lemon juice

3 egg yolks
Salt
1 tsp. tarragon

Boil vinegar, shallots and peppercorns for 3 minutes, in top of a double boiler. Whisk egg yolks and wine over heat. Whisk butter drop by drop, then add lemon juice salt and cayenne pepper.
*Good over beef, fish or vegetables.

****

BERRY SAUCE

Pinch of tarragon or cloves
4 cups fresh berries

1 cup sugar syrup
Sliced and scraped peel of 1 lemon

3 cups vodka

In place of 3 cups vodka, 2 cups vodka and 1 cup brandy or 1 cup sweet white wine can be used. Any berry can be used. Lightly crush berries with a fork. Add to vodka with lemon peel and cloves. Let stand 3 months, then strain. Crush the berries through a strainer to squeeze out all the juices. Add sugar syrup to taste. Mature 4-6 weeks.
*Good over desserts or ice cream.

****

BERRY WONDERFUL SAUCE

8-oz. cranberry sauce
1 tbsp. lemon juice

½ cup chili sauce
¼ tsp. pepper sauce

1 tbsp. brown sugar

Combine all ingredients in a saucepan. Bring to a boil over medium, stirring until well blended.
*Good over poultry.

BIGARADE SAUCE

¼ cup orange juice   ¼ cup lemon juice   1 cup sugar
½ duck or chicken stock   ¼ cup julienne of orange and lemon peel

Place sugar in saucepan and burn to caramel, add orange juice and lemon juice. Boil down stock until half.
*Good over duck or chicken.

****

BISMARCK SAUCE

¼ cup cheddar cheese   1 cup beef consume   1 tbsp. water
sliced mushroom   1 tbsp. arrow root   ½ cup Port

Heat consume and Port in a saucepan; bring to a boil. Mix in cheese, water and arrowroot or cornstarch until thickened.
*Good over ham.

****

BITTERSWEET CHOCOLATE SAUCE

¾ cup Dutch cocoa   ⅓ cup brown sugar   ¾ cup skim milk
1 tsp. vanilla extract

Combine cocoa and sugar in a saucepan, over low heat, stirring in milk. Mix until sugar is dissolved. Remove from heat and add vanilla.
*Good over fruit.

****

BLACK BEAN CLAMS SAUCE

2 tbsp. ginger, minced   1 oz. peanut oil   1 tbsp. dry sherry
2 tbsp. garlic, minced   1 tbsp. sesame oil   1 tbsp. hot pepper
1 tbsp. soy sauce   1 ½ cup clam stock

Heat oil in a saucepan, add garlic, ginger and hot pepper, lightly cook. Add remaining ingredients.
*Good over shrimp.

BLACK BEAN SAUCE I

1 tbsp. fermented black beans
2 tbsp. vegetable oil
2 lg. onions, sliced

2 sm. garlic cloves
1 tbsp. soy sauce
1 tsp. cornstarch

1 tsp. sugar
6 tbsp. water
2 tsp. water

Wash black beans in cold water, strain and place on flat surface; add garlic and sprinkle on sugar. Mash with a fork to blend thoroughly. Heat 1 tablespoon oil in large skillet over medium heat and stir fry bean mixture for 1 minute; stir in water and soy sauce. Bring to a boil, then reduce heat and simmer 2 minutes. In another saucepan, mix cornstarch with 2 teaspoons water. Stir into bean mixture; bring to a boil and cook for 1 minute. Remove from skillet and keep warm. Heat remaining 1 tablespoon oil; add onions and cook about 5 minutes, until soft and golden. Return bean mixture and stir fry until heated through.
*Good over pasta.

****

BLACK BEAN SAUCE II

½ cup dried black beans
2 ½ cups chicken broth
1 garlic clove

1 Serrano chili
1 tbsp. peanut oil

Salt and pepper
2 shallots

Soak beans in water over night. Drain and place in saucepan with chicken broth or stock and simmer until tender, about 1 hour. Drain beans, reserving 1 cup liquid. Heat oil in skillet over medium heat. Add chopped shallots, chili, and garlic; cook until softened, stirring frequently, about 5 minutes. Stir in black beans and reserved liquid from beans; boil until liquid is reduced by half. Transfer to blender and puree. Strain sauce into saucepan; season with salt and pepper.
*Good over pasta.

****

BLACK BEAN SAUCE III

1 tsp. vegetable oil
1 ½ garlic cloves
1 tbsp. fermented black beans

2 chopped shallots
2 tsp. rice vinegar
Ground white pepper

1 cup sake
1 tbsp. soy sauce
8 tbsp. butter

Warm oil over medium heat in a saucepan. Add shallots, mashed garlic and black beans; sauté until shallots soften, about 3 minutes. Add sake, soy sauce and rice vinegar. Cook until sauce reduces by 1/3, then remove from heat and whisk in butter. Season with pepper.
*Good for fish.

BLACK FRIAR'S SAUCE

¼ cup grated Parmesan   ¼ cup mushroom, puree   2 tbsp. butter
2 anchovy fillets, chopped

Heat all ingredients in a saucepan, for 4 minutes.
*Good over pasta.

****

BLACK OLIVE AND TOMATO SAUCE

28-oz. plum tomatoes   2 tbsp. olive oil   2 cloves garlic
7 oz. lg. black olives   1 sm. chili pepper   parsley
salt and pepper

Substitute 1 tsp. dried chili pepper for fresh pepper. Heat oil in skillet and sauté chopped garlic and chili.
Add tomatoes and cook for 20 minutes. Add chopped pitted olives, parsley, salt and pepper.
*Good over pasta.

****

BLACK OLIVE SAUCE

7 oz. pitted black olives   2 cloves garlic   parsley
4 tbsp. olive oil   salt

Chop garlic and olives, place in 2 tablespoons of olive oil and marinate for 3 to 4 hours. Heat the rest of
the oil and pour in olives and heat 2 minutes longer. Add parsley and salt.
*Good over pasta.

****

BLACK PEPPER SAUCE

½ cup dry red wine   2 lg. shallots, chopped   3 tbsp. butter
1 ½ cup duck sauce   2 tsp. crushed red or black peppercorns

Place wine, shallots and peppercorns in a saucepan, bring to a boil. Reduce heat. Add duck sauce and
whisk to blend. Whisk in butter and strain.
*Good over poultry.

BLACKBERRY BRANDY SAUCE

| 1 cup frozen blackberries | ⅓ cup blackberry brandy | ½ cup sugar |

Mix berries, sugar and brandy in a saucepan; let stand 2 hours. Bring to a boil. Reduce heat and simmer until syrupy.
*Good over ice cream.

****

BLACKBERRY CARAMEL CUSTARD SAUCE

1 cup granulated sugar	1 cup heavy cream	4 eggs
½ cup blackberry puree	⅓ cup sugar	2 egg yolks
2 ½ cups milk	1 tsp. vanilla	Fresh fruit

Pour sugar into skillet and cook over medium heat, without stirring, until sugar is brown and syrupy. Shake pan back and forth over burner occasionally to spread sugar evenly over bottom of pan. When sugar has melted, add puree. Stir to mix and set aside. Scald cream. Put eggs, yolks, and the ⅓ cup sugar into mixing bowl. Beat until smooth. Beat in cream, milk, and vanilla. Pour into first mixture. Chill.
*Good over ice cream or desserts.

****

BLACKBERRY SAUCE

| 1 sm. garlic clove | ½ pt. fresh blackberries | ¼ tsp. salt |
| 2 tsp. lemon juice | Pinch hot Hungarian paprika | 2 tbsp. coriander |

Mash the garlic with the salt. Using a wooden spoon, push the blackberries through a fine, nonmetallic sieve; discard the seeds. In a small glass bowl, combine the strained blackberries with the garlic, the fresh chopped coriander, paprika and fresh lemon juice. Set aside, covered, at room temperature for 5 to 6 hours to blend the flavors before serving.
*Good over poultry.

****

BLACKCURRANT CASSIS FONDUE SAUCE

| 1 ½ lbs. blackcurrants | 1 tbsp. cornstarch | ½ cup sugar |
| ¼ cup crème de cassis | 2 tbsp. half and half | ⅔ cup water |

Place blackcurrants in a medium size saucepan with sugar and water. Cook over medium heat until tender. Press through a sieve into fondue pot. In a small bowl blend cornstarch with half and half; stir into puree with crème de cassis and reheat until thickened. When ready to serve, swirl a little extra cream in for decoration.
*Good over poultry.

BLENDER BÉARNAISE SAUCE

2 tbsp. white wine vinegar
½ tsp. dried tarragon
½ cup unsalted butter

¼ cup dry white wine
1 tbsp. warm water
2 lg. egg yolks

¼ tsp. salt
ground pepper
2 tbsp. shallot

Place wine, vinegar, minced shallot and tarragon in small saucepan. Simmer, watching carefully, over low heat until liquid is almost completely evaporated, about 15 minutes. Transfer to blender; add egg yolks and warm water. Heat butter in small saucepan until foaming. Blend egg yolk mixture at low speed until smooth. Add butter in thin stream and process until emulsified. Season with salt and pepper. Serve warm.
*Good over all meats.

****

BLENDER MAYONNAISE SAUCE

2 tsp. fresh lemon juice
⅛ tsp. red pepper sauce

½ tsp. dry mustard
1 ¼ cups olive oil

1 lg. egg
¾ tsp. salt

Place all ingredients except oil in blender, beat until egg is foamy, about 10 seconds. Add oil slowly until emulsified.
*Good over fish or poultry.

****

BLUE CHEESE SAUCE I

4 oz. blue or Roquefort cheese
1 tsp. instant minced onion

1 cup sour cream
1 tsp. lemon juice

1 tsp. sugar
½ tsp. salt

Mix all ingredients together in a bowl, until well blended. Chill, preferably over-night, to allow flavors to blend.
*Good over salads or vegetables.

****

BLUE CHEESE SAUCE II

¼ cup chopped walnuts
¼ cup apricot liqueur or cassis liqueur

½ lb. unsalted butter

½ lb. blue cheese

Beat cheese and butter in a mixing bowl, until creamy. Beat in liqueur and stir in nuts. Chill.
*Good over pasta.

BLUE CHEESE SAUCE III

1 ½ tbsp. Worcestershire sauce
1 hard cooked egg, chopped
1 lg. stalk celery, chopped
Fresh dill sprigs or chopped parsley

¼ lb. blue cheese
½ cup fresh bread
⅓ cup sour cream

¼ cup butter
Lemon wedges
Pepper

Melt butter in top of a double boiler over simmering water. Add cheese and celery. Cook 5-6 minutes, stirring. Add Worcestershire sauce, sour cream, fresh breadcrumbs and pepper; combine well. Cool slightly and stir in egg.
*Good over pasta.

****

BLUE CHEESE SAUCE IV

1-8 oz. pkg. cream cheese
2 cups crumbled blue cheese

½ tsp. garlic salt
2 tbsp. half and half

1 cup milk
1 tbsp. cornstarch

Put milk and cream cheese in pot and beat with an electric mixer until creamy and smooth. Gradually stir in blue cheese; heat until smooth. In a small bowl, blend garlic salt and cornstarch with half and half. Blend into cheese and cook, stirring 2 to 3 minutes longer or until thick and creamy.
*Good over pasta.

****

BLUEBERRY AMARETTO SAUCE

2 tsp. lemon juice
2 tsp. cornstarch

½ cup water
¾ cup fresh blueberries

2 tbsp. amaretto

Combine water, amaretto, and cornstarch in a small saucepan; stir well. Add blueberries and cook over medium heat for 5 minutes or until thickened, stirring constantly. Remove from heat, stir in lemon juice. Cool.
*Good over dessert.

****

BLUEBERRY CINNAMON SAUCE

2 pints blueberries
2 tbsp. lemon juice
2 tsp. all purpose flour

½ cup apple cider
2 tsp. lemon peels
2 tbsp. blackberry or orange liqueur

6 tbsp. sugar
½ tsp. cinnamon

Heat first 7 ingredients together in a saucepan, for 5 minutes, then add liqueur.
*Good over desserts.

BLUEBERRY HONEY AND LIME SAUCE

2 tsp. fresh limejuice   3 cups blueberries   1 tbsp. honey

Mix all ingredients together, in a bowl, until well blended. Let stand 3 hours.
*Good over poultry.

****

BLUEBERRY SAUCE I

1 pint blueberries   ⅓ cup sugar   Pinch of salt
1 tbsp. lemon juice   1 tbsp. cornstarch   2 tbsp. water

Mix sugar, salt, and cornstarch in saucepan. Add water and lemon juice; stir until dissolved. Add berries; bring to boil. Boil 2 to 3 minutes, until clear and slightly thickened; stir carefully to avoid crushing berries.
*Good over dessert or ice cream.

****

BLUEBERRY SAUCE II

½ cup corn syrup   1 cup water   1 cup sugar
1 pint blueberries   2 lemon slices

Combine the water, sugar, corn syrup and lemon slices in a medium saucepan. Bring to a boil, stirring until sugar dissolves. Lower heat; simmer 5 minutes. Add blueberries; simmer 5 minutes or until berries burst. Cool slightly. Discard lemon slices. Puree blueberry mixture in blender until smooth. For a smoother sauce, press the puree through a sieve.
*Good over dessert or ice cream.

****

BLUEBERRY WINE SAUCE

½ cup dry white wine   1 tbsp. cornstarch   3 tbsp. sugar
2 cups blueberries

Boil all ingredients in a saucepan, for 2 minutes. Reduce heat and simmer 2 minutes, until thickened.
*Good over desserts.

BOLOGNA SAUCE

¼ cup Parmesan cheese
1 cup tomato puree

1 onion, chopped
3 cups beef

1 cup veal gravy

Sauté beef with chopped onions in a saucepan. Add the remaining ingredients and heat 5 minutes.
*Good over pasta.

****

BOLOGNESE SAUCE I

5 oz. beef and pork, ground
1 carrot, minced
4 oz. chopped bacon
1 tbsp. tomato paste
¼ cup Parmesan cheese

2 tbsp. olive oil
1 celery, minced
3 oz. sausage meat
5 tbsp. heavy cream
salt and pepper

3 tbsp. butter
1 onion, minced
4 oz. white wine
4 oz. stock

Heat oil and butter in a saucepan; add carrot, celery, onion and bacon for 10 minutes. Add pork, beef, sausage and wine; simmer for 10 minutes more, stir occasionally. Add stock and pasta; cook 1 ½ hours. Add cream.
*Good over pasta.

****

BOLOGNESE SAUCE II

1 celery stalk, chopped
¼ lb. bacon, chopped
½ cup whipping cream
½ lb. lean ground beef
½ cup dry white wine

1 sm. carrot, chopped
1 med. onion, chopped
Pinch of grated nutmeg
1 tbsp. chopped oregano
2 tbsp. tomato paste

¼ cup butter
2 chicken livers
Salt and pepper
1 cup beef stock

Melt butter in a large saucepan. Add onion, celery, carrot and bacon. Cook over medium heat until the onion is golden and soft. Add beef and cook until well done, stirring often to prevent sticking. Add salt, pepper, nutmeg and oregano. Increase heat to high and pour in wine. Bring to a boil, stirring constantly, and cook until the wine has almost evaporated. Add beef stock and tomato paste, and simmer for 35 to 40 minutes, stirring often. A few minutes before serving, add the chicken livers, if desired. Add cream and stir. Serve hot.
*Good over pasta.

BOLOGNESE SAUCE III

5 oz. lean boneless pork
5 oz. lean boneless beef
2 oz. fresh sausage
5 tbsp. heavy cream
Freshly grated Parmesan cheese (optional)

2 tbsp. olive oil
1 med. onion
2 tbsp. tomato paste
1 cup white wine

6 tbsp. butter
4 oz. bacon
1 cup stock
Salt & pepper

Mince pork and beef in a food processor. Heat oil in a large skillet, 2 tablespoons butter, minced onion, and finely chopped bacon. Cook gently for about 10 minutes, then add pork, beef, sausage meat with skin removed and wine. Cook for 10 minutes more, stirring occasionally. Add tomato paste, diluted in the stock. Add seasoning to taste. Cook 1 ½ hours. Stir in cream until it has been absorbed by the sauce; then remove from heat and keep warm.
*Good over pasta.

****

BOLOGNESE SAUCE IV

1 cup chopped carrots
⅔ cup chopped celery
2 tbsp. tomato paste
1 cup heavy cream

10 tbsp. tomato puree
½ cup chopped onion
½ cup beef stock
salt and pepper

5 oz. fatty pork
10 oz. lean pork
½ cup dry wine
1 cup milk

Brown pork in a skillet and cook for 5 minutes; add vegetables and continue to cook 3 minutes over medium heat. Add wine and tomato puree, reduce heat and simmer for 2 hours. Add milk a little at a time during the two hours. Heat cream 5 to 10 minutes, then add to sauce and mix.
*Good over pasta.

****

BOMBAY SAUCE

1 cup plain yogurt
1 tsp. ground coriander

1 tsp. ground cumin
salt and pepper

1 tbsp. paprika

Blend all ingredients in a food processor.
*Use to marinate fish, for 1 hour.

****

BOOTHBAY BLUEBERRY SAUCE

1 cup blueberry puree
2 tbsp. grated orange rind
1 tbsp. grated lemon rind

2 tbsp. orange juice
½ tsp. allspice

1 tsp. sugar
½ tsp. cinnamon

Combine all ingredients in a saucepan and bring to a boil. Reduce heat and simmer for 10 minutes. Serve hot.
*Good over desserts or ice cream.

BOUILLABAISSE SAUCE

1 lb. various fish	2 cloves garlic	1 onion
8 oz. can tomatoes	½ tsp. fennel seed	1 leek
1 qt. water	salt and pepper	1 bay leaf
1 tbsp. oil		

Use several kinds of fish, crustaceans and shellfish. Heat oil in a saucepan and brown garlic for about 1 minute. Add remaining ingredients and cook for ½ hour over a medium heat. Strain.
*Good over pork.

****

BOURBON BARBECUE SAUCE

1 cup ketchup	¼ cup molasses	⅓ cup bourbon
2 tbsp. vinegar	1 tbsp. Worcestershire sauce	2 tsp. soy sauce
½ tsp. dry mustard	1 tbsp. lemon juice	¼ tsp. pepper
1 clove garlic, crushed		

Mix all ingredients together, in a bowl, until well blended; let stand for several hours.
*Good over chicken, pork or ribs.

****

BOURBON JELLY SAUCE

4 tsp. unflavored gelatin	1 ½ cup water	½ cup sugar
½ cup orange juice	¾ cup bourbon	

Place ½ cup water in a small bowl with gelatin and mix well. Place in a saucepan and bring to a boil adding sugar, stirring constantly. Add orange juice and bourbon.
*Good over chicken or pork.

****

BOURBON SAUCE

1 cup superfine sugar	½ cup butter	1 egg
½ cup bourbon		

Melt butter in top of a double boiler; add mixed egg with superfine sugar. Pour in saucepan with butter and cook for 3 minutes. Remove from heat and add bourbon.
*Good for dessert.

BRANDY CHOCOLATE SAUCE

8 oz. cooking chocolate   ¼ cup sugar   ¼ cup brandy
¾ cup hot water

Melt chocolate in a double boiler. Stir in sugar, brandy and hot water, and continue stirring until sugar is dissolved. For a thinner sauce, add additional hot water.
*Good over desserts or ice cream.

****

BRANDY CREAM SAUCE

2 tbsp. butter   2 tbsp. onion   ½ cup Brandy
1 cup cream   salt and pepper

Heat butter and onion together, in a saucepan, for 1 minute. Add Brandy and heat another minute. Add cream, salt and pepper.
*Good over poultry.

****

BRANDY MASCARPONE CREAM SAUCE

1 ½ tsp. brandy or vanilla   8 oz. mascarpone cheese   2 egg whites
3 egg yolks   ½ cup + 2 tbsp. granulated sugar

Beat yolks and sugar in a large bowl, 2 minutes. Beat in brandy, sugar and add small pieces of cheese. Beat egg whites and 2 tbsp. sugar in small bowl until foamy, fold whites into yolk mixture.
*Good over dessert.

****

BRAZILIAN BARBECUE SAUCE

6 cloves garlic   1 tsp. Tabasco sauce   1 tbsp. salt
⅔ cup lime juice   1 tsp. black pepper   3 scallions
1 cup coarse sea salt

Mince garlic and scallion, mash to a paste with the salt. Stir in pepper, Tabasco sauce and lime juice.
*Use to marinate pork, chicken, ribs or steak over night.

BREAD SAUCE I

Pinch of ground mace	6 whole cloves	1 med. onion
1 cup white bread	Salt and pepper	2 tbsp. cream
Pinch of red (cayenne) pepper	2 tbsp. butter	2 cups milk

Use extra butter in place of cream, if desired. Break up fresh white bread, without crusts. Stick cloves in onion. Place milk and mace in a saucepan; add onion and bring to a boil. Simmer 15 minutes or more to flavor milk thoroughly. Remove onion and any loose cloves with a slotted spoon. Add butter, cream, seasonings, and breadcrumbs; beat constantly over low heat until the sauce thickens.
*Good over poultry.

****

BREAD SAUCE II

½ grated onion	2 slices of white bread	2 cups milk
salt and pepper	⅛ tsp. nutmeg	1 tbsp. butter
½ cup cream	⅛ tsp. cayenne pepper	

Boil milk with onion and bread for 5 minutes in a saucepan. Add the remaining ingredients, cook for 2 minutes more.
*Good for fish or chicken.

****

BREADCRUMB SAUCE

¼ cup grated Parmesan	1 cup breadcrumbs	4 tbsp. butter
2 tbsp. oil		

Place butter and breadcrumbs in a saucepan and heat until brown. Add oil and cheese to mixture.
*Good over pasta.

****

BREAM BEER SAUCE

½ oz. pale beer	½ cup onions	1 bay leaf
¼ cup lemon juice	½ tbsp. Rowe	1 tbsp. butter
salt and pepper		

Heat butter in a saucepan, cook onion until transparent. Add beer, lemon juice and bay leaf; simmer for 5 minutes. Add Rowe and continue to simmer until sauce thickened.
*Good over fish.

BROAD BEAN SAUCE

2 cups broad beans (Fava)	¼ cup cook bacon	2 tbsp. olive oil
¼ cup chopped celery	½ cup chopped onion	1 tsp. sugar
¼ cup wine vinegar	cooked thin strips ham	

Heat oil and onion in a saucepan. Add the remaining ingredients and simmer for 3 minutes.
*Good over pasta.

****

BROCCOLI AND TOMATO SAUCE

1 cup Parmesan cheese	1 cup cooked broccoli	2 cups tomato sauce

Heat all ingredients in a saucepan, for 5 minutes.
*Good over pasta.

****

BROCCOLI SAUCE I

Juice of 1 lemon	Chicken bouillon	8 tbsp. butter
½ cup sour cream	2 tbsp. flour	1 tsp. salt
3 cups broccoli puree	2 egg yolks	Fresh pepper
½ tsp. ground nutmeg	½ cup cream	Salt to taste

Measure and add chicken bouillon to make 1 ½ cups liquid. Heat 2 tablespoons butter in saucepan and add flour. Cook stirring for 2 minutes. Add the 1 ½ cups of liquid and cook, stirring until thickened. Beat egg yolks with cream. Remove saucepan from heat and whisk in egg mixture. Return to heat and cook, stirring until smooth and golden. Beat remaining butter and sour cream into broccoli puree. Season with nutmeg, salt and pepper.
*Good over poultry, pasta or vegetables.

****

BROCCOLI SAUCE II

1 cup cooked broccoli	2 cloves garlic	2 tbsp. oil
¼ cup Parmesan cheese		

Place oil and broccoli in a skillet; add crush garlic and heat for 3 minutes. Take off heat and stir in cheese.
*Good over pasta or poultry.

BROWN SAUCE I

4 cups basic beef stock   ¼ cup flour   2 tbsp. butter
1 cup chopped tomatoes   1 cup Mirepoix

Melt butter in small saucepan; blend in flour to make smooth paste. Cook and stir over low heat until mixture is browned. Add stock gradually, stirring constantly until smooth. Add tomatoes; simmer 3 minutes. Add Mirepoix; simmer until sauce is reduced by half, stirring occasionally. Strain sauce through fine sieve; serve immediately.
*Good over beef or poultry.

****

BROWN SAUCE II

4 lbs. veal bones   1 lg. carrot   1 diced leek
1 rib of diced celery   3 cloves crushed garlic

Place all the ingredients in a large shallow cooking pan and place in a preheated 425° oven for 1 hour. Turn bones with a spoon after ½ hour.

¾ cups all-purpose flour   4 tbsp. tomato paste   1 ¾ gallons water
1 cup dry white wine   1 tsp. crushed thyme   3 bay leaves
1 tsp. black peppercorns   Caramel coloring   2 tsp. salt
1 tsp. crushed tarragon

Transfer all the ingredients to a large kettle, place-cooking pan on stove. Add 1 quart of water; bring to a boil to melt all the solidified juices. Add the flour and tomato paste to the ingredients in the kettle and mix well. Add the boiling water, the remaining ingredients, and bring to a boil, stirring to dilute the flour. Simmer the sauce slowly, uncovered, for about 3 hours. Skim the foam, which comes up to the top every 15 to 20 minutes. Add 1 teaspoon of caramel coloring. Strain the sauce through a fine sieve.
*Good over veal, beef or poultry.

****

BROWN STOCK SAUCE III

10 black peppercorns   bouquet garni   3 quarts water
2 carrots, chopped   2 onions, halved   4 whole cloves
2 celery stalks   1 garlic clove   1 sm. turnip
3 or 4 lbs. beef or veal shank or neck bones   1 tsp. salt

To make bouquet garni, tie together herb sprigs with a piece of string or place in a cheesecloth bag; if string is used the bouquet garni can be tied to the saucepan handle for easy removal. Place bones and meat in roasting pan. Bake at 400F, turning once, until brown.

Place water, bones and pieces of meat into a 4-quart kettle. Stick cloves into onion halves and add them and all remaining ingredients, except salt and peppercorns, to kettle. Bring to a boil over medium heat; add salt and peppercorns. Skim surface as necessary. Reduce heat and simmer, uncovered, 3 ½ to 4 hours.
Remove bouquet garni and strain through a fine sieve and cool. Remove any fat that solidifies on surface. Cover and store in refrigerator for up to 1 week.
*Good over veal, beef or poultry.

BROWN SUGAR SAUCE

| ½ cup brown sugar | ½ cup water | Pinch of salt |
| ½ tsp. cornstarch | 2 tbsp. water | 2 tbsp. brandy |

Blend cornstarch with 2 tablespoons of water, in a cup. Cook sugar, water and salt in a small saucepan over medium heat 3 to 5 minutes or until sugar is dissolved. Stir in blended cornstarch, cook and stir until slightly thickened. Remove from heat and stir in flavoring.
*Good over fruit or dumplings.

****

BROWN SUGAR-CINNAMON SAUCE

| ¾ cup light brown sugar | ½ tsp. cinnamon | 3 tbsp. butter |
| ½ cup whipping cream | 2 egg yolks | |

Heat butter and sugar, in a saucepan, until melted, whisk in egg yolks quickly. Do Not Cook. Whisk in cream then add cinnamon.
*Good over desserts.

****

BUN SPICY PEANUT SAUCE

¼ cup smooth peanut butter	¼ cup soy sauce	3 tbsp. sugar
1 tsp. chile pepper flakes	1 tbsp. minced garlic	3 tbsp. corn oil
3 tbsp. toasted sesame oil		

Whisk together all the ingredients, in a bowl, until thoroughly blended. To simplify whisking, heat slightly.
*Good over poultry, pork or pasta.

****

BURGUNDY SAUCE

| ½ cup red Burgundy | 2 garlic cloves | 2 tsp. parsley |
| 2 cups tomato juice | 1 tsp. paprika | |

Heat all ingredients in a saucepan; bring to a boil.
*Good over poultry.

BUTTER SAUCE

2 tbsp. white roux
2 tbsp. lemon juice

1 egg yolk
½ cup cream

2 tbsp. water
1 tbsp. butter

Cook all ingredients in a saucepan, for about 5 minutes, then strain.
*Good for fish.

****

BUTTER GARLIC SAUCE

⅓ cup dry white wine
2 tbsp. white wine vinegar
3 tbsp. minced shallots

2 tbsp. minced garlic
2 tbsp. heavy cream

1 cup butter
salt and pepper

Heat garlic, shallot, wine and vinegar in a saucepan, for 1 minute. Add butter; cook 2 minutes longer.
Remove from heat and add heavy cream.
*Good over pasta, fish or chicken.

****

BUTTER WALNUT SAUCE

1 cup sweet butter
½ cup ground walnuts

1 tsp. brown sugar
Dash grated nutmeg

1 ½ tsp. brandy
1 tsp. lemon juice

Make a puree of the butter, sugar, brandy, nutmeg and lemon juice, in a bowl. Fold in the ground walnuts.
*Good over desserts or ice cream.

****

BUTTERED APPLESAUCE

2 cups chopped apples
¾ cup water

¼ cup brown sugar
½ tsp. rum extract

¼ cup butter

Sauté 2 cups chopped apples in butter, in a small skillet, until tender. Stir in brown sugar and water; cook
5 minutes; stir in rum extract.
*Good over ice cream.

BUTTERMILK-HERB SAUCE

¾ cup buttermilk
2 med. garlic cloves
⅛ tsp. curry powder

¾ cup mayonnaise
½ tsp. pepper
1 tbsp. basil

1 lg. shallot
½ tsp. salt
1 tsp. thyme

Mince shallot, garlic cloves, fresh basil and thyme. In a medium bowl, whisk together the buttermilk, mayonnaise, shallot and garlic. Whisk in the salt, pepper, curry powder, basil and thyme.
*Good over poultry.

****

BUTTERSCOTCH ALMOND SAUCE

2 cups light brown sugar
2 tbsp. lemon juice

½ cup whipping cream
2 tbsp. chopped blanched, toasted almonds

½ cup butter

Melt butter in the top half of a double boiler over simmering water. Add sugar and heat, stirring until sugar has absorbed butter. Add cream and carefully stir in lemon juice. Cook over barely simmering water for ½ to ¾ hour, stirring frequently. Add chopped almonds. Serve hot.
*Good over ice cream or desserts.

****

BUTTERSCOTCH FONDUE SAUCE

¾ cup packed brown sugar
14-oz. can evaporated milk

¼ cup light corn syrup
¼ cup unsalted peanuts

¼ cup butter
2 tbsp. cornstarch

Put butter, sugar and corn syrup in a medium size saucepan and heat until mixture begins to bubble; boil 1 minute. Stir in evaporated milk and cook 3 to 4 minutes or until sauce is hot and bubbly. Add chopped peanuts. In a small bowl, blend cornstarch with 2 tbsp. water. Add to sauce and heat until thickened.
*Good over desserts.

****

BUTTERSCOTCH SAUCE

½ cup dark corn syrup
2 tbsp. margarine

2 tbsp. cornstarch
1 tbsp. vanilla

½ cup milk
½ cup sugar

Combine sugar and cornstarch in a microwave bowl, then add corn syrup and milk. Microwave on high 2 ½ to 3 minutes, or until bubbling; whisk. Microwave on medium-high for 3 minutes, or until slightly thickened. Add margarine; whisk until melted. Blend in vanilla.
*Good over ice cream.

BUTTERSCOTCH SAUCE II

¾ cup heavy cream
3 cups seedless grapes
½ cups toasted almonds

½ cup brown sugar
2 tbsp. sour cream

⅛ tsp. salt
½ tsp. vanilla

Mix cream, salt and sugar in a saucepan, bring to a boil. Boil 10 minutes, then remove from heat and stir in sour cream, vanilla, grapes and almonds.
*Good over ice cream.

****

BUTTERY SAUCE

¾ cup sugar
¼ cup chocolate crème liqueur

½ cup butter

1 beaten egg

In a small saucepan combine sugar and butter. Cook mixture over medium heat, stirring constantly, until sugar dissolves, about 5 minutes. Remove from heat. Stir some of the mixture into the beaten egg. Return mixture to pan; cook and stir 2 minutes more. Cool slightly; stir in liqueur.
*Good over soufflé.

****

CACCIATORE SAUCE I

½ cup chopped onion   1 minced garlic clove   1 tbsp. oil
28-oz. can tomatoes   8-oz. tomato sauce   ½ tsp. salt
1 med. green pepper   ½ tsp. oregano   ½ tsp. basil
⅛ tsp. cayenne pepper

Sauté onion and garlic in oil in skillet. Add tomatoes, tomato sauce, salt, seasonings and green pepper.
Bring to a full boil. Cover, remove from heat and let stand 5 minutes.
*Good over chicken and pasta.

****

CACCIATORE SAUCE II

½ green pepper, diced   2 tbsp. olive oil   1 sliced onion
4 tbsp. tomato paste   28-oz. tomatoes   2 cloves garlic
½ cup dry red wine   12 oz. mushrooms   1 tsp. seasoning
3 ½ lbs. broiler   salt and pepper   parsley

Place olive oil, onion, green pepper and garlic in 3-quart micro proof baking dish. Micro cook on high 6
minutes or until onion is transparent, stirring after 3 minutes. Add remaining ingredients, except parsley.
Stir well and cover with plastic wrap, turning back one corner to vent. Micro cook on high 5 minutes.
Arrange chicken pieces in baking dish with thickest part of chicken and dark meat at outer edge of dish.
Spoon sauce over chicken, covering completely. Cover with vented plastic wrap and micro cook on high
12 minutes. Turn chicken over, recover, and micro cook on high 15 minutes or until chicken is tender.
Sprinkle with parsley.
*Good over chicken and pasta.

****

CAESAR NO-YOLK SAUCE

2 anchovy fillets   1 lg. minced garlic clove   ⅓ cup olive oil
Parmesan cheese   1 tbsp. fresh lemon juice   Fresh pepper
2 tbsp. Dijon mustard   3 tbsp. red wine vinegar

2 tsp. anchovy paste may substitute the anchovy fillets. Mash the anchovies with a fork, in a medium
bowl. Whisk in the garlic, lemon juice and mustard until combined. Whisk in the vinegar. Gradually add
oil in a thin stream, whisking vigorously until the sauce is thick and glossy. If the oil begins to separate
out, stop pouring and keep whisking until it is thoroughly incorporated; then whisk in the remaining oil in
a steady stream. Add cheese and pepper and refrigerate.
*Good over salads.

CAESAR SAUCE

2 tbsp. virgin olive oil
1 tbsp. Worcestershire sauce
2 tbsp. fresh lemon juice

1 ½ tsp. anchovy paste
2 tsp. red wine vinegar
¼ cup Parmesan cheese

1 clove garlic
2 eggs
¼ tsp. pepper

In a small bowl, place oil and anchovy paste. With a garlic press, squeeze garlic and add to oil mixture. Dip whole egg into boiling water for 30 seconds. Separate eggs; discard yolk and add white to oil mixture. Blend well. Add the pepper, lemon juice, Parmesan cheese, Worcestershire sauce, and vinegar and mix well.
*Good over pasta or salad.

****

CAFE MARIMBA TOMATILLO SAUCE

1 lb. tomatillos
1 jalapeno pepper

½ cup chopped onion
1 tbsp. chopped cilantro

Pinch of sugar
Salt to taste

Remove husks from fresh tomatillos. Put all ingredients in food processor and process for 30 seconds; leave some texture.
*Good over poultry, fish or shrimp.

****

CAJUN MAYONNAISE SAUCE

½ tsp. Tabasco sauce
1 tbsp. Cajun mustard
1 tbsp. horseradish
1 tsp. Worcestershire sauce

¾ cup mayonnaise
1 tbsp. ketchup
1 tbsp. celery
1 tbsp. parsley

1 tbsp. shallot
lemon juice
1 tbsp. paprika

Dijon mustard may be substituted for Cajun mustard. Finely chop shallot, celery and parsley. Combine shallot, celery and mayonnaise in a bowl, whisking to mix. Whisk in mustard, ketchup, horseradish, Worcestershire, paprika, Tabasco sauce and lemon juice.
*Good over fish or pork.

****

CAJUN MIX SAUCE

1 tsp. garlic powder
1 tsp. black pepper

1 tsp. cayenne pepper
½ tsp. dried thyme

1 tbsp. paprika
½ tsp. oregano

Combine paprika, garlic powder, cayenne, black pepper, thyme and oregano in a small bowl. Keep in a small jar, covered, for future use.
*Good over poultry.

CAJUN SAUCE

1 tbsp. cayenne pepper	1 ½ tsp. sweet paprika	½ tsp. salt
1 ¼ tsp. garlic powder	¾ tsp. onion powder	1 tbsp. butter
¾ tsp. cup white wine	¾ tsp. oregano	¾ tsp. thyme
1 tbsp. margarine	1 ½ tsp. black pepper	

Thoroughly combine red pepper, salt, paprika, pepper, garlic and onion powders, thyme and oregano, in a bowl. Heat skillet; add 1 tablespoon margarine and add wine, remove from heat and add 1 tablespoon cold butter and stir well. Stir in pepper mixture. Serve hot.
*Good over fish or poultry.

****

CALABANESE SAUCE

1 cup diced artichoke hearts	1 tbsp. oil	1 tbsp. butter
¼ cup Pecorino cheese		

Heat artichoke hearts in oil and butter for 3 minutes, in a saucepan. Add cheese and simmer for 3 minutes more.
*Good over pasta.

****

CALAMARI SAUCE

½ lb. calamari	28 oz. tomatoes	3 tsp. olive oil
½ cup chicken stock	3 cloves garlic	1 tsp. basil
½ tsp. oregano	1 tsp. sugar	

Sauté garlic in olive oil in a saucepan, over medium heat until lightly brown. Add crushed tomatoes, sugar, basil and chicken stock. Clean calamari and cut into pieces and boil in water for 15 minutes; remove and drain. Place calamari into tomato mixture, bring to a boil and simmer for 25 minutes.
*Good over pasta.

CALIFORNIAN FISH SAUCE

¼ cup all purpose flour
⅓ cup seedless raisins
¼ cup butter

Juice of 2 large lemons
¼ cup all purpose flour
¼ cup firmly packed light brown sugar

½ cup water
Lemon slice

Melt butter, and stir in flour over a low heat, in a saucepan. Stir for about 3 minutes, without letting the flour brown. Add salt and brown sugar. Warm water and lemon juice in a separate saucepan; stir into flour and butter mixture. Whisk; cook over medium heat for 5 to 6 minutes or until thick. Add raisins; continue cooking over low heat until raisins are warmed through. Pour into a warmed serving bowl; garnish with a lemon slice.
*Good over fish.

****

CANDIED CARROTS SAUCE

2 cups cooked carrots
¼ cup light brown sugar

Dash ground nutmeg

¼ cup butter

Melt butter in a saucepan, with cooked carrot slices. Sprinkle with sugar and nutmeg. Cook 5 minutes, until carrots are glazed.
*Good over capons and chicken.

****

CANNED APRICOT SAUCE

16 oz. canned apricots
5 crushed almonds or 1 tsp. almond extract

½ cup sugar syrup

1-3 cups vodka

Cut apricots in half and remove pits. Place the pits in a plastic or paper bag, hit with a hammer to open. Remove the nut and discard shell. Place the nuts in a bag and crush by hitting them to release the flavorful oils. (Any trace of the pit covering can impart a bitter taste.) Strain the juice, and add to the vodka to equal three cups. Combine fruit, almonds, vodka and let stand for one to two weeks. Strain and add sugar syrup to taste.

Optional flavorings. A pinch of cinnamon or cinnamon stick, a pinch of cloves or two whole cloves, ¼ cup flaked coconut, or a drop of coconut extract; small piece of sliced and scraped lemon peel.
*Good over desserts, fruit or ice cream.

CAPER SAUCE I

3 tbsp. bottled capers   ⅓ cup whipping cream   2 cups White Sauce

In a small saucepan, warm white sauce; stir in cream. Quickly add capers and liquid. Mix thoroughly. Do not cook any further, or the capers and pickling liquid may curdle the sauce.

If not serving at once, cover closely with plastic wrap to prevent skin forming. Reheat gently in top of double boiler.
*Good over fish, lamb or ham.

****

CAPER SAUCE II

8 sm. flounder fillets   Juice ½ lemon   salt and pepper
½ cup dry white wine   5 tbsp. butter   ½ cup flour
1 ½ tsp. Dijon mustard   1 ½ tbsp. capers   1 tsp. arrowroot
1 ½ tsp. minced shallots   ¼ cup heavy cream

Season fillets with salt and pepper, sprinkle with lemon juice and dredge in flour. Heat butter in a skillet and sauté fish about 2 minutes on each side, until golden brown. Remove fillets to a serving dish and keep warm. Add vermouth, capers, mustard and shallots to the skillet, blend well, bring to a boil while stirring. Simmer for 2 minutes; blend in cream and the arrowroot dissolved in a tablespoon of water. Bring to a simmer, stir for another minute.
*Spoon sauce over fish.

****

CARAMEL BRANDY SAUCE

2 lbs. caramel candies   ¾ cup heavy cream   2 tbsp. brandy

Place caramels over boiling water in a double boiler. In a separate pan bring the cream to a boil and pour over the caramels. Stir until caramels are melted and blend with the cream. Add brandy before serving.
*Good over desserts or ice cream.

****

CARAMEL SAUCE I

1 cup granulated sugar   1 cup heavy cream   ½ cup water
1 tsp. vanilla extract

Mix sugar and water in a 1-quart saucepan, over low heat. Stir often until sugar dissolves, then increase heat and bring syrup to a boil. Boil, without stirring, about 10 minutes until syrup is a rich, deep caramel color. Heat cream in a small saucepan just until bubbles form around edges. Stirring syrup constantly, slowly add cream. Stir in vanilla. Cool slightly, before pouring into a container and refrigerate.
*Good for ice cream and desserts

CARAMEL SAUCE II

| ½ cup sugar | 2 egg yolks | ¾ cup milk |
| ¾ cup cream | 1 tsp. vanilla | |

Heat sugar in a skillet until melted and light brown, stirring constantly. In a saucepan, scald milk and pour in sugar. Cook until the sugar dissolves. Beat egg yolks and add hot milk and sugar mixture slowly until thickened. Cool, then add cream and vanilla. Refrigerate.
*Good over ice cream and desserts.

****

CARAMEL SAUCE III

| 2 tbsp. condensed milk | 2 tsp. Golden Syrup | 1 tbsp. butter |
| 2 tbsp. brown sugar | 4 tbsp. hot water | Pinch of salt |

Melt butter in saucepan, then add all ingredients, except water. Stir over heat unit mixture is thick and turns rich caramel color. When mixture leaves sides of pan, remove from heat and add hot water, a little at a time. Return to heat, simmer 2 to 3 minutes. Let cool.
*Good over ice cream, pancakes, or cake.

****

CARAMEL SAUCE IV

| 2 cups brown sugar | ½ lb. butter | 2 tsp. vanilla |
| 2 tbsp. milk | | |

Combine ingredients in saucepan and cook over medium-low heat about 10 to 15 minutes.
*Good over ice cream and desserts.

****

CARAMEL TOPPING SAUCE

| ¼ cup whipping cream | 1 tbsp. light corn syrup | ½ cup sugar |
| 2 tbsp. unsalted butter | ½ cup toasted pecans | ½ tsp. vanilla |

Bring cream and butter to a simmer in a small saucepan; keep hot. Cook sugar in another small saucepan over low heat, stirring until sugar dissolves. Mix in corn syrup. Increase heat and boil without stirring until mixture turns deep tan, about 6 minutes. Remove from heat. Add warm cream mixture; stir until caramel dissolves. Return to high heat and stir until sauce is smooth and thickened, about 2 minutes. Pour into a bowl and mix in vanilla.
*Good over ice cream.

CARAMEL-MOCHA SAUCE

¾ cup light corn syrup	1 cup evaporated milk	¼ cup water
4 tbsp. unsalted butter	½ tsp. vanilla extract	1 cup sugar
¾ cup boiling water	1 tbsp. espresso coffee	Dash salt

Combine corn syrup, water, and sugar in a saucepan. Heat over medium-high heat, stirring until it is boiling vigorously. Add milk gradually, stirring continuously until it is thick and golden, about 10 minutes. Remove from heat and stir in coffee, vanilla and salt. Place the mixture into a food processor and blend it until smooth. Store the sauce covered in the refrigerator. Warm 1 minute in the microwave or warm at room temperature before serving.
*Good over ice cream or desserts.

****

CARAMELIZED ONIONS SAUCE

2 med. onions, chopped	3 tbsp. tomato paste	Salt and pepper
½ tsp. dry mustard	2 tbsp. dry Vermouth	3 tbsp. butter
1 ½ tbsp. all purpose flour		

Melt butter in a saucepan, then add onions and sauté for about 2 minutes. Add remaining ingredients, continue to cook until thickened.
*Good over pork.

****

CARAWAY SAUCE

| 1 ½ tsp. lightly crushed caraway seed | 1 ½ cups brandy or vodka |

Combine ingredients and let stand for 2 weeks, in a covered bowl or jar. Strain.
*Good over pork or poultry.

****

CARBONARA SAUCE I

4 oz. heavy cream	1 tbsp. olive oil	5 eggs
7 oz. diced bacon	2 tbsp. butter	Salt and pepper
4 oz. Parmesan and Romano cheese		

Beat the eggs and cream together with a pinch of salt. Heat the oil and butter in a large pan. Add the diced bacon and cook gently until the fat melts. Remove from heat, stir in the cream, eggs, cheese, salt and pepper to taste.
*Good over pasta.

CARBONARA SAUCE II

| 1 crushed garlic clove | 2 tbsp. olive oil | ½ lb. pancetta |
| ¾ cup Parmesan cheese | 3 eggs | |

In a deep skillet, gently cook crushed garlic in olive oil until golden brown. Remove the garlic and discard. Add diced pancetta and cook until the edges turn brown. Remove from the heat. In a warm bowl, beat 3 eggs with Parmesan cheese. Toss both mixtures together before serving.
*Good over pasta.

****

CARBONARA SAUCE III

2 eggs plus 2 egg yolks	½ cup heavy cream	¼ cup butter
1 cup Parmesan cheese	2 tbsp. olive oil	½ lb. bacon
1 tsp. red pepper flakes		

Cut about 8 slices of bacon into small strips. Cream butter in small bowl; set aside. In another bowl, beat eggs and egg yolks together; stir in ½ cup grated cheese; set aside. Fry bacon pieces over medium heat but do not let them get crisp. Reduce heat to low and pour off all but 1 tablespoon fat. Add olive oil and red pepper flakes; keep warm over low heat. Add cream to bacon, bring to a simmer. Stir all ingredients together and keep warm.
*Good over pasta.

****

CARIBBEAN CREOLE SAUCE

2 med. onions, chopped	½ cup vegetable oil	2 garlic cloves
1 med. green bell pepper	3 tomatoes, chopped	1 tsp. salt
½ cup dry white wine	6 oz. tomato paste	Pepper
1 tsp. fresh red chilies		

In medium saucepan, heat oil over low heat. Add onion, garlic, the cored, seeded and finely chopped pepper and chilies, and sauté until the peppers are soft. Add salt, pepper and tomatoes. Cook about 10 minutes over low heat, stirring occasionally. Stir in tomato paste and wine and simmer for another 10 minutes.
*Good over rice or pasta.

CARIBBEAN HOT AND SPICY BANANA SAUCE

1 cup seedless raisins
6-oz. tomato paste
½ cup light corn syrup
1 tsp. cayenne pepper
1 ½ tsp. grated nutmeg
¼ cup dark rum

1 cup chopped onions
2 ¼ cup vinegar
2 cloves garlic
1 cup brown sugar
1 ½ tsp. cinnamon
½ tsp. ground cloves

4 cups water
5 lg. bananas
1 tbsp. salt
1 tsp. pepper
4 tsp. allspices

Combine raisins, onion, garlic and tomato paste in a food processor. Add remaining ingredients to food processor, until well blended.
*Good over rice.

****

CARROT SAUCE

1 cup puree carrots

1 cup chicken stock

1 tbsp. butter

Heat carrots and chicken stock in a saucepan, for 2 minutes, then blend in butter.
*Good over pasta.

****

CATALONIAN CREAM SAUCE

2 cups whole milk
1 ½ tbsp. cornstarch

Peel of ½ lemon
1 cinnamon stick

4 egg yolks
7 tbsp. sugar

Combine the milk, lemon peel and cinnamon stick in a saucepan, bring to a boil and simmer for 10 minutes. Strain the milk and set aside. Discard the lemon peel and cinnamon stick. Combine the egg yolks and half the sugar, beating until slightly thickened and pale; yellow in color. Beat in the cornstarch. Add 3 tbsp. of the hot milk to the mixture. Stir to blend. Then stir the mixture into the rest of the hot milk. Cook over a low flame for 5 minutes, stirring constantly. The mixture should be kept just below the simmer stage. Do not let it boil. Cool.
*Good over ice cream.

CAULIFLOWER SAUCE

¾ lb. cauliflower
2 tbsp. dry white wine
¼ tsp. white pepper

1 tsp. fresh thyme
2 oz. Swiss cheese
Snipped parsley (optional)

Chicken stock
½ tsp. salt

Break cauliflower into flowerets. Simmer in a cup of stock, in a covered saucepan, until tender (about 8 minutes); drain. Puree cauliflower in a food processor or a blender, with remaining ingredients, except cheese and parsley. Heat thoroughly over low flame. Stir in cheese and continue to heat, stirring constantly, until cheese is melted (about 2 minutes). Stir parsley into sauce.
*Good over pasta.

****

CAVIAR SAUCE I

6 oz. heavy cream
¼ cup caviar

2 oz. butter

Dash black pepper

Melt butter, in a saucepan, over low heat, add cream and pepper, simmer for 3 minutes. Remove from heat and add caviar.
*Use over pasta.

****

CAVIAR SAUCE II

1 cup white vermouth
1 ½ lb. Gorgonzola

2 cups heavy cream
2 oz. Romanoff caviar

pepper to taste
pinch nutmeg

Bring vermouth to a boil in a small saucepan. Add cream, bring to a boil again, and lower heat. Season mixture with pepper and nutmeg, and simmer for about 15 minutes. Add Gorgonzola and caviar, mix well. Remove from heat.
*Good over pasta.

****

CEBOLLITA (PICKLED ONIONS) SAUCE

1 lg. white onion
¾ cup white vinegar

2 fresh jalapeno chilies
½ tsp. white pepper

¼ cup water
½ tsp. salt

Peel and cut onion, in ¼ inch wedges. Slice chilies paper-thin. Place onions and chilies in a non-aluminum bowl with vinegar, water, salt and sugar. Marinate at room temperature for 2 to 3 days.
You can substitute hot Italian sausage.
*Good over rice, beans or meats.

CELEBRATION CHAMPAGNE SAUCE

1 cup Emmentaler cheese
1 garlic clove, halved
1 cup champagne

¼ cup half and half
2 tbsp. cornstarch
3 cups Port du Salut Cheese

2 egg yolks
2 tbsp. brandy

Mash garlic clove and place in saucepan. Add champagne and heat until bubbly. Gradually add cheeses until melted, then add egg yolks and half and half. Blend cornstarch and brandy in a small bowl, stir into cheese mixture. Continue to cook, stirring constantly, until thick and creamy.
*Good over pasta or vegetables.

****

CELERY SAUCE I

½ cup chicken stock
1 - 2 tbsp. lemon juice
1 cup heavy cream

1 lb. celery stalks
¼ cup chopped parsley
salt and pepper

4 tbsp. butter
¼ tsp. nutmeg

Simmer celery in butter for 5 minutes, in a saucepan. Add all the remaining ingredients. Continue to cook until mixture is reduced to a sauce like consistency, then add salt and pepper.
*Good over pasta.

****

CELERY SAUCE II

1 cup pureed celery
1 cup pureed potatoes

½ cup milk

1 tbsp. butter

Heat all ingredients, in a saucepan, over a medium heat for 3 to 5 minutes.
*Good over rice.

****

CELERY SAUCE III

¼ cup blanched celery

½ cup chicken stock

1 cup cream sauce

Heat all ingredients together, until blended, in a saucepan, for about 5 minutes.
*Good over pasta.

CHAMPAGNE-HERB DRESSING SAUCE

2 cups brut champagne	¼ cup olive oil	¼ cup water
1 tsp. minced parsley	1 tsp. cornstarch	½ tsp. salt
1 tsp. minced tarragon	1 tsp. minced thyme	⅛ tsp. pepper
1 tsp. minced chives	2 tsp. honey	

Combine water and cornstarch, in a bowl; stir well and set aside. Place champagne in a small non-aluminum saucepan; bring to a boil. Cook 8 minutes or until reduced to 1 cup. Reduce heat and add cornstarch mixture, oil, honey and salt; cook 4 minutes, stirring frequently. Remove from heat; stir in remaining ingredients. Place in a small bowl; cover and chill. Stir well before using.
*Serve over salad.

****

CHARCUTERIE SAUCE

1 ½ cups Espagnole Sauce	1 sm. onion, chopped	2 tbsp. butter
½ cup dry white wine	2 dill pickles, cut in julienne strips	

Melt butter in a saucepan and sauté onion over medium heat until soft and golden, but not brown. Stir in Espagnole Sauce and wine, bringing to a boil. Reduce heat and simmer until the sauce has been reduced by about a quarter. Just before serving, add pickle and cook for about 1 minute. Serve hot.
*Good over rice or pasta.

****

CHASSEM SAUCE

1 ¼ cups beef stock	¼ lb. mushrooms	1 tbsp. butter
¼ cup dry white wine	1 tsp. tomato paste	½ cup bacon
2 tbsp. flour		

Heat butter and flour in a saucepan, for 2 minutes. Add the rest of the ingredients and heat for 5 to 8 minutes longer.
*Good over pasta.

****

CREAM SAUCE

1 tbsp. dry mustard	½ cup vinegar	1 egg yolk
2 tsp. flour	1 tbsp. butter	1 tsp. salt
1 ½ tsp. confectioners' sugar	1 cup whipped cream	pinch cayenne

Melt butter in a saucepan. Mix dry ingredients together in the top of a double boiler. Slowly add the vinegar, egg yolk and butter. Cook over boiling water until mixture thickens. Remove from heat and cool. Add whipped cream.
*Good over baked potatoes.

CREAMY PAPRIKA SAUCE

½ cup chicken broth
3 tsp. paprika

½ cup condensed milk
½ tsp. cornstarch

½ cup sliced onion
fresh pepper

Place chicken broth with onion in a saucepan over medium heat. Cook until onion is soft, about 3 to 5 minutes. Mix the milk and cornstarch together in a separate bowl. Pour into onion mixture and heat for 3 minutes until slightly thickened. Remove from heat; add paprika and pepper to taste.
*Good over meatballs, noodles or poultry.

****

CHEDDAR SAUCE

16-oz. pkg. peas and carrots
⅔ cup all-purpose flour
½ cup chopped green onion
8-oz. sharp cheddar cheese

½ tsp. paprika
¼ tsp. pepper
¾ cup white wine

½ cup butter
3 cups milk
Frozen patty shells

Melt butter or margarine, in a 3-quart saucepan; blend in flour, paprika, and pepper. Stir in milk and green onion. Cook and stir till mixture is thickened and bubbly. Continue to cook 1 minute more. Stir in wine, peas, carrots and cheese; stir till cheese is melted. Spoon mixture into patty shells. Serve immediately.
*Good over rice or pasta.

****

CHEESE & ONION SAUCE

2 tbsp. all purpose flour
2 cups Gruyere cheese
2 cups Cheddar cheese

1 lg. chopped onion
2 tbsp. snipped chives
⅔ cup sour cream

2 tbsp. butter
Pepper

Melt butter in a saucepan, add onion and cook 4 to 5 minutes or until soft but not brown. Add flour and sour cream, cook 2 minutes. Add cheeses and cook, stirring until mixture is smooth. Add chives and season with pepper.
*Good over hot dogs.

****

CHEESE AND CREAM SAUCE

2 cups Parmesan cheese
Black pepper

8-oz. heavy cream

4 tbsp. butter

Melt butter in a saucepan; stir in cream until thickened, about 5 minutes. Add cheese and black pepper.
*Good over pasta.

CHEESE DIP SAUCE

8-oz. pkg. cream cheese
¼ tsp. dry mustard

8-oz. pkg. American cheese
3 drops hot pepper sauce

½ cup milk
¼ tsp. onion salt

Melt cream cheese slowly in a saucepan, stirring constantly. Add shredded American cheese, milk, onion salt, mustard and hot pepper sauce. Cook, stirring constantly until cheese melts. Serve warm.
*Good over poultry.

****

CHEESE FONDUE SAUCE

2 tbsp. cherry liqueur
1 lb. Edam cheese

1 ½ cups white wine
2 tbsp. flour

1 lb. Swiss cheese
Salt and pepper

Pour wine into a saucepan, heat until it bubbles. Grate cheese, toss with flour and gradually add small amounts to the wine. Stir constantly. Add salt and pepper to taste. Stir for an additional 8 minutes.
*Good over pasta or as a dip.

****

CHEESE SAUCE I

½ cup Swiss cheese
¼ cup dry white wine
½ tsp. salt

1 tbsp. chopped pimento
1 cup milk
Dash white pepper and nutmeg

2 tbsp. butter
2 tbsp. flour

Melt butter in a saucepan and blend in flour and salt. Add milk, stirring until smooth; cook and stir until sauce boils and is thickened. Add wine, cheese, pepper, nutmeg, and pimento, if desired. Stir over low heat until cheese is melted. *Good over vegetables.

****

CHEESE SAUCE II

2 tbsp. all-purpose flour
½ tsp. prepared mustard
½ cup shredded Cheddar cheese

1 ¼ cups milk
Salt and Pepper

Dash cayenne pepper
1 tbsp. butter

Melt butter in a saucepan, stir in flour and cook 1 minute. Remove from heat and stir in milk gradually. Return to heat, and bring to a boil; simmer 2 minutes. Add mustard, cheese, cayenne, salt and pepper, heat just until cheese melts. Serve hot.
*Good over poultry.

CHEESE SAUCES (VARIATIONS)

MILD
Brick---Mild to moderately sharp flavor; semi soft to medium firm.
Cold-pack cheese food---Made from at least two natural cheeses with milk solids or whey added; sold in crocks, jars, and tubes.
Ricotta---Unripened; creamy texture, moist.
Muenster---Flavor varies from mild to mellow; porous texture.
Pepper cheese---Miló Monterey Jack cheese studded with black peppercorns.
Rope cheese---Process Monterey Jack cheese matted into ropes.
Triple-crème cheese---A 75-percent-fat cream cheese; rich flavor.
Pasteurized process American and Swiss cheeses---Blends of natural cheeses heated to kill bacteria and halt aging. Smooth texture. Mild flavor.
Limburger---Powerful aroma and flavor.

MELLOW
Gouda---Nutty to slightly acid flavor; usually has a red wax coating.
Havarti---Danish; slightly sour taste. Rich and creamy; hard rind.
Baby Swiss---Younger, slightly sweeter than regular Swiss.
Fontina---Italian; slightly smoky taste.
Jarlsberg---Semi soft; buttery flavor.
Cheddar---Originally English; smooth, firm texture.
Edam---Less buttery tasting than Gouda; has a cannonball shape.

SHARP
Sharp cheddar---Well-aged cheddar; bold flavor with a dry, grainy texture.
Sharp cheddar curds---Bite-size curds of aged cheddar cheese.
Chèvre---Goat cheese with distinctive tang.
Feta---Soft texture; salty flavor.
Roquefort---Imported; strong flavor, crumbly.
Gorgonzola---Creamy, spreadable; tangier than blue cheese.
Blue (or Bleu, when imported)---Blue streaked; sharp flavor.
Asiago---Slightly salty grating cheese.

PUNGENT
Provolone---Mild to salty, robust flavor reminiscent of fermented milk.
Liederkranz---Creamy spreading cheese; strong aroma. Less pungent than Limburger.
Sapsago---Tangy, hard cheese with a pale green color from cloverleaves.

SWEET
Gruyère---Mild and creamy tasting when young; older ones are stronger.
Brie---Edible crust. Mild aroma; slightly tangy.
French grape cheese---Fruity tasting; creamy white. Coated with an edible rind of grape seeds.
Port du Salut---Buttery, delicate flavor; zestier when aged.
Bel Paese---Soft, sweet, and mild.
Gourmandise---Creamy, sweet; nutty or fruity flavor.
Gjetost---Unripened; caramel flavor and color.

CHERRY CRANBERRY SAUCE

1 tbsp. crystallized ginger
12-oz. frozen cranberries

½ cup cranberry juice
½ cup dried cherries

½ cup sugar
½ cup water

Mix water, juice, and cherries in a bowl and let stand for 10 minutes. Heat cherries, cranberries, sugar and ginger together in a saucepan, for 15 minutes.
*Good over desserts or ice cream.

****

CHERRY JUBILEE SAUCE

¼ cup cherry liqueur
1 can pitted dark sweet cherries

1 tsp. cornstarch

1 tbsp. water

Drain cherries syrup into a blender and blend with cornstarch and water. Place in a saucepan and stir over low heat until thickened. Add cherries and heat 5 minutes longer. Pour cherry liqueur over cherries and ignite.
*Good over ice cream or desserts.

****

CHERRY MINT LIQUEUR SAUCE

2 ½ cups Bing cherries
10 fresh mint leaves

10 crushed cherry stones
Sliced peel of ½ lemon

2 cups vodka
½ cup sugar

Cut cherries in half, and remove the pits. Crush the cherries lightly. Then crush about 10 of the cherry stones by placing them in a plastic or cloth bag and hitting with a hammer. Place crushed pits and cherries in a quart jar. Add the sugar, then the vodka. Close the jar tightly and place in the sun daily for 1 week. Then set the jar in a cool dark place for 4 weeks. Strain and let mature at least 2 months.

Optional flavorings: add 5 cloves, ½ " stick of cinnamon, or a pinch of mace.
*Good over desserts or ice cream.

****

CHERRY SAUCE

1 cup Bing cherries
1 tbsp. lemon juice

3 tbsp. orange juice
¼ cup water, or juice from cherries

2 tbsp. sugar

If cherries are fresh, cook in water to cover, over medium heat until falling off the pits; drain. If canned, drain, reserving ¼ cup of juice. Place in a saucepan with juice or water, orange and lemon juices. Heat until warmed through. Press through sieve into a bowl. Stir in sugar until dissolved, while still hot. When ready to use, reheat over low heat.
*Good over ice cream or desserts.

CHERRY-LIME SAUCE

| 1 cup dark sweet cherries | ¼ cup + 1 tbsp. water | 1 tsp. cornstarch |
| 2 tbsp. light corn syrup | Limejuice to taste | |

Stir together pitted cherries and ¼ cup water in a microwave, uncovered on high power for 3 minutes. Puree cherry mixture in food processor or blender and press through a strainer into the clean bowl. Stir the remaining water with the cornstarch. Microwave the cherry sauce on high power for 1 minute, until boiling. Stir in cornstarch mixture and microwave, until boiling and slightly thickened, about 1 minute. Stir in corn syrup and limejuice. Cool and refrigerate until chilled.
*Serve over melon.

****

CHESTNUT DEVILED SAUCE

| 9 to 12 chestnuts | ¼ cup Masilot wine | 2 tbsp. Butter |
| ¼ tsp. cayenne pepper | 1 tbsp. oil | salt |

Place chestnuts in blender; add remaining ingredients and blend well. Heat all ingredients together in a saucepan, for 3 to 5 minutes.
*Good over veal.

****

CHESTNUT GLAZING SAUCE

| 1 cup veal stock | 9 to 12 chestnuts | 1 tbsp. ginger |
| 1 tbsp. butter | | |

Place chestnuts in blender; add remaining ingredients and blend well. Heat all ingredients together in a saucepan, for 5 minutes.
*Good over veal.

****

CHESTNUT PUREE SAUCE I

| 6 to 8 chestnuts | 1 cup veal stock | ½ cup white sauce |

Place chestnuts in blender; add remaining ingredients and blend well. Heat ingredients together, until well blended, in a saucepan for 5 minutes.
*Good over veal or chicken.

CHESTNUT PUREE SAUCE II

2 cups chicken stock
2 tbsp. unsalted butter
½ cup heavy cream

2 lbs. chestnuts
1 cup hot milk

1 rib celery
salt

Place chestnuts in a saucepan, with chicken stock and celery. Simmer, covered, for 20-30 minutes or until the chestnuts are soft. Drain and put through a food mill or ricer and whisk in the butter, hot milk and cream. Add salt to taste.
*Good over veal or chicken.

****

CHICK PEAS SAUCE

1 cup cooked chick peas
¼ cup carrots
8 oz. plum tomatoes
1 clove garlic, chopped

¼ cup onion
¼ cup celery
salt and pepper

1 bay leaf
¼ cup parsley
1 tbsp. oil

Heat oil; add chopped vegetables and cook in a saucepan, for 2 minutes. Add chickpeas, bay leaf and tomatoes; continue to cook for 10 minutes more.
*Good over pasta.

****

CHICKEN A LA KING SAUCE

1 cup cooked white chicken
¼ cup mushrooms
¼ cup green and red pepper

1 cup sweet cream
1 egg yolk
Dash of Cognac

1 tbsp. butter
¼ cup Sherry
salt and pepper

Dice chicken and toss in butter, add salt and pepper and heat in a saucepan. Add cream, mushrooms and peppers; continue to cook for 3 minutes. Add egg yolk, sherry and a dash of cognac. Remove from heat to prevent curdling.
*Good over toast or pasta.

****

CHICKEN AND OLIVE SAUCE

½ lb. diced chicken breast
¾ cup white wine
18 pitted black olives

2 tbsp. minced onion
2 tbsp. parsley.
1 tsp. minced garlic

1 tbsp. olive oil
Salt and pepper

Sauté ½ pound diced chicken breast in 1 tablespoon olive oil, in a skillet, until it loses its raw look. Add minced onion and garlic and cook another 30 seconds. Add wine and boil 1 minute. Add olives and cook another minute. Season to taste with salt and pepper and swirl in another tablespoon of olive oil and parsley.
*Good over pasta.

CHICKEN LIVER SAUCE I

¼ lb. bacon, minced
¼ cup minced parsley
¼ lb. mushrooms

1 sm. minced onion
½ lb. chicken livers
½ cup tomato puree

Salt and pepper
½ tsp. sage
¼ cup Marsala wine

Cut chicken livers into quarters, then thinly slice mushrooms. Chop the bacon, onion and parsley together to make a paste. Put into deep skillet and cook, stirring for 5 minutes. Add chicken livers and mushrooms. Cook over medium heat until livers are browned. Add remaining ingredients and cook for 10 minutes.
*Good over pasta.

****

CHICKEN LIVER SAUCE II

⅛ lb. bacon
½ lb. chicken livers
1 cup heavy cream

2 tbsp. minced onion
2 tbsp. Cognac
salt and pepper

2 tbsp. butter
1 bay leaf

Sauté diced bacon in butter in a skillet, until golden. Add onion, chicken livers and bay leaf, sauté over high heat until livers are barely done. Add Cognac and flame. Add cream and boil uncovered until it is reduced to sauce like consistency. Remove bay leaf. Season to taste.
*Good over pasta.

****

CHILE OIL SAUCE

1 or 2 Scotch bonnet chilies
2 scallions or chives
1 cup olive oil

2 cloves garlic
2 allspice berries
5 peppercorns

1 lg. shallot
2 cloves

Halve and seed chilies and cut into ¼ inch strips. Peel and cut garlic, shallot and scallions into thin slices. Combine ingredients in a bowl and let marinate for at least 24 hours. Flavor improves with age.
*Use over salads, grilled fish, rice, or any dish that needs a kick.

****

CHILE PEPPER SAUCE

6 tbsp. olive oil

5 cloves garlic

1 chile pepper

Heat oil in a small skillet and sauté garlic for 2 minutes. Add chopped up chile peppers, simmer 5 minutes longer.
*Good over poultry.

CHILE POWDER SAUCE

1 tbsp. Chile powder
1 minced garlic

¼ cup crushed tomatoes

1 onion, minced

Mix all ingredients together in a small saucepan, until well blended. Heat about 5 minutes.
*Use for pasta.

****

CHILI BUTTER SAUCE

½ cup unsalted butter
1 tsp. chili powder

2 tbsp. lemon juice

Pinch cayenne

Place butter and chili powder in a glass bowl, cover, melt in microwave on high 1 to 1 ½ minute. Stir in lemon juice and cayenne pepper, recover and microwave on low 2 to 3 minutes.
*Good over rice.

****

CHILI COCKTAIL SAUCE

⅓ cup chili sauce
2 tbsp. pineapple syrup

⅔ cup mayonnaise

2 tbsp. lemon juice

Mix all ingredients together in a bowl, until well blended. Chill and serve.
*Good over poultry.

****

CHILI CON CARNE SAUCE

1 ½ cups stewed tomatoes
1 ½ lbs. cooked beef
½ tsp. caraway seed
4 tbsp. tomato paste
12 oz. red kidney beans
Pinch of sugar

1 ¼ cups beef stock
½ tsp. celery seeds
Pinch cayenne
½ yellow pepper
Pinch red pepper

2 tbsp. oil
1 garlic clove
Pinch paprika
2 onions
salt and pepper

Chop yellow pepper, drain the kidney beans then cook all ingredients together in a saucepan, until well blended.
*Good over rice or pasta.

CHILI MAYONNAISE SAUCE

¼ tsp. white pepper
1 tbsp. olive or peanut oil
1 tbsp. minced hot chilies

1 ½ cups mayonnaise
2 tsp. chili powder

2 eggs yolks
2 tbsp. coriander

Heat oil in small skillet over low heat until rippling. Stir in chili powder and let cool at room temperature. Add chili powder mixture, coriander and hot chilies to mayonnaise; whisk until blended.
*Good over vegetables.

****

CHILI POWDER SAUCE

1 oz. hot chili powder
1 oz. cayenne pepper

3 oz. mild chili powder
1 tbsp. ground coriander

1 oz. ground cumin
1 tsp. celery salt

Mix the chili powders and ground spices together thoroughly. Heat an ungreased pan and carefully pour the chili mixture into the pan. Toast the mixture for about 90 seconds, moving it around with a spatula. Remove the pan from the heat and continue moving the mixture around.
*Good over ribs or chicken.

****

CHILI SAUCE I

1 ½ cups green peppers
2 minced garlic cloves
¼ tsp. ground cloves
1 cup brown sugar

1 cup minced onions
1 tsp. dry mustard
½ tsp. allspice
1 tsp. cinnamon

8 cups tomatoes
¼ cup salt
1 tsp. basil
1 cup vinegar

In a large saucepan, combine the peeled and chopped tomatoes, onion, minced green peppers and garlic together. Dissolve the seasonings in the vinegar; then add to the tomatoes. Blend in the sugar and bring to a boil. Reduce to a simmer until thick. Pour in sterilized jars, seal and place in a water bath for 30 minutes.
*Good over pork, shrimp or poultry.

****

CHILI SAUCE II

6 lg. onions, chopped
7 oz. fresh red chilies

½ cup vegetable oil
10 garlic cloves, finely chopped

1 ½ cups ketchup

In a medium saucepan, sauté onions in oil until they are soft; add the garlic and cook for 2 minutes. Add chilies and simmer for about 5 minutes. Place the mixture in a food processor and add ketchup and puree. Return mixture to saucepan and simmer 15 minutes. Cool.
*Good over ribs or poultry.

CHILI SAUCE III

½ cup Worcestershire sauce
1 tsp. ground coriander
1 ½ tsp. ground cumin
3 tbsp. chili powder
2 16-oz.cans tomatoes in puree

1 cup yellow onion
4 jalapeno peppers
2 red bell peppers
1 cup black olives

5 cloves garlic
5 tbsp. olive oil
pinch of cinnamon
1 cup beer

Heat half the oil in a large casserole. Add chopped onion and garlic and sauce over medium heat for 5 minutes. Add the cored, seeded and diced bell pepper and the seeded and minced jalapeno pepper; sauté 10 minutes. Stir in the chili powder, cumin, coriander and cinnamon and cook for 5 minutes more, stirring. Remove from heat.
*Good with chicken.

****

CHILI SAUCE IV

4 qts. ripe tomatoes
1 cup brown sugar
½ tbsp. allspice
3 lg. white onions
1 tsp. celery seed

3 green peppers
2 cups cider vinegar
½ tsp. ground cloves
1 tsp. cinnamon
1 tbsp. dry mustard

1 tsp. ginger
1 tbsp. salt
½ tbsp. pepper
1 tsp. nutmeg

Put tomatoes through a food grinder, seed and remove membrane, then place in a saucepan. Add the remaining ingredients. Slowly simmer until very thick, about 3 hours.
*Good over ribs or poultry.

****

CHILI TEXAS-STYLE SAUCE

2 ½ lbs. beef steak
10 ½ oz. can beef broth
½ cup chopped onion
½ tsp. ground cayenne
4 oz. can green chili peppers

2 tsp. dried oregano
1 ⅓ cup water
2 tsp. cumin seed
½ tsp. paprika
Cooked pinto beans

1 garlic clove
2 tsp. sugar
2 bay leaves
2 tsp. cornmeal
3 tbsp. cooking oil

In a large saucepan, brown cubes of beef, with onion and crushed garlic in hot oil. Stir in beef broth, water, sugar, oregano, cumin, cayenne, paprika, and bay leaves. Bring to a boil and reduce heat. Simmer, uncovered, 1 ¼ hours until meat is tender. Stir in the seeded and chopped chili peppers and cornmeal. Simmer 20 minutes, stirring occasionally. Remove bay leaves.
*Good over rice and beans.

CHILI-HORSERADISH SAUCE

3 tbsp. horseradish   ⅓ cup chili sauce   1 cup mayonnaise

Mix all ingredients together in a bowl, until well blended. Chill before serving.
*Good over shrimp.

****

CHINESE MARINADE SAUCE I

2 tbsp. oyster sauce   2 tbsp. hoisin sauce   2 tbsp. honey
2 tbsp. light soy sauce   Pinch white pepper   ¾ tsp. salt
2 tbsp. dark soy sauce   1 ½ tbsp. brandy or whisky

Mix all ingredients together in a bowl, until well blended.
*Good to marinate ribs, for at least 4 hours.

****

CHINESE MARINADE SAUCE II

1 cup apricot preserves   1 tbsp. 5-spice powder   3 lg. cloves garlic
⅓ cup dark soy sauce   ¼ cup vegetable oil

Orange marmalade may be used instead of apricot preserve. In a food processor or blender, combine preserves, spices, garlic and soy sauce, blend until smooth. Gradually add oil.
*Good to marinate spare ribs.

****

CHINESE SWEET 'N' SOUR SAUCE

1 tbsp. dry white wine   ¾ cup sugar   2 tbsp. soy sauce
2 tbsp. cornstarch   3 tbsp. ketchup   ½ cup water
3 tbsp. wine vinegar

Combine sugar, soy sauce, wine, vinegar, and ketchup in saucepan; bring to a boil. Dissolve cornstarch in water; add to sauce. Cook over low heat, stirring, until sauce has thickened.
*Good over poultry.

CHINESE-STYLE MUSTARD SAUCE

½ cup dry mustard   boiling water

In a small bowl place dry mustard and slowly add water, stir until mixture is a consistency you want. Set aside for 30 minutes, then use immediately. This mustard cannot be stored.
Options: Wine, cider, vinegar or beer can be substituted for the water.
*Good over poultry.

****

CHIVE AND CINNAMON SAUCE

½ tsp. cinnamon   1 tbsp. soy sauce   2 tbsp. water
2 tbsp. fresh chives   ½ cup cabbage   6 tbsp. butter
3 tbsp. heavy cream

Heat chopped chives, cabbage, soy sauce, butter, cinnamon and water in a saucepan for 3 minutes. Remove from heat and add cream, blend well.
*Good over poultry.

****

CHOCOLATE SAUCE I

1 ½ cups sugar   1 cup cocoa   ¼ tsp. salt
1 cup boiling water   1 tsp. vanilla

In a saucepan, mix cocoa, sugar and salt. Gradually stir in water; stir over medium heat about 8 minutes or until smooth and thickened. Remove from heat and stir in vanilla.
*Good over ice cream, plain cake or cut-up fruit.

****

CHOCOLATE SAUCE II

4 oz. milk chocolate candy bar   1 ¼ cups milk   1 tsp. sugar
Vanilla extract, to taste   4 egg yolks, well beaten

Chop or cut chocolate bar into pieces. Heat milk, chocolate, vanilla and sugar, in a saucepan, over low heat until chocolate melts, stirring continuously. When liquid is just bubbling around the edge of the saucepan, remove pan from heat. Spoon a small amount of the hot liquid into the yolks. Add yolks to chocolate. Return to heat and continue stirring for 2 to 3 minutes without simmering, until thickened. Serve hot.
*Good over desserts or ice cream.

CHOCOLATE SAUCE III

½ tsp. peppermint extract
¼ cup margarine

6 tbsp. cocoa power
¾ cups canned evaporated milk

1 cup sugar

Combine cocoa and sugar in a small saucepan; blend in evaporated milk. Add margarine and cook, stirring constantly, until mixture just begins to boil. Remove from heat and add peppermint extract.
*Good over desserts and ice cream.

****

CHOCOLATE SAUCE IV

3 tbsp. unsweetened cocoa
6 tbsp. half-and-half

½ cup sugar
1 tbsp. Amaretto di Saronno liqueur

2 tbsp. butter

Melt butter in a saucepan over low heat. Remove from heat, and stir in sugar and unsweetened cocoa. Add half-and-half, blending well. Cook over low heat, stirring constantly, until mixture just begins to boil. Remove from heat, and stir in amaretto liqueur. Cool slightly.
*Good over desserts and ice cream.

****

CHOCOLATE SAUCE V

6 oz. pkg. semi-sweet chocolate
¼ cup light corn syrup

¼ cup coffee liqueur
¼ cup milk

1 tbsp. butter

Melt chocolate and butter in top of a double boiler over hot water. Slowly stir in syrup and milk; beat until smooth. In a small saucepan warm liqueur. Ignite. Pour flaming liqueur into chocolate mixture. When flame subsides, stir well.
*Good over desserts and ice cream.

****

CHOCOLATE BRANDIED SAUCE

8 oz. cooking chocolate
¾ cup hot water

¼ cup sugar

¼ cup brandy

Melt chocolate in a double boiler. Stir in sugar, brandy and hot water, and continue stirring until sugar is dissolved. For a thinner sauce, add additional hot water.
*Good over ice cream or desserts.

CHOCOLATE BUTTER SAUCE

⅔ cups unsweetened cocoa powder   ½ cup hot water   1 cup sugar
⅛ tsp. almond extract   ½ tsp. vanilla   ½ cup butter
Dash Amaretto liqueur for flavoring.

Sift cocoa powder into top of double boiler. Add hot water stir until smooth. Place over simmering water. Stir in sugar and salt, cook to dissolved, about 1 minute. Whisk in butter and blend in. Whisk in vanilla extract and liqueur.
*Good over ice cream.

****

CHOCOLATE FONDUE SAUCE

12-oz. white chocolate   2 tbsp. orange liqueur   ½ cup heavy cream

Combine whipping cream and white chocolate in saucepan over low heat, stirring until chocolate melts and mixture is smooth. Remove from heat; stir in liqueur.
*Good over pasta or over desserts.

****

CHOCOLATE KAHLUA SAUCE

2-oz. semisweet chocolate   ¾ cup half and half   3 egg yolks
1-oz. baking chocolate   2 tbsp. Kahlua   ½ cup sugar

Place chocolate squares in a glass dish and microwave on 50 percent, 3 ½ to 4 minutes. Stir until melted; set aside. Mix half and half, whisk in egg yolks until well blended. Microwave on 70 percent 3 minutes, whisking every minute. Add sugar; whisk. Microwave on 70 percent 1 minute, or until sugar dissolves. Whisk in melted chocolate and Kahlua; whisk until smooth.
*Good over ice cream, plain cake or cut-up fruit.

****

CHOCOLATE MARSHMALLOW FUDGE SAUCE

⅔ cup evaporated milk   1 ½ cups sugar   2 tbsp. butter
18-oz. semi-sweet chocolate   7-oz. marshmallow cream   1 cup walnuts

Combine sugar, milk and butter in a saucepan. Bring to a boil over low heat, stirring constantly until sugar dissolves. Remove from heat, stir in chocolate bits and marshmallow cream, beating vigorously until thickens. Stir in nuts.
*Good over desserts.

CHOCOLATE MIGNONS A LA RITZ SAUCE

5 ½ oz. semisweet chocolate
1 ¾ cups half and half

4 lg. egg yolks
2 tbsp. vanilla

1 lg. egg
6 ½ tbsp. sugar

Melt chocolate with half and half in top of double boiler over barely simmering water, whisking until smooth. Whisk sugar, yolks and egg in medium bowl until thick and light colored. Stir in small amount of chocolate mixture. Return egg mixture to remaining chocolate mixture. Set over low heat and stir until slightly thickened, about 5 minutes. Remove from heat. Stir in vanilla extract.
*Good over desserts or ice cream.

****

CHOCOLATE WHITE SAUCE

9 oz. white chocolate

1 cup heavy cream

½ cup Dranbuie

Break up chocolate in small pieces. Scald cream in a saucepan. Remove from heat and place in a food processor with chocolate pieces for 3 seconds. Add Dranbuie.
*Good over pasta or desserts.

****

CHORON SAUCE

4 tbsp. dry white wine
4 tbsp. white wine vinegar
½ cup tomato paste, reduced by boiling to ¼ cup

1 green onion, chopped
¾ to cup butter

3 egg yolks
Salt & white pepper

In a small saucepan, combine wine and vinegar, green onion and cook over low heat until the liquid is reduced by half. Set aside to cool. Strain and put liquid in the top of a double boiler over simmering water. Whisk the egg yolks until light and fluffy. Add butter, one piece at a time, stirring thoroughly after each addition. Sauce should be like a smooth mayonnaise. More butter may be added if necessary. Add the tomato paste and season. Heat until warm.
*Good over pasta.

****

CHUNKY-CREAMY BLUE CHEESE SAUCE

½ cup low-fat plain yogurt
4 oz. Danish blue cheese

1 cup mayonnaise
¼ tsp. ground pepper

2 med. scallions

In a medium bowl, whisk together the mayonnaise and yogurt until smooth. Whisk in the vinegar and the pepper. Fold in the crumbled cheese and minced scallions. Season to taste with more pepper.
*Good over pasta.

CILANTRO, ORANGE AND TOMATO SAUCE

⅔ cup orange juice
¼ cup white wine
8 tbsp. unsalted butter

½ cup tomato
½ tsp. shallot
Salt and pepper

2 tsp. garlic
1 tbsp. cilantro

Simmer all ingredients, except butter, for 5 minutes over medium heat in a saucepan, to reduce slightly. Add salt and pepper to taste. Add the butter, 1 tablespoon at a time, beating after each spoon. Serve warm.
*Good over fish.

****

CILANTRO SAUCE

1 cup cilantro leaves
1-2 tsp. hot pepper sauce

¾ cup mayonnaise
6 med. cloves garlic

2 tsp. lemon juice

Simmer unpeeled garlic cloves in a small pot of water for 10 minutes, drain and peel. Process all ingredients in a blender or food processor until smooth. Cover and refrigerate.
*Good over poultry.

****

CINNAMON PLUM NUT SAUCE

2 cups plum puree
1 tbsp. lemon juice
½ cup chopped walnuts

1 cinnamon stick
1 tbsp. cornstarch

1 cup sugar
2 tbsp. water

Combine plum puree, sugar and cinnamon stick in a saucepan and simmer for 10 minutes. Mix cornstarch with lemon juice and water and stir into sauce. Cook, stirring, until sauce thickens. Stir in nuts. Remove cinnamon stick. Serve warm.
*Good over ice cream or desserts.

****

CINNAMON-CORIANDER SAUCE

1 ½ tsp. ground coriander seed
½ cup sugar syrup

2" cinnamon stick
1 ½ cups vodka

2 cloves

1 ½ tablespoons ground cinnamon may be substituted for cinnamon stick. You may substitute vodka with half vodka and half brandy. Soak the herbs in the alcohol, in a jar, for 10 days. Strain; add sugar syrup. This is especially good with brown sugar syrup. For other flavoring, add a few raisins or currants to the vodka and a slice of scraped lemon peel.
*Good over desserts or ice cream.

CLAM SAUCE I

1 tbsp. garlic salt
1 tbsp. parsley
2 8-oz. cans minced clams with liquid

1 tbsp. flour
½ tsp. pepper

2 tbsp. butter
1 tsp. salt

Melt butter in medium skillet over low heat, stir in flour and garlic salt with whisk. Add liquid from clams and continue to stir. Add seasoning then add clams last. Simmer 10 minutes.
*Good over thin spaghetti.

****

CLAM SAUCE II

2- 6 ½ oz. cans minced clams
½ cup pitted ripe olives

½ cup olive oil
¼ cup Parmesan cheese

1 lg. tomato
¼ cup parsley

In a large skillet, bring minced clams and olive oil to a boil, then boil 1 minute. Remove from heat and stir in tomato, pitted olives, cheese and parsley.
*Good for pasta.

****

CLAM SAUCE III

1 garlic clove, minced
2 tbsp. parsley, chopped
6 ½ oz. minced clams
Parmesan cheese, grated

¼ cup onion, chopped
½ tsp. oregano
¼ cup dry white wine

2 tbsp. olive oil
½ tsp. basil
⅛ tsp. pepper

Sauté onion and garlic in oil, in a large skillet, until tender. Stir in parsley, oregano, basil, pepper, wine and reserved clam liquid. Cook 5 minutes, stirring constantly. Add clams, and cook until thoroughly heated.
*Good over linguine with Parmesan cheese.

****

CLAM SAUCE IV

1 finely chopped onion
1 cup white wine
1 doz. littleneck clams

4 minced garlic cloves
2 tsp. dill leaves
¼ cup chopped parsley

2 tbsp. olive oil
Juice of 1 lemon
2 tbsp. butter

In a saucepan, cook onion and garlic in olive oil until soft. Add wine, dill leaves and lemon. Bring to a boil and add clams. Cover the pot and simmer until clams open, about 5 minutes. Remove the clams from their shells if desired. Stir in ¼ cup chopped parsley and 2 tbsp. of butter.
*Good over pasta.

CLARIFIED LEMON BUTTER SAUCE

½ cup butter   1 tbsp. lemon juice

Slowly melt butter in a saucepan. Remove from heat and let stand a few minutes until clear part can be spooned off into serving dish, discard the milky portion that is left. Add lemon juice to clarified butter.
*Good over shrimp or lobster.

****

CLASSIC CHEESE FONDUE SAUCE

½ lb. Emmentaler cheese	2 tbsp. lemon juice	3 tbsp. kirsch
½ lb. Gruyere cheese	1 clove garlic	2 tbsp. flour
1 ½ cups dry white wine	Pepper and nutmeg	Paprika

Coat cheeses with flour. Heat wine and lemon juice in a saucepan, over medium high heat. When just about to boil, add cheese. Stir to melt. Add pepper, nutmeg and paprika to taste. Stir in kirsch.
*Good over poultry or pasta.

****

CLASSIC HOLLANDAISE SAUCE

1 ½ cups clarified butter	4 egg yolks	2 tbsp. water
½ tbsp. lemon juice	Cayenne	Salt
Freshly ground white pepper		

Combine the egg yolks and water in the top of a double boiler. Whisk for 1 minute. Place over simmering water, (the bottom of the pan should not touch the water). Whipping vigorously, beat for 8 to 10 minutes or until the mixture is thick and creamy. Keep the temperature of the mixture warm, but never so hot you cannot dip your finger into it. Take the pan off the heat and add hot butter very slowly, whipping constantly. Season to taste with salt, pepper, and cayenne. Then stir in lemon juice. Serve lukewarm.
*Good over ham or eggs benedict.

CLASSIC SWISS FONDUE SAUCE

1 garlic clove, halved	1 cup dry white wine	1 tsp. lemon juice
2 cups Emmentaler cheese	2 cups Gruyere cheese	2 tbsp. kirsch
Pinch grated nutmeg	Dash of white pepper	2 tbsp. cornstarch

Rub inside of fondue pot with cut garlic clove. Shred the Gruyere and Emmentaler cheeses into the pot and pour in wine and lemon juice; cook over medium heat until bubbly. Reduce heat and gradually stir in cheeses with wooden spoon. In a small bowl blend cornstarch with kirsch. Blend into cheese and continue to cook, stirring 2 to 3 minutes or until mixture is thick and smooth. Season with white pepper and nutmeg.
*Good for cooked chicken.

****

CLASSIC WHITE BUTTER SAUCE

½ cup dry white wine	1 stick butter	2 shallots
½ cup white wine vinegar	Salt and pepper	

Peel and finely mince shallots; place in a saucepan with wine and vinegar. Bring to a boil; cook briskly until reduced to about 4 tablespoon. Cut cold butter into slices. Over low heat, using a wire whisk, beat in butter, one piece at a time, until sauce is thick and creamy. Season with salt and pepper to taste.
*Good over pasta.

****

COAMOISIER SAUCE

½ cup carrots	1 shallot, chopped	2 tbsp. butter
½ cup celery, diced	Drop of lime juice	3 tbsp. cognac
½ cup white wine	salt and pepper	1 tsp. tarragon
½ cup light cream		

Heat butter and dry ingredients in a saucepan; simmer for 5 minutes. Add cream, wine and lime juice; cook an additional 5 minutes.
*Good over pasta.

****

COCA-COLA BARBECUE SAUCE

¾ cup Coca-cola classic	¾ cup ketchup	2 med. onions
2 tbsp. Worcestershire sauce	2 tbsp. vinegar	½ tsp. salt
½ tsp. chili powder		

Finely chop onion. Combine ingredients in a saucepan and bring to a boil. Reduce heat and simmer, covered, for about 45 minutes or until the sauce is very thick. Stir occasionally.
*Good for ribs and poultry.

COCKTAIL SAUCE

1 tbsp. Worcestershire sauce
1 tbsp. grated horseradish
3 or 4 drops hot pepper sauce

1 tsp. cider vinegar
2 tbsp. whipping cream
1 tsp. prepared mustard

1 cup ketchup
Juice of 1 lemon
celery salt (pinch)

Thoroughly mix all the ingredients, except hot pepper sauce and cream in a medium size bowl, use a fork to lightly beat. Add hot pepper sauce to taste. Stir in cream. Cover and store in the refrigerator for up to 2 days. Serve chilled.
*Good over shrimp.

****

COCONUT HOLIDAY EGGNOG SAUCE

1 ½ cups cream of coconut
2 cups heavy cream
Ground nutmeg or coconut flakes

1 cup dark rum
1 tbsp. vanilla

1 qt. milk
6 eggs

Beat eggs in a bowl, until fluffy. Beat in cream of coconut. Gradually beat in milk; stir in vanilla and rum. Beat heavy cream until stiff and fold into egg mixture. Chill for several hours.
*Good over desserts or ice cream.

****

COCONUT HOT FUDGE SAUCE

6-oz. pkg. semisweet chocolate

14-oz. sweetened condensed milk

15-oz. cream of coconut

In a saucepan, over medium heat, melt chocolate with condensed milk. Cook stirring constantly, until sauce is slightly thickened, about 5 minutes. Gradually stir in cream of coconut; heat through. Serve warm.
*Good over ice cream, desserts or with fresh fruit.

****

COCONUT PINEAPPLE SAUCE

4 slices pineapple
1 tsp. curry powder

½ cup toasted coconut
2 tbsp. pineapple syrup

1 tbsp. butter

Heat butter and coconut in a saucepan, then add curry and syrup heating for 1 minute. Add slices of pineapple and continue to heat 1 more minute.
*Use over ham.

COCONUT PRALINE SAUCE

½ cup flaked coconut
1 cup cream of coconut

½ cup chopped pecans

¼ cup margarine

In a small saucepan, combine all ingredients, over a medium heat. Bring to a boil, then reduce heat and simmer uncovered for 5 minutes, stirring occasionally. Serve warm.
*Good over ice cream, pound cake or fruit.

****

COCONUT SAUCE I

1 tsp. coconut flavoring
¼ cup light corn syrup

1 cup granulated sugar

½ cup water

Heal all ingredients together in a saucepan, until well blended, about 5 minutes.
*Good over desserts, fruit or ice cream.

****

COCONUT SAUCE II

12 oz. fresh coconut
1" piece of vanilla bean

3 coriander seeds
3 oz. brandy

10 oz. vodka

Cut the coconut meat into small pieces or use a grater. Mix all the ingredients in a bottle. Soak 3 weeks and shake it gently every 3-4 days, then strain. Add sugar syrup if needed.
*Good over desserts or ice cream.

****

COFFEE & RUM SAUCE

⅓ cup whipping cream
2 egg yolks
½ cup hot strong black coffee

2 tbsp. dark rum
1 tsp. cornstarch

2 tsp. sugar
1 tbsp. milk

Have hot water just below simmering point in the bottom half of a double boiler, place coffee in the top half of the double boiler. Stir in sugar until dissolved; cool slightly. Add egg yolks one at a time, mixing thoroughly after each addition. Stir in cream and cook for 1 to 2 minutes. Mix cornstarch with milk; add to saucepan and stir constantly until sauce thickens. If serving hot, add rum, stir and serve immediately. If serving cold, allow to cool, stirring occasionally to prevent skin formation. Add rum just before serving.
*Good over desserts or ice cream.

COFFEE LIQUEUR SAUCE I

| 2 oz. instant espresso coffee | 1 ½ cups vodka | 1 cup brandy |
| 4 cups superfine sugar | 1 vanilla bean | 2 cups water |

Pour 2 cups boiling water over coffee in a bowl and stir until dissolved. Gradually add the sugar, stirring constantly. Add the vodka, brandy and the split vanilla bean. Pour the mixture into a ½ gallon jar and cover tightly. Let stand at room temperature for 30 days. Stir the mixture every 5 days. Remove the vanilla bean after the 30 days.
*Good over desserts or ice cream.

****

COFFEE LIQUEUR SAUCE II

| 2 tbsp. cold black coffee | 1 tbsp. coffee liqueur | Custard Sauce |

Make the custard sauce in a saucepan and remove it from heat; stir in 2 tablespoons cold strong black coffee and 1 tablespoon coffee flavored liqueur, whisking constantly.
*Good over desserts or ice cream.

****

COFFEE-VODKA SAUCE

| ½ chopped vanilla bean | 2 cups white sugar | 1 ½ cups vodka |
| ½ cup dry instant coffee | Caramel coloring | 2 cups water |

Rum or brandy can substitute for vodka. Boil water and sugar in a saucepan, until dissolved. Turn off heat. Slowly add dry instant coffee and continue stirring. Add chopped vanilla bean, the cooled sugar syrup and the coffee mixture to the vodka and add optional caramel coloring. Pour in jar and cover tightly and shake vigorously each day for 3 weeks. Strain.

Optional flavorings: a pinch of cinnamon, cloves, orange peel, cardamom, or mint.
*Good over desserts, fruit or ice cream.

****

CONEY ISLAND SAUCE

½ lb. ground beef	½ tsp. chili pepper	1 cup chopped onion
1 chopped garlic clove	8-oz. can tomato sauce	½ tsp. sugar
2 tsp. beef bouillon		

In a large skillet, brown beef, onion and garlic. Stir in remaining ingredients. Simmer uncovered 10 to 15 minutes.
*Good over frankfurters.

COURT BOUILLON SAUCE

2 qts. boiling water	6 cracked peppercorns	1 onion
6 dried pepper pods	½ cup amber rum	1 leek
Bouquet garni	2 whole cloves	1 carrot
5 parsley sprigs	3 celery stalks	1 basil sprig
2 tbsp. olive oil		

Finely chop fresh vegetables and herbs together. Heat oil in a large saucepan, add chopped mixture, and cook until lightly browned. Add boiling water, bouquet garni, peppercorns, cloves, pepper pods, and rum. Cover; boil 30 minutes. Boil uncovered to reduce by half.
*Good over pasta.

****

CRAB SAUCE

1 tsp. prepared mustard	1 cup White Sauce	4 oz. crabmeat
1 sm. bunch fresh chives	4 tbsp. tarragon vinegar	

In a bowl, combine mustard and vinegar; snip in 2 teaspoons chives, then add flaked crabmeat. Marinate for about 15 minutes. Carefully squeeze out the vinegar and discard. In a small saucepan, warm White Sauce then add crabmeat mixture. Cook for a few minutes. Serve warm.
*Good over pasta.

****

CRANBERRY KETCHUP SAUCE

1 ½ cups chopped onion	4 strips orange peel	4 cups water
1 cup cider vinegar	8 cups cranberries	1 ¾ tsp. salt
1 cup light brown sugar	1 ½ tsp. cinnamon	1 tsp. ginger
1 cup light corn syrup	1 ½ tsp. allspice	¼ tsp. cloves

Combine onion, water and orange peel in large saucepan or Dutch oven. Bring to a boil over medium-high heat. Lower heat and simmer, covered, until the onion is translucent, about 10 minutes. Add cranberries, bring to a boil again, and cook, partially covered, stirring occasionally for about 10 minutes. Pour mixture into a food processor or blender and chop until medium-fine texture. Return to a clean saucepan, adding the rest of the ingredients. Bring to a boil over medium-high heat. Boil, stirring to prevent sticking, until thick, 7 to 10 minutes.
*Good over turkey.

CRANBERRY DIP SAUCE

½ cup orange juice
¼ tsp. ground cinnamon

1 tbsp. cornstarch
1 lb. can whole cranberry sauce

1 tbsp. brown sugar

Blend orange juice and cornstarch in a saucepan. Add remaining ingredients and cook until thick, stirring constantly.
*Good over turkey.

****

CRANBERRY SAUCE I

1 lb. cranberries

2 cups sugar

½ cup water

Combine all ingredients in a rice bowl. Cover and steam in 1 ½ cups water for 30 minutes. Strain.
*Good over poultry.

****

CRANBERRY SAUCE II

1 tsp. cranberry liqueur
8-oz. bottle French dressing

1 tsp. orange liqueur
1 lb. can whole cranberry sauce

Salt & pepper

Mix all ingredients together in a bowl, until well blended.
*Good over poultry.

****

CRANBERRY SAUCE III

1 cup orange juice
2 tbsp. brown sugar
½ cup chicken broth

1 ½ cups cranberries
2 tbsp. red wine
1 tbsp. tomato paste

2 tbsp. butter
⅓ cup onion
1 tbsp. parsley

Blend orange juice and cranberries in a blender. Place 1 tablespoon butter in a skillet, add onion and brown sugar. Dissolve tomato paste and wine, stir until blended. Add cranberry and orange mixture, then add broth. Simmer 2 minutes.
*Use over pork or chicken.

CRANBERRY-APPLE SAUCE

3 oz. pkg. liquid fruit pectin   1 stick cinnamon   4 whole cloves
2 whole allspice   1 cup cranberry-apple juice drink

Combine juice drink and pectin in a medium, non aluminum saucepan; stir well. Add remaining ingredients; bring to a boil, stirring constantly. Remove from heat; cover and chill 8 hours. Discard spices. Serve chilled or at room temperature.
*Good over melon balls or apple salad.

****

CRANBERRY-ORANGE SAUCE

1 cup gouda cheese   ¾ cup cranberry-orange relish   2 tbsp. milk

Place gouda or edam cheese in small mixing bowl; cover and allow to come to room temperature. With an electric mixer beat cheese at low speed for 1 minute or until nearly smooth. Add milk and relish; beat until smooth and fluffy.
*Good with crepes, pancakes, or tortillas.

****

CRANBERRY-RAISIN SAUCE

¼ cup unsulphured molasses   1 tbsp. cornstarch   ¼ cup sugar
1 cup cranberry juice   2 tbsp. lemon juice   2 tbsp. raisins
¼ tsp. ground cloves

Mix sugar, molasses, cornstarch and cloves in a saucepan. Stir in juices and raisins. Cook about 3 minutes, until thick. Serve hot.
*Good over corned beef brisket or chicken.

****

CREAM 'N' BERRIES SAUCE

16-oz. pkg. raspberries   3 tbsp. low-fat sour cream   3 tbsp. sugar

Place raspberries in food processor or blender, process until smooth. Strain raspberry puree, and discard seeds. Combine puree and remaining ingredients in a small bowl; stir well.
*Good over ice cream, angel food cake.

CREAM AND SALMON SAUCE

4 oz. smoked salmon	2 tbsp. butter	½ sm. onion
7 oz. light cream	black pepper	

Melt butter in a saucepan; sauté finely chopped onion. Cook until soft but has not changed color. Add the smoked salmon, roughly chopped, and the cream. Warm gently, then blend or process together with the onion until smooth.
*Good over pasta.

****

CREAM OF CAULIFLOWER SAUCE

4 cups chicken broth	2 med. onions	½ cup flour
1 med. cauliflower	1 cup heavy cream	4 cups water
4 tbsp. chopped chervil	Ground white pepper	Salt
1 leek, peeled and sliced		

Cut cauliflower into chunks, and peel and slice onion. Parsley may be used in place of chervil. Mix the flour with 1 cup water until smooth. In a large saucepan place the mixed flour, remaining water, chicken broth, sliced onions, sliced leek, and cauliflower. Bring to a boil and simmer slowly for 1 ¼ hours. Puree a small amount at a time, in a blender. Add the cream and season to taste. Add chopped chervil and bring to a boil.

****

CREAM OF TOMATO SAUCE

4 tbsp. sweet butter	1 tbsp. olive oil	1 yellow onion
4 tbsp. all-purpose flour	3 ripe tomatoes	3 tbsp. tomato paste
2 ½ cups chicken broth	½ tsp. sugar	Dash salt
1 cup heavy cream	Ground white pepper	

Heat 2 tablespoons of the butter with oil in a saucepan. Add onion and sauté for about 5 minutes. Stir in tomatoes and tomato paste, cook for 2 to 3 minutes. Sprinkle with flour and mix well with a spatula. Add broth, sugar, salt, and pepper and simmer 15 minutes. Place in a blender at high speed for a couple of seconds. Pour into a saucepan and add the cream. Bring to a boil, then simmer 2 to 3 minutes. At serving time, stir in remaining butter.
*Good over pasta.

****

CREAM SAUCE

½ cup dry vermouth	1 cube chicken bouillon	1 cup cream
½ lb. mushrooms	4 tbsp. butter	2 tbsp. flour

Bring vermouth and chicken bouillon to a boil in a saucepan. Add cream and boil until thick. Add butter and flour; cook until thick.
*Good over fish or rice.

CREAMY BLUE CHEESE SAUCE

1 ½ cups sour cream
2 chopped scallions
1 tbsp. lemon juice
pinch of sugar

¼ lb. blue cheese
1 clove minced garlic
1 tbsp. white vinegar
salt, pepper and cayenne pepper

¼ cup mayonnaise
1 tbsp. olive oil
¼ cup parsley

Mix all ingredients together in a bowl, until well blended. Chill 4 hours to blend.
*Good over fish.

****

CREAMY CORN FONDUE SAUCE

1 16-oz. frozen corn kernel
3 tbsp. half and half

2 tsp. cornstarch
Salt and pepper

Tabasco sauce
2 tbsp. butter

Simmer corn with a little water in a medium size saucepan few minutes until tender. Drain and put in a blender or food processor until soft but not too smooth. In a medium size saucepan blend cornstarch with half and half, add corn puree and cook over low heat until smooth. Season with salt, pepper and a few drops Tabasco sauce. Beat in butter.
*Good over rice.

****

CREAMY CURRY SAUCE I

2 med. onions, chopped
½ tsp. grated gingerroot

1 tbsp. curry powder
2 cups White Sauce

1 garlic clove
2 tbsp. butter

In a medium saucepan, melt butter over low heat. Sauté onions, garlic, and ginger; remove garlic clove after 1 or 2 minutes. Continue cooking over low heat until the onion becomes soft and golden, but not brown. Stir in curry powder. Cook a few minutes longer over low heat, taking care not to brown onions. Add White Sauce and mix thoroughly.
Alternatively, increase butter to ¼ cup. Add ½ cup all purpose flour with the curry powder; stir into the onions, ginger and butter. Cook about 3 minutes until bubbly. Stir in 2 cups warm milk and bring to a boil. Serve hot.   .
*Good over chicken.

****

CREAMY CURRY SAUCE II

1 tsp. Chicken bouillon
¼ tsp. curry powder

½ cup boiling water
½ cup light cream

2 tbsp. butter
2 tbsp. flour

Dissolve bouillon in water. In a small saucepan, melt butter and stir in flour. Add remaining ingredients, cook and stir over low heat until thickened.
*Good over vegetables or fish.

CREAMY GARLIC SAUCE

½ cup evaporated skim milk
1 tsp. concentrated apple juice
2 lg. minced garlic cloves

2 tbsp. lemon juice
1 tsp. dill weed
¼ tsp. white pepper

¼ tsp. salt
Cayenne
Sesame oil

Place all ingredients in a blender and process until smooth. Chill before serving.
*Good over pasta.

****

CREAMY HORSERADISH SAUCE

⅔ cup whipping cream

1 tbsp. grated horseradish

2 green onions

Whip cream until soft peaks form, then stir in rest of ingredients. Chill before serving.
*Good over fish.

****

CREAMY LOBSTER SAUCE

3 tbsp. unsalted butter
1 tbsp. Worcestershire
½ cup chicken broth
2 tbsp. fresh lemon juice

2 ½ lbs. lobsters
1 tsp. Dijon mustard
1 cup heavy cream
black pepper

¼ lb. onion
½ tsp. Tabasco
2 tbsp. tarragon
coarse salt

Melt butter in a souffle dish at 100 percent power in a microwave for 2 minutes. Stir in onion and cook for 3 minutes more. Remove from microwave, whisk in Worcestershire, mustard and Tabasco. Add cream and chicken broth to mixture. Heat, for 4 minutes in microwave. Add tarragon and chopped meat of lobster, cook 2 minutes longer. Season to taste with lemon juice, salt and pepper.
*Good over fettucine.

****

CREAMY MUSTARD SAUCE I

2 tbsp. butter
2 tbsp. Dijon mustard

2 cups chicken sauce
½ cup heavy cream

Grind of 1 lemon
Salt and white pepper

Melt butter in a small saucepan; whisk in flour, stirring until mixture is a smooth paste. Stir in chicken stock and cook over low heat until mixture comes to a boil. Cook another minute and remove from heat. Stir in the grated lemon rind.
*Good over hens.

CREAMY MUSTARD SAUCE II

1 ¼ cups low-fat yogurt
2 tbsp. spicy brown mustard
1 minced garlic clove
¼ tsp. dried marjoram

¼ cup red wine vinegar
1 tbsp. grated parmesan
1 tbsp. olive oil

⅛ tsp. salt
⅛ tsp. pepper
Parsley

Mix all ingredients together in a bowl, until well blended. Cover and chill.
*Good over fish or poultry.

****

CREAMY PARMESAN CHEESE SAUCE

8 oz. pkg. cream cheese
Dash ground nutmeg

½ cup Parmesan cheese
Dash pepper

¾ cup milk

Microwave cream cheese, milk and parmesan cheese in 1-quart glass bowl. Microwave on medium, 6 to 8 minutes or until sauce is smooth, stirring every 2 minutes. Stir in seasonings.
*Good over pasta.

****

CREAMY ROASTED-GARLIC SAUCE

2 tsp. mild olive oil
¾ tsp. ground pepper
1 tbsp. white wine vinegar

½ cup sour cream
¼ cup mayonnaise
1 med. head of garlic

1 med. scallion
½ tsp. salt

Preheat the oven to 375 degrees. Cut off top of the garlic head. Place the garlic on a small piece of aluminum foil and drizzle the oil on top. Wrap garlic in the foil and roast for 45 minutes, or until soft. Set aside to cool. In a medium bowl, stir sour cream and mayonnaise. Squeeze the flesh of the garlic into the bowl and mash the garlic into the sour cream and mayonnaise. Stir in the thinly sliced scallion, vinegar, pepper and salt.
*Good over pasta.

****

CREAMY TOMATO SAUCE

½ cup chopped onion
2 slices prosciutto
¼ cup parmesan cheese

½ cup sliced mushrooms
8-oz. can tomato sauce

1 tbsp. olive oil
¼ cup heavy cream

In a medium-size saucepan, sauté onion in olive oil until translucent. Add mushrooms and prosciutto or boiled ham and sauté for 3 minutes more. Then add remaining ingredients, and simmer for about 3 to 4 minutes.
*Good over pasta.

CRÈME ANGLAISE SAUCE

2 cups half and half   3 lg. egg yolks   ¼ cup sugar
½ tsp. vanilla extract

Microwave the half and half uncovered in a 2-quart glass bowl, on high power for 4 minutes, until very hot but not boiling. In a medium bowl, whisk yolks and sugar together until fluffy and pale, about 2 minutes. Gradually pour the hot half and half into the egg mixture, whisking constantly. Pour back into the glass bowl and microwave uncovered for 2 minutes, whisking once. If not thick enough to coat the back of a spoon, continue to microwave, checking and whisking at 20-second intervals. Whisk in the vanilla. Strain and serve warm or at room temperature.
*Serve over fruit.

****

CRÈME DE BANANA SAUCE

1 cup sugar syrup   2 med. banana, peeled   3 cups vodka
1 tsp. vanilla extract or a 2" length of vanilla bean

Mash the bananas and add the vanilla and cooled sugar syrup to the vodka. Place in a covered bowl or jar. Shake gently and let stand 1 week. Strain. It may be consumed now, but a two to three month maturing period will result in a richer flavor.
*Good over ice cream or desserts.

****

CRÈME DE DIJON SAUCE

⅔ cup Dijon mustard   2 cups heavy cream   4 eggs
½ cup chopped dill   1 tbsp. white vinegar

Combine mustard, lightly beaten eggs, heavy cream and vinegar in medium-size saucepan. Cook over medium-low heat, stirring constantly, until mixture thickens, about 8 to 10 minutes; do not boil or eggs will curdle. Remove from heat. Stir in dill.
*Good over fish.

****

CRÈME FRAICHE SAUCE

2 tbsp. buttermilk, or sour cream   2 cup heavy cream

Heat cream over low heat, in a saucepan. Add buttermilk or sour cream and mix well. Let sit at room temperature for 6 hours. Refrigerate 24 hours.
*Good over desserts or fruit.

CREOLE BARBECUE SAUCE

28-oz. can plum tomatoes
2 crushed garlic cloves
1 med. chopped onion
⅛ tsp. dried basil

¼ cup lime juice
⅔ cup olive oil
5 drops Tabasco

1 tsp. salt
Dash pepper
Bouquet garni

Drain and chop tomatoes; put into a saucepan with onion and cook over medium heat for 15 minutes. Force tomato mixture through a fine sieve into another saucepan. Discard remaining solids. Add remaining ingredients to saucepan. Stir until blended. Simmer about 1 hour, stirring occasionally.
*Good to baste meat for barbecuing.

****

CREOLE SAUCE I

2 tbsp. chopped green pepper
¼ cup sliced mushrooms
2 to 3 drops Tabasco sauce

2 tbsp. vegetable oil
2 cups canned tomatoes
2 tbsp. chopped onion

½ tsp. salt
⅛ tsp. pepper
½ tsp. basil

Cook onion, green pepper and mushrooms in oil, in a skillet, over low heat about 5 minutes. Add tomatoes and seasoning, cook until sauce is thick, about 40 minutes.
*Good over meat, fish or poultry.

****

CREOLE SAUCE II

¼ cup white wine
½ cup cooked onions

1 cup tomato sauce
1 tbsp. cayenne pepper

1 clove garlic

Heat all ingredients together in a saucepan, over low heat, until well blended for 5 minutes.
*Good over shrimp.

****

CREOLE STYLE SAUCE

1 sm. green bell pepper
1 crushed garlic clove
Dash of cayenne pepper

1 sm. chopped onion
16-oz. can tomatoes
Salt and pepper

2 tbsp. salad oil
4 tbsp. butter

Melt butter and oil in a saucepan; add crushed garlic, finely chopped onion and sauté until vegetables are limp and translucent. Stem and seed a small green bell pepper, chop finely, add to saucepan and sauté 5 minutes. Add drained and finely chopped plum tomatoes, salt, pepper and a dash of cayenne pepper. Cook over medium heat for 10 minutes.
*Good over fish.

CUCUMBER SAUCE I

1 cup cucumber puree	½ cup sour cream	½ cup mayonnaise
Juice of ½ lemon	1 tsp. sugar	Salt to taste
1 tsp. chopped tarragon	Fresh ground pepper	

Combine all ingredients in a bowl and chill. Serve very cold.
*Good over beef.

****

CUCUMBER SAUCE II

¼ cup all purpose flour	1 egg yolk, beaten	1 cup milk
½ cucumber, quartered	¼ cup butter	1 onion slice
½ tsp. chopped chervil	1 sprig fresh parsley	1 whole clove
1 tsp. snipped chives	½ bay leaf	Salt & pepper

In a medium saucepan, warm milk, add onion, clove and herbs. In another saucepan, melt butter; stir in flour until well blended. Cook over low heat for 3 minutes, stirring occasionally. Season lightly with salt and pepper. Remove onion, clove and herbs from milk; pour flavored milk all at once into flour mixture. Whisk to produce a smooth sauce. Stir continually over low heat until the sauce just begins to bubble and become thick. Remove from heat. Mix a little of the hot sauce with the egg yolk; quickly whisk in the egg yolk. Finely chop the cucumber. Add to the sauce with the chervil and chives. Cook for 1 to 2 minutes, without allowing it to boil. Pour into a gravy boat and serve hot.
*Good over all meats.

****

CUCUMBER-DILL SAUCE I

⅓ cup green onions	2 cups sour cream	2 med. cucumbers
⅓ cup fresh dill	2 tbsp. milk	½ tsp. salt

Peel, half lengthwise, and seed the cucumber; finely chop cucumbers, onions and dill. Mix all ingredients together in a bowl, until well blended. Refrigerate.
*Good over ham.

****

CUCUMBER-DILL SAUCE II

8 oz. cream cheese	1 cup mayonnaise	2 med. cucumbers
2 tbsp. green onion	2 tsp. fresh dill	1 tbsp. lemon juice
½ tsp. hot pepper sauce		

Peel, seed and chop cucumbers; slice green onion. Beat softened cream cheese until smooth. Stir in remaining ingredients until well blended. Cover; chill.
*Good over fish.

CUMBERLAND SAUCE I

½ cup fresh cranberries
2 tsp. grated orange peel
¼ cup orange juice

1 lg. navel orange
1 tsp. prepared mustard
¼ cup beef stock

2 tbsp. brandy
½ cup port white

Finely chop cranberries, orange peel, chopped orange, and brandy in a food processor or blender. Place mixture in a saucepan; stir in remaining ingredients. Simmer uncovered until sauce thickens slightly (about 15 minutes).
*Good over duck, pork, ham, fruit salads or cottage cheese.

****

CUMBERLAND SAUCE II

¾ cup red currant jelly
1 tbsp. red wine vinegar
6 candied cherries, chopped

½ cup port wine
Pinch of red pepper
½ tsp. prepared mustard

1 lemon
1 orange
Salt

Peel orange and lemon carefully so that no white pith is removed. Cut the peel into julienne strips. Place strips in a medium saucepan, and cover with water. Cook for about 5 minutes. Strain strips and set aside. Add lemon, orange and all ingredients, except the cherries in a medium saucepan. Add the drained strips and mustard (optional). Boil mixture gently for about 5 minutes over high heat. Remove from heat and cool. Add the cherries.
*Good over all meats.

****

CUMIN SAUCE

1 onion
1 celery stalk
1 cup white wine

1 garlic clove
3 tbsp. cumin powder
4 cups veal stock

3 tbsp. olive oil
1 tomato
salt and pepper

Mince the garlic, celery and onion; peel seed and dice the tomato. Chicken stock may substitute the veal stock. Sauté the onion, garlic and celery in olive oil in saucepan. Stir in the cumin, tomato, wine and stock. Bring to a boil, reduce to a simmer and cook for 15 minutes. Puree in a blender. Season with salt and pepper to taste. Heat before using.
*Good over lamb.

****

CURRANT AND RAISIN SAUCE

1 cup currants (or raisins)
¾ cup sugar syrup for cassis

2 cups vodka or brandy

1 cup water

Boil 1 cup water, add currants, cover and turn off heat. Let stand to plump, for about 5 minutes, then strain. Place currants and alcohol in a tightly closed jar for 1 week. Shake the jar occasionally during the week. Strain and add ¼ cup sugar syrup for cassis, 1 ¼ cups of crème de cassis. Mature for two weeks.
*Good over desserts, fruit or ice cream.

CURRIED CHEESE FONDUE SAUCE

⅔ cup dry white wine
8 oz. Cheddar cheese
1 tsp. lemon juice

1 garlic clove, halved
2 tbsp. curry paste
8 oz. process Gruyere cheese

⅔ cup dry white wine
1 tsp. cornstarch

Shred Cheddar and Gruyere cheeses. Rub inside of fondue pot with cut garlic clove. Pour in wine and lemon juice; cook over medium heat until bubbly. Turn heat to low and add curry paste. Gradually stir in shredded cheeses.
In a small bowl blend cornstarch with sherry. Blend into cheese and continue to cook, stirring 2 to 3 minutes or until mixture is thick and smooth. Do not allow mixture to boil.
*Good for chicken.

****

CURRIED CHICKEN SAUCE

2 tsp. grated fresh gingerroot
½ tsp. red (cayenne) pepper
2 cups sm. tomatoes
Hot water as needed
2 tbsp. fresh cilantro or parsley

1 ½ lb. cubed chicken
3 tbsp. vegetable oil
1 tsp. curry powder
½ tsp. turmeric

2 onions
2 garlic cloves
1 bay leaf
½ tsp. salt

Brown chicken on all sides in oil in a skillet, then set aside. Sauté onions, garlic and ginger root until the onions are golden brown, stirring often. Add red pepper, turmeric, curry powder and bay leaf; cook 1-2 minutes. Add tomatoes and salt and mix well. Add chicken; bring to a simmer, half covered, over low heat. Simmer 30 minutes or until chicken is tender, stirring occasionally to prevent sticking. Stir in finely chopped cilantro. If sauce is too thick, add a little water.
*Good over rice.

****

CURRY COCONUT SAUCE

1 cup chopped onion
2 tbsp. lemon juice
1 tbsp. curry powder

1 clove garlic, chopped
¾ cup cream of coconut
1 cup chicken bouillon

¼ cup butter
2 ½ cups milk
¼ cup flour

In skillet, cook onion and garlic in butter until tender. Stir in flour and milk, until thickened, add lemon juice. Cook about 10 minutes.
Options: Add toasted flaked coconut, cashews, pecans, peanuts, chopped hard cooked eggs, crumbled bacon, or raisins.
*Use over chicken.

CURRY, GINGER, TOMATO SAUCE

1 tbsp. vegetable oil
2 tsp. curry powder
2 pinches cayenne pepper
¼ cup dry white wine
½ lb. shrimp, cleaned

3 garlic cloves
1 cup heavy cream
1 piece ginger
8 sprigs coriander

1 onion
⅛ tsp. pepper
2 lb. tomatoes
¼ tsp. salt

Use a 4 pound can of tomatoes, chopped and drained, or fresh tomatoes. Heat oil over medium-low heat in a skillet. Add chopped onion and gently cook until softened, about 5 minutes. Add chopped garlic, peeled and chopped fresh ginger, curry powder and cayenne pepper and stir. Add wine and boil until reduced by half. Stir in cream and season with salt and pepper. Bring sauce to a boil, add shrimp, and cook rapidly, turning the shrimp occasionally, until they change color and begin to curl, 2 to 3 minutes. Stir in peeled and seeded tomatoes and ⬚ of the fresh chopped coriander. Do not boil the sauce after the tomatoes are added or it will become watery.
*Good over pasta.

****

CURRY SAUCE I

⅓ cup chopped onion
¼ cup all purpose flour
⅛ tsp. white pepper
2 tbsp. lemon juice

4 tsp. curry powder
¼ tsp. ginger
2 cups milk

¼ cup butter
2 tbsp. sugar
1 tbsp. salt

Melt butter in medium saucepan over low heat. Sauté onion, stirring occasionally, about 5 minutes, until golden. Remove from heat. Combine flour, curry powder, sugar, salt, ginger, and pepper, stir into onion mixture. Return to heat. Add milk gradually, stirring constantly until mixture comes to a boil. Simmer until thick. Stir in lemon juice.
*Good over poultry, rice or potatoes.

****

CURRY SAUCE II

¼ cup curry powder
⅛ tsp. ground cinnamon
1 red pepper, diced
2 cups chicken broth

½ cup butter
⅛ tbsp. salt and pepper
1 cup apple, diced
1 cup apple juice

2 lg. onions
¼ cup cumin
½ tsp. cayenne
½ cup raisins

Melt butter and onions in a saucepan, for 5 minutes. Add curry, cumin, cinnamon, cayenne, salt and pepper, cook 5 minutes longer. Add peppers, apples and raisins, cook 5 minutes longer. Add broth and cook 2 additional minutes. Add apple juice.
*Good over rice.

CURRY-SOUR CREAM SAUCE

1 cup sour cream   1 tsp. curry powder   ¼ tsp. salt
Dash hot pepper sauce

Mix all ingredients together in a mixing bowl, until well blended. Refrigerate.
*Good over rice.

****

CUSTARD SAUCE I

3 egg yolks   1 cup milk   ½ cup sugar
1 tsp. vanilla

Combine yolks, milk, and sugar in saucepan. Cook over medium heat, stirring constantly, until thick and smooth. Sauce should coat back of spoon. Cool. Add vanilla.
*Good over desserts or ice cream.

****

CUSTARD SAUCE II

3 tbsp. Vanilla Sugar   2 cups milk, warm   4 egg yolks

Beat vanilla sugar and egg yolks together, in a medium bowl, until light pale, smooth and creamy. Add warm milk, stirring constantly. Transfer to top of a double boiler over barely simmering water. Continue cooking, stirring, until sauce is thick enough to coat back of metal spoon; check frequently because the sauce can separate if overcooked. Serve hot with desserts.

(VANILLA SUGAR - Place three 3-inch vanilla beans upright in a screw top jar. Cover with sugar. Seal and leave for at least 1 week until the flavor has time to blend.)
*Good over desserts or ice cream.

****

CUSTARD SAUCE WITH ALMONDS

½ cup toasted almonds   2 cups milk   4 egg yolks
¼ tbsp. almond extract   ½ cup sugar

Scald milk in top of double boiler, mix in egg yolks and sugar. Cook for another minute. Remove from heat and add in extract and toasted almonds.
*Good over desserts or ice cream.

DAIQUIRI SAUCE

| 1 ½ cups superfine granulated sugar | 3 cups light rum | 4 limes |

Peel a very thin layer from the limes and carefully scrape away the white; cut into strips. Blot the peel on a paper towel. Let stand in 2 cups of rum for 2 days or until the rum absorbs the color from the peel. Remove peel; add sugar and shake vigorously until dissolved. Add remaining cup of rum and stir until the liquid is clear. Store at least 1 week.
*Good over ice cream.

****

DANISH CHEESE SAUCE

9 slices chopped lean bacon	1 sm. onion, chopped	2 tbsp. butter
2 cups shredded Havarti cheese	2 cups shredded Samso cheese	½ cup beet juice
1 tbsp. all purpose flour	¼ cup beer	

Put bacon, onion and butter in a large saucepan and cook until bacon is golden and onion is soft. Stir in flour. Gradually add beer and cook until thickened. Add cheeses and cook, stirring constantly, until melted and the mixture is smooth. Add beet juice and cook 1 minute more.
*Good over pasta.

****

DARK BEER SAUCE

| 2 slices bacon, chopped | 1 sliced onion | 1 cup sauerkraut |
| 2 tsp. brown sugar | 1 pint dark beer | |

Fry bacon and onion, until bacon is crisp. Skim off fat from skillet, then add brown sugar, sauerkraut and beer. Cook 10 minutes.
*Use over pork or chicken.

****

DARK CHERRY SAUCE

| 16 oz. dark sweet cherries | 5 tbsp. cornstarch | 2 tbsp. sugar |
| 5 tbsp. almond-flavored liqueur | ¼ cup water | Dash salt |

If using frozen cherries, partially thaw and do not drain. 3 cups of fresh bing cherries, pitted, can be substituted, increase water to ½ cup. Combine sugar, cornstarch and salt in a medium saucepan. Stir in water, then cherries and cook over medium heat until mixture becomes clear and thickened, about 7 to 8 minutes. Stir in liqueur. Cool.
*Good over dessert or pork.

DARK CHOCOLATE SAUCE

½ lb. semisweet chocolate
¼ cup whipping cream

4 tbsp. unsalted butter
2 tbsp. dark rum

¼ cup milk

Melt the chocolate in the top of a double boiler over hot water. Stir in the milk; add the cream and rum. Stir until smooth. Serve warm.
*Good over desserts and ice cream.

****

DELUXE PINEAPPLE-RUM SAUCE

½ cup light brown sugar
8 ¼ oz. Crushed pineapple

1 tbsp. lemon juice
3 tbsp. amber rum

2 tbsp. butter
Ground cinnamon

Heat butter and brown sugar in a skillet until sugar is melted and lightly caramelized. Stir in cinnamon, undrained pineapple, lemon juice and 2 tbsp. rum. Heat to simmering. Cook, stirring frequently, until slightly thickened, 5 to 10 minutes. Add remaining tablespoon rum and simmer a minute longer. Serve warm or cold.
*Good over ice cream or desserts.

****

DELUXE SOUR CREAM SAUCE

3 tbsp. Dijon Mustard
¾ cup Italian bread crumbs

3 tbsp. sour cream

5 tbsp. butter

Heat bread crumbs with butter in a skillet, about 2 minutes. Mix in mustard and sour cream; continue to cook for 1 minute.
*Use for chicken, pork or beef.

****

DEVILED CHEESE SAUCE

3 cups smoky cheddar cheese
2 tsp. Worcestershire sauce

2 tsp. prepared horseradish
2 tbsp. all purpose flour

¾ cup milk
1 tsp. mustard

Place milk in saucepan and heat until bubbly. Toss cheese in flour and add to milk. Stir constantly over low heat until cheese melts and mixture is thick and smooth. Stir in Worcestershire sauce, horseradish and prepared mustard.
*Good over steak.

DEVILED SAUCE II

1 tbsp. all purpose flour
1 tbsp. red wine vinegar
Dash cayenne pepper
1 tbsp. Worcestershire sauce

⅔ cup chicken broth
1 tbsp. tomato paste
½ tsp. paprika
4 med. tomatoes, skinned, chopped

2 tsp. sugar
1 tbsp. butter
1 shallot

Melt butter in a medium saucepan, add shallot and cook until soft. Stir in flour, then add remaining ingredients. Simmer 15 minutes.
*Good over steak.

****

DEVILED SAUCE II

2 hot red chile peppers
16 oz. water

6 cloves garlic
½ cup Parmesan cheese, grated

3 tbsp. oil

Grind up garlic and chile in blender with 16 ounces of water. Pour into saucepan; boil then simmer for 15 minutes. Put through fine sieve and save water to cook pasta. Drain and add oil, sieve garlic, pepper and cheese.
*Use over pasta.

****

DILL SAUCE I

½ cup sour cream
2 tbsp. chopped dill pickle

½ cup mayonnaise

1 tsp. dill weed

Mix all ingredients together in a mixing bowl, until well blended. Let stand at room temperature for 1 to 2 hours to blend flavors.
*Good over fish.

****

DILL SAUCE II

4 tsp. cornstarch
2 tbsp. chopped fresh dill

⅔ cup milk
⅔ cup fish stock or clam juice

Salt and Pepper

Blend cornstarch with a portion of fish stock and milk in a saucepan; simmer until thickened. Stir in dill, salt and pepper. Serve hot.
*Good over fish.

DILLY CHEESE SAUCE

1 pkg. cheese sauce mix   ⅛ tsp. dill weed   1 cup milk
¼ cup chopped cucumber

Empty cheese sauce mix into a small saucepan; gradually blend in milk. Add dill weed and cook over medium heat, stirring constantly, until mixture comes to a boil. Add cucumber. Reduce heat; simmer 1 minute. Serve hot.
*Good over poultry.

****

DRIED APRICOT SAUCE

½ lb. dried apricots   1 cup boiled water   1 cup sugar syrup
2-3 cups vodka or brandy   5 whole almonds, or 1 tsp. almond extract

Pit apricots; soak them in enough boiling water to cover them, about 10 minutes or until water is absorbed. Cool. Pour remaining liquid into a measuring cup; add enough vodka to make a total of three cups. Combine apricot liquid mixture, apricots and almonds. Pour into a covered jar and let stand 2 weeks, shaking occasionally, strain and add sugar syrup.
*Good over ice cream and desserts.

****

DUTCH CHEESE SAUCE

4 cups shredded Gouda cheese   1 tbsp. cornstarch   1 cup milk
2 tsp. caraway seeds   3 tbsp. gin   Pepper

Place milk in a saucepan and heat until bubbly, then gradually stir in cheese. Continue to heat until cheese melts. Stir in caraway seeds. In a small bowl blend cornstarch with gin. Blend into cheese mixture and cook, stirring 2 to 3 minutes or until smooth and creamy.
*Good over pork.

****

EGG SAUCE I

| ½ cup granulated sugar | 1 ½ cups milk | 4 egg yolks |
| 2 tbsp. peach liqueur | | |

Mix egg yolks and sugar together in a double boiler, whisking in milk. Incorporate over hot water, until back of spoon is coated. Mix in liqueur and cool.
*Good over desserts.

****

EGG SAUCE II

| 1 tbsp. parsley, chopped | 2 eggs, hard cooked | 1 tsp. lemon juice |
| 1 ½ cups Béchamel Sauce, kept hot | | |

Remove yolks from hard cooked eggs and rub through a coarse sieve. Cut whites into thin, short strips, and combine the two in a bowl. Add parsley to eggs an set aside. In a saucepan over medium heat, add lemon juice to the hot Béchamel Sauce, Stirring to prevent separation. Add egg and parsley mixture. Serve hot.
*Good over pasta.

****

EGGPLANT WALNUT SAUCE

¾ lb. shelled walnuts	1 lg. clove garlic	¾ cup water
½ tsp. Hungarian paprika	1 tsp. coriander	Salt and pepper
1 tsp. fenugreek-coriander	½ tsp. turmeric	Pinch sugar
½ cup fresh coriander	6 lg. eggplants	1 sm. onion
2 tbsp. sour cream	olive oil	

Grind walnuts very fine in a food processor. Add fenugreek-coriander mixture, additional ground coriander, paprika, sugar and ¾ cup water, and process again. Add peeled, quartered onion, garlic, turmeric, fresh coriander, salt and pepper and process. Blend in sour cream; cover and set aside. Trim eggplants and slice lengthwise into thick slices. Cook slowly over medium heat, in 4 tablespoons hot oil until golden brown. Chop eggplant in small pieces and add to sour cream mixture.
*Good over pasta.

EGGS AND MARSALA WINE SAUCE

1 cup dry Marsala wine	8 oz. vodka or brandy	5 egg yolks
½ tsp. vanilla extract	1 ½ cups sugar	1 cup milk

Beat egg yolks; in a double boiler or non-stick pan then add sugar. Slowly add milk, vanilla, and ½ of the wine. Heat and stir as the mixture thickens to remove any lumps. Bring to a boil slowly; simmer for 5 minutes, stirring to prevent scorching. Remove mixture from the stove and stir while cooling. Add remainder of the wine and all the alcohol. Pour into a bottle and seal tightly, shake it well, let it mature about 6 weeks.
*Good over desserts or ice cream.

****

ENGLISH-STYLE MINT SAUCE

½ cup mint leaves	¼ cup sugar	¼ cup water
¼ cup cider vinegar	Dash salt	

Combine sugar, water, and salt in a small saucepan. Bring to a boil; stir until sugar is dissolved. Remove from heat and stir in mint and vinegar. Set sauce aside to cool to room temperature before serving.
*Good for lamb.

****

ESPAGNOLE SAUCE

¼ cup all purpose flour	5 cups Brown Stock Sauce	¼ cup butter
2 tbsp. bacon fat	1 sm. onion, chopped	2 tbsp. butter
1 celery stalk, chopped	1 sm. carrot, sliced	Bouquet garni
Strips of orange rind	Salt and pepper	

Melt butter in a saucepan. Add flour and cook about 10 minutes, stirring constantly, until roux turns a rich peanut butter color. Whisking, gradually add stock and bring to a boil, over a medium heat, then reduce heat and cook for about 30 minutes. In a small saucepan, melt 2 tablespoons of butter and bacon fat, add vegetables and brown, stirring constantly, over medium heat. Add this mixture and bouquet garni to the stock sauce. Simmer over low heat for 1 ½ to 2 hours. Skim any foam that rises to surface. Season to taste. Remove bouquet garni and strain through a fine sieve and cool. Spoon off any fat on surface. Garnish with orange rind.
*Good over all meats.

FAZIO'S TOMATO SAUCE

12 oz. tomato paste
24 oz. water
fresh pepper to taste

4 cloves garlic
3 tsp. basil

2 tsp. olive oil
9 tsp. sugar

Stir fry garlic in oil, in a saucepan, until lightly brown; add tomato paste, water, basil, sugar and pepper. Mix together until well blended. Bring to a boil, reduce heat and let simmer for 20 minutes, stirring occasionally.
*Good over pasta.

****

FEISTY APRICOT SAUCE

1 cup apricot nectar
1 tbsp. cider vinegar

2 tbsp. Creole mustard

1 tsp. cornstarch

Whole-grain mustard may be used instead of the Creole mustard. Combine apricot nectar and mustard in a saucepan. Stir and bring to a boil over medium heat. In a small dish, combine vinegar and cornstarch and stir to make a paste. When nectar boils, stir in cornstarch mixture until it thickens slightly. Remove from heat and serve warm.
*Good over poultry or pork.

****

FIG SAUCE

½ cup water chestnuts
¼ cup green pepper, diced
½ cup chick peas
1 ½ tsp. cornstarch

8 fig halves
1 apple, diced
1 cup beef stock
drops Pickapepper

2 tbsp. oil
3 tbsp. cold water
salt and pepper

Heat oil, figs, apple, chestnuts, green pepper and drained chick peas for 2 minutes in a saucepan. Mix water and cornstarch, then add beef stock, salt, pepper and pickapepper and heat for 8 minutes more.
*Good over fish.

****

FISH MARINADE SAUCE

1 cup dry white wine
2 tsp. lemon peel
Sliver lemon peel. Place ingredients in a jar and shake well. Cover and store in refrigerator. Shake well before using.
*Good over fish.

¼ cup olive oil
4 stalks parsley

4 peppercorns

FISH STOCK SAUCE

2 lb. fish bones and trimmings	1 med. sliced onion	1 sliced leek
1 lb. white-fleshed fish	1 sliced carrot	2 tbsp. lemon juice
12 black peppercorns	2 qts. water	½ tsp. salt
bouquet garni		

Place ingredients in a large saucepan over medium heat. Bring to a boil, reduce heat and simmer for 30 minutes. Skim off foam, then strain through a fine sieve and cool. Cover tightly and store in the refrigerator for up to 2 days.

For richer stock use ¾ water and ¼ dry white wine. Strain liquid, return to clean saucepan and boil over high heat until reduced to two-thirds.

*Good over pasta.

****

FIVE-WAY CHILI SAUCE

1 tbsp. chili powder	1 minced onion	1 tbsp. sugar
1 tbsp. ground cumin	1 tbsp. paprika	⅓ cup ketchup
3 minced garlic cloves	1 tsp. oregano	1 bay leaf
2 cups tomato sauce	1 tsp. coriander	½ tsp. mace
2 tbsp. cider vinegar	2 tbsp. red wine	2 cups water
½ tsp. allspice	1 tsp. turmeric	2 tsp. pepper
½ tsp. ground cloves	1 tsp. cinnamon	½ tsp. nutmeg

Sauté the onions and garlic in a saucepan, for about 10 minutes. Add spices. Mix well and sauté for another few minutes. Add the water, tomato sauce, ketchup, vinegar, wine, sugar, pepper, and bay leaf. Cook for an hour, adjusting the spices as necessary, and add a little water if the chili is too thick.

*Good over chicken.

****

FLAMBE SAUCE

1 tbsp. Worcestershire sauce	5 tbsp. butter	1 tbsp. lemon juice
2 tbsp. parsley or chives	Salt and pepper	Dry mustard
¼ cup berry liqueur, warmed		

Mix all ingredients together in a bowl, until well blended and marinade.

*Good over poultry.

FLOWER PETALS SAUCE

1 ½ cups fresh petals	½ cup sugar syrup	1 ½ cups vodka

Use highly scented fresh petals, wash and dab dry on paper towels. Place the petals in a jar, in vodka and soak 2-3 weeks. Strain and squeeze out the juices. Add sugar syrup. Mature 1 week.
*Good over ice cream.

****

FOOD PROCESSOR MAYONNAISE SAUCE

1 tsp. Dijon mustard	2 egg yolks	Salt and white pepper
1 tsp. white wine vinegar	1 cup oil	

Tarragon vinegar or lemon juice can be used in place of white wine vinegar. Place the mustard, egg yolks, ⅛ tsp. vinegar, salt and white pepper into a food processor. With motor running, add the oil slowly. Then add remaining vinegar. Do not over beat or it will be too thick.
*Good over fish or pasta.

****

FOUR CHEESE SAUCE

2 oz. Parmesan cheese	2 oz. gruyere cheese	2 oz. Edam cheese
2 oz. Fontina cheese	4 oz. butter	black pepper
¼ cup hot water		

Grate all the cheeses together. Melt butter in a saucepan; add water, and cheeses, stirring often. Once the cheese begins to melt remove the pan from the heat. Add more water if you prefer a thinner sauce.
*Good over pasta.

****

FRENCH CHOCOLATE SAUCE

2 cups cream	3 egg yolks	1 cup sugar
½ cup milk	⅓ cup cocoa	1 tsp. vanilla

Beat milk and egg yolks together; place in saucepan. Blend in sugar and cook over medium heat, stirring constantly, until thick. Remove from heat, sift cocoa into mix and beat until well blended. Cool.
*Good over desserts or ice cream.

FRENCH GREEN SAUCE

½ cup fresh chervil, chopped	4 spinach leaves	1 cup mayonnaise
½ cup fresh parsley, chopped	Few drops onion juice	1 tsp. parsley
½ cup fresh tarragon, chopped	½ cup watercress	8 capers, drained

Wash herbs and spinach well, and place into a medium saucepan of boiling water and cook for 1 minute; drain. Press with a wooden spoon in fine sieve to extract all liquid from greens, reserving liquid. Discard cooked leaves. Set liquid aside until cool. Carefully add liquid to mayonnaise taking care not to let it separate. Add 2 to 3 drops onion juice and the finely chopped capers. Cool, then transfer to a gravy boat and garnish with chopped parsley.
*Good over fish or vegetables.

****

FRENCH HERB SAUCE

½ cup white wine vinegar	1 cup nonfat milk	⅛ tsp. salt
2 tbsp. tomato puree	2 tbsp. shallot	1 tbsp. tarragon
1 tbsp. dried chervil	2 tbsp. arrowroot	1 cup water
¼ tsp. lemon juice	Dash of white pepper	Dash of paprika
2 tbsp. cooked cream of rice cereal		

Blend cooked cereal until smooth. Set aside. Combine herbs, pepper, vinegar, tomato puree and shallot in a saucepan over a medium heat and reduce to one third of original volume. Allow mixture to cool to room temperature. Mix arrowroot with water until dissolved. Cook over medium heat until it becomes clear and thickened. Remove from heat and allow to cool, then combine herb sauce mixture. Mix thoroughly with a wire whisk and pour into a large mixing bowl. Add white sauce mixture to thickened herb sauce mixture and blend thoroughly with wire whisk. Pour sauce through a sieve. Before serving add lemon juice and mix, sprinkle paprika.
*Good over fish.

****

FRENCH MUSHROOM MARINADE SAUCE

1 tbsp. chopped parsley	2 tbsp. white wine	3 tbsp. butter
2 tbsp. chopped shallot	¼ cup heavy cream	⅛ tsp. salt
1 ½ cups fresh mushrooms	¼ dried marjoram	¼ tsp. thyme
¼ tsp. ground pepper		

Mix all ingredients together in a bowl, until well blended. Marinade fish 30 to 60 minutes.
*Good over fish or pasta.

FRENCH-STYLE MUSTARD SAUCE

2 cups dry white wine   1 cup chopped onion   2 tbsp. honey
1 tsp. chopped garlic   Tabasco sauce   1 tsp. salt
1 ½ tbsp. vegetable oil   3-3 ¼ oz. cans dry mustard

In a medium saucepan combine wine, onion and garlic. Bring to a boil, lower heat, and simmer 5 minutes. Strain, discarding onion and garlic, and cool. Slowly stir in dry mustard until it forms a paste. Add honey, oil, salt and Tabasco to taste. Remove from heat and cool. Spoon into a jar and refrigerate.

*Good over poultry.

****

FRESH APRICOT SAUCE

1 lb. fresh apricots   1 cup sugar syrup   3 cups vodka

Cut apricots in half and remove pits. Place the pits in a plastic or paper bag, and hit them with a hammer to open. Remove the inner nut and discard the pit covers. Place the nuts in a bag and hit them to crush them and release the flavorful oils. (Any trace of the pit covering can impart a bitter taste.) Combine the fruit and nuts in alcohol, in a jar. Let stand two weeks, and shake gently two or three times a week. Strain and squeeze all the juice from the fruit. Strain until clear, then add sugar syrup. Mature 2-3 months.
*Good over ice cream, desserts or poultry.

****

FRESH BERRY SAUCE

3 cups strawberries   ½ cup powdered sugar   2 tbsp. lemon juice
3 tbsp. powdered sugar   3 tsp. crème de cassis liqueur

Lime juice or kirsch, raspberry brandy or Grand Marnier may be used in place of lemon juice. Raspberries, blackberries or blueberries may be substituted for fresh strawberries. Gently rinse and hull strawberries. Puree fruit in food processor or blender. Add ½ cup powered sugar and process until very smooth. Strawberry puree can be left unstrained. Strain other purees into bowl, pressing on pulp in strainer. Add powdered sugar to taste, if needed. Cover and refrigerate 30 minutes. Stir before serving, adding lemon juice or liqueur. Add water by teaspoons to thin sauce if necessary. Serve cold.
*Good over ice cream or desserts.

FRESH CORIANDER SAUCE

½ tsp. cayenne pepper
½ lb. sm. mushrooms
1 tsp. caraway seeds
½ cup fresh coriander

1 cup plain yogurt
2 tbsp. mustard or veg. oil
1 tsp. turmeric

Salt to taste
1 tbsp. garlic
½ tsp. cumin

Drain yogurt 5 minutes in cheesecloth. Finely chop garlic and coriander. Combine the yogurt, cayenne, garlic, turmeric, salt, cumin and caraway seeds in a bowl. Blend well, cover and refrigerate until ready to use. Heat oil in a large skillet. Add the mushrooms and salt and cook, stirring 2 minutes. Add coriander and cook 2 to 3 minutes. Serve hot.
*Good over poultry or fish.

****

FRESH HERB AND TOMATO VINAIGRETTE SAUCE

¼ cup virgin olive oil
⅛ cup red wine vinegar

2 cups ripe tomatoes
2 tbsp. chopped herbs

Crushed red pepper
Salt and pepper

Basil, tarragon, mint, dill or any herbs may be used. Peel, seed and finely chop the tomatoes. Mix all ingredients together in a bowl, until well blended.
*Good over fish, chicken, meats, seafood, or as a salad dressing.

****

FRESH MELON SAUCE

4 tbsp. powdered sugar
1 ½ lbs. melon or mango

2 tbsp. lemon juice

3 tbsp. melon liqueur

Peel fruit. Remove seeds and cut into chunks. Puree fruit in food processor or blender. Add powdered sugar and process until very smooth. Strain puree into bowl. Add more powdered sugar if needed. Cover and refrigerate 30 minutes. Stir before serving, adding lemon juice or liqueur. Server cold.
*Serve over cake or ice cream.

****

FRESH RASPBERRY SAUCE

2 tsp. orange or lemon juice
Light cream

2 lb. raspberries
1 tbsp. cornstarch

3 tbsp. sugar

Puree berries in a food processor or blender. Press through a sieve into a glass bowl; discard seeds. In a bowl, mix cornstarch with a little juice; and set aside. Pour balance of juice into a saucepan; add sugar, orange or lemon juice. Heat to dissolve sugar, stirring constantly. Bring to a boil, remove from heat and stir in cornstarch mixture. Simmer, stirring, and cook 1 to 2 minutes or until sauce is smooth and thickened. Cool to room temperature and add cream.
*Good over desserts or ice cream.

FROZEN BERRY LIQUEURS SAUCE

| 10 oz. pkg. strawberries, or any berry | ¼ cup sugar syrup | 1 ½ cups vodka |

1 cup vodka & ½ cup brandy may be used in place of 1 ½ cups vodka. Add juice and berries to alcohol. Stir and let stand one week in a jar, then strain. Crush berries through strainer, taste. Add sugar syrup as necessary. Many frozen fruits are already heavily pre-sugared. If using unsugared fruits without syrup treat them as fresh fruits, but reduce the amount of water when making the sugar syrup because of the water content in the frozen fruits.
*Good over ice cream or desserts.

****

FRUIT SAUCE

| ½ cup boiling water | ¼ cup raisins | 3 ripe bananas |
| Juice of 1 lemon | Dash of nutmeg | 2 oranges |

Pour water over the raisins and let stand in a bowl, until plump. Combine raisins with bananas, oranges, lemon juice and nutmeg in a blender. Puree until smooth.
*Good over poultry or desserts.

****

FRUITY LIQUEUR BASTING SAUCE

¼ tsp. each mace and nutmeg	1 tbsp. brown sugar	4 tbsp. butter
3 med. pitted peaches	2 tbsp. lemon juice	1 tsp. salt
2 tbsp. frozen orange juice	4 tbsp. fruit liqueur	

½ can pitted Bing cherries pureed in blender or food processor may be substituted for peaches. Peach, cherry, or lemon-lime fruit liqueur may be used. Melt butter or margarine in a saucepan and add spices, salt, sugar, stirring only until well blended. Mix in pureed fruit, then the remaining ingredients one at a time until well blended. Add to spice mixture, heat again and stir until smooth. Do not boil.
*Good over poultry.

GARLIC SAUCE I

2 cups fresh white bread crumbs
1 tbsp. white wine vinegar

2 garlic cloves
4 tsp. lemon juice

½ tsp. salt
1 cup olive oil

Dampen bread crumbs with water. Put in a blender or food processor with garlic and salt; puree. Add olive oil a little at a time and continue to process until it has all been added. Add lemon juice and vinegar to the sauce and process until it is a smooth and creamy consistency. Pour sauce into a serving bowl.
*Good over pasta, salad or vegetables.

****

GARLIC SAUCE II

½ cup red-wine vinegar
2 tbsp. chopped garlic
1 tsp. Worcestershire
¼ cup fresh herbs

4 lg. cloves garlic
¼ cup brown sugar
½ cup minced chives
1 tbsp. lemon juice

¾ cup olive oil
Salt and pepper
1 tsp. Dijon mustard
2 tbsp. fresh mint

Combine vinegar, garlic, oil, sugar, mustard and Worcestershire sauce in a food processor and blend until smooth. Add salt and pepper to taste. Add mixed herbs (parsley, oregano, dill, tarragon, and thyme), chives, 2 tablespoons of the mint and 1 teaspoon of the lemon juice, and process briefly. Use to marinade meat at least 45 minutes.
*Good for marinade.

****

GARLIC SAUCE III

2 tbsp. tomato sauce
¼ tsp. cayenne pepper
1 clove garlic, crushed

½ tsp. pepper
dash of tabasco sauce
¼ tsp. dry mustard

1 tsp. salt
1 cup salad oil
2 tbsp. vinegar

Place all ingredients into a bowl and mix together until well blended. Chill.
*Good over salad or all meats.

****

GARLIC MAYONNAISE SAUCE

4 crushed garlic cloves
Juice of ½ lemon

1 cup olive oil
Salt and white pepper

¼ tsp. salt
2 egg yolks

Combine garlic, salt and egg yolks in a bowl. Slowly add 3 tablespoons oil, beating vigorously. Add remaining oil in a steady stream, then add lemon juice, beating well. Season with salt and pepper.
*Good over poultry.

GARLIC SAUTÉED SHIITAKE MUSHROOMS SAUCE

4 tbsp. unsalted butter
Salt and pepper

2 lg. cloves garlic
6 oz. lg. shiitake mushrooms

1 tbsp. parsley

Combine butter and garlic in saucepan. Heat until butter is melted and garlic starts to sizzle, about 30 seconds. Do not let garlic brown. Add mushrooms and sauté 3 to 4 minutes, turning until lightly browned. Season to taste with salt and pepper, sprinkle with parsley and serve.
*Good over poultry or vegetables.

****

GENOA SAUCE

2 lbs. chopped onion
2 lbs. lean beef
1 cup white wine
4 oz. grated Parmesan cheese

4 oz. ham
4 oz. olive oil
1 cup water
Salt and pepper

1 sm. carrot
1 stalk celery
½ cup stock

Finely chop the carrot, celery and ham. Thinly slice the onions and cut up beef. Heat the oil in a saucepan until hot. Add the ham and vegetables and stir over a low heat for 5 minutes. Stir in meat and onions. Then add the water, salt and pepper to taste. Cover and cook over low heat for about 2 hours. Alternating, add wine and stock each time the sauce is stirred.
*Good over pasta.

****

GÉNOISE SAUCE

1 ½ cups onions
½ cup diced celery
½ lb. fresh mushrooms
2 tbsp. all-purpose flour

½ cup olive oil
1 carrot, grated
2 cups skinned tomatoes
¾ cup dry red wine

2 tbsp. Butter
1 lb. ground veal
1 cup beef broth
salt and fresh pepper

Finely chop onions, mushrooms and tomatoes. Combine butter and oil in a fry pan; heat until sizzling. Add onions; cook 3 minutes. Add carrot, celery, and mushrooms; continue to cook, about 5 minutes. Stir in veal; cook, stirring constantly, until well broken up and lightly browned. Add tomatoes, then sprinkle flour over mixture, mix well. Stir in wine gradually, then beef broth. Season with salt and pepper. Simmer about 2 hours, until thick; stir occasionally.
*Good over pasta.

GENOVESE SAUCE

4 oz. chopped raw ham
2 thinly sliced onions
2 lbs. lean beef pieces
4 oz. Parmesan cheese

1 carrot, chopped
4 oz. olive oil
4 oz. white wine
salt and pepper

1 celery, chopped
4 oz. water
2 oz. stock

Heat oil in a skillet, stirring in carrots, celery, ham and onions, simmer 5 minutes. Brown and sauté beef, add water, salt and pepper for 10 minutes over very low heat. Add wine and stock stirring with wooden spoon about 2 hours.
*Good over pasta.

****

GERMAN CHEESE SAUCE

1 tsp. German style mustard
1 cup Emmentaler cheese

3 cups smoky cheese
1 tbsp. cornstarch

3 tbsp. milk
1 cup light ale

Shred the Emmentaler and smoky cheeses. Pour ale in a saucepan and warm over medium heat until bubbly. Lower heat and gradually stir in cheeses. Continue to heat until cheese melts. In a small bowl blend cornstarch with milk, blend into cheese mixture. Add mustard and continue to cook, stirring until mixture is thick and creamy, 2-3 minutes.
*Good over chicken, vegetables or pasta.

****

GERMAN-STYLE MUSTARD SAUCE

1-3 ¼ oz. can dry mustard
4 tbsp. cider vinegar
1 tsp. horseradish

1 tsp. brown sugar
1 tbsp. vegetable oil

½ tsp. salt
4 tbsp. beer

In a small bowl combine mustard, salt and sugar. Blend in beer, cider vinegar, oil and horseradish. Chill for 30 minutes. Store in refrigerator. If mustard becomes thick, thin with beer.
*Good over poultry.

****

GINGER CREAM SAUCE

1 cup heavy cream
2 tbsp. candied ginger

2 egg yolks
1 tsp. vanilla

2 tbsp. butter

Finely chop the candied ginger. Whisk egg yolks and cream on top of a double boiler, over simmering water. Add butter, ginger and vanilla, mix until smooth and thickened.
*Use over ice cream.

GINGER LIME SAUCE

½ cup mayonnaise   ½ cup sour cream   1 tbsp. lime juice
2 tsp. grated lime peel   ½ tsp. ground ginger   1 tbsp. honey

Stir all ingredients in a bowl, until well blended. Cover and chill until ready to use.
*Good over fruit or use as a dip.

****

GINGER LIQUEUR SAUCE

½ tsp. dried ginger   ¾ cups sugar syrup   1 ½ cups vodka

1 teaspoon fresh ginger may be substituted for dried ginger. Brandy or whiskey may substitute vodka.
Soak the ginger in the alcohol for 1 week in a jar, shaking occasionally. Strain; add sugar syrup.
*Good over poultry or vegetables.

****

GINGER PEAR SAUCE

Grated rind and juice of 3 lemons   6 lbs. ripe pears   6 cups sugar
1 lb. crystallized ginger, chopped fine.

Peel, core and stem pears, then quarter and put into a large saucepan with ginger, sugar, lemon juice, and rind. Cook uncovered over medium heat until soft. About 30 to 45 minutes. Put through food mill or food processor. Return to saucepan and cook until thickened.
*Good over pork.

****

GLAZED CRANBERRY SAUCE

½ tsp. cranberry liqueur   ½ cup dry red wine   ½ cup brown sugar
¼ tsp. allspice liqueur   1 tbsp. cornstarch   ¼ tsp. cloves
1 1-lb. can whole berry cranberry sauce

Mix all ingredients together in a bowl. Use for marinade.
*Good over poultry or as a marinade.

GOLDEN VEGETABLE PUREE SAUCE

½ med. rutabaga	½ lb. carrots	1 sm. turnip
1 ¼ cups chicken broth	2 celery stalks	1 sm. onion
¼ cup butter	Dash nutmeg	¼ cup butter

Finely chop all vegetables; put in a medium size saucepan with broth. Bring to a boil then simmer just until vegetables are tender.
*Good over pasta.

****

GOOSEBERRY & WINE SAUCE

2 tbsp. half and half	2 tsp. cornstarch	½ cup sugar
⅔ cup dry white wine	1 ½ lbs. gooseberries, trimmed	

Place gooseberries in a saucepan with sugar and wine. Simmer until tender then press through a sieve to make a puree. In a saucepan, blend cornstarch with half and half, stir in gooseberry puree and heat until smooth and thick.
*Good over duck.

****

GORGONZOLA SAUCE

½ cup chopped walnuts	1 cup heavy cream	Parmesan cheese
¼ lb. unsalted butter	1 cup Gorgonzola cheese	

Place walnuts in baking pan, in a 350 degree oven. Bake, shaking occasionally, until golden brown. Heat cream and butter in a saucepan. Add ¾ cup crumbled cheese and stir over low heat until melted. Blend all ingredients together, and keep warm.
*Good over linguine.

****

GOULASH SAUCE

3 sliced onions	¼ cup vinegar	2 tbsp. butter
¼ cup paprika	2 tbsp. tomato paste	2 tbsp. oil
¼ cup water	salt and pepper	Pinch thyme
2 cloves garlic	1 tsp. caraway seeds	1 lemon zest

Melt butter and oil in a saucepan, sauté the onions about 5 minutes. Mix paprika and vinegar, add to onions and continue to cook a few minutes. Mix water with tomato paste and seasoning. Cook 15 minutes, add caraway seeds, garlic and lemon zest.
*Good over poultry.

GRAND MARNIER SAUCE

1 cup heavy cream, whipped   6 egg yolks   ¼ cup sugar
⅓ cup Grand Marnier or any orange liqueur

Beat yolks and sugar in top of double boiler until creamy. Place over hot water and beat until mixture forms a ribbon when dropped from a spoon. Remove from heat and beat until cool. Beat in liqueur gradually. Fold in cream. Chill.
*Good over desserts or ice cream.

****

GRAPEFRUIT SAUCE I

2 grapefruit peels   ½ cup sugar syrup   3 cups brandy

Scrape outer peel of 2 grapefruits and cut into pieces. Let peels stand in brandy for 10 days in a jar. Add sugar syrup gradually by tasting and establishing a ratio of flavor to sweetener.
*Good over fruit or desserts.

****

GRAPEFRUIT SAUCE II

1 ¼ cups grapefruit juice   2 tbsp. cornstarch   ½ cup sugar
¾ cup water

Place all ingredients in a saucepan, over a low heat and simmer for 3 minutes.
*Good over grapefruit sections.

****

GRAPES-BUTTERSCOTCH SAUCE

¾ cup heavy cream   ½ cup brown sugar   ⅛ tsp. salt
3 cups seedless grapes   2 tbsp. sour cream   ½ tsp. vanilla

In a small saucepan mix cream, grapes, salt and sugar. Bring to a boil, stirring frequently, for about 10 minutes. Remove from heat; stir in sour cream and vanilla.
*Good over desserts or ice cream.

GREEK MARINADE SAUCE

½ cup olive oil
Rind and juice of 2 lemons

3 lg. garlic cloves
1 tsp. dried oregano

½ tsp. pepper
½ tsp. salt

Mix all ingredients together in a bowl, until well blended. Marinate lamb at least 6 hours.
*Good for marinating.

****

GREEK TOMATO SAUCE

1 ½ lbs. plum tomatoes
1 tsp. lemon juice
Pinch of cinnamon

2 cloves garlic
1 tbsp. olive oil
½ cup Feta cheese

2 scallions
1 tsp. dill weed

Blend all ingredients together, except Feta cheese, in a saucepan, for 10 minutes. Then add cheese.
*Good over pasta.

****

GREEN PARSLEY SAUCE

2 minced shallots
1 cup chopped parsley

1 minced garlic clove
Parmesan cheese

⅓ cup olive oil
Salt and pepper

Cook shallots and minced garlic clove in a skillet, in olive oil over low heat, until soft. Add chopped parsley and season to taste with salt and pepper. Add grated Parmesan cheese just before serving.
*Good over pasta.

****

GREEN PEPPERCORN SAUCE I

3 tsp. green peppercorns
1 cup Brown Stock Sauce
3 tbsp. whipping cream

1 green onion, chopped
1 tbsp. beurre manie
2 tbsp. brandy

2 tbsp. butter
Salt and pepper

Sauté green onion in butter over medium heat until soft. Increase heat slightly, add brandy. Stir in stock and bring to a boil. Continue cooking until liquid is reduced to 1 cup. Remove onions with a slotted spoon. Bring liquid back to a boil. Whisk in the beurre manie a little at a time, combine well with liquid. When sauce begins to thicken, add the peppercorns, 1 tsp. lightly crushed and 2 tsp. uncrushed. Simmer for about 5 minutes. Add cream, stir and season.
*Good over steak.

GREEN PEPPERCORN SAUCE II

½ tsp. peppercorn, uncrushed
1 tsp. peppercorn, crushed
1 tbsp. Cognac

⅓ cup dry white wine
2 tsp. Dijon mustard
¼ cup cream, whipped

¼ cup milk
Salt
¾ cup poaching liquid

Poaching liquid can be from fish, chicken or White Stock Sauce. Place green peppercorns in a small sieve; strain, then dry on pepper towels. Place milk and poaching liquid in a saucepan, bring to a boil. In another small saucepan boil wine and Cognac. When milk mixture has reduced to less than half, add wine and brandy. Continue cooking over low heat; add mustard and cream. Stir constantly for 1 to 2 minutes. Add crushed and uncrushed peppercorns.
*Good over steak.

****

GREEN SAUCE I

2 white onions
1 green pepper
Juice of 1 lime

8 scallions
4 garlic cloves
30 lg. romaine lettuce leaves

white pepper
salt

Puree lettuce leaves, green pepper, onions, garlic, scallions, lime juice, salt and white pepper, in a blender.
*Good to marinate fish.

****

GREEN SAUCE II

2 cups mayonnaise
10 spinach leaves
1 tbsp. chopped chives

10 sprigs watercress
4 sprigs tarragon
Boiling water

4 sprigs parsley
4 sprigs chervil

Drop watercress, tarragon, parsley and chervil into boiling water. Add the spinach leaves and blanch for 1 minute. Drain; then refresh in cold water. Drain again and squeeze dry. Chop into a fine puree. Stir into mayonnaise along with 1 tablespoon of chopped chives.
*Good over fish or pasta.

GREEN TOMATO CHUTNEY SAUCE

2 8-oz. pkgs. tamarind	4 cups cider vinegar	10 cloves garlic
10 cups green tomatoes	6 cups brown sugar	2 whole lemons
1 ½ cups seeded raisins	1 ½ cups gingerroot	1 tbsp. salt
1 tsp. cayenne pepper	1 ½ cups seeded Muscat raisins	

Pour about 2 cups boiling water over the tamarind and let stand until cool. Place a sieve over a bowl and work the tamarind in it with your fingers, pressing the pulp through the sieve and leaving the seeds in it. Add hot water as you work the separation of seeds from pulp. Put the tamarind pulp and liquid into a deep, heavy pot, add the chopped raisins, chopped green tomatoes, peeled, chopped gingerroot and other ingredients and simmer, uncovered, about 1 hour, or until the mixture is reduced to a sauce like consistency.
*Good over pasta.

****

GREEN TOMATO SAUCE

1 can or 12 fresh tomatillos	2 cups garlic, minced	1 onion, chopped
1 tbsp. cilantro leaves	1 tsp. marjoram	salt and pepper
½ cup water	2-4 oz. cans green chilies, chopped	

Mix all ingredients together in a saucepan, bring to boil. Reduce heat and simmer 10 minutes.
*Good over pasta.

****

GRIBICHE SAUCE I

1 tsp. snipped fresh chives	½ tsp. Dijon mustard	1 cup olive oil
1 tsp. chopped fresh chervil	2 sweet pickles, chopped	4 tbsp. vinegar
1 tsp. chopped fresh tarragon	3 eggs, hard cooked	Salt
1 tsp. chopped fresh parsley	1 garlic clove, crushed	½ tsp. prepared
mustard		
8 capers, drained & chopped		

Separate yolks from whites. Cut whites in small thin strips; set aside. Place 3 eggs yolks in a bowl and mash to a paste. Add mustards and salt, mixing thoroughly. Whisk in oil, a little at a time. As mixture thicken, increase oil to a slow stream, and start adding vinegar, beating constantly. Use only the amount of oil required to reach a velvety consistency, not as thick as mayonnaise. Add garlic, pickles, herbs, capers and egg whites. Stir to mix through. Serve cold.
*Good over beef.

GRIBICHE SAUCE II

1 hard-cooked egg	1 tbsp. gherkins	2 cups mayonnaise
1 tbsp. capers	1 tbsp. shallots	3 sprigs parsley
4-5 tarragon leaves	⅓ tbsp. chives	salt and pepper

Chop all ingredients separately. Place the mayonnaise in a bowl and add chopped egg, gherkins or sour pickles, capers, shallot or green onion, minced parsley, tarragon leaves and chives. Add salt and pepper to taste.
*Good over shrimp.

****

GRILLING MARINADE SAUCE

¼ cup Worcestershire Sauce	1 cup dry red wine	½ cup soy sauce
4 lg. garlic cloves	½ cup parsley	2 tbsp. rosemary
1 tbsp. black pepper		

Fresh mint may be used in place of fresh chopped parsley. 2 teaspoons dried rosemary leaves may be substituted for fresh chopped rosemary leaves. Whisk all ingredients together in a bowl, until the marinade is well blended.
*Good over flank steak, London broil and spare ribs.

****

GUACAMOLE SAUCE

½ cup mayonnaise	1 sm. tomato, chopped	1 lg. avocado
¼ cup minced onion	¼ cup chopped green chilies	½ tsp. salt
1 tbsp. lemon juice		

Stir all ingredients in a bowl, until well mixed. Cover and chill until ready to use.
*Good for dipping or over vegetables.

****

HARD SAUCE

2 cups powdered sugar	½ cup butter	1 tbsp. hot water
1 tsp. vanilla	2 tsp. rum or brandy extract	

Rum or brandy liqueur may be used as a substitute for extracts. Combine all ingredients in a small bowl. Beat at highest speed until well blended. Cover and refrigerate until serving time.
*Good over desserts or ice cream.

****

HARE SAUCE

1 celery, chopped	1 tbsp. flour	4 tbsp. butter
1 onion, chopped	2 tbsp. olive oil	1 lb. meat (hare)
2 oz. cooked bacon	1 tsp. thyme	6 oz. wine
1 oz. Parmesan cheese	16 oz. stock	salt and pepper

Place oil and butter in a saucepan, add bacon, onion and celery. Add meat and brown. Add thyme, flour, wine and stock. Cook 2 hours. Season to taste. Add Parmesan cheese.
*Good over pasta.

****

HAZELNUT OIL SAUCE

1 tbsp. Dijon mustard	1 sm. egg yolk	salt to taste
2 tbsp. wine vinegar	1 ½ tsp. tarragon	1 tbsp. Cognac
¼ cup hazelnut oil	2 tbsp. hazelnut oil	ground pepper

Combine the mustard, salt, pepper and egg yolk, in a large salad bowl, and beat with whisk. Add the Cognac, vinegar, and tarragon and whisk until blended. Pour in the oil in a steady stream until thoroughly blended.
*Good over poultry.

****

HERB OIL SAUCE

¼ cup tarragon leaves	1 cup olive oil	2 tbsp. water

Mint leaves or Italian seasoning may be used as a substitute for the tarragon leaves. Vegetable oil may be used in place of olive oil. Combine herbs and water, then add to oil heated in a small saucepan, over a very low heat, just until warm. Remove from heat and pour into a non-plastic bowl. Cover and let stand at room temperature for one week. Strain mixture; discard herbs. Pour oil sauce into a covered bottle, and refrigerate.
*Good over fish or poultry.

HERBS, TOMATO AND CREAM SAUCE

2 tbsp. minced onion
½ cup heavy cream
12 lg. plum tomatoes
Salt and pepper

2 tbsp. olive oil
Pinch of basil
Pinch of thyme

½ cup parsley
Pinch of marjoram
1 tbsp. lemon zest

Cook minced onion in a skillet over moderate heat in olive oil until softened. Add chopped parsley, lemon zest and basil, marjoram and thyme. Cook 1 minute, stirring frequently. Add seeded, skinned, chopped tomatoes and cook until they release their liquid. Add cream and simmer a minute until sauce thickens lightly. Season with salt and pepper.
*Good over pasta.

****

HIGHLAND WHISKY SAUCE

4 cups Cheddar cheese
¼ cup whisky

1 sm. onion, chopped
1 tbsp. cornstarch

1 tbsp. butter
1 cup milk

In a medium saucepan cook onion in butter over low heat until soft. Add milk and heat until bubbly. Stir in cheese, cook until melted. Blend cornstarch in a small bowl, stir into cheese mixture; cook, stirring until thickened, 2-3 minutes.
*Good over steak.

****

HOLLANDAISE SAUCE

Paprika or red pepper
¾ cup butter, diced

2 tsp. lemon juice
Salt and white pepper

1 tbsp. water
3 egg yolks

In top of a double boiler over low heat, whisk egg yolks, water and lemon juice until fluffy. Add butter, piece by piece, melt one piece before adding the next. Season with salt and pepper, sprinkling with paprika or red pepper.
*Good over fish.

****

HOMEMADE HOT MUSTARD SAUCE

¾ cup wine vinegar
⅔ cup dry white wine
½ tsp. salt

1 cup mustard seed
¼ cup water

½ cup brown sugar
1 egg

Blend mustard seed in food processor or blender until smooth. Add wine vinegar, wine, sugar, water egg, and salt. Blend until smooth. Transfer mixture to saucepan; cook and stir 5 minutes or until thickened.
*Good over pork.

HOMEMADE WALNUT OIL SAUCE

⅔ cup warm toasted walnut pieces   1 ⅓ cups vegetable oil

Spread nuts on wax paper and crush with rolling pin. Combine with oil in a glass jar. Stir and store in cool room or refrigerator for 3 days. Strain through fine sieve.
*Good over salad or pasta.

****

HONEY BAKED APPLES WITH WALNUT SAUCE

3 apples   1 tsp. honey   ½ cup walnuts
3 tbsp. butter   ½ cup raisins   ½ cup apple juice

Core, peel and chop apples in small pieces. Sauté apples and apple juice in a pan for about 5 minutes. Add honey, walnuts, butter and raisins and continue to sauté for another 2 minutes.
*Good over poultry, ham or desserts.

****

HONEY VANILLA SAUCE

½ cup honey   2 cups cream   3 eggs
2 cups milk   2 tsp. vanilla

Beat eggs and milk together in large saucepan. Add honey and cook over low heat until thickened, stirring constantly, until mixture coats the back of a spoon, about 10 minutes. Cool, then add cream and vanilla. Refrigerate.
*Good over rice or desserts.

****

HONEY-ANISE SAUCE

½ cup nonfat buttermilk   1 vanilla bean, split   2 tbsp. honey
⅛ tsp. anise flavoring   ½ cup 1% low-fat cottage cheese

Scrape seeds from inside of vanilla bean. Combine seeds and remaining ingredients in blender; process until smooth. Pour into a bowl, cover and chill.
*Good with cabbage or apple or mixed fruit salad.

HONEY-LEMON DRESSING SAUCE

½ cup fresh lemon juice
¼ tsp. cider vinegar
½ tsp. white pepper

½ cup olive oil
1 tsp. sherry
Pinch of garlic powder

1 tbsp. honey
1 tsp. salt

Whisk the lemon juice and olive oil in a bowl, until combined. In another bowl, place honey and cider vinegar and stir until honey is dissolved. Add the honey and vinegar mixture to the lemon juice and oil. Add the remaining seasonings. Add the sherry, mix thoroughly, and refrigerate over-night.
*Good over salads or vegetables.

****

HORSERADISH CHEDDAR CHEESE SAUCE

1 tbsp. grated horseradish
½ lb. white cheddar cheese

¼ lb. cream cheese
¼ cup heavy cream

Salt and pepper

Combine the horseradish, cheddar cheese and cream cheese in the food processor and puree until smooth. Add enough cream to obtain a smooth consistency. Add salt and pepper to taste. Let mixture stand 3 to 4 hours.
*Good over pasta.

****

HORSERADISH SAUCE

1 piece fresh horseradish
¾ cup whipping cream
1 tbsp. red wine vinegar

2 tbsp. superfine sugar
½ tsp. dry mustard
½ cup fresh white bread crumbs

Salt
2 tbsp. milk

Cut any discolored pieces from the horseradish; cut away the outer part and finely grate 3 to 4 tablespoons. Combine horseradish with sugar, salt and mustard in a medium bowl. In another small bowl, pour milk over bread crumbs. Mix well, and squeeze out milk, leaving crumbs moist. Add crumbs to bowl with horseradish. Stir in cream and blend. At the last moment, stir in vinegar. Cover and refrigerate until ready to serve.
*Good over shrimp.

****

HOT ARTICHOKE SAUCE

⅛ tsp. hot pepper sauce
⅓ cup Parmesan cheese

½ cup mayonnaise
14 oz. artichoke hearts

½ cup sour cream

Chop artichoke hearts and place in a bowl; add remaining ingredients and stir until well blended. Bake at 350 degree for 30 minutes or until bubbly.
*Good over pasta, vegetables or as a dip.

HOT BUTTER DIPPING SAUCE

2 cloves garlic
8 oz. melted butter

2 pieces of ginger
pinch crushed chili

3 tbsp. soy sauce
2 tbsp. vinegar

Mince garlic and ginger, then sauté in butter in a saucepan, until golden brown. Add soy sauce and vinegar to mixture and stir well.
*Use for crabmeat, lobster or shrimp.

****

HOT CARAMEL SAUCE

⅓ cup packed brown sugar

1 cup whipping cream

⅓ cup butter

Heat whipping cream and butter, stirring constantly, in a heavy saucepan until butter melts. Add brown sugar; continue to stir until dissolved and the mixture comes to a boil. Boil 2 minutes or until thick and glossy.
*Good over ice cream.

****

HOT CHEDDAR BEAN SAUCE

16 oz. pinto beans
4 oz. chopped green chilies

1 cup shredded Cheddar cheese
¼ tsp. hot pepper sauce

½ cup mayonnaise

Stir all ingredients in a bowl, until well blended, place in baking dish. Bake at 350 degrees for 30 minutes or until bubbly.
*Good over rice or vegetables.

****

HOT CIDER SAUCE

½ cup purple onion
2 tbsp. brown sugar
2 tbsp. Dijon mustard

½ cup cider vinegar
2 tsp. poppy seeds
1 cup unsweetened apple juice

½ cup water
1 tbsp. cornstarch

Combine apple juice and onion in a medium, non aluminum saucepan; cook over medium heat 4 minutes or until onion is tender. Add remaining ingredients; stir well. Bring mixture to a boil over medium heat; cook 1 minute or until thickened, stirring constantly.
*Good over spinach salad.

HOT CRAB SAUCE

3 oz. cream cheese
⅛ tsp. hot pepper sauce

6 oz. crabmeat
¼ cup minced onion

½ cup mayonnaise
1 tbsp. lemon juice

Place softened cream cheese in a mixing bowl and beat until smooth. Stir in remaining ingredients. Bake at 350 degrees for 30 minutes or until bubbly.
*Good over pasta or use as a dip.

****

HOT DILL SAUCE

1 tbsp. onion, chopped
1 tsp. dill weed
1 ½ cups milk

2 tbsp. butter
⅛ tsp. pepper

2 tbsp. flour
1 tsp. salt

Sauté onion in butter until tender, in a small saucepan. Add flour, salt, dill weed and pepper, blend well. Add milk, gradually and cook until mixture boils and thickens, stirring constantly. Serve warm.
*Good over fish.

****

HOT FISH SAUCE

¼ cup white wine vinegar
1 tsp. lime or lemon juice

2 fresh red chilies
2 sm. onions, chopped

¼ cup olive oil
Salt and pepper

Place all ingredients, except the chilies in a blender or food processor and blend until the onions are pureed into the liquid. Cut chilies in half lengthwise and remove seeds; finely chop. Add chilies to onion mixture and stir through. Transfer to a serving dish and let stand for 1 to 2 hours before serving, to develop its maximum zest.
*Good over fish or vegetables.

****

HOT FUDGE SAUCE I

3 oz. semi-sweet chocolate
5 ½ oz. evaporated milk

⅔ cups sugar

Dash salt

Melt chocolate in a saucepan over very low heat, stirring constantly. Stir in sugar and salt. Gradually add milk, stirring constantly. Heat until thickened and hot, stirring constantly. Serve warm or cold.
*Good over ice cream or desserts.

HOT FUDGE SAUCE II

⅓ cup dark-brown sugar
½ cup unsweetened cocoa

⅓ cup granulated sugar
3 tbsp. sweet butter

Dash of salt
½ cup heavy cream

In a heavy 1-quart saucepan over medium heat, stir cream and butter until butter melts and cream barely boils. Stir in sugars until dissolved. Reduce heat; stir in salt and cocoa. Remove from heat. Serve immediately or reheat stirring frequently in heavy saucepan over lowest heat. If too thick when reheating, stir in a little hot water.
*Good over desserts or ice cream.

****

HOT FUDGE SAUCE III

2-oz. unsweetened chocolate
2-oz. semisweet chocolate
⅛ tsp. salt

½ cup butter
1 cup heavy cream

1 cup sugar
2 tsp. vanilla

In a large saucepan, melt butter and chocolates over very low heat. Blend in sugar, cream and salt. Stir over low heat until sugar is dissolved, about 5 minutes. Remove from heat; stir in vanilla. Serve warm.
*Good over ice cream, plain cake or cut-up fruit.

****

HOT FUDGE SAUCE IV

½ cup chocolate syrup

1 tbsp. butter

In a small saucepan, over low heat, stir chocolate syrup and butter until smooth, thick and shiny, about 4 minutes.
*Good over ice cream, plain cake or cut-up fruit.

****

HOT MUSTARD SAUCE

4 oz. dry mustard
1 cup cider or white vinegar

1 cup sugar

2 eggs

Mix all ingredients in blender or food processor until smooth. Transfer mixture to top of double boiler over simmering water. Stirring occasionally, cook until thick.
*Good over smoked ham.

HOT PEACH SAUCE

3 tbsp. brown sugar
1 tsp. vanilla

1 tbsp. lemon juice
3 med. ripe peaches, sliced

2 tbsp. butter

In small skillet over medium heat, stir butter, sugar, and juice until hot and bubbly. Add peaches and cook about 4 minutes or until peaches are heated through but still keep their shape. Remove from heat stir in vanilla.
*Good warm over ice cream, cake or pancakes.

****

HOT PEPPER AND LIME-JUICE SAUCE

⅓ cup fresh lime juice

1 med. Serrano pepper

3 tbsp. veg. oil

Jalapeno chili pepper, or 1 ½ tbsp. crushed red pepper may substitute the Serrano pepper. Seed and mince the hot pepper. Mix all ingredients together in a bowl, until well blended.
*Good to marinate fish about 15 minutes.

****

HOT STUFF BARBECUE SAUCE

1 tbsp. red wine vinegar
3 tbsp. dry mustard
1 tbsp. Tabasco sauce
¼ cup Worcestershire Sauce

1 cup chili sauce
2 tbsp. horseradish
1 tbsp. salsa relish

1 cup ketchup
1 tbsp. molasses
1 tbsp. garlic

Finely press garlic and drain horseradish well. Combine all ingredients in a bowl. Whisk until the sauce is well blended. Add seasoning to taste. Let sit covered for at least 1 hour for flavors to blend.
*Good for ribs and poultry.

****

HUNGARIAN SAUCE

1 cup cooked chop meat
3 tbsp. sour cream
½ cup chicken stock

½ tsp. ground cloves
½ tsp. marjoram
salt and pepper

1 tsp. basil
1 tbsp. flour
paprika

Add cloves, basil and marjoram to cooked meat and cook 5 minutes. Then add sour cream, flour, chicken stock, paprika, salt and pepper.
*Good over pasta.

****

INDIAN CURRY SAUCE

¼ cup coconut cream   ½ tsp. curry powder   1 cup chicken stock

Heat all ingredients together in a saucepan, about 3 minutes, until well blended.
*Good over rice or vegetables.

****

IRISH MIST SAUCE

2 tbsp. Irish whisky   ½ cup water   1 cup sugar
2 tbsp. Irish Mist liqueur   ¼ to ½ cup water

Put sugar and ½ cup of water in a saucepan, and stir over medium heat until sugar has dissolved. Cook without stirring until it caramelizes. Pour in whisky and Irish Mist. Simmer until caramel has dissolved. Add a little water to thin to a light pouring consistency. This sauce will keep almost indefinitely in a covered jar.
*Good over ice cream.

****

ISRAELI SOUR CREAM SAUCE

2 med. avocados, halved   2 tbsp. lemon juice   ⅓ cup sour cream
1 garlic clove, halved   ¾ cup dry white wine   2 tsp. cornstarch
3 cups shredded Edam cheese

Scoop flesh from avocados into a bowl with garlic clove and mash with lemon juice until smooth. Pour in wine and heat until bubbly. Over a low heat, stir in cheese, cook until melted. Blend cornstarch and sour cream in a small bowl. Mix the cornstarch and avocados with the cheese mixture. Continue to cook until thick and smooth, about 4 to 5 minutes.
*Good over fish.

ITALIAN SAUCE

1 to 2 garlic cloves
1 tbsp. chopped fresh basil

1 med. onion, chopped
5 tbsp. dry white wine

2 tbsp. olive oil
1 ½ lbs. tomatoes

Skin and chop the tomatoes and crush garlic. Heat oil in a medium saucepan, add onion and garlic; cook over low heat until soft. Add tomatoes and wine. Season with salt and pepper, simmer 30 minutes. Process sauce in a blender or food processor until smooth, or press through a sieve. Stir in basil and reheat sauce before serving.
*Good over pasta.

ITALIAN GREEN SAUCE

¼ cup fresh white bread
2 tbsp. white wine vinegar
2 anchovy fillets, drained

1 egg yolk, hard cooked
¾ cup chopped parsley
1 garlic clove, chopped

1 cup olive oil
Salt and pepper
1 tsp. capers

In a small bowl, soak bread crumbs in vinegar. Place egg yolk in a medium bowl and mash with parsley, chopped anchovies, garlic and finely chopped capers. Squeeze vinegar from bread crumbs and add to egg mixture. Add oil and blend until sauce is smooth and creamy. Add salt and pepper to taste. Let stand for 1 to 2 hours. Serve cold.
*Good over fish or salads.

****

ITALIAN MARINADE SAUCE

¼ cup tiny capers
1 cup dry vermouth

¼ cup chopped parsley
¼ cup olive oil

4 flat anchovies

Combine the capers, parsley, anchovies and vermouth in a food processor or blender, process until fine. Slowly add olive oil until well blended. Marinade fish 3 to 4 hours.
*Good for marinating.

**Also good over poultry.

ITALIAN MOZZARELLA CHEESE SAUCE

2 cups mozzarella cheese
8 oz. blue cheese, cubed
½ cup finely grated Parmesan cheese

1 garlic clove, halved
3 tbsp. dry white wine

1 ¼ cups milk
2 tbsp. cornstarch

Heat milk in a saucepan; mash garlic clove and add to milk until bubbly. Stir in all cheeses and continue to heat until melted. Blend cornstarch with wine, blend into cheese mixture and cook, stirring 2-3 minutes or until thick and creamy.
*Good over chicken.

****

ITALIAN SAUSAGE SAUCE

4 ½ lbs. sweet sausage
3 28-oz. cans whole tomatoes
1 ½ green bell peppers
3 8-oz. cans tomato sauce
3 6-oz. cans tomato paste
¾ lb. grated Cheddar cheese

¾ lb. mushrooms
1 ½ cups parsley
1 ½ tsp. oregano
1 ½ tsp. basil
¾ tsp. fennel seeds

3 cloves garlic
3 tbsp. olive oil
3 whole onions
1 tbsp. sugar
Salt

In a large Dutch oven, heat oil; sauté chopped garlic in oil until lightly browned. Add and brown sausage, removing casing, and crumble. Drain fat; remove sausage and set aside. Add undrained whole tomatoes, tomato sauce and paste to Dutch oven. Cook over medium heat 15 minutes, stirring occasionally. Return sausage to pan along with remaining ingredients except cheese and salt; simmer 15 minutes. Add cheese a little at a time; stir until cheese is blended. Simmer, covered, 1 ½ hours more. Remove and discard onions and peppers. Add salt to taste.
*Good over pasta.

JALAPENO CORN SAUCE

6 ears sweet corn
3 jalapeno peppers
2 bunches cilantro
½ cup virgin olive oil

2 lg. red peppers, diced
Salt and white pepper
2 tbsp. rice wine vinegar

3 ripe tomatoes
2 med. red onions
2 tbsp. lemon juice

Seed and mince jalapeno peppers, finely chop onions and cilantro. Husk, then blanch corn in rapidly boiling salted water for 5 to 6 minutes. Remove from water and let cool to room temperature. Quarter tomatoes, cut out and discard inside pulp, place in ice water to remove skin. Slice corn kernels from the cob. Combine corn, tomatoes, red and jalapeno peppers, onion and cilantro, in a large bowl. Add vinegar, lemon juice and olive oil and toss. Add salt and white pepper to taste; adjust lemon juice to taste.
*Good with lamb, shrimp, salmon or bluefish.

****

JAPANESE DIPPING SAUCE

¼ cup mirin (sweet rice wine)
1 cup water

2 tsp. grated ginger root
2 tbsp. grated daikon (white Japanese radish)

¼ cup soy sauce

In a small saucepan combine water, soy sauce, mirin, daikon and ginger root. Cook over medium heat until very hot.
*Good over all meats or poultry.

****

JAPANESE-STYLE SAUCE

4 tbsp. sugar
½ cup dashi or fish broth

4 tbsp. soy sauce

2 tbsp. mirin

Mix sugar, soy sauce, mirin and fish broth. Pour into large saucepan and cook over medium heat for about 15 to 20 minutes, with cover slightly ajar.
*Good over chicken or steak.

JARLSBERG VEGETABLE BISQUE SAUCE

2 cups chopped broccoli
1 sm. clove garlic, minced
1 ½ cups Jarlsberg cheese
4 cups chicken broth
1 sm. onion, chopped

1 cup heavy cream
¼ tsp. thyme
¾ cup carrots
½ cup celery
⅛ tsp. pepper

3 tbsp. butter
3 tbsp. flour
1 egg yolk
½ tsp. salt

Chop all vegetables. In a large saucepan, melt butter. Add flour and cook several minutes, stirring. Remove from heat, gradually blend in broth. Bring to a boil, add broccoli, carrots, celery, onion, garlic, thyme, salt and pepper. Cover, simmer 8 minutes until vegetables are tender. Blend cream and egg in a bowl; gradually blend in several tablespoons of sauce. Return to sauce and cook; stirring until thickened. Blend in cheese.
*Good over pasta.

****

JERK-STYLE JAMAICAN BARBECUE SAUCE

5 lbs. lg. white onions
¾ cup black pepper
4 cups white-wine vinegar

2 lbs. Jamaican peppers
1 cup ground allspice
1 cup dark soy sauce

1 cup thyme
½ lb. ginger

Place peeled and quartered onions, cored and quartered peppers and fresh peeled ginger in a blender or food processor and pulverize. Transfer mixture to a large bowl and stir in allspice, fresh thyme, black pepper, vinegar and soy sauce. Let rest at least an hour.
*Good to marinate pork, beef, chicken and fish.

****

JIFFY ALIOLI SUN-DRIED SAUCE

2 tbsp. sun dried tomatoes
½ cup butter, melted
1 tbsp. Dijon mustard

4 anchovies, minced
¼ cup olive oil

1 lg. garlic clove
2 tbsp. lemon juice

Blend garlic, butter, oil, lemon juice and mustard in a blender. Add drained, minced anchovies and tomatoes.
*Good over pasta.

****

JIFFY AMARETTO APRICOT SAUCE

¼ cup brown sugar
1 tsp. dry mustard

2 tbsp. lemon juice
½ cup apricot jam

2 tbsp. Amaretto

Heat all ingredients together in a saucepan, for 2 minutes.
*Good over poultry.

****

JIFFY AMARETTO MARINATE SAUCE

3 tbsp. chili sauce
2 tbsp. vegetable oil
¼ tsp. dry mustard

6 tbsp. orange juice
2 tbsp. soy sauce
1 glove garlic, minced

½ cup Amaretto
2 tbsp. honey

Mix all ingredients together in a bowl, until well blended.
*Use as marinate for chicken.

****

JIFFY ANCHOVY SAUCE

2 tsp. Dijon mustard
2 tbsp. red wine vinegar

1 tsp. anchovy paste
salt and pepper

¼ tsp. garlic
1 cup oil

Mix all ingredients together in a bowl, until well blended.
*Good over poultry.

JIFFY ANCHOVY BUTTER SAUCE

3 dashes onion powder   ½ cup minced anchovies   1 cup butter

Heat ingredients together in a saucepan, until well blended.
*Good over steak.

****

JIFFY ANCHOVY FRENCH SAUCE

2 tbsp. lemon juice	freshly ground black pepper	4 anchovy fillets
6 to 8 tbsp. olive oil	½ tsp. dry mustard	1 tsp. sugar
1 tbsp. Worcestershire sauce	1 tsp. paprika	

Mix lemon juice with minced anchovy fillets and pepper in a mixing bowl. Add remaining ingredients; beat with fork until mixture thickens. Mix well before using.
*Good over salad.

****

JIFFY ANCHOVY MAYONNAISE SAUCE

1 ½ can anchovies	6 tbsp. mayonnaise	2 tbsp. olive oil
2 tbsp. half and half	2 tsp. tomato paste	

Place all ingredients in a blender or food processor and process until smooth.
*Good over pork.

****

JIFFY ANCHOVY-CHEESE (LOW CAL) SAUCE

1 cup low fat cottage cheese	1 tbsp. lemon juice	½ tsp. salt
¼ cup skim milk	3 anchovy fillets	1 tsp. paprika
¼ tsp. dry mustard		

Mix all ingredients together in a blender, until well blended.
*Good over pasta.

JIFFY APFELKEN SAUCE

1 cup raw apples	⅛ cup Horseradish	1 tbsp. vinegar
¼ cup white wine	⅛ tbsp. paprika	2 tbsp. sugar

Mix all ingredients together in a bowl, until well blended.
*Good over ham or chicken.

****

JIFFY APPLE MARINADE SAUCE

¼ cup apple juice	2 tbsp. white wine vinegar	¼ cup water
2 tbsp. olive oil	1 tsp. dried savory, crushed	2 tbsp. soy sauce

Mix all ingredients together in a bowl, until well blended.
*Good over poultry or pork.

****

JIFFY APPLE SAUCE

1 cup apple puree	2 tbsp. cinnamon	1 tbsp. sugar

Mix all ingredients together in a bowl, until well blended.
*Good over ham.

****

JIFFY APPLE-MINT SAUCE

1 cup unsweetened applesauce	3 tbsp. mint jelly

Mix ingredients together in a bowl, until well blended.
*Good over pork.

JIFFY APPLE-SHERRY WINE VINEGAR SAUCE

½ cup chicken broth   3 tbsp. butter   2 tbsp. brown sugar
¼ cup Balsamic vinegar   ½ tsp. thyme   3 apples

Place all ingredients into a blender and mix well.
*Good over vegetables.

****

JIFFY APPLE-SOY SAUCE

½ cup light soy sauce   3 tbsp. cider vinegar   1 cup garlic clove
¾ cup unsweetened applesauce

Mix all ingredients together in a bowl, until well blended.
*Good for marinade.

****

JIFFY APRICOT SAUCE

1 cup apricot preserves   1 tbsp. Worcestershire sauce

Mix ingredients together in a bowl, until well blended.
*Good over poultry.

****

JIFFY APRICOT BRANDY SAUCE

2 tbsp. apricot brandy   1 tbsp. brown sugar   1 tbsp. butter

Heat all ingredients together in a bowl, until well blended.
*Good over chicken.

JIFFY APRICOT COCONUT GLAZING SAUCE

½ cup Cream of coconut
Grated rind of 1 orange

2 oz. apricot nectar

4 whole cloves

Mix all ingredients together in a bowl, until well blended.
*Good over ham.

****

JIFFY APRICOT GLAZE SAUCE

1 ½ tsp. whole cloves
½ cup angelica liqueur

½ tsp. potpourri liqueur
2 12-oz. jars apricot preserves

2 tbsp. lime juice

Mix all ingredients together in a bowl, until well blended.
*Good over poultry or pork.

****

JIFFY APRICOT GLAZING SAUCE

½ cup apricot preserves

¼ cup Dijon Mustard

Melt apricot preserves in a saucepan, then stir in mustard until well blended.
*Use over pork or ham.

****

JIFFY APRICOT-MINT SAUCE

5 oz. strained apricots

¼ cup mint apple jelly

1 drop green food coloring

Mix all ingredients together in a bowl, until well blended.
*Good over pork.

JIFFY ASPIC SAUCE

1 env. unflavored gelatin
2 tbsp. wine vinegar
⅛ tsp. thyme

2 cups beef stock
2 tbsp. sherry
salt and pepper

1 egg
½ tsp. parsley
1 egg white

Chicken stock can be substituted for beef stock. Lemon juice can be substituted for wine vinegar. Mix all ingredients together in a bowl, until well blended.
*Good for chicken or beef.

****

JIFFY AU VIN ROUGE SAUCE

½ cup dry red wine
1 glove garlic, crushed

1 tbsp. lime juice
salt and pepper

½ cup oil

Mix all ingredients together in a bowl, until well blended.
*Good for marinate.

****

JIFFY AVOCADO SAUCE

½ cup sour cream
¼ tsp. onion powder

1 tsp. lime juice
Dash chili powder

2 ripe avocados
salt and pepper

Mash the avocado in a bowl, then mix in remaining ingredients.
*Good over salad or vegetables.

****

JIFFY AVOCADO AND LIME SAUCE

½ cup olive oil
1 tbsp. chives

1 ripe avocado, diced
salt and pepper

½ lime

Squeeze the juice from the lime into a mixing bowl. Mix in the remaining ingredients until well blended.
*Good over broiled salmon.

JIFFY AVOCADO COCKTAIL SAUCE

1 cup sliced avocado
½ tsp. Worcestershire

1 tbsp. lemon juice
¼ cup chili sauce

⅓ cup mayonnaise

Mix all ingredients together in a bowl, until well blended.
*Good for marinade.

****

JIFFY BAGNIET SAUCE

1 cup chopped parsley
8 diced anchovy fillets
3 tsp. red wine vinegar
½ tsp. black pepper

½ cup red onions
1 tbsp. chopped garlic
1 tsp. dry oregano

¼ cup tomatoes
¼ cup olive oil
1 tsp. Tabasco

Chop up onions into small pieces and mix with remaining ingredients in a bowl, until well blended.
*Good over salads.

****

JIFFY BAILEYS IRISH CREAM SAUCE

1 cup Baileys Irish cream

¼ cup superfine sugar

½ cup heavy cream

Mix heavy cream and sugar in a bowl, whipping, fold in Baileys Irish Cream.
*Good over ice cream.

****

JIFFY BALTIMORE SAUCE

1 tbsp. horseradish
1 tsp. Worcestershire

½ cup chili sauce
½ tsp. celery salt

3 tbsp. lemon juice

Mix all ingredients together in a bowl, until well blended.
*Good over seafood.

****

JIFFY BANANA SAUCE

1 tbsp. fruit preserves
2 tbsp. creamy peanut butter

¼ cup chopped pistachio nuts

2 bananas

Chop banana into small chunks. Mix nuts, peanut butter and fruit preserves together in a bowl, then add banana to mixture.
*Good on top of desserts.

****

JIFFY BANKER'S SAUCE

1 cup tomato puree
¼ cup Madeira Wine

1 cup veal stock

1 tbsp. butter

Heat all ingredients together in a saucepan, until well blended.
*Good over meat and chicken.

****

JIFFY BARBECUE SAUCE

bottled barbecue sauce

prepared horseradish

Mix both ingredients together in a bowl, until well blended.
*Good over ribs, chicken or pork.

****

JIFFY BARBECUED GINGER SAUCE

¾ cup ginger liqueur
½ cup chicken broth

½ cup soy sauce
3 tbsp. lemon juice

¼ cup honey
Salt and pepper

Mix all ingredients together in a bowl, until well blended. Let stand to marinade.
*Good over poultry.

JIFFY BASTING SAUCE

¼ cup green onions
¼ cup fresh basil

1 piece garlic clove
¾ cup dry wine or tomato juice

¼ cup parsley

Chop onions, basil, garlic and parsley. Mix all ingredients together in a bowl, until well blended.
*Good over all meats.

****

JIFFY BÉARNAISE SAUCE

1 tbsp. parsley flakes
1 tsp. tarragon vinegar

¼ tsp. crushed tarragon
hollandaise sauce mix

½ tsp. grated onion

Prepare hollandaise sauce, in a bowl, from a mix according to package directions. Blend in parsley flakes, grated onion, tarragon and vinegar.
*Good over fish.

****

JIFFY BEAUE BLANC SAUCE

2 cups white wine
Salt and pepper

¼ cup wine vinegar

¼ lb. butter

Mix all ingredients together in a bowl, until well blended.
*Use for poaching fish.

****

JIFFY BEEF-BEER MARINADE SAUCE

1 12-oz. can beer
2 tbsp. beef bouillon

1 cup chopped onion
3 tbsp. vegetable oil

¼ cup lemon juice
2-3 cloves garlic

In a medium bowl, combine chopped garlic and instant beef bouillon add the rest of the ingredients; mix well.
*Good over pork.

JIFFY BLACK BUTTER SAUCE

3 tbsp. butter   1 tsp. vinegar

Brown butter in a saucepan until dark brown, add vinegar. Serve hot.
*Good for veal or chicken.

****

JIFFY BLACKBERRY SAUCE

¼ cup blackberry liqueur   2 tbsp. chopped parsley   6 tbsp. butter
1 tbsp. Worcestershire sauce   salt and pepper

Melt butter in a saucepan, add liqueur. Mix in remaining ingredients, stirring until well blended.
*Good over steak.

****

JIFFY BLACKBERRY BRANDY BROWN GRAY SAUCE

2 cups beef stock   3 oz. Blackberry Brandy

Place stock and brandy into a saucepan and heat.
*Use over meat.

****

JIFFY BLACKBERRY CASSIS SAUCE

2 cups fresh blackberries   1 tsp. lemon juice   ¼ cup sugar
2 tbsp. crème de cassis   1 ¼ cups whipping cream

Puree blackberries, lemon juice, sugar and crème de cassis in a food processor. Add cream.
*Good over ice cream and desserts.

JIFFY BLACKBERRY JAM SAUCE

½ cup onions, minced
¼ cup blackberry jam
1 tsp. ground coriander
½ tsp. hot pepper sauce

1 tsp. ground garlic
¼ cup lemon juice
1 tsp. ground ginger

¼ cup soy sauce
4 tbsp. peanut oil
¼ cup brown sugar

Mix all ingredients in a blender, pulse until well blended.
*Good over poultry or pork.

****

JIFFY BLACKENED RUBBING SAUCE

½ tsp. onion powder
½ tsp. basil, crushed
¼ tsp. white pepper

½ tsp. garlic salt
⅛ tsp. ground sage
½ tsp. red pepper

¼ cup butter
¼ tsp. thyme
¼ tsp. pepper

Mix all ingredients together in a bowl, until well blended.
*Rub on chicken or fish.

****

JIFFY BLUE CHEESE VINAIGRETTE SAUCE

¼ cup red wine vinegar
½ cup crumbled blue cheese

¾ cup olive oil
⅛ tsp. dry thyme

1 tsp. Dijon mustard
Salt and pepper

Combine all ingredients in a bowl and beat with a fork to mix.
*Good over vegetables.

****

JIFFY BLUEBERRY MALLOW SAUCE

2 cups blueberries

½ cup marshmallow cream

Puree or mash blueberries; fold in marshmallow cream until well blended.
*Good over ice cream.

JIFFY BOURBON SAUCE

2 tbsp. brown sugar   2 tbsp. maple syrup   1 tbsp. bourbon

Mix all ingredients together in a bowl, until well blended.
*Good over fruit and desserts.

****

JIFFY BOURBON FUDGE SAUCE

1-oz. unsweetened chocolate   ½ tsp. vanilla extract   2 tbsp. sugar
1-oz. semisweet chocolate   ½ cup heavy cream   2 tbsp. bourbon

Combine all ingredients in a saucepan, stirring constantly, until smooth.
*Good over desserts.

****

JIFFY BROWN SUGAR SAUCE

1 cup brown sugar   ⅔ cup light corn syrup

Spiced fruit juice or ginger ale may be substituted for corn syrup. Heat brown sugar and corn syrup together in a saucepan, stirring until sugar is dissolved.
*Good over pork or pancakes or desserts.

****

JIFFY BUTTER SAUCE

¾ cup half and half   1 cup sugar   ½ cup butter
½ tsp. rum extract

Combine all ingredients in a small saucepan and heat just to boiling, stirring occasionally. Serve warm.
*Good over poultry or french toast or desserts.

JIFFY BUTTER HERB SAUCE

1 tbsp. tarragon
1 tbsp. basil
1 tsp. lemon juice

2 tbsp. butter
1 tbsp. parsley

1 tbsp. chives
1 tbsp. dill

Melt butter and herbs together, in a saucepan, until well blended.
*Good over fish.

****

JIFFY BUTTER PARISIAN SAUCE

½ cup butter sauce
⅛ cup chopped parsley
4 drops Worcestershire sauce

1 shallot, chopped
⅛ tsp. tarragon

Pinch sage
Pinch paprika

Mix and heat all ingredients together in a bowl, until well blended.
*Good over meat, fish or chicken.

****

JIFFY BUTTER SAUCE

1 stick butter
Dash Tabasco sauce

1 tsp. lemon juice
Salt and pepper

2 tbsp. fresh parsley

Mince fresh parsley or coriander or other herb. Melt butter in a saucepan, season with salt, pepper, lemon juice, herb and Tabasco sauce.
*Good over fish.

****

JIFFY CALIFORNIAN SAUCE

5 drops Worcestershire
3 drops Tabasco

1 cup cream sauce (cold)
paprika

¼ cup ketchup
lemon juice

Mix all ingredients together in a bowl, until well blended.
*Good over salads.

JIFFY CALYPSO SAUCE

¼ cup pineapple juice   6 oz. V-8 juice   1 oz. light rum
1 tsp. brown sugar

Heat all ingredients together in a saucepan; bring to a boil. Serve hot.
*Use over pork chops.

****

JIFFY CANTONESE-STYLE SAUCE

½ tsp. five-spice powder   1 tbsp. rice wine   ¼ cup sugar
1 tbsp. Chinese oyster sauce   ¼ cup hoisin sauce

Mix all ingredients together in a bowl, until well blended.
*Good over pork or spareribs.

****

JIFFY CAPER SAUCE I

½ cup butter sauce   2 tbsp. lemon juice   ¼ cup caper

Mix warm butter sauce with the remaining ingredients in a bowl, until well blended.
*Good over fish.

****

JIFFY CAPER SAUCE II

½ cup sour cream   ½ cup mayonnaise   3 tbsp. milk
1 tsp. Dijon mustard   2 tbsp. capers   1 tbsp. parsley

In a small bowl, combine sour cream, mayonnaise or salad dressing, milk, capers, parsley and mustard.
*Good over fish.

JIFFY CAPER SAUCE III

| 1 tbsp. chopped capers | 1 cup tartar sauce | 1 tbsp. half-and-half |

Mix chopped capers and tartar sauce in a bowl; blend in half-and-half.
*Good over fish.

****

JIFFY CARAMELIZED GARLIC SAUCE

| 8 garlic cloves, sliced | ¼ tsp. thyme | 2 tbsp. oil |
| ¼ cup Balsam vinegar | salt and pepper | |

Heat all ingredients together, in a saucepan, heat for 2 minutes.
*Good over chicken.

****

JIFFY CASINO SAUCE I

| 2 tbsp. unsalted butter | 2 tbsp. anchovy paste | 2 tbsp. pimento |
| ¼ cup sweet pickle relish | ¼ cup minced crisply cooked bacon | |

Heat butter in saucepan, then mix in remaining ingredients, until well blended.
*Good over clams.

****

JIFFY CASINO SAUCE II

12 slices of bacon, pieces	1 tbsp. onion, minced	¼ lb. butter
2 tbsp. pimentos, minced	1 tbsp. chives, minced	1 tsp. lemon juice
3 tbsp. green pepper, minced	Pinch of pepper	

Mix all ingredients together, in a saucepan, until well blended.
*Use for oysters, shrimp or mushrooms.

JIFFY CAULIFLOWER SAUCE

1 cup cauliflower, pureed   1 cup milk   1 tbsp. butter

Substitution for milk is half and half. Heat cauliflower and milk in a saucepan, for 2 minutes, then add butter.
*Good over pasta.

****

JIFFY CHANTILLY SAUCE

½ cup heavy cream   1 cup mayonnaise

Whip heavy cream and mayonnaise together in a bowl, until well blended.
*Good over eggs.

****

JIFFY CHARCOAL BROILED MARINATE SAUCE

1 ½ cups olive oil   3 cloves garlic   2 cups ketchup
¼ cup Worcestershire   3 tbsp. dry mustard   ¾ cup Sherry
Juice of ½ lemon   3 drops Liquid Smoke   Pinch of thyme
salt and pepper

Mix all ingredients in a bowl, until well blended.
*Good to chicken or shrimp.

****

JIFFY CHATEAUBRIAND SAUCE

¼ cup sliced mushrooms   1 shallot, chopped   ⅛ tsp. thyme
1 cup white wine   ¼ cup parsley   1 bay leaf
¼ tsp. tarragon   ½ strained meat glaze

Heat all ingredients together in a saucepan, until well blended.
*Good over steak.

JIFFY CHIFFONADE FRENCH SAUCE

2 tbsp. white wine vinegar
6 to 8 tbsp. olive oil
2 tbsp. ripe olives
1 tbsp. Worcestershire sauce

freshly ground black pepper
1 hard-cooked egg, chopped
½ tsp. dry mustard
1 tsp. paprika

1 tsp. salt
4 tsp. parsley
1 tsp. sugar

Mix vinegar with salt and pepper, in a bowl. Add hard-cooked egg, finely chopped ripe olives, finely chopped parsley and the remaining ingredients; beat with fork until mixture thickens. Shake well before using.
*Good over salad.

****

JIFFY CHILI BUTTER SAUCE

¼ cup butter

2 tbsp. Chili sauce

Mix ingredients together in a bowl, until well blended.
*Good over poultry.

****

JIFFY CHIVE BUTTER SAUCE

4 drops Worcestershire sauce

½ cup butter

¼ cup chives

Mix all ingredients together in a bowl, until well blended.
*Good over steak.

****

JIFFY CHIVES DIPPING SAUCE

½ cup chives
2 tbsp. Balsamic vinegar

2 tsp. mustard

Salt and pepper

Mix all ingredients together in a bowl, until well blended.
*Good over salad.

JIFFY CHOCOLATE SORBET SAUCE

⅓ cup Port wine   ¼ cup sugar   2 cups warm water
1 ¼ cups unsweetened cocoa

Mix sugar and cocoa together in a bowl. Whisk in warm water, a little at a time until smooth. Add port and mix well.
*Use for chicken or ice cream.

****

JIFFY CILANTRO PESTO SAUCE

1 cup fresh cilantro   1 cup fresh parsley   3 tbsp. butter
12 shelled hazelnuts   ½ cup olive oil   2 cloves garlic
½ cup grated parmesan cheese   Salt and pepper

Mix all ingredients together in a food processor or blender, until well blended.
*Good over pasta.

****

JIFFY CLAM AND DILL SAUCE

1 can clams   1 tsp. dill leaves   1 tbsp. lemon juice

Mix all ingredients together in a saucepan, until well blended, about 2 to 3 minutes.
*Good over pasta.

****

JIFFY COCKTAIL SAUCE

½ cup heavy cream   ½ cup chili sauce   3 tbsp. lemon juice
½ cup mayonnaise   1 tbsp. Worcestershire sauce

Place cream in a bowl and whip; then fold in remaining ingredients and whip until well blended.
*Good over fish.

JIFFY COCONUT CHOCOLATE SAUCE

4 oz. semi-sweet chocolate   1 ½ cups coconut milk   1 tsp. vanilla

Heat all ingredients together in a saucepan, until well blended; about 3 to 4 minutes.
*Good over desserts or ice cream.

****

JIFFY COCONUT CREAM SAUCE

3 oz. all purpose flour   7 oz. powdered sugar   1 egg white
3 tbsp. shredded coconut   ⅔ cup heavy cream   ¾ oz. cornstarch

Combine dry ingredients in a bowl and beat in egg white. Then beat in heavy cream.
*Good over desserts, fruit or ice cream.

****

JIFFY COCONUT RUM BAR-B-Q SAUCE

½ cup coconut rum   3 tbsp. lime juice   ½ cup ketchup
1 glove garlic, minced   1 tbsp. brown sugar   2 tsp. oil
salt and pepper

Mix all ingredients together in a bowl, until well blended.
*Use for ribs, pork, chicken or beef.

****

JIFFY COLD HORSERADISH SAUCE

6 oz. creamy-style horseradish   ½ tsp. sugar   ¼ tsp. salt
1 ½ cups sour cream   1 lg. apple

Pare and shred the apple, then mix with horseradish, in a bowl. Add sour cream; stir in sugar and salt.
*Good with cold meat, hard-cooked eggs, and fish.

JIFFY CONFECTIONERS' GLAZE SAUCE

¼ cup skim milk   1 cup confectioners' sugar   ½ tsp. vanilla

Rum extract may be used as a substitute for vanilla. In a small bowl, stir confectioners' sugar and extract into the milk until mixture is thick.

Options: Use lemon or orange in place of milk. Or add 2 tablespoons of cocoa to the sugar for chocolate sauce.
*Good over desserts or ice cream.

****

JIFFY COOL AVOCADO SAUCE

2 tsp. lemon juice   ⅔ cup sour cream   1 med. avocado
1 sm. grated onion   Salt and pepper

Cut avocado in half, discard seed and scoop flesh into a bowl. Mash with lemon juice until smooth then stir in sour cream, salt and pepper.
*Good over salad.

****

JIFFY CORIANDER AND MINT CHUTNEY SAUCE

1 bunch fresh coriander   1 slice fresh ginger   ⅓ cup mint
1 minced hot green chili   1 tbsp. lemon juice   Salt and pepper
¾ cup plain yogurt

Finely mince ginger in a food processor; add the coriander, mint, chili and lemon juice, and then process until finely pureed. Add the yogurt and process until smooth. Season to taste with salt and pepper.
*Good over poultry or fish.

****

JIFFY COUNTRY HOT SAUCE

1 sm. green bell pepper   1 lg. ripe tomato   1 med. onion
2 pimentos malaguetas   2 tbsp. olive oil   ¼ cup water
2 tbsp. vinegar   Juice of 2 limes

Hot chilies may substitute the pimentos malaguetas. Seed the tomato, core the pepper, and finely chop the onion, tomato and pepper. Mince pimentos malaguetas. Mix all ingredients together in a bowl; add salt and pepper to taste.
*Use to marinate beef, pork or chicken.

JIFFY COURGETTE FLOWERS SAUCE

1 cup courgette flowers   4 tbsp. olive oil   3 cloves garlic

Chop flowers and heat all ingredients together, in a saucepan, for 2 minutes.
*Good over pasta.

****

JIFFY CREAMY BLUE CHEESE SAUCE

4 oz. blue cheese, crumbled   1 cup sour cream   1 tsp. lemon juice

Process all ingredients in a food processor or blender, process until smooth.
*Good over fish.

****

JIFFY CREAMY DILL SAUCE

½ cup sour cream   ¼ cup mayonnaise   ¼ tsp. dill weed

Salad dressing may substitute mayonnaise. Combine ingredients in a bowl and mix well.
*Good over fish.

****

JIFFY CREAMY FRENCH SAUCE

2 tbsp. white wine vinegar   freshly ground black pepper   1 tsp. salt
6 to 8 tbsp. olive oil   ½ tsp. dry mustard   1 tsp. sugar
1 tbsp. Worcestershire sauce   ¼ cup sour cream   1 tsp. paprika

Mix ¼ cup thick sour cream with salt and pepper in a bowl. Add remaining ingredients and beat with a fork until mixture thickens.
*Good over baked potato or vegetables.

JIFFY CREAMY FRUIT MAYONNAISE SAUCE

⅓ cup mayonnaise
⅓ cup sour cream

1 tbsp. lemon juice
1 tbsp. orange juice

¼ tsp. salt
1 tbsp. honey

Mix all ingredients together in a bowl, until well blended.
*Good over pasta.

****

JIFFY CREAMY ONION SAUCE

2 oz. Neufchatel cheese

⅔ cup plain low-fat yogurt

6 green onions

Finely chop green onions, then mix all ingredients together in a bowl, until well blended.
*Good over shrimp.

****

JIFFY CREAMY ROQUEFORT DRESSING SAUCE

¾ tsp. Worcestershire sauce
¾ cup Roquefort cheese
¼ tsp. fresh black pepper

1 cup sour cream
5 tsp. mayonnaise

Dash Tabasco
⅛ tsp. salt

Whisk together the sour cream, Worcestershire, Tabasco, salt, pepper and mayonnaise, in a bowl. Fold in the crumbled Roquefort cheese and serve.
*Good over salads or vegetables.

****

JIFFY CREAMY TOMATO VINAIGRETTE SAUCE

2 tbsp. tarragon mustard
1 tbsp. tarragon wine vinegar

2 tbsp. balsamic vinegar
2 tbsp. Dijon mustard

¼ cup buttermilk
¼ cup tomato juice

Mix all ingredients together in a bowl, until well blended.
*Good over pasta.

JIFFY CREAMY VINAIGRETTE SAUCE I

¼ cup white wine vinegar
1 tsp. Dijon mustard
⅛ tsp. hot pepper sauce
2 tbsp. virgin olive oil

2 tbsp. lemon juice
2 tbsp. plain yogurt
2 lg. garlic cloves
½ cup vegetable oil

½ tsp. sugar
½ tsp. salt
½ tsp. pepper

Mix all ingredients together in a bowl, until well blended.
*Good over salads.

****

JIFFY CREAMY VINAIGRETTE SAUCE II

½ cup red wine vinegar
2 tbsp. dry vermouth

2 tbsp. Dijon mustard
1 ⅓ cups olive oil

2 egg yolks
Salt and pepper

Mix in all ingredients in a blender, except oil. Gradually add oil and blend until thick.
*Good over salads.

****

JIFFY CRÈME DE MENTHE SAUCE

⅓ cup prepared mustard
4 oz. Crème De Menthe

2 tbsp. soy sauce
1 tsp. rosemary or thyme

1 clover garlic

Mix all ingredients together in a bowl, until well blended.
*Good over lamb.

****

JIFFY CRÈME FRAICHE LOW FAT SAUCE

1 cup low fat cottage cheese

¼ cup no salt buttermilk

Drain cottage cheese, then put into blender with buttermilk. Blend until smooth.
*Good over pasta.

JIFFY CREOLE DOG SAUCE

1 or 2 Scotch bonnet chilies
2 tbsp. chopped chives
4 tbsp. lime juice
Fresh black pepper

2 cloves garlic
2 tbsp. parsley
6 tbsp. olive oil

4 scallions
2 tbsp. cilantro
½ tsp. salt

Mince chilies, scallions, garlic, and herbs. Combine lime juice and salt in a bowl, stir until dissolved. Add remaining ingredients and stir.
*Use over grilled fish and chicken, salads and soups.

****

JIFFY CRIMSON GLAZE SAUCE

½ cup chopped pickle

2 tbsp. melted butter

½ cup ketchup

Combine ingredients in a saucepan, over medium heat, until bubbly.
*Good for fish omelets.

****

JIFFY CUCUMBER & YOGURT SAUCE

⅔ cup plain low fat yogurt
2 tsp. lemon juice

2 oz. Neufchatel cheese
⅔ cup peeled, diced cucumber

Salt and pepper

Beat cheese and yogurt together, in a bowl, until smooth. Blend in cucumber, lemon juice, salt and pepper.
*Good over fish.

****

JIFFY CUCUMBER-DILL YOGURT SAUCE

8 oz. plain yogurt
3 tbsp. fresh dill

2 tbsp. lemon juice

½ cucumber

Blend yogurt with ½ cucumber, peeled, seeded and finely chopped, lemon juice, and finely minced fresh dill, in a bowl.
*Good over fish.

JIFFY CURRIED FRENCH SAUCE

2 tbsp. white wine vinegar
6 to 8 tbsp. olive oil
1 tbsp. Worcestershire sauce

freshly ground black pepper
½ tsp. dry mustard
¼ tsp. curry powder

1 tsp. salt
1 tsp. sugar
1 tsp. paprika

Mix vinegar with curry powder, salt and pepper, in a bowl. Add the rest of the ingredients; beat with fork until mixture thickens. Place in a glass jar. Shake well before using.
*Good over rice.

****

JIFFY CURRIED MAYONNAISE SAUCE

1 garlic clove, crushed
1 tsp. chopped fresh cilantro

1 cup mayonnaise

1 tsp. curry powder

Place mayonnaise in a bowl, add garlic; sprinkle in curry powder, stirring well. Fold in cilantro or parsley.
*Good over shrimp.

****

JIFFY CURRY MAYONNAISE SAUCE

1 ½ cups mayonnaise

2 tsp. curry powder

Mix ingredients together in a bowl, until well blended.
*Good over poultry.

****

JIFFY CURRY SAUCE

1 tbsp. curry powder
1 cup mayonnaise

1 tsp. grated onion

½ tsp. lemon juice

Mix all ingredients together in a bowl, until well blended.
*Good over rice.

JIFFY DIANE SAUCE

3 fresh chives, chopped
3 tbsp. parsley, chopped
¼ cup chicken broth

½ cup lemon juice
2 tbsp. Dijon mustard
salt and pepper

2 tbsp. butter
2 tbsp. Cognac
2 tbsp. oil

Heat butter in a saucepan, adding the rest of the ingredients and simmer for 1 minute.
*Good over chicken or steak.

****

JIFFY DIJON VINAIGRETTE SAUCE

¼ cup Dijon mustard
¼ tsp. ground pepper

¼ cup red wine vinegar

½ cup olive oil

In a small bowl, stir together the mustard, vinegar, and pepper. Whisk in the oil in a thin stream until incorporated.
*Good over salads.

****

JIFFY EIGHT SPICE SAUCE

2 tbsp. Szechwan peppercorns
2 tbsp. green peppercorns
2 tbsp. black peppercorns
2 tsp. butter

3 tbsp. coarse salt
2 tsp. fennel seeds
½ ground turmeric

1 tsp. cinnamon
½ ground cloves
2 tsp. oil

Finely grind all ingredients, in a small bowl; add oil and butter.
*Good over or steak.

****

JIFFY ESCABECHE SAUCE

2 tbsp. olive oil
½ cup orange juice
1 tsp. tarragon
¼ cup red wine vinegar

1 chopped garlic clove
¼ cup lemon
1 tsp. hot pepper sauce

1 onion
⅛ cup lime
Salt and pepper

Place all ingredients in a bowl and mix until well blended.
*Good over salads.

JIFFY EVER-GREEN SAUCE

⅓ cup green onion
1 cup sour cream

1 tsp. horseradish
2 tsp. Worcestershire

⅓ cup parsley
⅓ cup spinach

Mix all ingredients together in a bowl, until well blended.
*Good over chicken.

****

JIFFY FIGARO SAUCE

1 cup Hollandaise sauce
Lemon juice

⅓ cup tomato puree

1 tsp. parsley

Warm tomato puree in a saucepan, then mix all ingredients together until well blended.
*Good over fish.

****

JIFFY FOAMY CREAM SAUCE

1 cup confectioners' sugar
1 cup heavy whipped cream

1 egg yolk
1 egg white

1 tsp. vanilla
Pinch of salt

Beat together the sugar, egg yolk and vanilla in a bowl. Beat egg white with a pinch of salt, in another bowl, until stiff, then fold into yolk mixture. Fold in whipped cream.
*Good over desserts, fruit or ice cream.

****

JIFFY FRENCH MARINADE SAUCE

1 tbsp. tarragon
½ cup dry white wine
2 tbsp. green peppercorns

1 tsp. thyme
4 cloves garlic

4 shallots
1 cup olive oil

Combine all ingredients, except for oil, in a food processor or blender, process until mixture is finely minced. Slowly add olive oil.
*Good for marinating vegetables for kebabs.

JIFFY FRENCH SAUCE

2 tbsp. white wine vinegar
6 to 8 tbsp. olive oil
1 tbsp. Worcestershire sauce

freshly ground black pepper
½ tsp. dry mustard
1 tsp. paprika

1 tsp. salt
1 tsp. sugar

Mix vinegar with salt and pepper in a bowl. Add the rest of the ingredients; beat with fork until mixture thickens.
*Good over salad.

****

JIFFY FRESH TOMATO SAUCE

4 med. skinned tomatoes
½ green bell pepper

½ red bell pepper
1 tbsp. fresh coriander, chopped

1 green chili

Put all ingredients in a blender or food processor and process until vegetables are finely chopped. Place sauce in a serving bowl.
*Good over pasta.

****

JIFFY FRUIT AND MIXED MUSTARDS SAUCE

½ cup Dijon mustard
1 tbsp. Chinese mustard
⅓ cup Bavarian mustard
2 cups melon balls

⅓ cup light cream
2 tbsp. margarine
¼ cup mayonnaise
4 kiwi fruit

⅓ cup honey
½ tsp. salt
Parsley
¼ tsp. pepper

Use honeydew and cantaloupe melon balls. Mix all ingredients together in a bowl, until well blended.
*Good over ham.

****

JIFFY FRUIT GLAZE SAUCE

1 sm. can frozen orange juice
1 tsp. lemon-lime liqueur

1 tsp. orange liqueur
1 sm. jar currant jelly

2 tbsp. butter
Salt and pepper

Melt butter in a saucepan; add remaining ingredients and mix until well blended.
*Good over poultry.

JIFFY FRUIT JUICE FRENCH SAUCE

2 tbsp. lemon juice
freshly ground black pepper
1 tbsp. Worcestershire sauce
1 tsp. salt

2 tbsp. orange juice
6 to 8 tbsp. olive oil
1 tsp. paprika

2 tbsp. pineapple juice
½ tsp. dry mustard
1 tsp. sugar

Mix all ingredients together in a glass bottle and shake well before using.
*Good over ham.

****

JIFFY FRUITY SHRIMP SAUCE

½ cup pineapple yogurt
1 cup cooked shrimp, finely chopped

1 oz. orange liqueur

3 oz. cream cheese

Mix all ingredients together in a bowl, until well blended.
*Good over shrimp or fish.

****

JIFFY GAME MARINADE SAUCE

1 ¼ cups olive oil
1 lg. celery stalk
1 tsp. lemon peel

3 sprigs tarragon
2 stalks parsley
1 sm. onion

¾ cup port
6 peppercorns
⅛ tsp. sage

Combine all ingredients together in a covered bottle or container and shake until well blended.
*Good to marinate game.

****

JIFFY GARLIC FRENCH SAUCE

2 tbsp. white wine vinegar
6 to 8 tbsp. olive oil
1 tbsp. Worcestershire sauce

freshly ground black pepper
½ tsp. dry mustard
1 peeled garlic clove

1 tsp. salt
1 tsp. sugar
1 tsp. paprika

Mix all ingredients together in a bowl, until well blended; let stand to blend flavors. Remove whole clove before serving.
*Good over chicken.

JIFFY GARLIC MAYONNAISE SAUCE

3 egg yolks
1 tbsp. Dijon mustard
⅔ cup olive oil

3 tbsp. lemon juice
1 cup corn oil
2 tbsp. sun-dried tomatoes

3 garlic cloves
¾ tsp. salt
fresh pepper

Blend yolks, lemon juice, mustard and salt in processor. Gradually add oils in a very slow steady stream and process until thickened. Season generously with pepper.
*Good over tuna.

****

JIFFY GARLIC-VINAIGRETTE SAUCE

1 lg. glove garlic
1 tbsp. Dijon mustard
Drops of hot pepper sauce

4 strips of lemon zest
1 tbsp. lemon juice
½ cup minced onion

¼ tsp. salt
1 tbsp. wine vinegar
½ cup olive oil

Mix all ingredients together, in a bowl, until well blended.

Options: Add 2 medium peppers, 1 green and 1 red. Thyme and oregano.
*Good over salads.

****

JIFFY GEORGINA SAUCE

1 cup pureed artichoke

1 cup half and half

1 tbsp. butter

Heat all ingredients together in a saucepan, for 3 minutes.
*Good over pasta.

****

JIFFY GIN SAUCE

2 tbsp. butter

2 tbsp. lemon juice

2 tbsp. gin

Mix all ingredients together in a saucepan and heat for 2 minutes.
*Good over poultry or vegetables.

JIFFY GINGER SAUCE

2 tbsp. dry sherry or rice wine   2 tsp. ginger root   2 tbsp. soy sauce

Chop ginger root, then mix all ingredients together in a bowl.
*Good over beef or pork.

****

JIFFY GINGER TERIYAKI SAUCE

1 tbsp. Teriyaki sauce   2 tbsp. fresh ginger   2 tbsp. olive oil
½ lemon, squeezed

Mix all ingredients together in a bowl, until well blended.
*Good over shrimp or chicken.

****

JIFFY GINGER-GARLIC SAUCE

2 med. garlic cloves   1 tbsp. plus 1 tsp. ginger   3 tbsp. peanut oil

In a serving bowl, whisk together all the ingredients until well blended.
*Good over poultry.

****

JIFFY GLOUCESTER SAUCE

2 cups mayonnaise   1 cup sour cream   Juice of 1 lemon
1 tsp. fennel leaves   1 tsp. Worcestershire sauce

Chop fresh fennel leaves. Mix all ingredients together in a bowl, until well blended.
*Good over fish.

JIFFY GREEN GODDESS SAUCE

¼ cup chopped chives
¼ cup parsley
2 anchovy fillets
4-5 watercress or spinach leaves

½ cup sour cream
1 garlic clove
1 tbsp. herb vinegar

1 cup mayonnaise
2 tsp. lemon juice
Salt and pepper

Combine all ingredients in a blender or food processor. Mix until well blended.
*Good over fish.

****

JIFFY GREEN ONION SAUCE

1 cup mayonnaise
½ cup green onions

1 cup sour cream
½ cup parsley sprigs

1 tsp. Dijon mustard
1 glove garlic

In a blender or food processor blend all ingredients until almost smooth. Cover; chill.
*Good over fish or use as a dip.

****

JIFFY GREEN SAUCE

⅔ cup mayonnaise
2 green onions, chopped

⅓ cup sour cream
½ cup watercress

1 sm. dill pickle
¼ cup parsley

Stir mayonnaise, sour cream, minced pickle, chopped onions, chopped watercress and parsley together, in a bowl, until well blended.
*Good over fish or steak.

****

JIFFY GUACAMOLE VINAIGRETTE SAUCE

2 avocados
Salt and pepper

2 cloves garlic
3 tbsp. white wine vinegar

Dash of cayenne

Mix all ingredients together in a mixing bowl, until well blended.
*Good over salads.

JIFFY HAM BUTTER SAUCE

2 hard cooked eggs   ¼ cup cooked ham   ½ cup butter
salt and pepper

Mix all ingredients together in a mixing bowl, until well blended.
*Good over poultry.

****

JIFFY HARD SAUCE

½ cup unsalted butter   ¾ cup powdered sugar

In a mixing bowl, cream butter until soft; slowly add sugar and beat until creamy and fluffy. Add flavoring of choice. *Good over desserts.

****

JIFFY HAZELNUT SAUCE

3 tbsp. sherry-wine vinegar   3 tbsp. Madeira   ½ tsp. sugar
1 tbsp. Dijon Mustard   1 cup hazelnut oil   Salt & white pepper
1 cup chopped toasted hazelnuts

Mix the vinegar, Madeira, mustard, sugar, salt, and pepper in a bowl. Slowly whisk in the oil, beating until thickened. Then whisk in the hazelnuts. Serve.
*Good over salad.

****

JIFFY HERB BUTTER SAUCE

¼ lb. unsalted butter   3 tbsp. minced parsley   1 tsp. lemon juice
¼ tsp. dried herbs

Place all ingredients in a bowl and mix until well blended.
*Good on fish.

JIFFY HOISIN ORANGE SAUCE

3 tbsp. hoisin sauce
2 tsp. orange peel
Salt and pepper

2 tbsp. orange juice
1 tbsp. ketchup

1 tbsp. oyster sauce
¾ tsp. sugar

Mix all ingredients together in a bowl, until well blended.
*Good over chicken or shrimp.

****

JIFFY HOISIN SAUCE

2 tbsp. Hoisin sauce

2 tsp. soy sauce

1 tsp. ketchup

Place all the ingredients in a bowl and mix until well blended.
*Good over poultry.

****

JIFFY HOLLANDAISE ANISE SAUCE

½ cup butter, melted
2 tbsp. anise liqueur
Dash cayenne

1 ½ tbsp. lemon juice
½ cup boiling water

4 egg yolks
¼ tsp. salt

Place all ingredients in a bowl and mix until well blended.
*Good over fish.

****

JIFFY HONEY FRENCH SAUCE

2 tbsp. lemon juice
6 to 8 tbsp. olive oil
¼ tsp. grated lemon peel
1 tbsp. Worcestershire sauce

freshly ground black pepper
½ cup honey
½ tsp. dry mustard
1 tsp. paprika

1 tsp. salt
½ tsp. celery seed
1 tsp. sugar

Mix lemon juice with salt and pepper in a bowl. Add remaining ingredients; beat with fork until mixture thickens. Pour into a bottle or pouring container.   Shake well before using.
*Good over salad.

JIFFY HONEY YOGURT SAUCE

1 cup honey yogurt
1 tbsp. minced chives

¼ cup mayonnaise
2 tbsp. mustard

2 tbsp. herb vinegar
½ tsp. salt

Mix all ingredients together in a bowl, until well blended.
*Good over poultry.

****

JIFFY HONEY-LIME FRENCH SAUCE

2 tbsp. lime juice
6 to 8 tbsp. olive oil
½ tsp. dry mustard
1 tsp. paprika

¼ tsp. grated lime peel
freshly ground black pepper
1 tbsp. Worcestershire sauce

½ cup honey
1 tsp. salt
1 tsp. sugar

Mix lime with honey, salt and pepper in a bowl. Add remaining ingredients slowly, until mixture thickens. Pour into a bottle or pouring container. Shake well before using.
*Good over chicken.

****

JIFFY HORSERADISH APPLESAUCE SAUCE

6 oz. jar of grated white horseradish   8 oz. jar applesauce

Mix both ingredients together in a bowl, until well blended.
*Good with pork.

****

JIFFY HORSERADISH CREAM SAUCE

2 tsp. Dijon mustard
1 tbsp. horseradish sauce
Salt and ground black pepper

1 cup heavy cream
Juice of ½ lime

1 tbsp. shallot
1 tbsp. fresh chives

Beat the cream to soft peaks, in a mixing bowl. Mince the shallot and chives and fold them into the cream with the lime juice, mustard, horseradish, salt and pepper.
*Good with smoked fish, clams or oysters.

JIFFY HORSERADISH MAYONNAISE SAUCE I

⅛ tsp. hot pepper sauce
1 ½ cups mayonnaise

2 tbsp. horseradish

1 tsp. lemon juice

Place mayonnaise in a bowl, add prepared white horseradish, lemon juice and hot red pepper sauce. Whisk until well blended.
*Good over shrimp.

****

JIFFY HORSERADISH MAYONNAISE SAUCE II

4 tbsp. fresh horseradish, finely grated

1 cup Mayonnaise

Stir together horseradish and Mayonnaise in a bowl, until well blended.
*Good over fish.

****

JIFFY HORSERADISH SAUCE

3 tbsp. prepared horseradish
1 cup mayonnaise

1 tsp. grated onion

½ tsp. lemon juice

Mix all ingredients together in a bowl, until well blended.
*Good over fish.

****

JIFFY HOT BLOODY MARY SAUCE

46-oz. can tomato juice
⅓ cup horseradish

46-oz. can V-8 juice
¾ cup Worcestershire sauce

4 cups beef stock

Mix all ingredients together in a bowl, until well blended.
*Good over pasta.

JIFFY HOT BUTTERED MAPLE SYRUP SAUCE

1 cup maple syrup   ¼ cup butter or margarine

Heat maple syrup and butter in a saucepan, until butter has melted. Stir and serve.
*Good over ice cream, plain cake or cut-up fruit.

****

JIFFY HOT FUDGE SAUCE

5 oz. semi-sweet chocolate   ½ cup whipping cream   ¼ cup butter
½ tsp. vanilla

Combine chocolate, cream, butter and vanilla, in a small saucepan over a medium heat. Stir until melted.
*Good over ice cream or desserts.

****

JIFFY HOT MIXER SAUCE

6 oz. V-8 juice   Dash chili powder   Dash of pepper
Dash cinnamon   Chopped cooked onion

Heat all ingredients together in a saucepan, until well blended.
*Use over chop meat or beef.

****

JIFFY INDIAN TURMERIC SAUCE

1 tsp. ground turmeric   1 tsp. ground cumin   1 tbsp. sugar
1 ½ tsp. ground ginger   1 tsp. cayenne pepper   2 tbsp. oil
1 tsp. minced garlic

Mix all ingredients together in a bowl, until well blended.
*Good over rice or vegetables.

JIFFY INDONESIAN SAUCE

⅓ cup chunky peanut butter
⅓ cup Teriyaki sauce
¼ cup crushed red pepper

¼ cup lemon juice
2 tsp. ground ginger
2 tsp. onion powder

vegetable oil
2 tsp. sweet basil
garlic powder

Place all ingredients in a bowl and mix until well blended.
*Good over poultry, vegetables or pasta.

****

JIFFY INDONESIAN SYRUP SAUCE

1 lb. brown sugar
1 oz. hot chili sauce

2 oz. Tamarind Paste

3 cups water

Place all ingredients in a saucepan and bring to a boil, heat until well blended.
*Good over poultry or rice.

****

JIFFY ITALIAN SAUCE

6 tbsp. white vinegar
½ sp. salt

freshly ground black pepper
1 tbsp. Worcestershire sauce

6 to 8 tbsp. olive oil

Mix vinegar with salt and pepper in a bowl. Add remaining ingredients; beat with fork until mixture thickens. Pour into a bottle or pouring container. Shake well before using.
*Good over salads or vegetables.

****

JIFFY JAM SAUCE

1 cup elderberry jam

⅓ cup very hot water

Quince or elderberry jelly or orange marmalade may be substituted for jam. Mix jam with hot water in a bowl, until well blended.
*Good over ham.

JIFFY JAMAICAN DELIGHT JERK SAUCE

½ up chopped onion
2 ½ z. fresh ginger
1 ½ bunches fresh thyme
½ tsp. grated nutmeg

2 med. scallions
2 cups cold water
1 med. chili pepper
6 tbsp. allspice berries

4 cloves garlic
½ tsp. cinnamon
1 tbsp. salt

Seed chili pepper. Combine all ingredients in a food processor or blender; process until fairly smooth.
*Good over poultry.

****

JIFFY JAPANESE SAUCE

½ cup Shoyu soy sauce
½ cup oil

½ cup Sakeor sherry

⅓ cup sugar

Mix all ingredients, in a bowl, until well blended.
*Good over shrimp.

****

JIFFY KAHLUA DIPPING SAUCE

8 oz. pkg. cream cheese
2 tbsp. toasted blanched almonds

¼ cup Kahlúa

2 tbsp. light cream

Chop the toasted almonds. Place softened cream cheese in a mixing bowl. Gradually beat in Kahlúa and cream until mixture is smooth. Stir in almonds.
*Good for dipping fruits or over desserts.

****

JIFFY KEY WEST RUM AND LIME SAUCE

¼ cup dark rum
Salt and pepper

¼ cup lime juice
⅛ cayenne pepper

¼ soy sauce
⅛ paprika

Mix all ingredients together in a bowl, until well blended.
*Good over poultry or fish.

JIFFY LEMON BUTTER SAUCE

2 tsp. Worcestershire sauce
2 tbsp. fresh parsley

3 to 4 tbsp. lemon juice
pepper

1 cup butter

Melt butter in a saucepan, adding lemon juice, Worcestershire sauce and pepper. Simmer for about 1 minute, then add fresh chopped parsley. Serve hot.
*Good over poultry or fish.

****

JIFFY LEMON SORBET SAUCE

1 tbsp. lemon zest

¾ cup lemon juice

2 cups champagne

Combine lemon zest and juice in a bowl, adding in champagne.
*Use to marinade chicken or fish.

****

JIFFY LEMON VERONIQUE SAUCE

1 tbsp. clarified butter
¼ cup seedless grapes

1 ½ cups chicken stock

1 squeeze of lemon

Mix all ingredients together in a bowl, until well blended.
*Good over poultry.

****

JIFFY LEMON VINAIGRETTE SAUCE

¼ cup fresh lemon juice
½ cup sesame oil

1 Tbsp. Dijon mustard
1 tbsp. black pepper

4 tbsp. water
1 shallot

Blend all ingredients, except oil, in blender and beat at high speed. Slowly add oil until smooth.
*Good over poultry or vegetables.

JIFFY LEMON-APPLE SAUCE

⅔ cup apple jelly   ¼ cup lemon juice   16 marshmallows
¼ cup butter

Heat marshmallows, jelly and lemon juice in a saucepan, until smooth. Add butter and whisk.
*Good over poultry or pork.

****

JIFFY LEMON-SESAME SAUCE

½ cup tahini   ¼ cup sesame paste   2 tbsp. lemon juice
½ tbsp. salt   ¼ cup water

Slowly mix all ingredients together in a bowl, until well blended.
*Good over poultry, pork or shrimps.

****

JIFFY LIME MARINADE SAUCE

½ cup chicken broth   1 tsp. shredded lime peel   ⅓ cup lime juice
2 tbsp. cooking oil   1 tbsp. brown sugar   2 cloves garlic
⅛ tsp. red pepper

Mince garlic and mix all ingredients together in a bowl, until well blended.
*Good over poultry or fish.

****

JIFFY LIME SEASONING SAUCE

¼ cup lime juice   ¼ cup oil   1 tbsp. water
2 tsp. sesame oil   1 tbsp. soy sauce   2 tsp. honey
1 tbsp. toasted sesame seed 1 chopped green chili

Mix all ingredients together in a small mixing bowl. Place fish in plastic bag with all the seasonings. Fry in all its juices.
*Good over fish.

JIFFY LIME-THYME SAUCE

1 ½ cups chicken stock
2 tbsp. limejuice

1 tbsp. butter

1 tsp. thyme

Mix all ingredients together in a bowl, until well blended.
*Good over rich or vegetables.

****

JIFFY LIQUEUR DELIGHT SAUCE

¼ oz. cherry liqueur
¼ oz. green crème de menthe liqueur

¼ oz. orange liqueur

¼ oz. heavy cream

Mix all ingredients together in a bowl, until well blended.
*Good over desserts or ice cream.

****

JIFFY LORENZO FRENCH SAUCE

2 tbsp. white wine vinegar
6 to 8 tbsp. olive oil
1 tbsp. Worcestershire sauce
2 tbsp. chili sauce

freshly ground black pepper
½ tsp. dry mustard
1 tsp. paprika

1 tsp. salt
1 tsp. sugar
¼ cup watercress

Mix vinegar with chili sauce, watercress, salt and pepper in a mixing bowl. Add remaining ingredients; beat with fork until mixture thickens. Place in a bottle or pouring container. Shake well before using.
*Good over fish.

****

JIFFY MACADAMIA NUT PESTO SAUCE

½ cup fresh parsley
⅔ cup macadamia nuts
1 tsp. hot pepper flakes

1 cup fresh basil
5 sm. garlic cloves

1 cup olive oil
1 ½ tsp. salt

Mix all ingredients together in a blender or food processor, mix until well blended.
*Good over pasta.

JIFFY MALTAISE SAUCE

2 cups hollandaise sauce   1 lg. navel orange

Place the hollandaise sauce in a mixing bowl. Stir in the grated rind and strained juice of the orange. Mix until well blended.
*Good over eggs.

****

JIFFY MANHATTAN SAUCE

2 tsp. prepared horseradish	2 tbsp. tomato ketchup	2 tbsp. vinegar
¼ cup lemon juice	¼ tsp. Tabasco sauce	1 tsp. salt

Mix all ingredients together in a bowl, until well blended.
*Good over shrimp.

****

JIFFY MAPLE APPLESAUCE SAUCE

8 oz. applesauce   ½ tbsp. maple extract   1 tbsp. brown sugar

Mix all ingredients together in a bowl, until well blended.
*Use over ham or pork.

****

JIFFY MAPLE BUTTER SAUCE

½ cup butter   ½ cup maple syrup

Place butter in a bowl and beat until creamy, then beat in maple syrup.
*Good over ice cream or desserts.

JIFFY MAPLE SYRUP SAUCE

1 cup maple-flavored syrup   ⅓ cup sugar   1 tsp. cinnamon
½ cup nuts

Mix all ingredients together in a bowl, until well blended.
*Good over cake or desserts.

****

JIFFY MARINADE SAUCE

¼ cup brown sugar   ½ cup soy sauce   ½ tsp. salt
1 tsp. ginger liqueur   2 tbsp. lemon juice   1 tbsp. salad oil
1 glove garlic, minced

Place all ingredients in a bowl and mix until well blended.
*Good for marinade.

****

JIFFY MARSHMALLOW CRÈME FUDGE SAUCE

7 oz. jar marshmallow crème   Chocolate mixture   1 tsp. vanilla

Mix all ingredients together in a bowl, until well blended.
*Good over desserts, cakes and ice cream.

****

JIFFY MASCARPONE DIPPING SAUCE

½ cup mascarpone cheese   1 tbsp. hazelnut liqueur   3 tbsp. sugar
1 pint fresh strawberries

Hull, rinse and blend strawberries. Mix all ingredients together in a bowl, until well blended.
*Good for dipping fruit or over desserts.

JIFFY MAYONNAISE AND CHILI SAUCE

½ cup mayonnaise
3 tbsp. chili sauce
juice of half lemon

½ cup cream
1 tbsp. Worcestershire sauce
1 tbsp. chives, chopped

1 tsp. salt
pinch paprika
pinch cayenne pepper

Combine all ingredients in a bowl and mix until well blended.
*Good over hot dogs or all meats.

****

JIFFY MAYONNAISE LIGHT SAUCE

1 tbsp. Dijon mustard
4 tbsp. cider vinegar
4 tbsp. low-fat yogurt

2 cups vegetable oil
4 tbsp. white wine

1 egg yolk
White pepper

Combine all ingredients in a bowl and mix until well blended.
*Good over vegetables.

****

JIFFY MAYONNAISE RED-WINE VINEGAR SAUCE

1 tbsp. red-wine vinegar
¼ tsp. dry mustard
½ tsp. salt

1 tbsp. lemon juice
⅛ tsp. paprika
Dash of cayenne pepper

1 cup salad oil
1 egg

Pour ¼ cup oil into blender, and add vinegar, lemon juice, egg, and seasonings. Blend 5 seconds.
*Good over vegetables.

****

JIFFY MINT JULEP SAUCE

¼ cup white wine vinegar
3 tbsp. vegetable oil

1 cup mint leaves
2 tbsp. bourbon

½ cup sugar
Salt and pepper

Finely chop mint in processor using on/off button. Blend in remaining ingredients. Transfer to bowl and chill.
*Good for lamb.

JIFFY MINT MAYONNAISE SAUCE

3 tsp. fresh mint, finely chopped   1 cup Mayonnaise   ¼ tsp. sugar
2 tbsp. white wine vinegar, warmed   ½ tsp. boiling water

Sprinkle water on mint and sugar, in a small bowl. Crush with back of spoon to extract as much mint flavor as possible. Add vinegar and stir mixture with mayonnaise.
*Good over salads.

****

JIFFY MINTED MARINADE SAUCE

⅓ cup of Dijon mustard   1 glove garlic, crushed   2 tbsp. soy sauce
1 tsp. rosemary liqueur   ½ cup mint liqueur

Mix all ingredients together in a mixing bowl, until well blended.
*Good over all meats and poultry.

****

JIFFY MINTED MELON SAUCE

1 sm. ripe honeydew or cantaloupe   ½ cup fresh mint leaves

Peel, seed and coarsely chop the melon. Put in a food processor or blender with the mint leaves and puree until they are smooth.
*Good over ice cream.

****

JIFFY MIXED OIL SAUCE

1 tbsp. white wine vinegar   2 tbsp. sunflower oil   Salt and pepper
½ tsp. Dijon mustard   2 tbsp. walnut oil

Mix all ingredients together in a bowl, until well blended.
*Good over salads.

JIFFY MOCHA SAUCE I

1 tsp. white crème de cacao   1 tsp. white crème de menthe   ¾ oz. coffee liqueur
1 tsp. orange liqueur

Mix all ingredients together in a bowl, until well blended.
*Good over desserts, fruit or ice cream.

****

JIFFY MOCHA SAUCE II

6 oz. semi-sweet chocolate   1 cup hot coffee   ¼ tsp. salt

Melt all ingredients in a saucepan, over medium heat until well blended.
*Good over desserts, fruit or ice cream.

****

JIFFY MOLASSES GLAZE SAUCE

2 tbsp. light molasses   ½ cup ketchup   1 tbsp. lemon juice
1 tbsp. soy sauce   Several dashes hot pepper sauce

Sit all ingredients together in a small bowl. Mix until well blended.
*Good for ribs.

****

JIFFY MUSTARD CREAM SAUCE

1 cup mayonnaise   2 tbsp. prepared mustard   2 tbsp. vinegar
½ cup cream   ¼ tsp. pepper   1 tsp. salt

Mix all ingredients together in a bowl, until well blended.
*Good over shredded cabbage.

JIFFY MUSTARD GLAZE SAUCE

1 cup brown sugar   1 tsp. dry mustard   1 tbsp. flour
2 tbsp. cider vinegar

Mix all ingredients in a saucepan, over medium heat, until well blended.
*Good over ham or pork.

****

JIFFY MUSTARD SAUCE

1 tbsp. half-and-half   1 cup mayonnaise   prepared mustard
Blend half-and-half with mayonnaise in a small mixing bowl, then stir in prepared mustard to taste.
*Good over ham.

****

JIFFY MUSTARD VINAIGRETTE SAUCE

3 tbsp. whole grain mustard   2 tbsp. Dijon mustard   1 tsp. pepper
½ cup apple cider vinegar   ¾ cup sesame oil

Blend all ingredients, except oil, in blender at high speed. Slowly add oil until smooth.
*Good over poultry or vegetables.

****

JIFFY NIPPY PINEAPPLE SAUCE

12-oz. jar pineapple preserves   ¼ cup prepared mustard   ¼ cup prepared horseradish

In a saucepan, mix all ingredients and heat for 3 minutes.
*Good over poultry.

JIFFY NO-CALORIE SALAD SAUCE

½ cup wine vinegar
1 tbsp. chopped parsley

½ glove garlic, crushed
¼ tsp. oregano

¼ tsp. tarragon
¼ tsp. salt

Shake all ingredients together in a bottle or pouring container, until well blended. Can be stored in refrigerator several weeks.
*Good over salad.

****

JIFFY OIL AND EGG SAUCE

2 tbsp. white wine vinegar
½ tsp. fresh lemon juice
4 chopped hard-cooked eggs

2 tbsp. Dijon mustard
¾ cup olive oil
¼ cup fresh chives

¾ tsp. salt
½ tsp. pepper

In a bowl, whisk together the vinegar, mustard, salt and lemon juice. Slowly whisk in the oil until incorporated. Stir in the eggs, chives and pepper.
*Good over salads.

****

JIFFY OLIVE FRENCH SAUCE

2 tbsp. white wine vinegar
6 to 8 tbsp. olive oil
1 tbsp. Worcestershire sauce

freshly ground black pepper
½ tsp. dry mustard
½ cup stuffed olives

1 tsp. salt
1 tsp. sugar
1 tsp. paprika

Mix vinegar with chopped stuffed olives, salt and pepper in a mixing bowl. Add the remaining ingredients; beat with fork until mixture thickens. Pour into a bottle or pouring container. Shake well before using.
*Good over salad.

****

JIFFY ONION MARINADE SAUCE

1 cup fruity olive oil
1 grated onion

2 tbsp. fresh lemon juice

2 tsp. garlic

Mix all ingredients together in a bowl, until well blended.
*Good for seafood or poultry.

JIFFY ONION-HORSERADISH SAUCE

½ envelope dry onion soup mix
1 cup sour cream

2 tsp. prepared horseradish
snipped parsley

1 tbsp. milk

Blend onion soup mix with milk and horseradish in a blender; blend in the parsley and sour cream.
*Good over vegetables.

****

JIFFY ORANGE GLAZE SAUCE

1 cup orange marmalade

½ cup orange liqueur

1 tsp. dry mustard

Mix all ingredients together in a bowl, until well blended.
*Good over poultry.

****

JIFFY PALERMA SAUCE

1 clove crushed garlic
¼ cup oil

1 egg yolk
⅛ tsp. cayenne pepper

¼ cup lemon juice

Place all ingredients in a bowl and mix until well blended.
*Good over beef, chicken or fish.

****

JIFFY PAPRIKA MAYONNAISE SAUCE

1 ½ cups mayonnaise

1 tsp. paprika

Mix ingredients together in a bowl, until well blended.
*Good over poultry or potatoes.

JIFFY PEACH SAUCE I

⅔ cup peach preserves
4 med. peaches, ripe

4 tsp. lemon juice
2 tsp. water

2 tsp. orange liqueur

Mix all ingredients together in a bowl, until well blended.
*Good over meat or desserts.

****

JIFFY PEACH SAUCE II

1 can of peach halves
¼ tsp. cinnamon

2 tbsp. brown sugar
salt to taste

2 tbsp. butter

Mix syrup from can peaches, butter, brown sugar and cinnamon in a saucepan. Chop and add peaches and warm all together until well blended, about 1 minute.
*Pour over meat or desserts.

****

JIFFY PEACHY MARINADE SAUCE

½ tsp. ginger liqueur
1 glove garlic, minced

3 tbsp. peach liqueur
4 canned peach halves

½ cup soy sauce
⅓ cup peach syrup

Place all ingredients in a bowl and mix until well blended.
*Good over pork.

****

JIFFY PEANUT BUTTER SAUCE

2 cups roasted shelled peanuts
1 tbsp. peanut oil
½ tsp. salt

Place all ingredients in a food processor, and process for 3 minutes.
*Good over chicken.

JIFFY PEANUT BUTTER DELIGHT SAUCE

1 cup part-skim ricotta cheese
¼ cup smooth peanut butter

2 tbsp. skim milk
2 ¼ tsp. vanilla

½ tsp. cinnamon
2 tbsp. sugar

½ teaspoon of sweet and low can substitute the 2 teaspoons sugar. Mix all ingredients together in a food processor, until satin smooth.
*Good over pasta.

****

JIFFY PEANUT-BUTTER BARBECUE SAUCE

1 tbsp. Worcestershire
3 tbsp. cooking oil
½ cup vinegar

3 tbsp. peanut butter
1 tbsp. mustard
Juice of 1 lemon

3 tbsp. mayonnaise
2 tsp. salt
2 tsp. pepper

Mix all ingredients well in a small saucepan and bring to boil. Mix until well blended.
*Good over chicken.

****

JIFFY PEANUTTY PESTO-SAUCE

¼ cup Parmesan cheese
¾ cup creamy peanut butter
1 cup sharp cheddar cheese

1 ½ cups parsley
2 lg. garlic cloves
¾ cup peanut oil

1 egg
2 tbsp. oregano

Place oil, parsley, garlic and oregano in a blender, on high speed until partially blended. Add peanut butter; about ¼ cup at a time, blend well. Add Parmesan cheese and blend until smooth.
*Good over pasta.

****

JIFFY PECAN BUTTER SAUCE

½ cup chopped pecans
1 tsp. Worcestershire sauce

1 tbsp. lemon juice

¼ cup butter

Combine pecans, butter, lemon juice and Worcestershire in a blender, and blend until smooth.
*Good over poultry.

JIFFY PECAN MUSTARD SAUCE

5 tbsp. ground pecans
⅓ cup sour cream

4 tbsp. butter
1 tsp. peanut oil

2 tbsp. mustard
Salt and pepper

Mix and heat oil, butter and ground pecans for 1 minute, in a small mixing bowl. Mix in sour cream, salt and pepper.
*Good over pasta.

****

JIFFY PEPPERMINT CREAM SAUCE

1 cup heavy cream
2 tbsp. peppermint candies

½ tsp. vanilla

1 tbsp. sugar

Whip cream, in a mixing bowl, until frothy; gradually beat in sugar, vanilla and crushed hard peppermint candies until soft peaks form.
*Good over chocolate ice cream.

****

JIFFY PESTO SAUCE I

¼ lb. pine nuts
2 cups oil

2 cloves chopped garlic
½ cup Parmesan cheese

1 lb. basil

Place basil, pine nuts and garlic in a blender, adding oil blend well.
*Good over pasta.

****

JIFFY PESTO SAUCE II

10 oz. frozen chopped spinach
⅓ cup grated Parmesan cheese
1 tsp. dried basil

1 cup sour cream
¼ cup walnut pieces
1 glove garlic, crushed

1 cup mayonnaise
¼ tsp. salt

In blender or food processor blend all ingredients until almost smooth. Cover; chill.
*Good over pasta or use as a dip.

JIFFY PESTO SAUCE III

¾ cup part-skim ricotta cheese
2 tbsp. grated Parmesan cheese
Dash of white pepper

¼ cup parsley
¼ cup skim milk

¼ cup basil
1 med. shallot

Mix all ingredients together in a blender, until well blended and smooth. Pour into a bowl, cover and chill.
*Good with spinach salad or over pasta.

****

JIFFY PESTO VINAIGRETTE SAUCE

½ cup Parmesan cheese
¾ cup champagne vinegar
¼ cup parsley leaves

2 cups basil leaves
¼ cup lemon juice

3 med. cloves garlic
1 ¾ cups olive oil

Combine all ingredients in a food processor or blender and puree. Add oil in a steady stream; process until smooth.
*Good over salad.

****

JIFFY PIMENTO BUTTER SAUCE

½ cup butter

¼ cup mashed Pimento

2 tsp. relish

Mix all ingredients together in a mixing bowl, until well blended.
*Good over poultry.

****

JIFFY PINE NUT SAUCE

⅛ cup mayonnaise
1 tbsp. tomato paste
Salt and pepper

4 drops sesame oil
¼ cup toasted pine nuts

¼ cup wine vinegar
1 scallion, sliced

Place all ingredients together in a bowl and mix until well blended.
*Good over pasta.

JIFFY PINEAPPLE CHILI SAUCE

¼ cup pineapple syrup
3 tbsp. vegetable oil
1 sm. glove garlic, pressed

3 tbsp. cider vinegar
1 tsp. chili powder

1 tsp. salt
⅛ tsp. oregano

Mix all ingredients together in a bowl, until well blended.
*Good over poultry.

****

JIFFY PINEAPPLE GINGER SAUCE

½ cup dry white wine
1 tbsp. soy sauce
1 cup unsweetened pineapple juice

1 tsp. sesame oil
1 glove garlic

1 tbsp. ginger
1 tbsp. grainy mustard

Mix all ingredients together in a bowl, until well blended.
*Use to marinade.

****

JIFFY PINEAPPLE GRAPEFRUIT SAUCE

⅔ cup pineapple syrup

⅓ cup grapefruit juice

⅓ cup grenadine syrup

Mix all ingredients together in a bowl, until well blended.
*Good over fruit or ice cream.

****

JIFFY PLUM SAUCE

½ tsp. red pepper sauce

½ cup chili sauce

½ cup plum jam

Grape jelly can substitute plum jam. Mix all ingredients together in a bowl, until well blended.
*Good over duck, poultry or pork.

JIFFY PLUM SWEET AND SPICY SAUCE

½ tsp. ground ginger
¼ tsp. ground cloves
½ cup plum jelly

½ tsp. ground cinnamon
¼ cup soy sauce
2 tsp. vinegar

½ tsp. pepper
2 tbsp. honey
2 tsp. sugar

Mix all ingredients together in a bowl, until well blended.
*Good over duck, poultry or pork.

****

JIFFY POLISH SAUCE

½ up sour cream
1 tbsp. lemon juice

1 tbsp. grated horseradish

¼ up chopped fennel

Mix sour cream with horseradish in a bowl; add lemon juice and fennel. Mix until well blended.
*Good over fish.

****

JIFFY PUTTANESCA SAUCE

½ up black olives
½ sp. red pepper flakes

3 mashed anchovies
2 cups tomato sauce

2 tbsp. capers

Rinse capers and place in a bowl, add sliced black oliver, anchovies, red pepper flakes and tomato sauce.
Mix until well blended.
*Good over pasta.

****

JIFFY RASPBERRY GRAND MARNIER SAUCE

12-oz. frozen raspberries
2 tbsp. Grand Marnier

Juice of 1 orange

Sugar to taste

Puree raspberries in blender or food processor. Strain. Add orange juice, Grand Marnier and sugar.
*Good over desserts or ice cream.

JIFFY RASPBERRY SAUCE

1 tbsp. granulated sugar   2 tbsp. dry white wine   1 cup raspberries

Puree raspberries, wine and sugar in a food processor.
*Good over desserts, sliced fresh fruit or ice cream.

****

JIFFY RASPBERRY VINAIGRETTE SAUCE

½ pt. fresh raspberries   1 cup sesame oil   ½ tsp. pepper
½ cup raspberry vinegar   1 tsp. Dijon mustard   1 shallot

Blend all ingredients, except oil, in blender at high speed. Slowly add oil until smooth.
*Good over salads, poultry or vegetables.

****

JIFFY RATTLESNAKE CLUB BARBECUE SAUCE

½ cup prepared chili sauce   ¼ cup steak sauce   1 ½ cups ketchup
1 tbsp. red wine vinegar   2 tbsp. horseradish   3 tbsp. dry mustard
1 tbsp. jalapeno chili   1 tbsp. garlic juice   1 tbsp. molasses
1 tbsp. tamarind paste   1 tbsp. hot pepper sauce

Whisk all ingredients together in a bowl, except hot pepper sauce. When well blended add hot pepper sauce to taste. *Good over poultry and ribs.

****

JIFFY RAW TOMATO SAUCE

Red-ripe tomatoes   salad oil   salt and pepper
1 tbsp. fresh basil

Skin and remove seeds from tomatoes. Place in a food processor and finely chop. Add a little salad oil, salt, pepper and finely chopped fresh basil or tarragon, parsley or coriander.
*Good over fish.

JIFFY RED SAUCE

1 ½ tbsp. horseradish
1 ½ tsp. lemon juice

¼ cup chili sauce
¼ tsp. hot pepper sauce

¼ cup ketchup

Mix all ingredients together in a bowl, until well blended. Serve cold or warm.
*Good over fish.

****

JIFFY REMOULADE SAUCE I

¼ cup white-wine vinegar
2 tbsp. horseradish
⅓ cup chopped scallions
1 tsp. chopped garlic

3 tbsp. Dijon mustard
1 cup vegetable oil
⅓ cup chopped celery
2 tbsp. chopped parsley

1 lg. egg yolk
1 tbsp. paprika
2 tbsp. ketchup
Salt and pepper

Put the egg yolk, mustard, vinegar, and paprika in a mixing bowl. Blend briskly, then add the remaining ingredients and blend well.
*Good over fish or poultry.

****

JIFFY REMOULADE SAUCE II

1 ½ cups mayonnaise
1 tsp. Dijon mustard
⅛ tsp. anchovy paste

2 tbsp. gherkins
2 tbsp. parsley

2 tbsp. capers
2 tbsp. tarragon

Chop gherkins, capers, parsley and tarragon. Mix all ingredients together in a bowl, until well blended.
*Good over pasta, fish or poultry.

****

JIFFY REMOULADE SAUCE III

½ tsp. peppercorns
2 tbsp. prepared mustard
1 tbsp. horseradish
¼ tsp. garlic powder
1 tbsp. chopped parsley

1 sm. sliced onions
2 tbsp. chopped onion
2 tbsp. chopped celery
⅔ cup olive oil

3 tbsp. vinegar
¼ tsp. pepper
1 ½ tsp. salt
Dash of cayenne

Stir the vinegar in a bowl, with the mustard, onion, celery, horseradish, parsley, salt, garlic powder, pepper and cayenne. Gradually beat in the oil.
*Good over fish or poultry.

JIFFY REMOULADE SAUCE IV

½ tsp. anchovy paste
1 tsp. Dijon mustard
1 tbsp. pickle, finely chopped

1 tsp. chopped chervil
1 tsp. minced parsley

1 cup mayonnaise
1 tbsp. capers

Mix all ingredients together in a bowl, until well blended.
*Good over fish, pasta or poultry.

****

JIFFY RICOTTA SAUCE

½ cup heavy sweet cream
½ lb. ricotta cheese

1 cup Parmesan cheese
¼ lb. diced prosciutto

Salt and pepper

Combine the cream, cheeses, prosciutto, salt and pepper and place in a serving bowl that can be kept warm. Set bowl over simmering water, about 3-4 minutes.
*Good over pasta.

****

JIFFY RICOTTA AND ROASTED PEPPERS SAUCE

1 jar roasted peppers
1 tsp. hot pepper oil
½ cup ricotta cheese

1 tbsp. olive oil
1 tbsp. butter
2 tbsp. Parmesan

Salt and pepper
2 tbsp. parsley

Sauté the peppers in olive oil for 2 minutes in a saucepan. Season with salt, pepper and hot pepper oil. Toss this mixture with butter, room temperature ricotta, parmesan and chopped parsley.
*Good over pasta.

****

JIFFY ROCKEFELLER SAUCE

1 cup chopped raw spinach
¼ cup bread crumbs

3 tbsp. onion, minced
salt and pepper

½ cup butter

Mix all ingredients together in a bowl, until well blended.
*Use for oysters, clams, shrimps or mushrooms.

JIFFY ROQUEFORT FRENCH SAUCE

¾ Roquefort cheese
6 to 8 tbsp. olive oil
1 tbsp. Worcestershire sauce
1 tsp. paprika

2 tbsp. white wine vinegar
freshly ground black pepper
½ tsp. dry mustard

1 tsp. salt
2 tsp. water
1 tsp. sugar

Blend together in a bowl, the Roquefort cheese and water until smooth. Mix the remaining ingredients; beat with fork until mixture thickens. Add this mixture slowly to the cheese mixtures.
*Good over salad or vegetables.

****

JIFFY ROSEMARY SAUCE

3 med. cloves garlic
2 anchovy fillets
1 tsp. Dijon mustard

⅓ cup parsley
2 tbsp. rosemary
¼ cup olive oil

½ tsp. pepper
¾ tsp. thyme
2 tbsp. red wine

In a food processor, puree all ingredients.
*Good over pasta.

****

JIFFY RUM GLAZE SAUCE

6 tbsp. Virgin Island Rum

4 tbsp. brown sugar

6 tbsp. butter

Place all ingredients in a saucepan and blend over medium heat.
*Good over ice cream.

****

JIFFY RUSSIAN DRESSING SAUCE

¼ cup chili sauce
1 tsp. onion, grated

1 tbsp. horseradish

1 cup mayonnaise

Stir the mayonnaise, chili sauce, horseradish and grated onion together in a bowl, until well blended.
*Good over salads or vegetables.

JIFFY RUSSIAN SAUCE

½ cup red chili sauce
Dash Worcestershire sauce

Hot pepper sauce
1 hard cooked egg

1 cup mayonnaise
2 tbsp. red pepper

Mix all ingredients together in a bowl, until well blended.
*Good over cold pasta, salads or vegetables.

****

JIFFY S'MORES SAUCE

1 Hershey bar

3 graham crackers

3 marshmallows

Crush Graham crackers. Melt Hershey bar and marshmallows in a small saucepan. Mix all ingredients together until well blended.
*Good over ice cream.

****

JIFFY SAGE BUTTER SAUCE

12 tbsp. sweet butter

15 lg. sage leaves

Salt and pepper

Melt butter in a small saucepan over medium heat. Add sage leaves and sauté 1 minute. Season with salt and pepper.
*Good over steak.

****

JIFFY SALSA SAUCE I

¼ bunch parsley
1 jalapeno pepper
½ tsp. sugar
Dash nutmeg

1 bunch cilantro
2 tbsp. lemon juice
Dash cardamom
Dash coriander

2 scallions
1 tbsp. water
Dash cumin
Dash clove

Combine all ingredients in food processor and blend until smooth.
*Good on top of fish.

JIFFY SALSA SAUCE II

1 cup chopped red onion	2 tbsp. jalapeno chilies	4 med. tomatoes
1 tbsp. red wine vinegar	1 tbsp. fresh lime juice	½ tsp. salt
2 tbsp. chopped cilantro	1 minced garlic clove	

Peel, seed and chop tomatoes. Place tomatoes and juice in a medium bowl. Mix in onion, 1 tablespoon chilies, cilantro, vinegar, lime juice, garlic and salt. Taste and add remaining chilies if desired. Cover and refrigerate.
*Good over pasta.

****

JIFFY SALSA AL PRADO SAUCE

3 avocadoes	3 chopped tomatoes	6 tbsp. cilantro
3 tbsp. fresh chives	1 jalapeno chili	3 cucumbers
Salt and pepper		

Peel and finely chop avocadoes. Chop cilantro and chives. Peel, seed and dice cucumbers, seed and mince jalapeno chili. Mix all ingredients together in a mixing bowl, you will probably need a lot of salt.
*Good with shrimp.

****

JIFFY SAVORY ONION TOPER SAUCE

3 cups sweet Spanish onions	1 ¼ cups chili sauce	3 tbsp. butter
¼ cup bottled meat sauce		

Sauté chopped onion in butter in a skillet until tender. Mix in chili sauce and meat sauce; heat thoroughly.
*Good over hamburgers.

****

JIFFY SAVVY SAUCE

1 ½ tsp. brown sugar	1 ½ tbsp. butter	1 lg. onion
¾ cup Salad dressing	½ tsp. paprika	1 egg

Mix all ingredients together in a bowl, until well blended.
*Good over rice.

JIFFY SCAMPI SAUCE

2 cloves pureed garlic	½ tsp. dry mustard	1 tsp. salt
3 tbsp. lemon juice	1 cup olive oil	⅛ tsp. pepper
2 tbsp. parsley, finely chopped		

Combine garlic, salt, mustard and pepper in a bowl. Add parsley, lemon juice and olive oil, mix well.
*Good over shrimp and pasta.

****

JIFFY SCOTCH SAUCE

½ cup vegetable oil	3 tbsp. fresh lemon juice	½ tsp. sugar
3 tbsp. Scotch whisky	pinch white pepper	½ tsp. salt

Mix all ingredients together in a saucepan, until well blended. Heat 2 minutes.
*Good over all meats.

****

JIFFY SEAFOOD COCKTAIL SAUCE

½ cup chili sauce	2 tbsp. lemon juice	1 tsp. horseradish
½ tsp. Worcestershire	½ tsp. celery seed	

Mix all ingredients together in a bowl, until well blended. Chill.
*Good over shrimp or any shellfish.

****

JIFFY SEAFOOD SAUCE

4 tbsp. white horseradish	1 tsp. chili powder	¾ cup ketchup
2 tbsp. green pickle relish	1 tbsp. lemon juice	¼ tsp. pepper
½ tsp. Worcestershire sauce	Sliver of lemon	cayenne pepper

Mix all ingredients together in a mixing bowl, until well blended. Use lemon as garnish.
*Good over seafood.

JIFFY SEMI-SWEET CHOCOLATE GLAZE SAUCE

6 oz. semi-sweet chocolate morsels   ¼ cup butter   2 tsp. oil

Melt chocolate, oil and butter in a saucepan, over low heat until well blended.
*Good over ice cream, plain cake or cut-up fruit.

****

JIFFY SESAME DRESSING SAUCE

¼ cup red wine vinegar   1 tbsp. black pepper   ¼ cup soy sauce
¼ cup rice wine vinegar   5 tbsp. dark sesame oil   1 cup sesame oil

Mix all ingredients, except oil together in blender. Slowly add oil until smooth.
*Good over poultry.

****

JIFFY SESAME MAPLE SAUCE

⅓ cup maple syrup   ¼ cup soy sauce   1 tbsp. chili oil
3 drops sesame oil   2 cloves garlic   1 tsp. ginger

Mix all ingredients together in a bowl, until well blended.
*Use as marinate.

****

JIFFY SESAME SAUCE

4 dashes Sesame oil   1 cup sesame seeds   Salt and pepper
½ tsp. minced garlic   ½ tsp. cayenne   3 tbsp. peanut oil
2 tbsp. soy sauce

Heat peanut oil and sesame seeds for 1 minutes in a saucepan. Add garlic, salt, cayenne pepper, sesame oil and soy sauce.
*Good over chicken.

JIFFY SHERRY SAUCE

¼ cup mushroom
¼ tsp. tarragon
1 ½ cups beef gravy

¼ tsp. chili powder
4 tbsp. Sherry

1 ½ tbsp. oil
salt and pepper

Heat all ingredients together in a bowl, until well blended.
*Good over poultry or any meat.

****

JIFFY SHRIMP SAUCE

⅓ cup chopped green pepper
1 tbsp. prepared horseradish
2 cups chopped cooked shrimp

1 cup mayonnaise
¼ cup chili sauce
⅛ tsp. ground pepper

1 cup sour cream
¼ tsp. salt

Finely chop green pepper and shrimp and place in a bowl; add remaining ingredients and blend well. Cover; chill.
*Good over pasta or use as a dip.

****

JIFFY SIMPLE SYRUP SAUCE

2 cups sugar

1 cup water

Mix together in a saucepan and bring to a boil. Reduce heat and simmer until sugar dissolves, about 3 minutes.
*Good over ice cream.

****

JIFFY SKORDALIA SAUCE

4 tsp. garlic puree
Juice of 2 lemons

2 cups potato puree
Freshly ground pepper

1 cup vegetable oil
Salt to taste

In a medium bowl, beat garlic into warm potatoes. Gradually beat in oil and lemon juice, adding in small amounts and beating well between additions. Season with salt and pepper.
*Good over pasta.

JIFFY SMOKED TOMATO SAUCE

1 can tomatoes	2 tbsp. olive oil	2 oz. bacon
1 glove garlic	2 tsp. Liquid smoke	1 lg. onion

Cook the bacon and set aside. Sauté garlic in oil, in a medium skillet, then add tomatoes, onion, bacon and liquid smoke together, until well blended, about 1 minute.
*Good over poultry.

****

JIFFY SOLE ANGELICA SAUCE

⅔ cup slivered almonds	¼ up angelica liqueur	⅔ cup butter
¼ cup fresh lemon juice	freshly ground pepper	½ tsp. dill

Blanch almonds by sautéing in butter in large skillet until toasted lightly. When butter browns, stir in angelica liqueur, lemon juice, dill, and pepper.
*Good over fish.

****

JIFFY SORRENTO SAUCE

¼ tsp. garlic powder	½ cup white wine	1 cup milk
1 cup grated Parmesan or Romano cheese		

Mix all ingredients together in a bowl, heat until well blended.
*Good over pasta.

****

JIFFY SOUR CREAM BEET SAUCE

1 tbsp. prepared horseradish	¼ cup cubed beets	⅔ cup sour cream

Put sour cream in a small bowl. Stir in beets and horseradish. Season with salt and pepper.
*Good over veal.

JIFFY SOUR CREAM SAUCE

1 cup sour cream   ½ lemon juice   ½ cup yogurt
¼ tbsp. sugar

Blend all ingredients together in a mixing bowl, until well blended.
*Good over desserts or ice cream.

****

JIFFY SOUR CREAM APRICOT SAUCE

½ cup apricot jam   3 tbsp. Dijon mustard   ¾ cup sour cream

Mix all ingredients together in a bowl, until well blended. Serve at room temperature.
*Good over poultry or pork.

****

JIFFY SOUR CREAM SAUCE

1 cup sour cream   ½ cup mayonnaise   2 tsp. lemon juice
2 tsp. prepared horseradish sauce   ¼ tsp. dry mustard   pinch of cayenne
salt and paprika

Combine all ingredients in a bowl and mix until thoroughly combined.
*Good over baked potatoes or vegetables.

****

JIFFY SOY SAUCE

½ cup soy sauce   2 tsp. sugar   1 cup sherry
2 tbsp. powdered ginger

Blend all ingredients together in a mixing bowl for 30 seconds until smooth.
*Good over poultry.

JIFFY SPANISH-STYLE HOT SAUCE

1 sm. chopped onion
2 tbsp. white wine vinegar
1 minced garlic clove

2 tbsp. chopped parsley
1 ½ tsp. paprika

½ cup olive oil
salt and pepper

Mix all ingredients together in a bowl, until well blended.
*Good with fish.

****

JIFFY SPICY COLD SESAME SAUCE

¼ cup light soy sauce
1 tbsp. rice vinegar
2 crushed cloves garlic

2 tbsp. sesame paste
2 tbsp. sesame oil
2 tsp. crushed peppercorns

1 tbsp. chili oil
2 tbsp. ginger root

Mix all ingredients together in a bowl, until well blended.
*Good over poultry.

****

JIFFY SPICY FISH SAUCE

2 tbsp. fresh lime juice
1 sm. red chili pepper

2 sm. garlic cloves
¼ cup nuoc mam

2 tbsp. sugar
Water

In a food processor or blender, combine peeled and crushed garlic, seeded and minced chili and sugar.
Add lime (or lemon) juice, vinegar, nuoc mam (fish sauce) and ¼ cup water.
*Good over fish.

****

JIFFY SPICY HONEY SAUCE

⅔ cup maple syrup
1 tsp. ground cinnamon

½ tsp. ground allspice
Pinch of caraway seeds

⅓ up honey

Stir syrup with honey in a small saucepan, over low heat. Add spices to hot sauce and cook over medium heat, stirring, until the sauce boils. Serve hot.
*Good over poultry.

JIFFY SPICY ORIENTAL SAUCE

1 minced garlic clove
2 green chili peppers

2 tbsp. soy sauce
1 tbsp. sesame oil

2 tbsp. lemon juice

Mince chili peppers; put all ingredients in a small bowl and mix together.
*Good over poultry.

****

JIFFY SPINACH HERBED SAUCE

2 cups chopped spinach
½ up Parmesan cheese
1 ½ sp. sweet basil

¾ up olive oil
1 sm. garlic clove
½ up walnut

½ up parsley
1 tsp. salt
½ sp. pepper

Place all ingredients except walnuts in a food processor or blender. Blend until smooth, then stir in chopped walnuts. *Good over pasta.

****

JIFFY STIR FRIED ORANGE SAUCE

2 tbsp. hoisin sauce
2 tsp. orange marmalade

2 tbsp. cornstarch
½ up orange juice

½ up water
1 tsp. garlic

Stir-fry all ingredients together in a skillet until well blended.
*Good over pork.

****

JIFFY STRAWBERRY SAUCE

1 tbsp. strawberry preserves
1 ½ sp. balsamic vinegar

1 pint strawberries

2 tbsp. powdered sugar

Puree berries in a food processor. Blend in sugar, preserves and vinegar until smooth.
*Good over salads.

JIFFY STRAWBERRY-LIME SAUCE

2 pints strawberries   3 tbsp. lime juice   ¼ up sugar

Puree strawberries and sugar in food processor or blender until sugar is dissolved. Strain into bowl. Stir in limejuice.
*Good over ice cream.

****

JIFFY SUBSTITUTE SOY SAUCE

1 ½ ups boiling water   4 tbsp. cider vinegar   4 tbsp. beef bouillon
1 tsp. sesame seed oil   1 tbsp. dark molasses   salt and pepper

Mix all ingredients together in a bowl, until well blended.
*Good over poultry.

****

JIFFY SUEDOISE SAUCE

1 cup mayonnaise   1 cup thick applesauce   1 tbsp. horseradish

Mix all ingredients together in a bowl, until well blended.
*Good over pork.

****

JIFFY SUN-DRIED TOMATO ROUILLE SAUCE

2 tbsp. parmesan cheese   1 tsp. minced garlic   1 bunch basil
1 tbsp. virgin olive oil   10 sun-dried tomatoes   Salt and pepper

Puree in food processor or blender, sun-dried tomatoes in ⅓ up of its own oil. Combine with 1 bunch basil leaves, finely chopped, garlic and grated Parmesan cheese, olive oil, salt and pepper to taste.
*Good over pasta.

JIFFY SUPREME MUSTARD CREAM SAUCE

2 tbsp. dry Vermouth   2 tbsp. heavy cream   ⅛ sp. thyme
1 tbsp. Dijon mustard   ⅛ sp. black pepper

Heat all ingredients together in a saucepan, for 3 minutes.
*Good over fish.

****

JIFFY SUPREME SAUCE

½ b. American cheese   ½ cup mayonnaise   ¼ cup milk
1 tsp. dry mustard

Combine cheese, mayonnaise and milk in a saucepan, over low heat until smooth. Stir in mustard.
Use ½ teaspoon of dill weed, horseradish, dried tarragon, oregano or basil for alternate flavor.
*Use over vegetables.

****

JIFFY SUZETTE SAUCE

½ cup butter   ½ cup sugar   1 orange
3 tbsp. orange flavored liqueur

Melt butter in a saucepan and stir in sugar. Using a citrus zester, add about 2 teaspoons finely shredded orange peel; add about 1 tablespoon orange juice, then add liqueur. Bring to a boil; lower heat and cook for 1 minute.
*Good over desserts or ice cream.

****

JIFFY SWEET 'N SASSY SAUCE

16 oz. V-8 juice   2 tsp. maple syrup

Place ingredients in a saucepan and heat until well blended, about 2-3 minutes.
*Use for chicken.

JIFFY SWEET AND SOUR PRESERVE SAUCE

1 env. onion soup   5 oz. apricot preserves   ½ cup water
½ bottle Russian dressing

Mix all ingredients together in a bowl, until well blended.
*Use over chicken for baking.

****

JIFFY SWEET CREAM CHEESE SAUCE

2 3-oz. pkg. cream cheese   3 tbsp. heavy cream   1 tsp. vanilla
1 egg white   ⅛ tsp. salt   2 tbsp. sugar

Blend heavy cream into cream cheese in a mixing bowl. Add vanilla. Beat egg white until firm. Add sugar and salt; fold into cheese mixture.
*Good over fruit or desserts.

****

JIFFY SWEET MUSTARD SAUCE

2 tbsp. prepared mustard   2 tbsp. mayonnaise   ½ cup salsa
2 tbsp. honey

Mix all ingredients together in a saucepan; heat until well blended. Cook 2 to 3 minutes or till sauce is heated through.
*Good over poultry or pork.

****

JIFFY SZECHUAN PEANUT SAUCE

½ cup nonfat yogurt   6 tbsp. peanut butter   2 tsp. sugar
¼ tsp. red pepper flakes   1 tsp. soy sauce   ½ garlic clove
¼ tsp. dark sesame oil   2 tbsp. rice wine vinegar

One half teaspoon of sweet and low can substitute the 2 teaspoons sugar. Mix all ingredients in a blender until smooth.
*Good over pasta, noodles or vegetables.

JIFFY TAHINI SAUCE

Juice of 2 to 3 lemons
1 tbsp. chopped parsley
Dash black & cayenne peppers

2 tbsp. olive oil
2 garlic cloves

1 cup tahini
¼ tsp. salt

Place tahini in a medium bowl and stir in lemon juice a little at a time, until mixture thickens. Add ½ cup water, slowly, until mixture is pourable. Stir in oil, parsley, salt, peppers and parsley.
*Good over poultry.

****

JIFFY TAMARIND SAUCE

2 tbsp. Tamarind

1 cup light beer

1 tsp. sugar

Use fresh cooked tamarind or 2 tablespoons dried, soaked and drained tamarind; heat, in a saucepan, 2 minutes with light beer and sugar.
*Use with lobster.

****

JIFFY TAMPA TINGLER SAUCE

6 oz. V-8 juice

½ cup orange juice

1 tbsp. brown sugar

Heat all ingredients together in a bowl, until well blended.
*Use for chicken.

****

JIFFY TANDOORI MARINADE SAUCE I

½ cup fresh lemon juice
1 tbsp. minced garlic
½ tsp. black pepper
1-1 ½ tsp. cayenne pepper

1 cup plain yogurt
1 tbsp. minced ginger
½ tsp. cardamom

1 tbsp. paprika
1 ½ tsp. cumin
1 tsp. turmeric

Mix all ingredients together in a bowl, until well blended.
*Good for poultry or lamb.

JIFFY TANDOORI MARINADE SAUCE II

¼ cup vegetable oil   1 cup plain yogurt   8 cloves garlic
½ cup fresh coriander   2 tbsp. curry powder   2 tbsp. honey

Combine all the ingredients in a food processor or blender, and blend until finely minced.
*Good for marinating chicken.

****

JIFFY TANGERINE SAUCE

¼ cup orange juice   1 tbsp. brown sugar   ½ tsp. cinnamon
1 tsp. apricot liqueur   ¼ cup melted butter   ¼ tsp. nutmeg
¼ cup tangerine liqueur

Mix all ingredients together in a bowl, until well blended.
*Good over desserts and ice cream.

****

JIFFY TANGY BUTTER SAUCE

1 tbsp. butter   1 tsp. lemon juice   2 tbsp. plum brandy

Heat all ingredients together in a bowl, until well blended.
*Good over poultry, all meats or ice cream.

****

JIFFY TANGY COCKTAIL SAUCE

¼ cup Horseradish   1 cup chili sauce   1 ½ cups ketchup
2 tsp. Worcestershire sauce   ¼ cup lemon juice   2 tbsp. basil

Combine all ingredients together in a mixing bowl, until well blended.
*Good over fish.

JIFFY TANGY COCONUT SAUCE

¾ cup cream of coconut   2 tbsp. prepared mustard   1 ½ tsp. cornstarch

Heat all ingredients in a small saucepan and bring to a boil, about 2 to 3 minutes.
*Use over ham.

****

JIFFY TANGY FRENCH SAUCE

2 tbsp. white wine vinegar	freshly ground black pepper	1 tsp. salt
6 to 8 tbsp. olive oil	½ tsp. dry mustard	1 tsp. sugar
1 tbsp. Worcestershire sauce	4 tbsp. prepared horseradish	1 tsp. paprika

Mix vinegar with horseradish, salt and pepper, in a mixing bowl. Add the remaining ingredients; beat with fork until mixture thickens. Mix well before using.
*Good over steak.

****

JIFFY TAPENADE SAUCE

20 pitted olives   1 tsp. garlic   6 tbsp. olive oil
Salt and pepper

Chop olives and garlic; place in a small bowl and add remaining ingredients, mix until well blended.
*Good over pasta.

****

JIFFY TARRAGON FRENCH SAUCE

2 tbsp. tarragon vinegar	freshly ground black pepper	1 tsp. salt
6 to 8 tbsp. olive oil	1 tsp. sugar	1 glove garlic
¼ tsp. Worcestershire sauce	⅛ tsp. thyme	½ tsp. paprika

Mix vinegar with salt and pepper in a small bowl. Add remaining ingredients; beat with fork until mixture thickens. Pour into a bottle or pouring container. Shake well before using.
*Good over salad or poultry.

JIFFY TARTAR SAUCE I

½ cup mayonnaise   2 tsp. pickle relish   1 tsp. horseradish.

Mix all ingredients together in a bowl, until well blended.
*Good with shrimp.

****

JIFFY TARTAR SAUCE II

1 ⅔ cups mayonnaise   3 tbsp. sweet pickle   1 tbsp. capers
3 tbsp. stuffed olives   1 tsp. lemon juice   1 tbsp. parsley
1 tbsp. minced onion   1 tsp. vinegar

Chop pickles, olives, parsley and capers. Mix all ingredients together in a bowl, until well blended.
*Good with shrimp.

****

JIFFY TARTAR SAUCE III

1 tbsp. capers, drained   1 tbsp. dill pickles   Salt and pepper
1 cup Mayonnaise Sauce 1 tsp. lemon juice   1 tbsp. parsley

Finely chop the capers, parsley and pickles. Add chopped ingredients to the Mayonnaise Sauce in a bowl. Stir in lemon juice. Adjust the flavor if necessary, with salt and pepper, or more lemon juice. Serve cold.
*Good over fish.

****

JIFFY TEMPURA DIPPING SAUCE

1 cup chicken broth   2 tbsp. dry sherry   2 tbsp. soy sauce

Mix together all ingredients in a bowl, then place in a serving bowl.
*Good over shrimp or poultry.

JIFFY TERIYAKI MARINADE SAUCE

½ cup sweet sake
1 tsp. brown sugar

½ cup soy sauce
1 tsp. white sugar

2 tbsp. dry sherry
Dash ginger juice

Mix all ingredients together in a bowl, until well blended.
*Good over all meats.

****

JIFFY TERIYAKI SAUCE

⅓ cup mirin (rice wine)

⅓ cup soy sauce

⅓ cup sake

Combine the soy sauce, sake and mirin in a saucepan and bring to a boil over medium heat. Let cool.
*Good over fish.

****

JIFFY TEXAS BARBEQUED SAUCE

3 tbsp. prepared brown mustard
2 tbsp. Worcestershire
1 tsp. Liquid Smoke
½ cup vinegar

½ tsp. pepper
¼ cup ketchup
3 tbsp. brown sugar
1 cup butter

1 tbsp. salt
1 cup water
2 tbsp. chili sauce

Melt butter in a saucepan; add all ingredients and heat until well blended.
*Good over poultry or pork.

****

JIFFY TEXAS GARLIC SAUCE

7 cloves garlic

egg yolk

½ cup oil

Boil and drain garlic clove in a small saucepan, then mash and add egg yolk and oil. Mix well.
*Good over pasta or to baste poultry or meats for grill.

JIFFY THAI GREEN CURRY SAUCE

4 lg. fresh green chilies
1 tsp. black peppercorns
2 tsp. grated lemon peel
2 tsp. dried shrimp paste
2 tsp. coriander powder

1 sm. onion, chopped
2 tbsp. fresh cilantro
1 tbsp. garlic, chopped
1 tsp. ground cinnamon

1 tsp. cumin powder
1 tsp. salt
1 tsp. tumeric
1 tbsp. vegetable oil

Coarsely chop chilies and remove seeds. Put into a food processor or blender with remaining ingredients. Blend to a paste, adding extra oil or water if necessary.
*Good over pasta, rice or meats.

****

JIFFY THANKSGIVING SAUCE

½ cup orange juice
2 cups raw cranberries

¼ cup orange rind
1 diced apple

2 cups sugar

Cut orange rind into small pieces. Place in blender and blend about 2 minutes. Add diced apple and raw cranberries. Blend until desired consistency is achieved. Place all ingredients in a saucepan and heat 1 minute.
*Good over poultry.

****

JIFFY THICK WHITE SAUCE

1 cup light cream
½ tsp. salt

4 tbsp. butter
⅛ tsp. pepper

4 tbsp. flour

Heat butter in a saucepan. Blend in flour, salt, and pepper; heat and stir until bubbly. Gradually add the milk, stirring until smooth. Bring to a boil, cook and stir 1 to 2 minutes longer.
*Good over pasta or vegetables.

****

JIFFY THOUSAND ISLAND SAUCE I

2 tbsp. stuffed olives
2 tbsp. onion, finely chopped

1 cup mayonnaise
1 hard-boiled egg

1 tsp. tomato paste
1 tbsp. parsley

Chop olives, onions, parsley and eggs. Place all ingredients in a small bowl and mix together. Season with salt and pepper, then spoon into a serving dish.
*Good over vegetables and salads.

JIFFY THOUSAND ISLAND SAUCE II

1 cup mayonnaise	½ cup chili sauce	1 tsp. paprika
2 hard-boiled eggs, chopped	1 tsp. Worcestershire sauce	¼ cup celery, chopped
¼ cup sweet pickle relish	¼ green pepper, chopped	½ onion, grated

Mix all ingredients together in a bowl and mix until well blended.
*Good over salad.

****

JIFFY TOMATILLO, TOMATO AND AVOCADO SALSA SAUCE

½ lb. tomatillos	1 lb. ripe tomato	1 sm. avocado
1 tbsp. red-wine vinegar	1 lg. glove garlic	

Finely chop tomatillos and tomatoes; mash avocado and garlic. Combine ingredients in a mixing bowl, and mix until well blended.
*Good over fish and chicken.

****

JIFFY TOMATO MAYONNAISE SAUCE

1 ½ cups mayonnaise	2 tbsp. tomato paste

Mix ingredients together in a bowl, until well blended.
*Good over pasta.

****

JIFFY TOMATO SALSA SAUCE

3 tbsp. red-wine vinegar	⅓ cup cilantro	1 jalapeno chili
2 tbsp. fruity olive oil	2 lbs. ripe tomatoes	

Seed and quarter chili, mince in a food processor. Add cilantro. Peel tomatoes and cut in half and squeeze to extract juice and most of the seeds. Add to processor and process to a rough puree. Blend vinegar and oil into tomatoes. *Good over linguine, with fish or chicken.

JIFFY TOMATO SOUP FRENCH SAUCE

2 tbsp. white wine vinegar
6 to 8 tbsp. olive oil
1 tbsp. chopped onion
1 tbsp. Worcestershire sauce

freshly ground black pepper
⅔ cup condensed tomato soup
½ tsp. dry mustard
1 tsp. paprika

1 tsp. salt
½ tsp. marjoram
1 tsp. sugar

Mix vinegar with tomato soup, salt and pepper in a small bowl. Add remaining ingredients; beat with fork until mixture thickens. Pour into a bottle or pouring container. Shake well before using.
*Good over rice.

****

JIFFY TOMATO VINAIGRETTE SAUCE

1 cup tomato puree
2 tbsp. chopped parsley

¼ cup olive oil
Salt and pepper

2 tbsp. wine vinegar

Place all ingredients in a bowl and mix until well blended.
*Use for poaching fish.

****

JIFFY TOMATO-WINE CREAM SAUCE

1 ¼ cups heavy cream
2 tbsp. dry white wine

2 tbsp. green onions
2 tbsp. diced tomato

Dash of sugar
salt

Mix cream, minced green onion, sugar and salt with a fork, in a mixing bowl. Gradually beat in wine; stir in tomato.
*Good over fish.

****

JIFFY TRIPLE SEC GLAZING SAUCE

4 oz. Triple Sec

1 tbsp. butter

1 tsp. sugar

Simmer all ingredients in a saucepan, for 2 minutes.
*Use over carrots.

JIFFY TUNA, CAPERS AND TOMATO SAUCE

6 oz. can tuna in oil
½ cup gaeta olives
Salt and pepper

2 cups plum tomatoes
¼ cup fresh parsley

1 tbsp. capers
1 shallot

Pour oil from tuna into a bowl. Flake tuna and add to oil with peeled, chopped and seeded tomatoes, capers, chopped olives, parsley and chopped shallot. Season with salt and pepper. Mix well.
*Good over pasta.

****

JIFFY VERMOUTH AND TARRAGON SAUCE

2 tbsp. minced onion
1 cup dry Vermouth

1 tbsp. clarified butter
2 tbsp. wine vinegar

3 tbsp. butter
1 tbsp. tarragon

Heat all ingredients, except 3 tbsp. butter, together in a saucepan, for 2 minutes. Then add butter, mix until melted and well blended.
*Good over steak.

****

JIFFY VINAIGRETTE DE MENTHE SAUCE

1 tbsp. Crème de Menthe (white)
salt and pepper

8 tbsp. olive oil

1 tbsp. vinegar

Mix all ingredients together in a bowl, until well blended.
*Good over pork.

****

JIFFY VINAIGRETTE FRENCH SAUCE

2 tbsp. white wine vinegar
freshly ground black pepper
1 hard-cooked egg, chopped
1 tsp. sugar

6 to 8 tbsp. olive oil
2 tbsp. chopped dill pickle
1 tbsp. Worcestershire sauce
1 tsp. paprika

1 tsp. salt
1 tbsp. chopped chives
½ tsp. dry mustard

Mix vinegar with salt and pepper in a bowl. Add oil; beat with fork until mixture thickens. Add remaining ingredients. Pour into a bottle or pouring container. Shake well before using.
*Good over salad.

JIFFY VINAIGRETTE-MUSTARD SAUCE

1 tbsp. red wine vinegar

1 tbsp. lemon juice

1 tsp. Dijon mustard

6 tbsp. virgin olive oil

2 tbsp. heavy cream

Salt and pepper

Put the vinegar and lemon juice in a bowl. Whisk in the mustard, salt and pepper. Add the oil and whisk vigorously until smooth and thickened. For a creamier dressing that is also a little less acid, whisk in the cream.

*Good over poultry.

****

JIFFY VIRGIN MARY SAUCE

3 tbsp. red wine vinegar

1 tsp. tomato paste

½ tsp. pepper

1 tsp. Worcestershire sauce

½ cup olive oil

1 garlic clove

½ cup tomato juice

¼ cup celery leaves

¾ tsp. salt

2 Dashes hot pepper sauce

Mash garlic and salt together to form a paste, in a small bowl. Whisk in tomato juice, vinegar, Worcestershire sauce, tomato paste and pepper; add oil in a thin stream until incorporated. Stir in minced celery leaves and hot pepper sauce.

*Good over pasta.

****

JIFFY VOLCANIC HORSERADISH SAUCE

2 cups grated horseradish root

2 tbsp. sugar

Salt to taste

⅔ cups white wine vinegar

6 tbsp. dry white wine

Peel and finely chop horseradish in a food processor, or grate by hand. Mix in enough vinegar and wine to obtain a creamy sauce. Add sugar and salt to taste.

*Good over pasta.

****

JIFFY WALDORF SAUCE

½ lg. lemon celery diced

½ cup walnuts

1 diced apple

⅓ cup mayonnaise

⅓ cup sour cream

salt and pepper

Mix all ingredients, except walnuts, together in a blender, until well blended. Then add walnuts.

*Use over pasta.

JIFFY WALNUT CREAM SAUCE

8 oz. cream cheese   1 cup sour cream   salt
1 cup walnuts

Finely grind walnut in a food processor or blender; add cream cheese and sour cream until smooth; season with salt. *Good over pasta.

****

JIFFY WALNUT SAUCE I

1 cup Parmesan cheese   1 cup heavy cream   2 eggs
1 cup toasted walnuts   ¼ cup walnut oil   Pinch nutmeg
2 smashed garlic cloves   Salt and pepper

Beat eggs with a whisk in a bowl; add heavy cream and walnut oil. Stir in ground walnuts, cheese, garlic, salt, pepper and nutmeg.
*Good over pasta or vegetables.

****

JIFFY WALNUT SAUCE II

2 tbsp. wine vinegar   2 tbsp. sugar   1 tsp. garlic
1 tbsp. peanut oil   3 tbsp. walnut oil

Mix all ingredients together in a bowl, until well blended.
*Use with salad.

****

JIFFY WARM HERBED VINAIGRETTE SAUCE

⅓ cup salad oil   ⅓ cup white wine vinegar   1 tbsp. chives
1 tbsp. dill   1 tbsp. parsley   Salt and pepper

In a small saucepan, blend salad oil, vinegar and finely minced chives, dill and parsley. Season to taste with salt and pepper; and gently heat over low flame for 1 minute.
*Good over fish.

JIFFY WARM YELLOW SAUCE

½ cup melted butter
1 tsp. Worcestershire sauce

2 tbsp. prepared mustard

Juice of 1 lemon

Mix and heat all ingredients together in a saucepan, for about 2 minutes.
*Good over ham.

****

JIFFY WEST INDIAN HOT SAUCE

10 Scotch bonnet chilies
2 tbsp. orange juice
2 tbsp. molasses or brown sugar

½ cup Dijon mustard
2 tbsp. lime juice

2 tbsp. vinegar
Salt

Mix all ingredients together in a blender, until well blended.
Warning: Take care not to get sauce on your hands or in your eyes.
*Good over pork.

****

JIFFY WHITE WINE SAUCE

¼ cup dry white wine
¼ tsp. dry mustard
½ tsp. minced onion

½ cup olive oil
¼ tsp. black pepper
pinch of cayenne

2 tsp. lemon juice
1 tsp. salt
¼ tsp. sugar

Mix all ingredients together in a bowl, until well blended and chill.
*Good over steak.

****

JIFFY WINE MARINADE SAUCE I

3 tbsp. fresh parsley
½ tsp. black pepper
¼ tsp. tarragon
1 tsp. Worcestershire sauce

½ cup olive oil
3 tbsp. scallion
¼ tsp. thyme

1 cup dry wine
3 cloves garlic
1 tsp. salt

Chop parsley, scallions and garlic, then combine all ingredients together in a bowl, until well blended.

Use white wine for chicken or fish and red wine for beef, pork or lamb.
*Good over chicken, fish or any meat.

JIFFY WINE MARINADE SAUCE II

¼ cup olive oil
½ tsp. dried basil

¼ cup dry white wine
½ tsp. dried rosemary

1 tbsp. dried onion
¼ tsp. pepper

Mix all ingredients together in a bowl, until well blended.
*Good over beef.

****

JIFFY UNCOOKED FRESH TOMATO SAUCE

6 lg. ripe tomatoes
1 lg. glove garlic
½ cup olive oil

Juice of 1 lemon
½ cup fresh basil
Sprigs of basil

½ tsp. salt
Salt and pepper
Grated Parmesan

Peel skin off tomatoes, remove seeds and squeeze out juice. Put the coarsely chopped tomatoes into a bowl; add lemon juice, minced garlic, fresh basil, salt and pepper, adjusting seasoning to taste. Garnish with a sprig of basil and grated Parmesan.
*Good over pasta.

****

JIFFY UNCOOKED TOMATO SAUCE

1 ½ tbsp. red-wine vinegar
¼ cup sliced scallions

3 tbsp. olive oil
¼ cup pimento-stuffed olives

1 lb. tomatoes

In a bowl, whisk together the vinegar, oil, salt and pepper to taste and stir in the peeled, seeded, chopped tomatoes, scallions, and thinly sliced olives. Mix ingredients together until well blended.
*Good over pasta.

JIFFY UNCOOKED TUNA SAUCE

6 ½ oz. can tuna fish
Grated rind of 1 lemon
Salt and pepper

½ cup walnuts
4 tbsp. chopped parsley
1 tsp. Worcestershire sauce

6 oz. olive oil
4 basil leaves

Put the drained tuna, walnuts, lemon rind, Worcestershire sauce and herbs into the food processor or blender and process until smooth. Add the olive oil gradually, and season to taste.
*Good over pasta.

****

JIFFY WINE GLAZE SAUCE

¼ cup currant jelly
1 tbsp. cornstarch

1 tsp. Dijon mustard
¼ cup port or med. dry sherry

½ cup red wine

Blend all ingredients in a saucepan; simmer over medium heat until the sauce has thickened and is clear. About 3 minutes.
*Good over ham.

****

JIFFY YAKITORI SAUCE

3 tbsp. light soy sauce
2 tbsp. fresh coriander

2 tbsp. dry fino sherry
¼ tsp. gingerroot

3 tbsp. peanut oil

Blend peanut oil, soy sauce, sherry, finely minced coriander and freshly grated gingerroot, in a bowl. Mix well.
*Good over fish.

****

JIFFY YELLOW BEAN SAUCE

2 tbsp. yellow bean sauce
1 tbsp. dry sherry

1 tbsp. soy sauce
1 green chili, finely chopped

2 tbsp. water

Combine all ingredients together in a bowl, until well blended.
*Good over rice.

JIFFY YOGURT SAUCE I

2 tbsp. chopped garlic   1 cup plain yogurt   ¼ cup fresh mint
1 tsp. lemon juice

Puree the chopped garlic, the lemon juice and half cup of the yogurt together in a food processor. Stir in the remaining yogurt and mint.
*Serve over grilled meat and vegetables.

****

JIFFY YOGURT SAUCE II

1 cup plain yogurt   1 garlic clove, mashed   salt to taste
1 tbsp. grated onion

Mix all ingredients together in a small bowl, until well blended and smooth.
*Good over fish.

****

JIFFY YOGURT DILL SAUCE

8 oz. plain yogurt   1/6 cup chopped dill   1 tbsp. lemon juice
1 cucumber   salt and pepper

Mix all ingredients together in blender, until almost smooth.
*Good over fish.

****

JIFFY YOGURT SPICY MARINADE SAUCE

1 tsp. coriander seeds   ½ tsp. cumin   ¼ tsp. turmeric
¼ tsp. ground red pepper   ⅛ tsp. ginger   ⅛ tsp. black pepper
1 cup plain low-fat yogurt

Put spices in a small saucepan, over medium heat. Stir about 2 minutes to cut rawness and bring out flavors. Cool 1 minute; add to yogurt and stir until well blended.
*Good to marinate fish.

KETCHUP LEMON SAUCE

2 tbsp. mustard seeds	2 tsp. black peppercorn	9 lg. lemons
¼ tsp. whole cloves	¼ tsp. grated nutmeg	¼ tsp. mace
2 oz. fresh horseradish	3 tbsp. kosher salt	1 qt. White vinegar

Thinly slice lemons and remove seeds. Coarsely chop mustard seeds, peppercorns and cloves in a food processor or a spice grinder. Combine mixture with the remaining ingredients in a saucepan. Bring to a boil; cook 20 minutes over moderate heat, stirring occasionally. Let cool to room temperature. Place in a wide-mouth jar and cover tightly. Let steep at least two weeks in the refrigerator. Shake jar well every day. Strain through a filter and ladle into a clean jar. Store in refrigerator.
*Good over fish.

****

KETCHUP MUSHROOM SAUCE

4 lbs. Mushrooms	½ tsp. crushed peppercorns	½ cup kosher salt
2 tbsp. shallots, chopped	¼ tsp. grated lemon zest	1 tsp. garlic, chopped
¼ tsp. grated fresh ginger		

Break up all the mushrooms by hand and place in a saucepan and sprinkle with salt. Cover tightly and let stand in a cool place for three days, stirring and mashing twice a day with a wooden spoon. This is important. If you don't stir mixture ever day, mold may form over the mushrooms. Uncover and slowly bring mixture to a boil. Let simmer over low heat for 45 minutes, stirring occasionally. Cool to room temperature. Strain through a fine sieve, extracting all mushroom liquid. Transfer to a clean saucepan; add remaining ingredients and bring to a boil. Cook, stirring, until ketchup is reduced by half. Strain through a fine sieve into hot sterilized jars, filling to within ¼ inch of rim; seal and process in a hot-water bath 10 minutes. Store in a cool, dark, dry place. Refrigerate after opening.
*Good over all meats.

****

KETCHUP NO-SUGAR, LOW-SODIUM SAUCE

½ cup apple juice, undiluted	6 oz. can tomato paste	3 tbsp. white vinegar
2 tsp. fresh lemon juice	¾ tsp. salt	

Combine all ingredients in a saucepan and simmer very slowly until thickened, about 30 minutes.
*Good over all meats.

KETCHUP TOMATO SAUCE

10 lbs. Ripe tomatoes, quartered
1 tsp. whole cloves
1 tsp. whole black peppercorns
2 tsp. dry mustard
1 ½ cups cider vinegar

5 med. Onions, sliced thin
1 tsp. whole allspice
1 2 inch stick cinnamon, broken
¼ tsp. cayenne pepper

2 cloves garlic
2 bay leaves
½ tsp. mace
1 tbsp. salt

Combine tomatoes, onions and garlic in a saucepan and simmer until very soft, about 30 to 45 minutes, stirring occasionally. Strain through a food mill. Return to the saucepan and simmer uncovered about an hour, until the liquid is reduced by half, stirring often to prevent burning. In another saucepan, place the bay leaves, cloves, allspice, peppercorns, cinnamon and ginger into a cheesecloth bag, tie it, and add vinegar, and cook over a low heat for about 30 minutes. Remove the spice bag. Gradually add the spiced vinegar to first saucepan, to taste. Add mustard, mace, salt and cayenne. Continue to cook, stirring often, until desired consistency, about 20 minutes to an hour. Pour immediately into, sterile jars, leaving ¼ inch headroom. Seal and process in a boiling-water bath for 10 minutes. Allow to stand at least 24 hours before using. Store in a cool, dark, dry place. Refrigerate after opening.
*good over all meats.

****

KOREAN STEAK TARTER (YUK KWE) SAUCE

1 lb. beef filet
1 crushed garlic clove
Julienne pears and cucumbers

2 tsp. sesame seeds
½ tsp. sesame oil

1 tsp. sugar
6 egg yolks

Place beef in freezer 1 hour, then slice into slivers. Place in a bowl and mix with sugar, sesame seeds, garlic sesame oil. Chill 30 minutes. Serve over pears and cucumbers and top with raw egg yolk.
*Good over steak.

LAMB SAUCE

2 lbs. of lamb
4 oz. olive oil
2 oz. freshly grated Sardo or Romano cheese

few sprigs of rosemary
14 oz. plum tomatoes

2 cloves garlic
1 sm. onion

Pour oil in a skillet; cut lamb into small pieces and sauté until brown. Then add the remaining ingredients and cook for 1 ½ hours.
*Good over pasta.

****

LEEK PUREE SAUCE

2 lbs. leeks, chopped
2 tbsp. green onions, chopped

⅔ cup chicken broth
Salt and pepper

¼ cup butter
Dash nutmeg

Wash leeks well, put in a medium size saucepan with a little water and simmer 10 to 15 minutes or until soft. Drain leeks and allow to cool slightly. In a blender or food processor puree leeks with broth.
*Good over pasta.

****

LEMON MUSTARD SAUCE

⅓ cup all purpose flour
2 tsp. Dijon mustard
Red (cayenne) pepper

2 tbsp. lemon juice
3 egg yolks
1 ½ cups chicken or beef stock

⅓ cup butter
Salt

In a medium saucepan, melt butter and add the flour all at once. Cook, stirring constantly, for 3 minutes. Add stock, whisk to blend. Cook over low heat, stirring often, for 5 to 6 minutes. Gently beat in egg yolks and lemon juice, whisking constantly. Add mustard and salt. Cook 1 to 2 minutes longer; add red pepper, a little a time, stirring constantly. Serve hot.
*Good over poultry or vegetables.

****

LEMON PARSLEY SAUCE

2 tbsp. all purpose flour
1 cup fish stock or clam juice
Grated peel and juice of ½ lemon

3 tbsp. half and half
1 tbsp. parsley, chopped

2 tbsp. butter
Salt & pepper

Melt butter in a small saucepan, stir in flour and cook 1 minute. Gradually add fish stock or clam juice then bring to a boil and simmer 1 to 2 minutes, or until thickened. Stir in lemon peel and juice, parsley, salt and pepper. Heat for 1 minute then add half and half.
*Good over fish.

LEMON SAUCE

3 tbsp. lemon juice
1 cup boiling water
1 tsp. grated lemon peel

1 tbsp. cornstarch
⅛ tsp. salt

½ cup sugar
2 tbsp. butter

Mix sugar, cornstarch and salt in a saucepan. Stir in boiling water, gradually. Bring to a boil and cook 5 minutes or until thickened, stirring constantly; remove from heat. Mix in butter, lemon peel and lemon juice. Serve warm or cold.
*Good over ice cream or ices.

****

LEMON-HAZELNUT BUTTER SAUCE

½ lb. + 2 tbsp. butter
4 tbsp. hazelnut liqueur
⅓ cup toasted hazelnuts

½ cup dry white wine
2 tbsp. lemon juice
ground pepper

2 tbsp. shallots
salt

Heat 2 tablespoons of butter in a saucepan and add the finely chopped shallots. Cook briefly, stirring, add wine, 3 tablespoons hazelnut liqueur and lemon juice. Bring to a boil, cook about 5 minutes or until reduced to 4 tablespoons. Gradually add the remaining butter, stirring constantly with whisk. When thickened remove from heat and add remaining liqueur, salt and pepper. Process the hazelnut as finely as possible. Add to sauce.
*Good over ham or poultry.

****

LEMON-LIME SAUCE

Peels of 4 lemons and 4 limes

1 ½ cups vodka

1 cup sugar syrup***

Scrape and slice the lemon and lime peels. Place lemon and lime peels in the vodka for 2 weeks. Divide into two separate bottles and add sweetener to one bottle only, if desired.
Note: substitute 2 teaspoons each lemon and lime extract. No steeping or filtering will be necessary.
*Good over ice cream.

****

LEMONY-CHEESE SAUCE

8-oz. cream cheese
½ tsp. dry mustard
¼ cup Parmesan cheese

2 tbsp. lemon juice
¼ tsp. tarragon
½ cup buttermilk salad dressing

1 egg, beaten
1 tsp. sugar

In a medium saucepan combine all ingredients except salad dressing and Parmesan cheese. Cook over low heat until cream cheese has melted and sauce is smooth. Stir in salad dressing and Parmesan cheese.
*Good over salads.
***Sugar syrup is made from equal parts sugar and water, boiled down to syrup.

LICORICE ROOT SAUCE

2 ½ tbsp. licorice root   ½ cup sugar syrup   1 ½ cups vodka

Wash and chop the root into small pieces. Soak in vodka, in a covered bowl or bottle for 1 week. Strain and add sugar syrup.
*Good over desserts or ice cream.

****

LIGHT MARINARA SAUCE

2 tsp. olive oil   1 sliced garlic clove   1 tsp. salt
2 16-oz. can tomatoes   Fresh black pepper

In a saucepan, heat the oil and sauté the garlic. Do not let it brown. Add the drained tomatoes, bring to a boil, season with salt and pepper and simmer, covered, for 15 minutes. Put the sauce in a blender and puree until it is smooth.
*Good over pasta.

****

LIGHT TARTAR SAUCE

1 cup plain low-fat yogurt   1 tsp. Dijon mustard   ¼ tsp. Tabasco
2 tbsp. green bell pepper   1 med. green onion   black pepper
2 tbsp. light mayonnaise

In a mixing bowl, stir yogurt, mayonnaise, finely minced green pepper, minced green onion, mustard, Tabasco sauce and fresh black pepper, together. Refrigerate at least 30 minutes to blend flavors.
*Good over shrimp or fish.

****

LORD CHESTERFIELD SAUCE

2 oz. Sherry wine   1 tsp. turtle herbs   1 tbsp. butter
Dash cayenne pepper   1 cup beef stock

Heat all ingredients together in a saucepan, until reduced by half.
*Good over rice or vegetables.

LOW-CAL SAUCE

4 med. tomatoes
1 tbsp. cilantro, chopped
½ tsp. black pepper

¼ cup scallions, chopped
½ tsp. whole oregano

1-2 tsp. chili flakes
½ tsp. sea salt

Combine all ingredients in a bowl, mixing until well blended. Refrigerate for 1 day before using. Will keep several days in the refrigerator.
*Good over beans, egg dishes, cottage cheese, salad or fish.

****

LOW-CAL BLUE CHEESE SAUCE

¾ cup plain, low-fat yogurt
1 ½ oz. Danish blue cheese, crumbled

½ tsp. garlic, minced

1 tsp. black pepper

Blend yogurt, garlic and pepper in a blender until smooth; add cheese and use pulse cycle, making sure cheese stays crumbly.
*Good over salad, vegetables or use as dip.

****

LOW-CAL BOLOGNESE SAUCE

½ lb. chopped beef
1 med. carrot, quartered
¼ cup dry white wine
1 tbsp. tomato paste

2 sprigs parsley
½ tsp. oregano
1 sm. garlic clove
1 tbsp. plus 1 tsp. low-fat ricotta

1 med. onion
1 celery rib
Salt and pepper

Lightly brown meat in saucepan, stirring to prevent sticking. Put parsley, onion, celery, carrot and garlic in a food processor and process until they are pureed. When the meat is lightly browned, add the vegetable puree and oregano; cook, stirring frequently, about 5 minutes. Add the wine and cook until it evaporates. Add the tomatoes, tomato paste, salt and pepper; simmer, covered, stirring occasionally for 1 hour. Put the low-fat ricotta in the food processor with about ¼ cup sauce and process. Stir into the pot of sauce and heat through, but do not boil.
*Good over pasta.

****

LOW-CAL BUTTERMILK SAUCE I

1 ½ cups buttermilk
½ cup green bell pepper
2 tsp. minced onion

½ cup tomato paste
1 tbsp. lemon juice

¼ tsp. salt
black pepper

Finely chop green peppers. In a medium bowl, whisk together buttermilk and tomato paste until smooth. Stir in remaining ingredients until well blended; cover and chill several hours.
*Good over fish or vegetables.

LOW-CAL BUTTERMILK SAUCE II

2 tbsp. scallions, minced
¼ cup cucumber, grated
¼ tsp. black peeper

1 tbsp. Dijon mustard
2 tsp. parsley, chopped
2 tsp. lemon juice

1 cup buttermilk
¼ tsp. dill weed

Mix all ingredients in a jar; shake to blend. Chill in freezer 10 minutes.
*Good over salad or vegetables.

****

LOW-CAL CHINESE SAUCE

1 ½ tsp. soy sauce
1 thin slice ginger
¼ tsp. sesame oil
2-13 ¾ oz. cans chicken broth
2 cups vegetables: peeled, slice broccoli, bok choy, pea pods and celery

few sprigs parsley
2 tsp. dry sherry
Dash hot oil
½ chicken breast on bone

2 scallions
1 sm. onion
½ pkg. peas

In a large saucepan, simmer the chicken broth, chicken, onion and parsley for 20 minutes. Remove the chicken and vegetable and set the chicken in the refrigerator to cool. Add the ginger to the broth and reheat with sherry, soy sauce, sesame oil and hot oil to taste. Dice chicken after it cools, and add to the broth with the 2 cups of vegetables and peas.
*Good over rice.

****

LOW-CAL CLAM SAUCE

1 cup white wine
½ tsp. oregano

2 lg. cloves garlic
Salt and black pepper

2 doz. clams
1 cup parsley

Place clams in a saucepan, with about an inch of white wine, the sliced garlic and oregano. Cover and steam for 5 to 10 minutes, until all the clams are open. Remove the clams and keep warm, season with salt, pepper and parsley to the liquid.
*Good over spaghetti.

****

LOW-CAL CHOCOLATE FRUIT SAUCE

1 cup plain yogurt
2 tsp. unsweetened cocoa

½ cup pineapple juice

2 bananas

Place all ingredients in a blender and mix until smooth.
*Good over ice cream.

LOW-CAL CREAMY CHILI SAUCE

½ cup fat-free mayonnaise
2 drops hot sauce

3 tbsp. chili sauce
dash ground cumin

1 tbsp. coriander

Plain low-fat yogurt may be substituted for mayonnaise. Chop fresh coriander. Place all ingredients in a small bowl and mix until well blended. Cover and chill.
*Good over beans, lettuce or fish.

****

LOW-CAL EGGPLANT SAUCE

2 cups eggplant, chopped
1 tsp. oregano
12 oz. tomatoes, chopped

½ onion
3 cloves garlic
pepper

2 tbsp. basil
1 tsp. olive oil
½ cup mushrooms

Peel eggplant and chop onion. Place all ingredients in a large microwave bowl. Cook for 20 minutes, on high, in a microwave oven. Remove from microwave oven and mash all ingredients together.
*Good over chicken or pasta.

****

LOW-CAL GORGONZOLA SAUCE

½ cup low-fat mayonnaise
2 oz. Gorgonzola cheese

½ cup plain yogurt
1 tsp. white wine vinegar

1 garlic clove
salt and pepper

Coarsely chop Gorgonzola cheese and mince garlic clove. Combine mayonnaise with remaining ingredients in a medium bowl, until well blended.
*Good over red cabbage or chicken salad.

****

LOW-CAL HONEY SAUCE

2 tbsp. fresh parsley
3 tbsp. cider vinegar
½ tsp. powdered mustard
½ tsp. celery seed

⅓ cup + 2 tsp. safflower oil
1 tbsp. lemon juice
½ tsp. paprika

1 sm. onion
3 tbsp. honey
½ tsp. salt

In a food processor, process onion and parsley until finely chopped. Gradually add liquids until blended. Add seasonings and process just long enough to mix through.
*Good over fruit salads or lettuce.

****

LOW-CAL ISLAND SAUCE

1 cup non-fat mayonnaise
2 tbsp. chives
2 tbsp. cornichons, chopped (optional)

2 ripe tomatoes
1 tbsp. cilantro (optional)

3 tbsp. pimento
cayenne pepper

Chopped red bell pepper may be used in place of pimento and scallions may be substituted for chives. Peel and chop the tomatoes; mix all ingredients in a mixing bowl. Do not use blender.
*Good over shrimp or seafood dishes.

****

LOW-CAL LEMON SAUCE

4 tbsp. sesame seed oil
½ tsp. vegetable seasoning

3 tbsp. lemon juice
2-3 tbsp. Parmesan cheese

2 tbsp. parsley
¼ tsp. black pepper

Safflower oil may be substituted for sesame seed oil and Romano cheese may be used in place of Parmesan cheese. Place all ingredients except cheese into a blender. Blend until parsley is finely chopped. Add cheese.
*Good over salad.

****

LOW-CAL LEMON-CURRY SAUCE

1 cup plain yogurt
½ tsp. grated lemon peel

½ tsp. curry powder

2-3 drops hot sauce

Combine all ingredients in a small bowl and mix until well blended.
*Good over shrimp salad or over greens.

****

LOW-CAL MADRAS SAUCE

1 cup low-fat mayonnaise
1-2 tsp. curry powder

1 tbsp. shallots, chopped
½ ripe banana

1 tsp. sesame-seed oil
cayenne pepper

Puree banana and mayonnaise together. In a small skillet, lightly sauté shallots in oil until they are glazed. Add curry powder; add and mix the remaining ingredients.
*Good over fish.

****

LOW-CAL MICHEL SAUCE

1 sm. celery stalk	½ cup broth	1 onion
3 oz. low-fat cream cheese	1 tbsp. arrowroot	water
2 tsp. fresh lemon juice	grated nutmeg	cayenne pepper

Place onion and celery in saucepan with water to cover. Simmer until tender, about 45 minutes, covered. Drain, reserving ½ cup of broth. In a blender or food processor, puree onion, celery, broth, cream cheese, arrowroot, lemon juice and dash of nutmeg and cayenne pepper. Reheat before using.
*Good over poultry, fish or vegetables.

****

LOW-CAL MOCK BÉARNAISE SAUCE

½ cup plain, low-fat yogurt	2 tbsp. shallots, chopped	2 tbsp. dried tarragon
3 tbsp. tarragon vinegar	¼ cup dry white wine	2 tsp. dijon mustard
1 hard-cooked egg, chopped	3 tbsp. parsley, minced	1 tsp. black pepper
3 tbsp. tarragon (optional)		

Place yogurt in blender. In a small saucepan combine shallots, tarragon, white wine, vinegar, and pepper. Simmer until reduced by about half. Cool. Strain mixture over mustard and egg. Add mixture to yogurt in a blender. Blend until smooth. Add parsley and tarragon to mixture and blend briefly.
*Good over fish, seafood or all meats.

****

LOW-CAL NO-OIL ROQUEFORT SAUCE

1 cup tomato juice	¼ cup lemon juice	2 tbsp. grated onion
1 oz. Roquefort cheese, crumbled		

Combine all ingredients in blender and mix until smooth and creamy.
*Good over lettuce.

****

LOW-CAL POPPY-SEED SAUCE

⅓ cup fat-free mayonnaise	⅓ cup plain yogurt	¼ tsp. salt
1 tsp. shredded orange peel	1 tsp. poppy seeds	2 tsp. sugar

Combine all ingredients in a small bowl, and mix until well blended.
*Good over poultry, salads or over vegetables.

****

LOW-CAL PRIMAVERA SAUCE

2 cups light marinara sauce   ½ cup mushroom   2 tbsp. pesto
½ cups asparagus tips   ½ cup zucchini   ½ cup peas
2 tbsp. low-fat ricotta

Put the marinara sauce, ricotta and pesto in the blender and puree until smooth. In saucepan, heat the creamy sauce with mushrooms, zucchini, asparagus and peas.
*Good over fettuccine.

****

LOW-CAL RAIFORT SAUCE

½ cup plain, low-fat yogurt   2 tbsp. creamed horseradish   1 tbsp. Dijon mustard
Cayenne pepper   radish, sliced   2 scallions, chopped

Place all ingredients in a bowl and with a wire whisk, mix until smooth. Top with radish and/or scallions.
*Good over fish or as a dip.

****

LOW-CAL RASPBERRY SAUCE I

½ cup plain, low-fat yogurt   ¼ cup raspberries   2 tsp. honey

Place all ingredients in a blender and mix until just blended (over-blending raspberry seeds will make the sauce tart).
*Good over fruit salad.

****

LOW-CAL RASPBERRY SAUCE II

½ cup raspberry preserve   2 tsp. raspberry liqueur   ¼ cup water

Chambord liqueur may be used in place of raspberry liqueur. Mix water and raspberry preserve in a bowl, then add liqueur and continue to mix until well blended.
*Good over desserts or ice cream.

****

LOW-CAL TOMATO PIMENTO SAUCE

½ cup plain, low-fat yogurt
¼ cup scallions, diced
1 tsp. dried whole oregano

½ cup plum tomatoes
1 tsp. garlic, minced

¼ cup pimento, diced
cayenne pepper

Peel and chop tomatoes. Whisk yogurt in a bowl, until smooth. Add other ingredients and mix until well blended.
*Good over salad or fish.

****

LOW-CAL VEGETARIAN SAUCE

1 celery stalk, chopped
¼ cup parsley, chopped
¼ cup onion, chopped

¼ cup chives, chopped
4 tbsp. cider vinegar
2 tsp. vegetable seasoning

1 med. tomato
1 cup water

Peel and quarter the tomato. Place all ingredients in a saucepan and bring to a boil. Simmer 5 minutes. Place the mixture in a blender and puree. Chill before serving.
*Good over salad, vegetables or as a dip.

****

LOW-CAL VINCENT SAUCE

1 cup low-fat mayonnaise mixture

1 tbsp. fresh lemon juice

1 cup fresh herb

Use parsley, chives or scallions, mint, sweet basil, and tarragon to make the fresh herb mixture. Place all ingredients into a blender and mix until well combined, but herbs are still leafy. Serve immediately.
*Good over salmon or any fish.

****

LOW-FAT YOGURT SAUCE

¼ cup instant nonfat dry-milk

2 tbsp. low-fat yogurt

1 qt. 2% milk

Mix milk and dry-milk solids in a medium saucepan. Heat to scalding; cool and stir in yogurt. Transfer mixture to a glass bowl, cover with plastic wrap; wrap bowl securely in a heavy bath towel. Set in warm place for 4 to 6 hours, (an oven with a pilot light is a good place) until yogurt has formed. Place several layers of paper toweling directly on yogurt; refrigerate covered until cold.
*Good over pasta or vegetables.

****

LYONNAISE SAUCE

2 onions, thinly sliced
1 garlic clove, pressed
½ tsp. celery seeds
¼ cup mozzarella, grated

1 tbsp. parsley
1 tsp. cumin
2 cups chicken stock
salt and pepper

1 tbsp. oil
1 tbsp. butter
2 tbsp. flour

Heat all ingredients, except mozzarella, in a saucepan, for 5 minutes. Then add cheese and cook for 2 minutes more.
*Good over veal.

****

MADEIRA SAUCE I

| 1 ½ cups Espagnole Sauce | ⅓ cup Madeira | 2 tbsp. butter |

In a skillet, over low heat, add all but 1 tablespoon Madeira to the drippings of cooked meat, stir with wooden spoon. In a small saucepan, simmer Espagnole Sauce over low heat until reduced to about 1 cup; add to skillet, stir well. Melt in butter. Add remaining tablespoon of Madeira immediately before serving. Serve hot.
*Good over poultry.

****

MADEIRA SAUCE II

1 cup Chicken stock	Juice of 1 lemon	¼ tsp. salt
⅓ cup Madeira wine	1 tbsp. arrowroot	Cold water
1 tsp. Worcestershire Sauce	1 tbsp. parsley	

Heat stock, lemon juice, Worcestershire sauce, salt and Madeira in a saucepan. Mix arrowroot with a little cold water, stir into stock. Simmer, stirring constantly, until thickened, about 3 minutes. Stir in parsley. Serve immediately.
*Good over poultry.

****

MADEIRA SAUCE III

| ½ med. Bermuda onion | 1 cup Madeira | 1 tbsp. butter |
| Salt, pepper and basil | 1 tsp. cornstarch | 1 apple |

Peel, core and mince apple. Mince onion. Mix all ingredients together in a saucepan, cook over medium heat, stirring constantly, about 5 minutes until sauce thickens.
*Good over poultry or pork.

****

MADEIRA SAUCE IV

¼ cup celery	¼ cup carrot	½ bay leaf
2 tbsp. green onion	1 tbsp. cooking oil	Pinch thyme
1 chicken bouillon cube	2 beef bouillon cubes	1 qt. water
1 tbsp. tomato sauce	⅓ cup Madeira	2 tbsp. flour
black pepper to taste	¼ cup water	

Cook chopped celery, carrot and green onion in hot oil in a large saucepan until dark brown, but not burned. Stir in 1 quart water, bouillon cubes, bay leaf, thyme, and pepper. Bring to a boil and simmer until liquid is reduced by half. Strain the liquid. Stir in tomato sauce and bring to a boil. Shake ¼ cup of water and flour in a covered jar. Stir the flour, slowly into the boiling mixture, continue stirring. Cook 1 to 2 minutes, then simmer about 30 minutes, stirring occasionally. Just before serving, stir Madeira into sauce and bring sauce to a boil.
*Good over poultry.

MADEIRA SAUCE V

4 lg. sliced mushrooms
1 ½ cups brown sauce

2 tbsp. shallots, chopped
⅓ cup Madeira

1 tbsp. butter
Salt and pepper

Heat butter in a skillet and add the mushrooms. Sprinkle with salt and pepper to taste and cook until the mushrooms give up their liquid. Add the shallots and cook, stirring, until most of the liquid evaporates. Add the wine and cook 1 minute, add the brown sauce and simmer 15 minutes longer. Serve hot.
*Good for Roasts and sautéed meat dishes.

****

MAGIC MARINADE SAUCE

½ cup balsamic vinegar
2 pressed garlic cloves

½ cup soy sauce

2 tbsp. ginger

Rice wine vinegar may substitute balsamic vinegar. Mix all ingredients together, in a bowl, until well blended. Use for marinating, skinless chicken breasts; fish, like tuna, salmon and swordfish, or vegetables. Soak ingredients in marinade for at least 1 hour before cooking.
*Good over poultry, fish or vegetables.

****

MALTAISE SAUCE

8 tbsp. melted butter
1 tsp. lemon juice
Salt and pepper

2 tbsp. orange juice
1 tsp. grated orange rind

3 egg yolks
1 tbsp. water

Put the yolks, water and lemon juice into the top of a double boiler, over simmering water. Beat the mixture with a whisk until it is light colored and fluffy. Gradually add the butter, beating rapidly with the whisk. Add salt and pepper to taste. Beat in the orange juice and orange rind and remove from the heat.
*Good over desserts.

****

MAMA MIA TOMATO SAUCE

1 lb. ground beef or pork
2 lbs. 3-oz. Italian tomatoes
1 cup dry red wine

1 lg. onion, chopped
1 garlic clove, minced
2 tsp. mixed Italian herbs

6 oz. tomato paste
1 tsp. salt

Brown chopped meat in large saucepan, 10 minutes. Drain on paper towels. Pour off all but 3 tablespoons of fat. Sauté onion and garlic in the fat until soft; stir in tomatoes, tomato paste, Italian herbs, salt and wine. Crumble meat into sauce; bring to a boil; reduce heat; simmer, uncovered, stirring frequently, 45 minutes, or until sauce thickens.
*Good for lasagna, over ravioli or pasta.

MANDARIN SAUCE

¾ cup orange juice
2 tsp. Dijon mustard
Dash nutmeg

1 tbsp. cornstarch
2 tbsp. lemon juice
11 oz. can mandarin oranges, drained

2 tbsp. sugar
¼ tsp. ginger

Combine all ingredients, except mandarin oranges, in small saucepan. Cook over medium heat, stirring constantly, until thickened. Gently stir in oranges and heat.
*Good over poultry.

****

MANGO SAUCE I

2 tsp. lime juice
2 tbsp. sugar

1 med. mango

2 tbsp. rum

Peel and seed mango, then combine all ingredients in a food processor and puree until smooth. Transfer to a bowl, cover and refrigerate until serving time.
*Good over ice cream, pound cake or custard.

****

MANGO SAUCE II

1 lg. ripe mango
1 sm. garlic clove
1 cup chicken stock

1 tbsp. peanut oil
¼ tsp. minced ginger

1 shallot
Salt and pepper

Heat oil in medium skillet, over medium heat. Add mango, shallot, garlic and ginger and cook until softened, stirring frequently, about 5 minutes. Add stock and boil until reduced by half; cool, cover and refrigerate. Transfer to blender and puree. Strain into small saucepan and heat; season with salt and pepper.
*Good on fish.

****

MANGO GLAZING SAUCE

1 lg. crushed garlic clove
1 tsp. grated ginger
½ cup med. dry sherry
1 ½ tbsp. vegetable oil

1 tsp. dry rosemary
1 tsp. Dijon mustard
½ cup mango chutney
1 ½ tbsp. soy sauce

½ tsp. thyme
1 ½ tsp. paprika
pepper to taste

Mix all ingredients together in a bowl, until well blended. Let stand for an hour before using.
*Good over ham.

****

MANGO VINAIGRETTE SAUCE

⅓ cup rice-wine vinegar
1 ½ tbsp. fresh chives
¼ tsp. white pepper

⅓ cup vegetable oil
1 tbsp. marjoram, chopped
¼ tsp. anise seed

2 med. mangoes
2 tbsp. honey
½ tsp. salt

One teaspoon-dried marjoram may be used in place of fresh marjoram. Peel, seed and puree the mangoes. Chop the fresh chives and marjoram. Mix all ingredients together in a bowl, until well blended. *Good over vegetables.

****

MAPLE CRANBERRY SAUCE

12 oz. fresh cranberries
Grated zest of 1 orange

1 cup maple syrup
1 cup cranberry-raspberry juice

1 cup walnut halves

Combine cranberries, maple syrup, juice and orange zest in a saucepan. Bring to a boil, lower heat and cook for about 10 minutes, or until cranberries pop open. Carefully skim off any foam that forms on the surface. Stir in the walnuts. *Good over poultry.

****

MAPLE MUSTARD SAUCE

¾ cup cider vinegar
2 lg. egg yolks

¾ cup dry mustard

⅔ cup maple syrup

Place vinegar in a small saucepan and bring to a boil. Remove from heat and stir in mustard. Cover and let stand overnight at room temperature. Beat in maple syrup and egg yolks. Place pan over low heat and cook, stirring constantly, until thickened.
*Good over poultry.

****

MAPLE QUICK SAUCE

1 ¼ cups granulated sugar
1 ¼ cups brown sugar

3 tbsp. margarine
¾ tsp. maple flavoring

1 ¼ cups water

Combine water and sugars in a small saucepan. Bring to a boil; stir to dissolve sugars. Lower heat and simmer 5 minutes. Remove from heat, and stir in margarine and maple flavoring until blended.
*Good over bananas.

****

MARCHAND DE VIN BUTTER SAUCE

1 ½ tsp. minced shallots
½ cup dry red wine
1 tbsp. minced parsley

3 tbsp. beef broth
2 tsp. lemon juice
salt and pepper

2 tbsp. butter
1 tsp. Cognac

Place wine and shallots in a small saucepan, simmer until the mixture is almost dry. Add beef broth, reduce again by half. Stir in butter, add pepper and salt. Just before serving stir in Cognac, lemon juice and parsley.
*Good over steak.

****

MARINADE DARK SAUCE

1 ¾ cups dark brown sugar
1 tsp. ground ginger
1 cup chunky peanut butter
½ tsp. grated coriander

1 ⅓ cups soy sauce
¾ cup dark molasses
½ cup onion, chopped
1 med. lemon

2 cups water
½ tsp. pepper
1 tsp. sugar

Stir water and sugar in a 2-quart saucepan over medium-high heat until sugar dissolves. Bring to a brisk boil; boil 5 minutes. Reduce heat to medium-low; stir in soy sauce, molasses, ginger, pepper and coriander. Simmer 3 minutes. Pour 1 ½ cups into a small bowl; blend in peanut butter. Cover and set aside for dipping sauce. Reserve remainder.
*Good over pork.

****

MARINADE SAUCE

½ cup dark brown sugar
½ tsp. ground ginger
1 tbsp. gin or rum

1 cup pineapple juice
½ tsp. garlic powder
½ cup cold water

1 cup soy sauce
2 tbsp. cornstarch

Combine pineapple juice, soy sauce, sugar, ginger, garlic powder and liquor in a saucepan. Stir and bring to a boil. Blend cornstarch and cold water in a bowl; stir into boiling sauce and simmer 2 minutes. Cool to room temperature.
*Good for chicken, beef or pork.

****

MARINARA SAUCE I

1 to 2 sm. fresh red chilies
1 tbsp. drained capers
2 cloves garlic

2 tsp. oregano, chopped
1 med. onion, chopped
12 lg. pitted, chopped ripe olives

1 lb. ripe tomatoes
½ cup olive oil

Strain canned tomatoes may be used in place of fresh tomatoes. Slice chilies and remove seeds. Marinate the olives, chilies and capers in 4 tablespoons oil for at least 1 hour, in a glass bowl. Sauté the onion and garlic in the remaining oil until golden. Add the oregano. Peel, seed and chop fresh tomatoes. Turn all ingredients into a large skillet and cook over medium-high heat until the mixture thickens and darkens slightly. Remove chilies. Serve the sauce hot.
*Good over pasta.

****

MARINARA SAUCE II

2-4 cloves garlic, sliced
⅛ tsp. black pepper
1 ½ tsp. salt

3 ½ cups tomatoes
½ cup olive oil

1 tsp. oregano
1 tsp. parsley

Heat olive oil in a saucepan, add garlic cloves and sauté until light brown. Discard them. Add tomatoes slowly, stirring constantly. Cook rapidly for about ½ hour, or until thickened. Stir occasionally to avoid sticking. Then add oregano and parsley and cook for another ½ hour. If sauce becomes too thick, add up to ½ cup water.
*Good for pasta.

****

MARINATED ROASTED PEPPER SAUCE

4 roasted red peppers
1 tbsp. parsley, chopped

2 tbsp. red wine vinegar
2 cloves garlic

¼ cup olive oil

Mix oil, vinegar and garlic in a bowl. Add pepper strips and marinate for 2 hours. Add parsley and put in blender. *Good over vegetables.

****

MARMALADE LIQUEUR SAUCE

4 oz. marmalade
2 tbsp. Grand Marnier

2 tbsp. lemon juice

2 tbsp. water

In a small saucepan, combine marmalade, juice and water; bring to a boil over medium heat. Simmer over low heat for 1 to 2 minutes, stirring occasionally. Remove from heat. If serving hot, stir in the liqueur and serve at once. If using warm, cool to desired temperature, then stir in the liqueur.
*Good over ice cream or desserts.

MARMALADE SAUCE

¼ cup raisins, chopped
¼ cup orange marmalade

⅔ cup orange juice
3 tbsp. lemon juice

1 tbsp. brown sugar

Simmer brown sugar, orange juice, marmalade, lemon juice and raisins in a small saucepan for 5 minutes.
*Good over ice cream or desserts.

****

MARSHMALLOW CREAM SAUCE

1 6-oz. pkg. marshmallows

1 pint half and half

2 tbsp. cornstarch

Blend cornstarch with a portion of half and half in a medium size saucepan. Stir in remaining half and half and marshmallows. Cook over medium heat, stirring constantly, until mixture thickens and marshmallows melt.
*Good over desserts or fruit.

****

MASCARPONE SAUCE

4 tbsp. mascarpone cheese
Parmesan cheese to taste

2 tbsp. heavy cream
1 lb. spinach

Pepper

Puree spinach in a blender or food processor until smooth. Combine spinach, cheese, cream and pepper to taste in a saucepan over low heat.
*Good for pasta.

****

MATELOTE SAUCE

3 cups red or white wine
½ cup Fish Stock
1 ½ tbsp. all purpose flour

Red (cayenne) pepper
2 tbsp. butter

1 garlic clove
Extra butter

Melt 1 tablespoon of butter in a saucepan and sauté crushed garlic until golden. Remove garlic and add Fish Stock. Bring to a boil and reduce sauce to about half. Pour in wine and continue cooking over medium heat until the liquid has reduced to about 1 ½ cups. Combine remaining butter with flour to make a paste. Add paste, a little at a time, stirring constantly. Bring to a boil. Float a little extra butter on top. Sprinkle with red pepper and serve hot.
*Good over pasta.

MAYONNAISE SAUCE I

| 1 tsp. Dijon mustard | Ground white pepper | 2 egg yolks |
| 1 tbsp. tarragon or white wine | 1 ½ cups oil | salt |

Place the yolks, mustard, half the vinegar, salt and pepper to taste in a large bowl. Beat for 1 minute with a wire whisk. Add oil slowly, whipping vigorously until all the oil is incorporated. If too thick, beat in remainder of the vinegar.
*Good over fish.

****

MAYONNAISE SAUCE II

| 4 medium egg yolks | ⅛ tsp. white pepper | 1 tsp. salt |
| 2 cups vegetable oil | 1 tbsp. wine vinegar | |

Place egg yolks, salt, and pepper in bowl, beat at medium speed until thick, pale and fluffy. Add 5 ounces of oil in a very thin stream, beating constantly, until thickened and oil is absorbed. Beat in vinegar. Add remaining oil slowly, beating constantly, until all oil is blended into mixture.
*Good over hot or cold pasta.

****

MAYONNAISE SAUCE III

| 1 ½ tsp. wine vinegar | ¼ tsp. dry mustard | 2 egg yolks |
| 1 cup olive oil | ½ tsp. lemon juice | ½ tsp. salt |

Place egg yolks, salt, mustard and 1 teaspoon of vinegar; beat vigorously or at low speed with an electric mixer. Add half the oil, drop by drop and remaining vinegar. Beat in the rest of the oil in steady stream. Add lemon juice.
*Good over hot or cold pasta.

****

MAYONNAISE SAUCE IV

1 tbsp. red-wine vinegar	1 cup salad oil	1 egg
1 tbsp. lemon juice	½ tsp. salt	⅛ tsp. paprika
¼ tsp. dry mustard	Dash cayenne pepper	

Pour ¼ cup oil into electric blender. Add vinegar, lemon juice, egg, and seasonings, blend 5 seconds. Add remaining ingredients and beat well.
*Good over vegetables or pasta.

MAYONNAISE SAUCE V

1 ½ cups Mayonnaise
1 lemon, sectioned

Strained juice of 1 lemon

1 tsp. dry mustard

Place mayonnaise in large bowl. Combine lemon juice and mustard in small bowl; stir until well blended. Fold lemon juice mixture into mayonnaise until blended. Chop lemon segments fine; fold into mayonnaise
*Good over hot or cold pasta.

****

MAYONNAISE SAUCE VI

½ tsp. Worcestershire sauce
1 tsp. white vinegar
Several drops Tabasco sauce

Juice of ½ lemon
1 cup peanut oil
1 tbsp. Dijon mustard

1 egg yolk
Salt and pepper

Put mustard, egg yolk, Worcestershire sauce, vinegar, salt, pepper and Tabasco in mixing bowl. Beat with wire whisk, then gradually beat in oil. Add lemon juice; blend well.
*Good over poultry.

****

MEAT SAUCE I

1 ½ lbs. beef round
12 pieces dried mushrooms
1 tbsp. minced parsley
½ cup dry red wine
4 cups beef consommé

½ sm. minced onion
1 garlic clove
Dash of nutmeg
1 cup tomato paste

3 tbsp. olive oil
½ cup butter
½ tsp. salt
Ground pepper

Heat oil in large skillet and brown meat; set aside. In saucepan, sauté onion and garlic in butter over low heat. Discard garlic when golden brown. Add parsley, salt, nutmeg and pepper, cook 5 minutes. Add mushrooms; cook 5 minutes longer. Add wine and cook until wine evaporates, 5 to 6 minutes. Add tomato paste and just enough consommé for a thick sauce; cook 10 to 15 minutes. Add meat; cover and cook 20 minutes, turning meat often. Stir in remaining consommé a little at a time. Cover and cook 35 minutes. Remove meat, cut in serving portions and serve as desired.
*Good over pasta.

****

MEAT SAUCE II

2 35-oz. cans plum tomatoes
3 lbs. pork neck bones
Pinch crushed red pepper
1 lb. ground chuck
Fresh ground pepper

4 cloves garlic
2 cans tomato paste
1 ½ cups water
1 garlic clove

2 lg. onions
Olive oil
Salt
2 lg. eggs

Put tomatoes through a food mill, then into a 6-quart saucepan, discard seeds, simmer over medium heat. Rinse neck bones under cold water, dry and set aside. Heat olive oil in skillet, over medium heat. Carefully slip pork bones into hot oil and brown; add them to the simmering tomatoes. Pour off all but a thin film of oil into a bowl and set aside. Lightly brown garlic in remaining oil, then add to simmering mixture. Add chopped onions to pan and cook until soft and golden, about 10 minutes, stirring occasionally. Stir in tomato paste and cook 10 minutes longer, stirring constantly. Add water and seasoning. Partially cover and allow to simmer for about 1 ½ hours. Stir occasionally.
*Good over pasta.

****

MEDITERRANEAN SAUCE

½ cup dry white wine
¼ cup tomato paste
¼ cup black olives
⅛ tsp. red pepper flakes

½ cup minced onion
1 tbsp. minced garlic
¼ cup green olives
½ cup clam juice

1 tbsp. olive oil
1 cup tomato
½ tsp. capers

Put olive oil, onion and garlic in a 2-quart casserole. Microwave on high, uncovered, 2 to 3 minutes to soften. Stir in all ingredients and microwave on high, uncovered, 13 to 15 minutes to thicken, stirring twice. Set aside.
*Good over fish.

****

MEDIUM WHITE SAUCE

1 cup milk
½ tsp. salt

2 tbsp. butter
⅛ tsp. pepper

2 tbsp. flour

Heat butter in a saucepan. Blend in flour, salt, and pepper; heat and stir until bubbly. Gradually add the milk, stirring until smooth. Bring to a boil; cook and stir 1 to 2 minutes longer.

Optional: for thin white sauce, use 2 tbsp. flour and 1 tbsp. butter.
*Good over pasta.

MELBA SAUCE I

2 cups raspberries
1 tsp. arrowroot

Juice of ½ lemon
1 tbsp. cold water

2 tbsp. sugar
2 tbsp. water

Strawberries may be used as a substitution for raspberries. Cornstarch may substitute arrowroot. Wash berries; place in small saucepan with water, sugar and lemon juice. Simmer gently 5 minutes; press through fine sieve. Return to clean saucepan; thicken with arrowroot dissolved in cold water. Chill before serving.
*Good over ice cream or desserts.

****

MELBA SAUCE II

1 pkg. frozen raspberries
1 ½ tsp. cornstarch

½ cup currant jelly

1 tbsp. cold water

In a saucepan, stir together raspberries and jelly. Bring to a boil, stirring occasionally. Blend cornstarch with water. Add to saucepan and cook, stirring, until clear. Serve slightly warm or cold.
*Good over ice cream or desserts.

****

MELISSA BRANDY SAUCE

Sliced peel of ¼ lemon
½ cup sugar syrup

2 tbsp. dried Melissa

1 ½ cups brandy

Soak the Melissa and lemon peel in brandy, in a covered bowl or jar, for 2 days. Strain and sweeten. Mature several weeks.
*Good over ice cream or desserts.

****

MELISSA VODKA SAUCE

2 ½ tsp. dried Melissa
2 peppermint leaves
½ cup sugar syrup

Pinch of coriander
Pinch of cinnamon

Peel of ¼ lemon
1 cup vodka

Place all ingredients in a bottle and soak for 3 weeks. Shake the jar daily during the 3 weeks. Strain into a dark bottle, adding more sugar to taste. Mature for 2 months.
*Good over ice cream or desserts.

MELONS MARINES SAUCE

1 sm. mature coconut
½ lb. fresh cherries
4 tbsp. white rum

1 sm. honeydew
3 tbsp. coconut milk
1 lg. pineapple

1 sm. cantaloupe
3 tbsp. amaretto

Mix all ingredients together in a food processor, until well blended. Marinade.
*Good over ice cream or desserts.

****

MEUNIERE SAUCE

2 tbsp. green onions, chopped
1 tbsp. parsley, chopped
Dash Worcestershire sauce

2 tbsp. lemon juice
½ tsp. white pepper
Dash liquid hot pepper sauce

½ cup margarine
½ tsp. salt

Mix all ingredients together in a saucepan, until well blended. Simmer for 2 to 3 minutes over low heat.
*Good over steak.

****

MEXICAN MARINADE SAUCE

1 garlic clove, chopped
2 tbsp. fresh lime juice

10 ancho chilies
½ cup olive oil

½ tsp. salt
2 tbsp. tequila

Place chilies in a heatproof bowl and cover with boiling water. Weigh chilies down with a plate so they are fully submerged; let stand 2 hours to soften. Remove and discard stems and seeds from chilies. In a food processor, puree chilies with garlic, salt, tequila and lime juice. Slowly pour in oil.
*Good over poultry or fish.

****

MEXICAN SAUCE

¼ cup yellow onion, chopped
1 16 oz. can peeled tomatoes
1 green chili, finely chopped

½ tsp. chili powder
2 tbsp. tomato paste
1 tbsp. vegetable oil

1 garlic clove
Salt and pepper

Heat vegetable oil in a medium-size saucepan, add and sauté onion and garlic until softened. Stir in tomato paste, chili powder, tomatoes and their juice. Simmer uncovered 10 minutes. Remove sauce from heat and puree in a blender or food processor until smooth, or press through a sieve to give a smooth sauce. Return to heat, add chopped green chili and simmer 15 minutes. Season with salt and pepper to taste.
*Good over all meats.

MEXICAN STYLE SAUCE I

1 red bell pepper	1 sm. white onion	1 med. tomato
Salt and pepper	Hot pepper flakes	salad oil

Process cored and seeded pepper until finely minced in a food processor; place in a bowl. Mince onion and peeled and seeded tomato. Combine with minced pepper. Season to taste with salt and pepper and drizzle in a little salad oil.
*Good with fish.

****

MEXICAN STYLE SAUCE II

2 sm. onions, chopped	¼ cup vegetable oil	1 ¼ cups water
¾ lb. lean round beef	1 ¼ cups tomato sauce	2 lg. tomatoes
1 tsp. chili powder	2 tsp. ground cumin	½ tsp. pepper
1 garlic clove, chopped	2 tbsp. parsley, chopped	½ tsp. salt
½ cup grated Cheddar cheese		

Heat oil in a saucepan; sauté onions and garlic until light gold and soft. Cut meat into small pieces, add to the onions; cook over medium heat until well browned. Mix the tomato sauce and water; add the rest of ingredients. Bring just to boil; reduce heat and cook gently for 2 to 3 hours.
*Good over pasta or rice.

****

MIMOSA SAUCE

½ cup strawberries	1 cup orange juice	1 tbsp. cornstarch
½ cup dry champagne	1 orange, sliced	2 tbsp. honey

Whisk orange juice and cornstarch in a saucepan, until well blended, over medium heat. Add champagne, stirring until thickened, boil 1 minute. Remove from heat, stir in honey, orange slice and strawberries. Serve warm.
*Good over desserts.

****

MINT GRAPEFRUIT SAUCE

1 cup mint jelly	1 ¼ cups sugar	1 ½ cups water

Melt mint jelly in double boiler and beat with hand mixer. Boil water and sugar together 10 minutes and add to mint jelly.
*Good over grapefruit sections.

MINT JELLY SAUCE

4 tbsp. mint jelly
4 tbsp. apple juice

1 garlic clove, minced
½ tsp. Rosemary, crushed

1 tsp. oil

Brown garlic in oil for 1 minute, remove saucepan from heat, then add all ingredients and mix well.
*Good over ham or fresh pork.

****

MINT LIQUEURS SAUCE

12-14 tbsp. fresh peppermint
1 tsp. glycerin (optional)

1 cup sugar syrup

3 cups vodka

Substitute fresh peppermint or spearmint leaves with 6 teaspoons of dried well-crumpled mint, peppermint, or spearmint leaves or 2-3 teaspoons pure mint or peppermint extract. Soak the leaves in vodka for 10 days and shake the bottle occasionally. Strain. Be sure to press all the juices from the leaves with a spoon against the strainer. Mature 2 weeks.
*Good over pork.

****

MINT SAUCE

3 tbsp. fresh mint, chopped
½ cup vinegar

1 tbsp. sugar

2 tbsp. water

Combine ingredients in a non-metal saucepan, bring to boil, cover and turn off heat. Let sit for 2 hours.
*Good over lamb.

****

MINT YOGURT SAUCE

1 cup plain yogurt
3 tbsp. lemon juice

¼ cup minced mint

¼ tsp. salt

Whisk ingredients together in a bowl. Let stand 1 hour before using.
*Good over salads.

****

MIREPOIX BROWN SAUCE

2 tbsp. cooking oil	2 tbsp. butter	1 med. carrot
1 med. onion	1 stalk celery	⅛ tsp. thyme
2 tbsp. sherry	1 bay leaf, crushed	

Coarsely grate carrot and onion. Finely chop celery. Melt butter in small saucepan; add oil. Add carrot, onion and celery; sauté until soft. Add remaining ingredients; simmer until vegetables are tender.
*Good over pasta.

****

MIXED FRUIT FLAVORS SAUCE

3 med. oranges	1 lemon	½ lime
1 cup sugar syrup	3 cups vodka or brandy or gin	

Place the fruit in a bowl or jar with alcohol; cover and let stand for 2 weeks. Strain, add sugar syrup and mature 2 more weeks.

Optional flavorings: mace, cloves, cinnamon, cardamom or vanilla.
*Good over fruit or ice cream.

****

MIZUTAKI SAUCE

2 tbsp. white wine vinegar	¼ tsp. dry mustard	1 egg
1 cup peanut oil	⅓ cup sour cream	2 tbsp. sherry
⅓ cup chicken broth	2 tbsp. soy sauce	

Combine the egg, vinegar, dry mustard and ¼ cup of oil in a blender or food processor. Process until blended, then add remaining oil in a slow steady stream. After oil is added, blend 30 seconds and pour into a bowl. Stir in sour cream, soy sauce, sherry and broth. Refrigerate several hours.
*Good over rice.

****

MOBILE SAUCE

¼ cup mayonnaise	2 tbsp. chili sauce	¼ cup ketchup
2 tbsp. minced green pepper	2 tbsp. fresh tomato	

Mix all ingredients together in a bowl, until well blended, chill and serve.
*Good over shrimp.

MOCHA CREAM SAUCE

3 tbsp. chocolate syrup
⅓ cup coffee liqueur
12 oz. can sweetened condensed milk

1 cup Irish whiskey
1 tbsp. instant coffee

2 cups light cream
1 beaten egg yolk

Combine condensed milk, cream and instant coffee in a 2-quart saucepan. Stir in coffee crystals and dissolve over medium heat. Gradually stir half the hot sauce into egg yolk; return egg-yolk mixture to the saucepan, and bring to a boil. Stir until bubbly, over medium heat, 2 minutes more. Remove from heat. Stir in whiskey, liqueur and syrup.
*Good over ice cream.

****

MOCK BÉARNAISE SAUCE

½ cup Neufchatel cheese
3 tbsp. low-fat yogurt

Juice of ½ lemon
½ tsp. dried tarragon

Dash salt
½ tsp. shallots

Substitute 1 ½ teaspoons snipped fresh tarragon leaves in place of dried tarragon. Mince shallots then process all ingredients in a blender or food processor until smooth and fluffy. Cook over simmering water until hot and thickened. Serve immediately or refrigerate and serve cold. Stir before using.
*Good over pasta.

****

MOCK CABANARA SAUCE

¼ stick sweet butter
2 eggs
¼ cup reserve pasta water

3 tbsp. flour
¼ Parmesan cheese
½ lb. cooked bacon

1 cup skim milk
fresh pepper
1 tsp. bacon fat

Beat eggs in a medium bowl, add cheese, chopped cooked bacon and fresh pepper together and set aside. Melt butter, bacon fat and flour in a saucepan until it forms a roux. Add milk and bring to a boil, add reserved pasta water, then simmer about 3 minutes or until sauce coats spoon. Add milk mixture to hot pasta, toss in egg mixture and mix well.
*Good over pasta.

****

MOCK CRÈME FRAICHE SAUCE

1 ½ cups Neufchatel cheese

6 tbsp. low-fat yogurt

Mix cheese and yogurt in a blender or food processor until smooth and fluffy. Place in covered jar and set in warm water for 2 hours. Cool and refrigerate. Stir before using.
*Good over desserts or ice cream.

MOCK HOLLANDAISE SAUCE

½ cup Neufchatel cheese   Juice of ½ lemon   Dash salt
3 tbsp. low-fat yogurt

Mix all ingredients in a blender or food processor until smooth and fluffy. Cook over simmering water until hot and thickened. Serve immediately or refrigerate and serve cold. Stir before using.
*Good over ham.

****

MOCK MAYONNAISE SAUCE

½ cup Neufchatel cheese   Juice of ½ lemon   Dash salt
3 tbsp. low-fat yogurt   1 ½ tsp. Dijon mustard   ½ tsp. sugar

Mix all ingredients in a blender or food processor until smooth and fluffy. Cook over simmering water until hot and thickened. Serve immediately or refrigerate and serve cold. Stir before using.
*Good on sandwiches, cold pasta or hard cooked eggs.

****

MOCK SOUR CREAM SAUCE

2 tbsp. skim milk   1 tbsp. lemon juice   ¼ tsp. salt
1 cup low-fat cottage cheese

Place all ingredients in a blender and mix on medium-high speed until smooth and creamy.
*Good over baked potatoes.

****

MOLASSES BARBECUE SAUCE

¼ cup grated onion   2 tbsp. cider vinegar   ¾ cup ketchup
1 tbsp. mustard   Worcestershire sauce   Molasses
Hot pepper sauce

Mix all ingredients in a bowl, until well blended.
*Good over ribs or chicken.

MOLHO DE PIMENTA SAUCE

2 tbsp. fresh lime juice   2 tbsp. olive oil   ½ sm. onion
1 tbsp. hot red peppers preserved in vinegar

Place all ingredients except the oil in a small bowl. Allow to stand for 20 minutes or longer. Just before serving, mash to a paste, and stir in the olive oil.
*Good over shrimp.

****

MOREL SAUCE

1 ½ cups boiling water   1 oz. dried morels   1 lg. shallot
5 tbsp. unsalted butter   ½ cup white wine   Salt and pepper
3 cups heavy cream   1 cup chicken stock   1 tbsp. port wine
1 tsp. lemon juice

Pour boiling water over morels and let steep about 1 hour. Drain, separate morels and liquid. Slice morels in half lengthwise. Strain liquid and boil over medium-high heat until reduced to ½ cup, about 5 minutes. In a saucepan, sauté shallot in 2 tablespoons butter over low heat until lightly browned, about 5 minutes. Deglaze pan with wine. Reduce mixture over high heat until syrupy, about 3 minutes. Reduce cream to 1 ½ cups over medium heat, about 30 minutes. Also reduce chicken stock to 2 tablespoons over medium-high heat, about 10 minutes. Stir in morels, cream, and stock. Simmer, stirring often, 3 to 5 minutes. Add morel liquid and lemon juice; simmer, stirring often, 5 minutes. Add salt and pepper to taste. Just before serving, add port and swirl in remaining 3 tablespoons butter, bit by bit, over low heat.
*Good over pasta.

****

MORNAY CHEESE SAUCE

3 tbsp. grated Swiss   1 tbsp. butter   1 tbsp. flour
1 tbsp. Parmesan cheese   1 cup milk   Salt and pepper
½ tsp. Dijon mustard

Gruyere cheese may substitute the Swiss. Melt butter in a small saucepan; remove from heat. Add flour, stirring with wire whisk. Over moderate heat, add milk gradually. Stir constantly until thickened. Add remaining ingredients.
*Good over poultry or fish.

****

MORNAY SAUCE I

3 egg yolks, lightly beaten   2 cups Béchamel Sauce, warm   ¼ cup whipping cream
1 oz. Parmesan cheese, freshly grated

Mix together, beaten egg yolks and whipping cream in a saucepan. Add Béchamel Sauce over low heat, stirring constantly, until just boiling. Remove from heat and mix in grated cheese; stir to melt. Serve hot.
*Good over poultry or vegetables.

MORNAY SAUCE II

¼ cup grated Swiss
2 cups med. béchamel or veloute
(optional)

Pinch of nutmeg
cayenne (optional)

Salt and pepper
1-2 tbsp. butter

Bring béchamel to a boil in a saucepan. Remove from heat, and beat in the cheese until it melts and is well blended. Season to taste with salt, pepper, nutmeg, and optional cayenne. Just before serving, stir in the optional butter a bit at a time.
*Good over poultry or vegetables.

****

MORNAY SAUCE III

½ cup grated Parmesan
½ cup grated Gruyere

1 cup heavy cream
4 tbsp. unsalted butter

2 cups béchamel
2 egg yolks

Beat egg yolks, and ¼ cup cream, in a bowl, until well blended. Beat in ½ cup heated béchamel, until smooth. Place over low heat, in a saucepan, until hot. Remove from heat; blend in cheese with whisk until melted. Before serving, heat and whisk in butter.
*Good over poultry or vegetables.

****

MUSHROOM AND HAZELNUT SAUCE

3 tbsp. unsalted butter
3 tbsp. all purpose flour
4 cups chicken stock
¼ lb. shiitake mushrooms
¼ tbsp. fresh basil

¾ lb. mushrooms
½ tsp. fresh thyme
1 cup half and half
¼ tbsp. fresh oregano
Salt and white pepper

2 celery stalks
1 sm. onion
⅔ cup hazelnuts
1 leak
1 bay leaf

Melt butter in saucepan over medium heat. Add ¾ pound mushrooms, celery, onion and leek and sauté 10 minutes. Add flour and stir 5 minutes, gradually mix in stock. Add thyme, basil, oregano and bay leaf and bring to boil. Reduce heat, cover partially and simmer 45 minutes. Strain sauce through fine sieve into medium saucepan, pressing on solids with back of spoon; cool. Add half and half and hazelnuts to sauce and bring to a simmer. Season with salt and pepper.
*Good over poultry.

****

MUSHROOM FONDUE SAUCE

1 lb. mushrooms, chopped
²⁄₃ cup chicken broth
²⁄₃ cup whipping cream

¼ cup butter
1 tbsp. cornstarch
Dash cayenne pepper

2 garlic cloves
Salt and pepper

Melt butter in a medium size saucepan, add mushrooms and garlic and sauce over medium heat 10 minutes. Add broth and simmer 10 minutes. Cool slightly then puree in a blender or food processor. Blend a portion of the whipping cream with cornstarch in fondue pot. Simmer over medium heat until thickened. Season with salt, pepper and cayenne pepper.
*Good over pasta.

****

MUSHROOM PUREE SAUCE

1 tsp. lemon juice
Pinch ground nutmeg
1 tbsp. sour cream

1 tsp. water
Pinch pepper

2 oz. mushrooms
¼ tsp. salt

Put all ingredients except sour cream in a small saucepan. Simmer, uncovered, over low heat for 10 minutes. Stir in sour cream and then puree in a blender or food processor.
*Good over veal, pork or poultry.

****

MUSHROOM SAUCE I

1 cup chicken broth
½ cup sour cream
1 lg. onion, chopped

2 tbsp. melted butter
1 tsp. lemon juice
3 tbsp. flour

1 lb. mushrooms
Salt and pepper

Simmer mushrooms with onion in bouillon, in a saucepan for 15 minutes. Stir flour into mushrooms and bring to a boil, stirring. Remove from heat and stir in remaining ingredients.
*Good over all meats.

****

MUSHROOM SAUCE II

2 cups Béchamel Sauce   ⅓ lb. mushrooms   3 tbsp. butter
Salt and pepper   Paprika (optional)

Remove the stems from mushrooms and reserve for other uses. Wash caps and dry on a paper towel; finely slice. Melt butter, and sauté the mushrooms until lightly browned, over a low heat, in a medium skillet. Add mushrooms to the hot Béchamel Sauce. Season to taste with salt and pepper. Sprinkle with paprika before serving. Serve hot.
*Good over all meats.

****

MUSHROOM SAUCE III

⅓ lb. mushrooms, chopped   ¼ cup butter   1 ¼ cups milk
1 tbsp. dry sherry   2 tbsp. flour

Melt butter in a small saucepan; add mushrooms and sauté over low heat 5 minutes. Stir in flour then slowly add milk. Simmer for 5 minutes longer; add sherry. Serve warm.
*Good over poultry.

****

MUSHROOM SAUCE IV

Juice of half a lemon   ¼ lb. mushrooms   1 tbsp. butter
3 tbsp. shallots, chopped   ¾ cup heavy cream   Salt
¼ cup dry white wine   ⅛ tsp. nutmeg   Ground pepper
Pinch of cayenne pepper

Thinly slice mushrooms and sprinkle with lemon juice. Heat butter in a saucepan and add shallots. Cook briefly while stirring; add mushrooms and cook until liquid evaporates. Add wine and cook until almost evaporated. Add cream, nutmeg, cayenne, salt and pepper and cook over high heat 3 minutes.
*Good over poultry.

****

MUSTARD CREAM SAUCE

2 tbsp. butter
1 cup heavy cream
1 ½ tbsp. grainy mustard

Juice of ½ lemon
½ cup white wine

Black pepper
2 tbsp. oil

Heat butter and oil in a saucepan, add wine and stir constantly over high heat. Pour in cream and reduce until mixture coats the back of spoon. Reduce heat and stir in mustard, do not boil. Use just enough mustard for a hint of flavor.
*Good over pasta.

****

MUSTARD SAUCE I

¼ cup whipping cream
1 tsp. prepared mustard

1 cup Béchamel Sauce
1 tsp. Dijon mustard

½ lemon
Fresh herb sprigs

Combine Béchamel Sauce and cream in a saucepan. Squeeze in juice from the lemon, removing seeds. Stir in mustards. Serve hot and garnish with fresh herb.
*Good over fish.

****

MUSTARD SAUCE II

¼ cup dry mustard

¼ cup cold water

¼ cup honey

Combine dry mustard and cold water in a cup until smooth. Stir in honey until well blended. Refrigerate.
*Good over fish.

****

MUSTARD SAUCE III

2 tbsp. prepared mustard
3 tbsp. cider vinegar

1 cup brown sugar

1 tbsp. butter

Mix all ingredients together in a saucepan, until sugar is dissolved. Heat for 5 minutes.
*Good over fish.

****

MUSTARD SAUCE IV

2 tsp. Dijon mustard
½ cup dry white wine

1 cup whipping cream
3 tbsp. butter

1 cup fish stock
Salt and pepper

Combine all ingredients in a saucepan and bring to a boil, then simmer.
*Good over fish.

****

MUSTARD SAUCE V

1 tbsp. Dijon mustard
3 tbsp. mayonnaise

⅔ cup sour cream

Salt and pepper

Put mustard, sour cream and mayonnaise in a small bowl and mix together until smooth. Season with salt and pepper.
*Good over fish.

****

MUSTARD SAUCE VI

3 tbsp. mustard powder
¼ tsp. white pepper
2 tbsp. fresh lime juice

2 tbsp. olive oil
1 tsp. mint leaves
½ cup cream

1 tsp. honey
Pinch of salt

Mix mustard powder, honey, pepper and oil in a small bowl. Add cream, a spoon at a time, whisk until thick and creamy. Whisk in the mint, lime juice and salt, cover and refrigerate.
*Good over poultry.

****

MUSTARD-DILL SAUCE

4 tbsp. clarified butter
Dash hot pepper sauce
1 tsp. fresh lemon juice

2 tbsp. dry Vermouth
1 tbsp. Dijon mustard
2 tsp. fresh dill

Salt and pepper
1 cup heavy cream
2 tbsp. shallots

Heat butter in a saucepan; sauté finely chopped shallots until translucent. Add vermouth, mustard, cream, pepper sauce and lemon juice; simmer until thick enough to coat a spoon. Add dill.
*Good over fish.

****

NAPA NO TSUKEMONO SAUCE

1 head Napa cabbage	½ cup raisins	2 tbsp. coarse salt
Candied ginger, grated	3 red chilies	1 cup water

Thinly slice cabbage; place in a bowl and sprinkle with raisins and salt. Add water and chilies. Weight with plate and chill overnight. Drain and discard raisins and chilies. Serve with grated ginger.
*Good over poultry.

****

NASU NO KARASKI SAUCE

1 med. eggplant	2 tbsp. dry mustard	3 tbsp. light soy sauce
3 tbsp. mirin	1 tbsp. sugar	Salt and water

Soak eggplant in salted water for 1 hour. In a bowl, mix mustard, soy sauce, mirin and sugar. Drain eggplant, place in bowl and pour in dressing. Cover with plastic wrap and chill overnight.
*Good over pasta.

****

NEAPOLITAN CLAM SAUCE

2 ½ cups plum tomatoes	1 sm. green pepper	4 tbsp. olive oil
½ tsp. red pepper flakes	2 cups clam juice	1 lg. garlic clove
1 cup dry white wine	½ cup onion, chopped	1 cup water
2 tbsp. minced parsley	½ tsp. marjoram	½ tsp. basil
2 cups canned minced clams with juice		

Sauté onion and garlic in oil, in a saucepan, until soft and just starts to color. Add white wine and cook over high heat, stirring, until reduced by half. Add tomatoes, green pepper, clam juice, water, red pepper flakes, basil and marjoram. Stir well and bring to a boil. Simmer for 10 minutes. Add clams and their juice and parsley. Heat 2 minutes and serve.
*Good over pasta.

****

NEW ORLEANS BÉARNAISE SAUCE

½ tsp. Worcestershire	¼ cup margarine	1 tsp. tarragon
3 tbsp. + 2 tsp. white wine	2 tsp. lemon juice	4 egg yolks
½ tsp. liquid red-pepper	2 cups unsalted butter	½ tsp. parsley

Use clarified butter. Cook tarragon and parsley in 3 tablespoons of wine over high heat, in a saucepan, stirring occasionally, until liquid has almost evaporated, about 2 minutes. Let cool 5 minutes. Combine remaining 2 teaspoons wine, egg yolks, lemon juice, red-pepper and Worcestershire sauce in top of double broiler, whisking until mixture is light, creamy and shiny, 6 to 8 minutes. Remove from heat.
*Good over poultry.

NEWBURG SAUCE

5 tbsp. dry sherry or Madeira
Pinch of red (cayenne) pepper

1 cup whipping cream
3 egg yolks, beaten

2 tbsp. butter
½ tsp. salt

In top half of a double boiler over very low heat, melt butter and add cream. When cream is hot but not boiling, stir in 4 tablespoons sherry and season with salt and red pepper. Bring almost to a boil. Place over simmering water in the lower half of the double boiler. Stir in egg yolks and beat with a whisk until the sauce has thickened and is smooth. Add 1 tablespoon or sherry just before serving. Serve hot.
*Good over rice or vegetables.

****

NORCIA SAUCE

4 oz. white wine
8 oz. heavy cream
2 oz. grated Parmesan cheese

7 oz. pork sausages
1 tbsp. olive oil

1 sm. onion
Salt and pepper

Sauté finely sliced onion in olive oil in a covered pan. The onion should not be allowed to change color. Remove the skin from sausages and chop meat into small pieces; putting them in pan with onion. Add wine. After 10 minutes, add cream and simmer gently, uncovered; about 10 minutes. Remove from heat, add salt and pepper to taste; keep warm.
*Good over pasta.

****

NORMANDY SAUCE

½ cup dry white wine
¼ cup calvados brandy

12 oz. Camembert cheese
1 garlic clove, halved

1 tbsp. cornstarch
⅔ cup half & half

Mash garlic clove with wine and half and half in a saucepan; heat until bubbly. Cut cheese in small pieces and add to wine mixture. Stir over low heat until melted. Blend cornstarch with calvados in a small bowl, then add to cheese mixture. Continue to cook, stirring 2 to 3 minutes or until thick and creamy.
*Good over fish.

****

OLIVE SAUCE

¼ cup all purpose flour
1 tbsp. chopped fresh parsley
½ tsp. chopped fresh oregano

¼ cup butter
½ cup Fish Stock Sauce

20 ripe olives
½ cup milk

Pit the olives, then cut olive flesh in thin strips. Melt butter in a small saucepan and stir in flour. Cook over low heat for about 3 minutes, stirring continually, until bubbly. Warm Fish Stock Sauce with milk in a separate saucepan. Add milk stock liquid all at once; whisk to blend into a smooth sauce. Continue whisking gently until the sauce thickens. Simmer, stirring often, for 10 minutes. Add olives, parsley and oregano and heat through well.
*Good over pasta.

****

ONION-CHILI SAUCES

½ envelope dry onion soup mix
2 tbsp. chili sauce

¾ cup boiling water
¼ cup water

1 ½ tbsp. flour

Combine onion soup mix and boiling water in a saucepan. Cover partially and cook 10 minutes. Mix flour and ¼ cup water, then gradually add to the soup mixture. Bring to a boil, stirring constantly; cook until thick. Remove from heat; mix in chili sauce.
*Good over hot dogs.

****

ONION CREAM SAUCE

4 oz. butter
4 oz. heavy cream

½ lb. sliced onions
salt and pepper

½ cup chicken stock
⅛ tsp. grated nutmeg

Sauté onions in butter, in a saucepan, until soft. Add chicken stock and continue to cook for 15 minutes. Puree onion mixture in a blender. Add cream, nutmeg, salt and pepper; mix and serve.
*Good over steak, pasta or vegetables.

ONION SAUCE

2 med. to large onions
½ tsp. grated nutmeg
½ cup all purpose flour

2 cups milk
¼ cup butter

Salt and pepper
1 bay leaf

In a saucepan, over medium heat, cook onions in milk, seasoned with nutmeg, salt, pepper and bay leaf. Cook until onions are soft. Remove bay leaf. Melt butter in another saucepan; add flour, stirring for 3 minutes or until bubbly. Add flavored milk all at once and whisk to combine ingredients smoothly. Cook over medium heat, stirring often, until just boiling, reduce heat and simmer for 5 to 7 minutes. Serve hot.
*Good over all meats.

****

ORANGE & GRAPEFRUIT SAUCE

2 green onions, chopped
1 sm. celery stalk, chopped
1 ¼ cups whipping cream

2 tbsp. unsalted butter
1 cup dry white wine
1 lg. grapefruit

½ lb. fish bones
1 lg. orange
Salt and pepper

Melt butter, in a saucepan, over medium heat. Add fish bones, trimmings, green onions and celery. Sauté over medium heat for a few minutes, stirring occasionally, until onion is golden and the celery is becoming soft. Add wine, and simmer for 15 to 20 minutes. If liquid reduces too much, add a little water. Strain stock into a bowl. Discard bones and vegetables. Peel and segment orange and grapefruit. Return stock to saucepan and add orange and grapefruit segments; heat through over medium heat. Reduce heat, add cream, salt and pepper. Serve hot.
*Good over fish.

****

ORANGE BUTTER SAUCE

½ cup unsalted butter
¼ cup orange juice

¼ cup sugar
2 tbsp. Cointreau

1 orange

Remove orange peel, cut into pieces and place in food processor with sugar. Process until peel is finely chopped and well blended with sugar. Add butter, a piece at a time, processing until smooth and fluffy. Add orange juice, drop by drop, then Cointreau, until fully incorporated.
*Good over warm crepes.

ORANGE CRANBERRY SAUCE

2 cups fresh orange juice
Zest of 1 orange
1 lb. fresh cranberries

1 ½ cups sugar
4 cloves garlic

Zest of 1 lemon
1 cinnamon stick

In a large saucepan, add orange juice, sugar, cloves, cinnamon, lemon and orange zest. Reduce this mixture by half, over medium high heat. Add cranberries and let simmer for 5 minutes. Allow to cool and serve.
*Good over poultry.

****

ORANGE EXTRACT SAUCE

1 ½ tsp. extract
1 ½ cups brandy

½ cup sugar syrup
1 pinch coriander

1 pinch caraway
1 pinch cinnamon

Mix all the ingredients in a bottle and let stand for a few days.
*Good over desserts.

****

ORANGE JUICE SAUCE

12 oz. freshly squeezed orange juice
6 oz. vodka & 6 oz. brandy

1 cup sugar syrup

peel of one orange

Scrape and slice orange peel. Combine juice, orange peel, and alcohol in a bowl or jar. Cover and let stand for 4 weeks, then strain. Add sugar syrup.
*Good over ice cream.

****

ORANGE SAUCE

2 tbsp. butter
1 tbsp. light corn syrup

1 cup brown sugar
½ cup sour cream

½ cup orange juice
½ cup chopped pecans

Combine butter, sugar, corn syrup and orange juice in a saucepan; cook over a low heat, stirring constantly until sugar is dissolved. Bring mixture to a boil and cook 5 minutes. Remove from heat and stir in sour cream and pecans.
*Good over desserts, pound cake or fruit.

ORANGE SAUCE

1 orange
⅛ tsp. orange zest
¼ cup port wine

¼ cup lemon juice
1 tbsp. butter
pinch of cayenne pepper

2 tbsp. red current jelly
1 tsp. dry mustard

Cut orange into julienne strips. Place all ingredients into a saucepan and heat for 5 minutes.
*Good over poultry.

****

ORANGE TEQUILA SAUCE

½ cup tequila

2 cups orange juice

Place tequila and orange juice into a saucepan and boil down to ½ cup.
*Good over rice or desserts.

****

ORANGE TOMATO SAUCE

1 cup onion, chopped
1 cup orange juice
1 tbsp. sugar

2 cups tomatoes
salt and pepper

¼ cup butter
1 tbsp. thyme

Sauté onions in butter, in a saucepan, until tender; add tomatoes and simmer 10 minutes. Add the remaining ingredients and cook 5 minutes.
*Use to bake chicken.

****

ORANGE-FLAVORED VINEGAR SAUCE

12-4 in. strips orange rind

3 cups white wine vinegar

3 medium oranges

Peel and section the orange. Combine orange rind strips and orange sections in a jar. Place vinegar in a medium saucepan and bring to a boil. Pour vinegar over rind and orange sections in jar; cover with an air tight lid and let stand 10 days.
*Good over poultry.

ORANGE-PEACH SAUCE

½ cup peach syrup   ½ cup orange juice   ⅓ cup sugar
2 tsp. cornstarch

In a medium saucepan, place orange juice and peach syrup, bring to a boil. Combine sugar and cornstarch, stir into boiling liquid. Stir over medium heat until clear and thickened.
*Good over desserts.

****

ORIENT PEANUT SAUCE

2 tsp. fresh gingerroot   1 tsp. coriander seeds   1 tsp. sesame seeds
⅛ tsp. hot red pepper   ¼ tsp. cinnamon   ⅛ tsp. nutmeg
½ cup peanut butter   3 tbsp. cider vinegar   1 garlic clove
1 tsp. low-sodium soy sauce

Finely chop gingerroot and garlic. Mix all ingredients together in a saucepan, until well blended. Heat 3 minutes.
*Good over poultry.

****

ORIENTAL APRICOT SAUCE

1 garlic clove, crushed   ¼ cup soy sauce   ¼ cup oil
3 oz. Apricot Brandy   salt and pepper   1 tsp. ginger
¼ cup apricot jam

Heat all ingredients together in a saucepan, until well blended, about 3 minutes.
*Use over chicken or pork.

****

ORIENTAL BARBECUE GLAZE SAUCE

2 tsp. instant bouillon   ¼ tsp. garlic powder   ⅓ cup honey
¼ cup soy sauce   1 cup boiling water   2 tbsp. sherry
½ cup vinegar   ½ tsp. ginger

Boil water in a medium saucepan; add instant bouillon and stir to dissolve. Add remaining ingredients; stir to blend.
*Good to marinate chicken, pork, beef or ribs.

ORIENTAL CRANBERRY SAUCE

½ cup cranberry liqueur
2 tbsp. orange liqueur or tangerine liqueur

9-oz. jar chutney

¼ cup water

Blend all ingredients in blender or food processor until smooth. Pour into a 2-quart saucepan. Simmer and stir 5 minutes until dipping consistency.
*Good over poultry.

****

ORIENTAL PLUM SAUCE

1 ½ lbs. ripe plums
⅛ tsp. red pepper flakes
2 garlic clove, chopped

2 tsp. gingerroot
3 tbsp. soy sauce

1 tbsp. water
3 tbsp. honey

Combine plums, water, honey, gingerroot, red pepper flakes and garlic in medium-size saucepan. Bring to boiling. Lower heat; cover and simmer 5 to 10 minutes until plums are soft. Remove from heat and stir in soy sauce. Cool slightly; process mixture in blender or food processor until smooth.
*Good on spareribs, pork chops and chicken.

****

ORIENTAL SAUCE

¼ cup sesame oil
2 tbsp. rice wine vinegar
2 tbsp. chopped scallions

½ cup peanut oil
1 tbsp. grated ginger
2 cloves garlic

¼ cup soy sauce
2 tbsp. dry sherry

Put 2 cloves garlic through a garlic press, then combine oils, soy sauce, vinegar, sherry, grated ginger, and scallions in a covered jar. Cover tightly and shake well. Chill.
*Good over poultry.

****

ORIENTAL VINAIGRETTE SAUCE

½ tsp. unflavored gelatin
1 tsp. chicken bouillon
⅓ cup rice vinegar

1 tsp. sesame seeds
1 tsp. gingerroot
⅔ cup plus 1 tsp. cold water

1 tsp. honey
1 tbsp. soy sauce

Use low-sodium soy sauce and chicken bouillon granules. Dissolve gelatin in 1 tablespoon water; stir well and set aside. Combine remaining ⅔ cup water and remaining ingredients, except gelatin mixture, in a non aluminum saucepan; bring to a boil over medium-heat; add gelatin mixture, stirring well.
*Good over chicken salad.

****

PALOISE SAUCE

1 cup white wine
2 shallots, chopped

⅓ cup white wine vinegar
½ lb. melted butter

¼ mint leaves
2 egg yolks

Heat wine, vinegar and shallot in a saucepan, then add mint. Whisk egg yolks until fluffy and thick, over simmering water. Add ½ lb. melted butter, whisking in slowly.
*Use for poaching.

****

PANG PANG SAUCE

¼ cup chunky peanut butter
2 tsp. Chinese Black vinegar
4 to 6 tbsp. chicken broth
1 tbsp. chili paste

3 tbsp. soy sauce
2 tbsp. sesame oil
1 tbsp. ginger root

1 tbsp. sugar
1 tbsp. garlic
1 tbsp. scallion

In a blender or food processor, combine all the ingredients except for the minced scallion. Blend until smooth. Add the minced scallion. The sauce should have the consistency of lightly whipped cream.
*Good with noodles, chicken, beef or as salad dressing.

****

PAPAL SAUCE

10 tbsp. butter
salt and pepper
4 oz. grated Parmesan cheese

1 sm. onion
7 oz. cream

7 oz. ham
4 eggs

Cut the ham into fine strips and chop the onion very fine. Melt half the butter in a saucepan and gently cook the onion until it becomes transparent. Add the ham and cook gently for 5 minutes. Keep hot. Beat the eggs together with the cream and half the cheese. Melt the remaining butter in a large pan and add the egg mixture. Remove from heat and add salt and pepper to taste.
*Good over pasta.

****

PAPAYA, MANGO, AND MELON SAUCE

½ med. ripe melon
Peel of ¼ lemon or lime

⅓ cup sugar syrup

1 cup vodka

Scrape and cut up peel of ¼ lemon or lime. Cut melon and remove the peel and seeds. Cut in ½ inch pieces. Place the cut-up fruit pieces in the vodka and let stand 1 week in a covered bowl or jar. Strain and squeeze the softened fruit to extract as much juice as possible. Add the sugar syrup (which is equal parts water and sugar, boiled down to a syrup). Mature 3 weeks.
*Good over desserts or ice cream.

PAPAYA RELISH SAUCE

½ cup red bell pepper
1 tbsp. vegetable oil
2 tbsp. limejuice

½ cup red onion
¼ cup mint leaves

1 sm. red chili
1 papaya

Pare, seed and cut papaya into ½ inch cubes. Seed and finely chop red chili, bell pepper and onion. Cook onion, bell pepper and chili in oil, in a skillet, over medium heat, stirring frequently, until tender. Stir in remaining ingredients. Cover and refrigerate 2 hours.
*Good over ham.

****

PAPAYA-GLACE LIME MARINADE SAUCE

4 tsp. green peppercorns
1 tsp. hot pepper flakes
14 ½ oz. can chicken broth

1 tsp. dried sage leaves
½ cup vegetable oil
¼ cup plus ⅔ cup lime juice

1 tsp. salt
2 shallots
1 lb. papaya

Peel and seed papaya, then place in a food processor or blender. Add vegetables, ¼ cup lime juice, shallots, sage, pepper flakes and salt. Set aside for glaze. Chop the peppercorns and mix the ⅔ cup lime juice, to marinate chicken for half an hour.
*Good over poultry.

****

PAPRIKA SAUCE

1 tbsp. onion, chopped
¼ cup whipping cream

1 cup Béchamel Sauce
½ tbsp. butter

1 tbsp. paprika

Melt butter over low heat, in a small saucepan. Sauté onion and paprika until onion is soft and golden. In a separate saucepan, simmer Béchamel Sauce, stirring often, for 1 to 2 minutes. Add cooked onion and paprika. Add cream, stirring constantly until heated through. Transfer to a serving dish, sprinkle with extra paprika.
*Good over pasta.

****

PARFAIT AMOUR SAUCE

1 ½ tsp. lemon extract
⅛ tsp. vanilla extract

⅛ tsp. orange extract
1 ½ cups sugar syrup

3 cups vodka
6 fresh flower petals

½ inch length of fresh vanilla bean may substitute extract. Put all ingredients, except the sugar syrup, in a jar with the vodka for 2 weeks. Remove vanilla bean and petals after 2 weeks, add sugar syrup. Mature approximately 1 week.
*Good over fruit or ice cream.

PARMESAN CREAM SAUCE

1 cup heavy cream
⅛ tsp. white pepper

¼ cup Parmesan cheese
⅛ tsp. salt

1 egg yolk

Simmer cream gently, in a saucepan for about 20 minutes, until it reduces to about ⅔ cup. Remove from heat. Blend in remaining ingredients. Keep warm until served.
*Good over pasta.

****

PEACH BRANDY SAUCE

½ can sliced peaches
¼ cup Peach Brandy

2 tbsp. butter
salt and pepper

2 tbsp. flour
¼ tsp. thyme

Heat butter and flour, in a saucepan, until dissolved; add peaches and heat until it boils, about 5 minutes. Add remaining ingredients.
*Use over pork or ice cream.

****

PEACH PRESERVES SAUCE

5 lbs. ripe peaches
1 tsp. almond extract

¼ cup lemon juice

6 cups sugar

Add peaches to boiling water. After 30 seconds, remove to a bowl of cold water and slip off skins. Halve and stone peaches. Cut ¾ of the peaches into thin slices and place in a metal pan with lemon juice and sugar. Cut remaining peaches into 1-inch dice and reserve. Bring to a boil over medium heat, stirring occasionally to make sure sugar is melting evenly and preserves are not scorching. Skim foam from surface with a skimmer or large spoon. Raise heat to high and boil rapidly, continuing to skim, until preserves reach a temperature of 220 degrees on a candy thermometer, or until a spoonful dropped onto a chilled plate does not remain runny after cooling, about 10 minutes. Add diced peaches and almond extract and cook 5 minutes longer. Lower heat.
*Good over ice cream or desserts.

****

PEACH SALSA SAUCE

½ cup diced red onion
½ cup diced red pepper
½ tsp. jalapeno chili

2 cups ripe peaches
¼ cup minced mint
2 tsp. grated ginger

2 tsp. olive oil
2 tbsp. lemon juice

Combine all ingredients in a bowl, let mellow for half an hour then serve.
*Good over fruit.

PEACH SAUCE I

10 med. ripe peaches	1 cup sugar syrup	3 cups vodka

Remove skin and pits from fruit and discard; cut into quarters. Place the cut up peaches in vodka in a tightly covered jar for 1 week and shake a few times. Strain through cloth, squeezing all juices from the fruit. Add the sugar syrup. (Sugar syrup is equal parts of sugar and water, boiled down to a syrup) Mature 4-6 weeks.
*Good over meat, desserts or ice cream.

****

PEACH SAUCE II

1 tbsp. powdered sugar	1 tbsp. lemon juice	2 cups peaches
1 tsp. almond extract	1 tbsp. cornstarch	¼ cup honey
¼ cup toasted sliced almonds		

Reserve 1 ½ cups of peach slices. Sprinkle remaining peach slices with powdered sugar and lemon juice. Rub reserved ½ cup peach slices through sieve. Mix peach puree, honey, cornstarch and extract in saucepan. Heat to boiling, stirring occasionally, cool slightly. Pour over peach slices and almonds; fold gently. Refrigerate until chilled.
*Good over ice cream or desserts.

****

PEANUT BUTTER FUDGE SAUCE

1 can sweetened condensed milk	4 oz. chocolate	2 tbsp. vanilla
¼ cup smooth peanut butter	¼ cup heavy cream	

Use bittersweet, unsweetened or semi-sweet chocolate. Microwave milk uncovered in a microwave-safe, two-quart glass pan on medium power for 10 minutes, whisking four times. Whisk in chocolate and peanut butter until melted and completely smooth. Whisk in heavy cream and vanilla. Serve warm.
*Good over ice cream.

****

PEANUT BUTTER SAUCE

½ cup creamy peanut butter	½ cup butter	¼ tsp. cumin
¼ cup roasted peanuts	⅓ cup chili sauce	1 tbsp. shallots

Chop roasted peanuts and mince shallots. Mix all ingredients together in a bowl, until well blended. Cover and refrigerate 24 hours to allow flavors to blend.
*Good over poultry.

PEANUT CHILI SAUCE

⅔ cup shredded coconut
1 garlic clove, crushed
5 tbsp. crunch peanut butter

1 ¼ cups boiling water
1 green chili, chopped

2 tsp. sugar
1 tsp. lemon juice

Put coconut in a medium size bowl and pour boiling water over. Let stand 15 minutes. Pour through a sieve into a medium size bowl pressing the liquid through the sieve; discard coconut. Pour liquid into a saucepan. Add remaining ingredients to coconut liquid and mix well. Cook over low heat stirring until sauce boils. Serve hot.
*Good over poultry.

****

PEANUT LIQUEUR SAUCE

3" piece of vanilla bean
4 oz. fresh unsalted, unroasted peanuts, shelled

½ cup sugar syrup

1 ½ cups vodka

Chop the peanuts with the vanilla bean, slightly, add to the vodka. Soak in a covered bowl or jar for 2 weeks, then strain. Add sugar syrup and mature 2 months.
*Good over poultry, desserts or ice cream.

****

PEANUT ORIENTAL SAUCE

¼ cup creamy peanut butter
2 tbsp. Oriental sesame oil
¼ tsp. cayenne pepper
¼ cup olive oil

2 tbsp. lemon juice
¼ cup peanut oil
1 tbsp. soy sauce
1 tbsp. distilled white vinegar

2 tbsp. ginger
½ tsp. salt
1 garlic clove

In a medium bowl, whisk together the peanut butter, sesame oil, lemon juice, ginger, garlic, salt and cayenne, until well blended. Whisk in the vinegar and soy sauce; then the olive and peanut oils in a thin stream until incorporated.
*Good over poultry.

****

PEANUT SAUCE

½ cup creamy peanut butter
½ cup dry sherry
1 tsp. red chili peppers

½ cup soy sauce
2 tbsp. ginger root

½ cup honey
1 garlic clove

Blend in a saucepan, peanut butter, soy sauce, honey, minced garlic, minced ginger root, sherry, crushed red chili peppers. Simmer, stirring, 5 to 6 minutes. Cool slightly.
*Good over chicken.

PEANUT SAUCE MARINADE

½ cup teriyaki sauce
¼ cup vegetable oil
1 tbsp. fresh ginger

¼ cup lemon juice
2 tbsp. fresh basil
½ cup chunky peanut butter

¼ tsp. hot oil
3 cloves garlic

In a food processor or blender, mix all ingredients, until smooth. Place turkey breast in a large resealable plastic pouch. Pour all but ¾ cup of sauce on top to thoroughly coat poultry. Seal bag. Marinate in refrigerator for at least 1 hour. Cook for 25 minutes.
*Good over poultry.

****

PEAR BRANDY SAUCE

¼ cup fresh lemon juice
4 Bartlett pears

2 cups water
¼ cup poire Williams Cognac or brandy

1 lemon

Remove peel from lemon in strips with vegetable peeler. Transfer to large saucepan. Add water, sugar and juice and stir over medium heat until sugar dissolves. Add pears and cook until knife pierces centers easily, about 20 minutes. Transfer to bowl using slotted spoon. Simmer poaching syrup until reduced to ¾ cup if necessary. Transfer half of the lemon peel to processor. Discard remaining peel. Add pears and syrup to processor and puree until smooth. Strain sauce through sieve; pressing with back of spoon. Mix in poire Williams. Cover and refrigerate. Bring to room temperature before serving.
*Good over desserts.

****

PEAR SAUCE

½ lb. ripe firm pears
½ " cinnamon stick
1 ½ cups vodka or brandy

2 coriander seeds
1 cup granulated sugar
Pinch nutmeg

2 apples
1 clove

A pinch of cinnamon can replace the cinnamon stick. Cut the pears in strips (do not pare) and place in a jar with all the other dry ingredients including sugar and the apple peels. Add alcohol to cover and let stand 2 weeks. Shake the jar every two days to mix the ingredients, then strain through a cheesecloth. Add sugar syrup in small quantities, to taste. Mature about 2 month.
*Good over desserts or ice cream.

PEARS BURGUNDY SAUCE

1 cup dry red wine
3 tbsp. walnuts, chopped
1 piece lemon peel

1 tbsp. butter
1 stick cinnamon
½ cup rum

4 pears
1 ¼ cups sugar

Mix all ingredients together in a saucepan, heat until well blended about 5 minutes.
*Good over poultry.

****

PEAS AND PROSCIUTTO SAUCE

⅓ cup minced onion
1 cup diced prosciutto
2-10 ½ oz. pkg. peas
Freshly parmesan cheese

2 tbsp. olive oil
⅔ cup parsley
¾ cups heavy cream
½ cup tomato sauce

2 tbsp. butter
Salt
Fresh pepper

Heat the butter and olive oil in a saucepan. Add the onion and ⅓ cup of parsley. Cook over low heat, Stirring frequently, until onion is soft. Add the prosciutto and cook 5 minutes longer. Add the frozen peas and the tomato sauce and continue to cook, covered, for about 10 minutes or until the peas are tender. Stir in heavy cream and season to taste. Simmer about 3 to 5 minutes, uncovered. Stir in the remaining parsley.
*Good for pasta.

****

PEAS SAUCE

4 cups fresh cooked peas
¼ cup grated Parmesan cheese

½ cup cooked onion
½ cup cooked bacon

4 oz. butter

Heat peas, onion and bacon in butter, in a saucepan, for about 2 minutes. Then add cheese and serve.
*Good over pasta.

****

PEPPERMINT FONDUE SAUCE

1 ¼ pints half and half
1 cup powdered sugar

2 tbsp. cornstarch

Peppermint extract

Put half and half and sugar in a medium size saucepan. Heat until almost boiling. Blend cornstarch with a little water and stir into mixture. Continue to heat, stirring until thickened, then add peppermint extract to taste. Pour into fondue pot and serve hot.
*Good over desserts.

PEPPERONATA SAUCE

¼ cup fresh oregano
2 tbsp. minced garlic
2 green bell peppers

½ cup olive oil
2 red bell peppers
1 yellow bell pepper

½ yellow onion
2 tomatoes
2 tsp. salt

Sauté garlic and onion in oil, in a large skillet, until lightly colored, about 3 minutes. Halve, seed and trim peppers; and cut into strips. Add peppers, tomatoes, salt and oregano, cover and simmer until peppers are soft, 12 to 15 minutes. *Good over pasta.

****

PHILADELPHIA PEPPER POT SAUCE

½ cup onion, chopped
¼ cup green peppers
¼ cup white dry wine

½ diced ham
¼ cup leeks, chopped
salt and pepper

¼ cup celery, chopped
2 tbsp. sweet butter

Sauté onions, peppers and leeks in butter for about 2 minutes, in a saucepan. Add remaining ingredients, and bring to a boil. Reduce heat and simmer for 1 minute.
*Good over chicken or steak.

****

PICKLE SAUCE

1 shallot, chopped
2 tbsp. red wine vinegar
¼ cup dry white wine

2 onion, sliced
2 lg. dill pickles
1 ½ cups beef gravy

1 tbsp. butter
½ red pepper
1 tbsp. oil

Thinly slice pepper and pickles, then heat all ingredients in a saucepan, for a few minutes.
*Good over steak.

****

PICKLED BEETS SAUCE

¼ tsp. cinnamon
2 cups beets

¼ cup water
2 to 3 whole cloves

⅓ cup cider

Mix all ingredients except beets together in a saucepan and bring a boil. Add cooked sliced beets about 10 minutes. Chill before serving.
*Good over pork.

PICKLED CUCUMBER SAUCE

| 2 whole cucumbers | 1 cup rice wine vinegar | 2 tbsp. sugar |
| Sliced onion, optional | | |

Dissolve sugar in vinegar (to taste). Place cucumber slices and onion, if using, in bowl and pour sweetened vinegar over. Marinate for ½ hour. Serve in small bowls with some of the marinade.
*Good over ham or beef.

****

PICO DE GALLO SAUCE

2 lg. ripe tomatoes	1 med. red onion	2 garlic cloves
2-4 serrano chilies	3 tbsp. cilantro	Pinch of sugar
2 tbsp. fresh lime juice	Salt to taste	

In a glass bowl, combine all ingredients and mix well. Allow to stand for 1 hour for the flavors to blend.
*Good over rice or pasta.

****

PINEAPPLE AND BRANDY SAUCE

| 1 med. ripe pineapple | 2 tbsp. sugar | 1 cup brandy |

Cut pineapple into thin slices and place in a wide-mouth jar. Add sugar until it reaches half the height of the fruit. Cover with brandy to reach the top of the fruit. There should be more brandy than sugar. Let stand for 2 months. Strain. Mature 1 month.
*Good over desserts, fruit or ice cream.

****

PINEAPPLE AND RUM SAUCE

| ½ lb. fresh pineapple | 3 cups rum |

Peel and cut up the pineapple into small pieces and place in a jar with the rum. Let stand for 3 weeks. Strain. Mature at lease 1 month.
*Good over desserts or ice cream.

PINEAPPLE AND VODKA SAUCE

2 cups fresh pineapple ½ cup sugar syrup 2 ½ cups vodka
¼ tsp. vanilla or 1" vanilla bean

Combine the pineapple, vanilla, and vodka in a jar and let stand about 1 week. Strain and squeeze out all the juice from the pineapple by mashing it through the strainer. Sweeten with sugar and strain through finer mesh strainer, if any pulp remains. Add sweetened pineapple juice or sugar syrup, to taste. Mature 1 month.
*Good over desserts or ice cream.

****

PINEAPPLE LIQUEUR SAUCE

¼ cup light brown sugar 1 slice canned pineapple ¼ cup water
¼ cup Benedictine liqueur Pinch of allspice ½ tbsp. butter
1 tbsp. walnuts, chopped 2 tbsp. cornstarch 6 pitted dates
½ cup unsweetened pineapple juice

Heat juice and sugar over low heat, stirring occasionally, in a saucepan. Blend water with the cornstarch, and add to saucepan. Stir over a medium heat until sauce begins to thicken. Increase heat and bring to a boil. Reduce heat, add all remaining ingredients, except the butter, and stir for 1 to 2 minutes. Add butter; stir to melt. Serve hot.
*Good over desserts or ice cream.

****

PINEAPPLE PLUM SAUCE

2 8-oz. cans crushed pineapple, drained 1 7-oz. jar plum sauce

Combine pineapple and plum sauce in small bowl. Refrigerate until ready to use.
*Good over desserts or ice cream.

****

PINEAPPLE SAUCE

15 oz. crushed pineapple ⅓ cup cider vinegar ¼ cup dry sherry
½ cup onions, chopped ½ tsp. grated ginger ¼ tsp. pepper
½ cup dark-brown sugar 2 tbsp. cornstarch 2 tbsp. water
Salt to taste

In a small saucepan, combine pineapple, its juice, vinegar, sherry, onions, sugar, salt and pepper and ginger. Simmer about 10 minutes, stirring occasionally. Mix cornstarch with water; add to sauce, stirring until thickens. Serve warm.
*Good over ice cream or desserts.

PIQUANT SAUCE I

3 tbsp. all purpose flour
1 tsp. fresh tarragon, chopped
2 tsp. fresh parsley, chopped
1 tsp. fresh chervil, chopped

1 cup dry white wine
2 dill pickles, diced
1 beef bouillon cube
1 cup red wine vinegar

1 lg. onion
¼ cup butter
¼ cup water
Salt and pepper

Thinly slice and dice onion, and place in a saucepan, where butter was melted. Cook over medium heat until golden. Sprinkle in flour, cook, stirring, for 8 to 10 minutes until flour turns brown. Mix wine and vinegar together. Gradually add to flour mixtures, stirring constantly to make a smooth, creamy brown sauce. Add salt and pepper and simmer for 15 minutes. Add pickles and herbs. Dissolve bouillon cube in water and add to sauce; stir through. Continue simmering for 10 minutes.
*Good over fish.

****

PIQUANT SAUCE II

1 ¼ cups tomato juice
¼ tsp. ground cinnamon

¼ tsp. ground ginger
2 tsp. red wine vinegar

2 tsp. brown sugar
1 sm. red chili

Put all ingredients in a small saucepan and simmer 15 minutes.
*Good over poultry.

****

PIRAO SAUCE

2 ½ cups fish broth
1 ½ cups manioc flour

1 tbsp. tomato paste
Salt and black pepper

Pepper to taste

In a medium saucepan, bring the fish broth to a rapid boil, and stir in a little salt and pepper. Add the tomato paste, and stir to incorporate thoroughly. Sprinkle in the manioc flour, a little at a time, stirring vigorously and continuously until all the flour has been incorporated and the mixture has the consistency of soft ice cream. Serve immediately.
*Good over fish.

****

PISTACHIO AND WALNUT SAUCE

3-4 oz. walnuts & pistachio nuts
12 raisins or currants

1 ½ cups vodka
½ cup sugar syrup

pinch of cloves
pinch of cinnamon

Soak the nuts, raisins, and spices in vodka for 2 weeks, in a covered bowl or jar. Shake occasionally. Strain; add the sugar syrup. Mature 2-3 weeks. (Equal parts sugar and water boiled down to a syrup is sugar syrup)
*Good over poultry.

PIZZA SAUCE

1 lg. onion, chopped
4 cups plum tomatoes
Pinch granulated sugar

¼ cup olive oil
½ tsp. oregano
Salt and pepper

2 cloves garlic
½ tsp. basil

In a medium saucepan heat oil and sauté onion and garlic 5 minutes. Add tomatoes and simmer 20 minutes. Add basil, oregano, salt, pepper and sugar. Cook 10 minutes longer. If sauce becomes too thick, add a few tablespoons water. *Good over veal, poultry, beef or English muffin and mozzarella.

****

PLUM DESSERT SAUCE

1 ½ cups plum puree
1 tbsp. cornstarch

¼ cup port wine
2 tbsp. grated orange rind

2 tbsp. sugar

Place sugar in a saucepan and stir it into a puree, until bubbling. Dissolve cornstarch in wine and stir into hot mixture. Cook, stirring, until slightly thickened and smooth. Stir in orange rind.
*Serve warm or cold over poached peaches or pears or hot winter puddings.

****

PLUM JAM SAUCE

½ cup soy sauce
¼ cup orange juice

½ cup plum jam
1 garlic clove

½ cup honey

Mix all ingredients together in a bowl, until well blended. Pour mixture into a saucepan and heat about 2 minutes.
*Pour over cooked meat.

****

PLUM SAUCE I

2 green onions, sliced
1 tbsp. lemon juice

½ cup plum jelly
2 tbsp. dry sherry

1 tbsp. cornstarch
2 tbsp. soy sauce

In a small saucepan combine jelly, green onions, sherry, soy sauce, cornstarch, and lemon juice. Cook and stir until thickened and bubbly. Cook and stir for 1 to 2 minutes more. Remove from heat.
*Good over duck, poultry, fish or pork.

PLUM SAUCE II

1 lb. plums
1 cup sugar

2 cups vodka
¼ " piece of cinnamon stick

3 cloves

Place cut up plums and pits in a jar with flavorings, sugar and vodka. Be sure vodka covers the plums.
Let stand for 3 months, shaking occasionally to mix all the ingredients. Strain.
½ pound dried prunes may be substituted for plums.
*Good over duck, poultry, pork or ice cream.

****

PLUM SAUCE III

1 ½ cups plum puree
Freshly ground pepper

4 lg. garlic clove, minced

Salt to taste

Put puree in a saucepan and add garlic, salt, and pepper. Bring to a boil. Reduce heat and simmer 5
minutes, stirring frequently. Serve at room temperature.
*Good over duck, poultry or pork.

****

PLUMS WITH SOFT CUSTARD SAUCE

1 cup heavy cream
6 med. plums, pitted

6 lg. egg yolks
½ cup sugar

1 cup milk
pinch of salt

Heat cream and milk in a saucepan, until just beginning to scald. In another saucepan, whisk in egg
yolks, sugar and salt. Continue whisking, slowly pour in hot milk-cream mixture. Place pan over low to
medium heat stirring constantly, cook until it thickens and coats the spoon. Stir in brandy. Cool, then
refrigerate. Add plums before serving.
*Good over ice cream or desserts.

****

POLPETTI SAUCE

1 cup beef broth

¼ cup Parmesan cheese

1 tbsp. tomato paste

Place all ingredients into a saucepan. Bring to a boil and simmer for 5 minutes.
*Good over poultry or all meats.

POLYNESIAN SAUCE

½ cup pineapple liqueur   ½ cup soy sauce   ½ cup oil
1 garlic clove, minced   ½ tsp. ginger

Mix all ingredients together, in a bowl, until well blended. Use to marinate. (About 2 hours)
*Good over chicken or shrimp.

****

POOR MAN'S SAUCE

1 cup beef or chicken stock   1 shallot, chopped   1 tsp. parsley
¼ tsp. chives   ¼ cup breadcrumbs   1 tbsp. butter

Heat butter with breadcrumbs in a skillet; add shallots, stock, parsley and chives. Cook for a few minutes.
*Good over poultry.

****

POPPY SEED SAUCE

1 ½ cups granulates sugar   2 tsp. dry mustard   1 tsp. salt
⅔ cup apple-cider vinegar   2 cups vegetable oil   3 tbsp. poppy seeds

Combine sugar, mustard, salt and vinegar in blender. Slowly add oil, blending until thick. Stir in poppy seeds and store in refrigerator.
*Good over ham.

****

PORK SAUCE

1 lg. onion, chopped   1 sm. chili pepper   2 oz. butter
4 oz. minced pork   10 oz. plum tomatoes   salt
1 cup Parmesan cheese

Melt butter, in a skillet and sauté onion and chili for 5 minutes. Add pork and brown. Add tomatoes and salt and simmer for 30 minutes.
*Good over pasta.

PORT & RASPBERRY SAUCE

½ cup red currant jelly
12 oz. raspberries

¼ cup port wine
2 tsp. cornstarch

2 tsp. lemon juice
pepper

Add port and lemon juice to jelly in a saucepan. Stirring over low heat until jelly melts and ingredients are combined. Reserve a few raspberries for garnish, press remainder through fine sieve. Add puree to red currant mixture in saucepan and heat gently. In a small bowl, mix cornstarch with a little of the warm sauce. Return to saucepan and cook, stirring until sauce thickens, then add pepper. Serve hot with reserved raspberries.
*Good over poultry.

****

POULETTE SAUCE

½ cup whipping cream
¾ cup Chicken Veloute Sauce
1 tsp. grated onion

⅓ cup dry white wine
4 sm. mushrooms, sliced
1 tbsp. parsley, chopped

1 tbsp. butter
3 egg yolks
2 tbsp. lemon juice

Melt butter and sauté mushrooms, in top half of a double boiler over direct medium heat, until softened. Add onion and wine; cook until wine has almost evaporated. Lower heat, stir in half the cream and cook for 5 minutes or until sauce has reduced by about half. Add the Veloute Sauce and bring to a boil. In another bowl lightly beat egg yolks into remaining cream; stir in a little hot sauce. Place the top of the double boiler over boiling water in bottom half of double boiler; stir in egg and cream mixture. Cook, stirring, until very hot but not boiling. Add lemon juice and parsley.
*Serve hot with cooked jumbo shrimp or other shellfish.

****

PRALINE SAUCE

⅓ cup brown sugar
1 cup pecans, chopped

⅓ cup boiling water

2 cups molasses

Bring all ingredients to a boil over medium heat in a saucepan. Remove from heat immediately.
*Good over desserts or ice cream.

****

PROVENCAL OLIVE PASTE SAUCE

1 cup black olives, pitted
½ tsp. Dijon mustard
½ cup fruity olive oil

2-oz. anchovies
1 tbsp. lemon juice
2 tbsp. cognac

2 tbsp. capers
black pepper

Place all ingredients, except oil, into a blender. Pour in enough oil in a steady stream for a smooth thick sauce. Chill.
*Good over fish.

PROVENCAL SAUCE

4 cloves of garlic
dash cayenne pepper

¼ cup sliced mushrooms
¼ cup lemon juice

2 tbsp. butter

Scald garlic in a saucepan, then sauté in butter. Add mushroom, cayenne pepper and lemon juice. Simmer a few minutes.
*Good over poultry or meats.

****

PROVENCALE OLIVE OIL SAUCE

15 sun-dried tomatoes
1 dried chili pepper

4 peppercorns
2 bay leaves

2 cloves garlic
Olive oil

Soak the sun-dried tomatoes in warm water for 15 minutes. Drain and pat dry. Put half the chili pepper, 1 garlic clove, 2 peppercorns and 1 bay leaf into a mason jar. Cover with ¼ cup of olive oil. Put in the rest of the ingredients and fill the jar with oil. Cover the jar and let sit in a cool place at least 24 hours before using.
*Good over pasta.

****

PROVENCE OIL SAUCE

½ tsp. Rosemary
½ tsp. Marjoram

½ tsp. sage
2 cups oil

½ tsp. thyme

Combine all ingredients in a jar, and leave in sunlight 2 weeks.
*Good over pasta.

****

PRUNE SAUCE I

1 tbsp. grated lemon peel
Pinch of ground cinnamon
Pinch of ground allspice
½ cup red wine vinegar

7 oz. pitted prunes
8 whole garlic cloves
½ tsp. fresh nutmeg

2 tbsp. lemon juice
1 cup water
½ cup sugar

Mix prunes, lemon juice and peel with cloves, cinnamon, allspice and nutmeg. Transfer to a medium saucepan. Add water, just enough to cover; heat until simmering, cook about 15 minutes or until soft. Stir occasionally. When liquid has reduced to about half, take off heat and remove the cloves. Pass through a fine sieve or puree in a food processor. Return to saucepan; add sugar and vinegar. Cook over low heat until smooth and warmed through.
*Good over poultry.

PRUNE SAUCE II

½ lb. prunes
1 celery rib
¾ cup red wine
1 tbsp. flour

1 carrot, chopped
2 tbsp. butter
2 tbsp. red wine vinegar
salt and pepper

1 onion, chopped
1 garlic clove
1 tbsp. butter

Soak prunes in cold water. Sauté vegetables 3 minutes in a saucepan; add vinegar and red wine. Simmer 20 minutes then strain. Poach prunes 20 minutes. Heat butter, flour, prunes and vegetables.
*Good over poultry or pork.

****

PRUNES AND BRANDY SAUCE

1" piece of cinnamon stick
¾ cup sugar syrup

½ lb. lg. prunes
Peel from ¼ orange

2 cups brandy

Scrape and slice peel from ¼ orange and add all the ingredients in a jar. Let stand 4 weeks. Strain out the prunes and use as dessert. Strain the liqueur. Mature 2-3 weeks.
*Good over pork chops.

****

PULP SAUCE

1 Idaho potato pulp
Ground white pepper
1 ½ cups olive oil

4 crushed garlic cloves
Juice of ½ lemon juice

3 egg yolks
Salt

Beat pulp with a beater, in a mixing bowl, until smooth; beat in egg yolks 1 at a time, add garlic, lemon juice, salt and pepper to taste, beating until the mixture is thoroughly combined and smooth. Begin adding the oil very slowly, beating constantly with a wooden spatula. When oil has been added the sauce should have the consistency of a firm mayonnaise.
*Good over pasta.

****

PUMPKIN SAUCE

1 lb. piece pumpkin
½ cup chicken stock
⅛ tsp. grated nutmeg

½ cup leek, chopped
½ cup Parmesan cheese
⅔ cup heavy cream

4 tbsp. butter
salt and pepper
¼ cup celery

Melt 2 tablespoons of butter in a saucepan, add leek and celery and cook for 2 minutes. Add pumpkin and stock. Cover and cook 20 minutes, then add nutmeg, salt and pepper. Place the hot mixture into a food processor and puree. Return to saucepan, add cream and continue to cook over a low heat for 2 minutes. Add cheese and serve.
*Good over pasta.

PUMPKIN SEED SAUCE

1 cup shelled pumpkin seed
2 tbsp. canned green chilies
½ cup whipping cream

1 slice white bread
2 tbsp. vegetable oil
14 oz. chicken broth

1 sm. onion
1 garlic clove
Dash of salt

Cook pumpkin seeds, onion, bread pieces and garlic in oil, in a skillet, stirring frequently, until bread is golden brown. Stir in chilies. Place mixture in food processor, and process until smooth. Stir in cream and salt.
*Good over pasta.

****

PUREE FRUIT SAUCE

2 apples, peeled and sliced
2 tbsp. maple syrup

1 tsp. cinnamon
½ cup raisins

1 tbsp. butter
½ orange

Heat butter in saucepan, add apples, maple syrup, cinnamon, raisins and orange. Cook 8 minutes, then pour into a blender and blend until pureed.
*Good over desserts or ice cream.

****

PUREE MUSHROOM SAUCE

½ cup sour cream
½ cup beef bouillon

¼ lb. mushrooms
2 tbsp. flour

2 tbsp. butter
Salt and pepper

Place all ingredients in blender or food processor, and process briefly. Pout into heavy saucepan and cook over medium heat, stirring, until thickened.
*Good over beef or veal.

****

PUTTANESCA SAUCE

3 anchovy fillets
4 oz. pitted black olives

1 ½ cups olive oil
14 oz. plum tomatoes

3 cloves garlic
4 tbsp. capers

Heat olive oil in saucepan, add chopped garlic and anchovy fillets, cook for 2 minutes. Add chopped tomatoes, black olives and capers, simmer 5 minutes.
*Good over pasta.

280

Quick Brown Sauce

2 tbsp. onions, chopped
1 tbsp. carrot, chopped
¼ cup all purpose flour

1 tbsp. celery, chopped
1 tsp. salt and pepper

¼ cup butter
Bouquet garni

Sauté butter, vegetables and garni 5-6 minutes, in a saucepan. Add remaining ingredients; boil; simmer for about 5 minutes.
*Good over all meats or mashed potatoes.

****

QUICK CHILI SAUCE

½ cup ground beef
1 green pepper, chopped
1-2 tsp. chili powder

1 onion, chopped
2 cups tomato sauce
pinch powdered cumin

2 cloves garlic
¼ tsp. oregano
Kidney beans

Brown beef, onion, pepper and garlic in a saucepan. Stir in tomato sauce, chili powder, oregano and cumin. Serve with kidney beans.
*Good over cooked chopped meat.

****

QUICK CURRY SAUCE

½ cup dairy sour cream
1 tsp. dehydrated onion, minced

⅛ tsp. curry powder

2 tbsp. milk

Mix all ingredients together, in a bowl, until well blended. Refrigerate. Substitute 2 tablespoons blue cheese instead of curry.
*Good over poultry.

****

QUICK MUSTARD SAUCE

2 tbsp. cider vinegar
1 tsp. red pepper flakes

2 tbsp. dry mustard
2 tbsp. soy sauce

1 cup ketchup
1 tbsp. brown sugar

Combine the ingredients in a saucepan and simmer slowly for 20 minutes.
*Good over pasta.

****

QUICK TOMATO SAUCE AND RED BEANS

1 cup onion, chopped
1 cup roasted bell pepper
cup cooked kidney beans

2 garlic cloves, minced
12 plum tomatoes
Salt and pepper

2 tbsp. olive oil
1 tbsp. tomato paste   1

Sauté onion, garlic and chili peppers in oil, in a saucepan. Add remaining ingredients; cook 6-7 minutes.
Remove the chili peppers.
*Good over pasta.

****

RAISIN SAUCE

¼ cup all purpose flour
1 ½ tbsp. light brown sugar
2 tbsp. white wine vinegar

1 ½ tbsp. dry mustard
Salt & white pepper
⅓ cup seedless raisins

1 ½ cups water
2 tbsp. butter
1 tbsp. lemon juice

Blend flour, brown sugar, mustard, salt and pepper in a saucepan. Bring water to a boil in separate saucepan and whisk in dry ingredients, a little at a time, stirring constantly. Add vinegar and lemon juice; bring to a simmer over medium heat. Cook 7 to 8 minutes. Add raisins. Reduce heat, cook 3 more minutes, or until raisins are soft and plump. Just before serving, stir in the butter until melted.
*Good over poultry, ham or fresh pork.

****

RAISIN AND CRANBERRY SAUCE

1 cup orange juice
⅛ tsp. ground cloves

½ cup cranberries
4 tbsp. raisins

1 tbsp. cornstarch
Cinnamon stick

Combine the juice and cranberries in a saucepan. Cook over medium heat just until the berries pop. Add the remaining ingredients and cook until the mixture is thick.
*Good over baked ham or poultry.

****

RAISINS AND PINE NUTS SAUCE

2 cups unseasoned bread crumbs
¼ cup sun-dried tomatoes
2 tbsp. balsamic vinegar

½ cup olive oil
¼ cup pine nuts

½ cup raisins
2 tbsp. parsley

Heat olive oil in skillet and cook bread crumbs until golden, taking care not to burn them. Stir in raisins, pine nuts, sun dried tomatoes and balsamic vinegar. Serve.
*Good over pork.

****

RASPBERRY AND GIN SAUCE

2 lbs. fresh raspberries

2 lbs. sugar

3 cups gin

Mix all the ingredients together in a covered jar. Turn every day until the sugar is dissolved. Strain.
*Good over poultry or desserts.

RASPBERRY BRANDY SAUCE

| 1 ½ cups ripe raspberries | ¾ cup sugar syrup | 3 cups vodka |
| Peel of ½ lemon, sliced and scraped | | |

In place of 3 cups vodka, 2 cups vodka and 1 cup brandy or 1 cup sweet white wine can be used. Lightly crush berries, add lemon peel and berries to alcohol. Place in a jar and let stand 2-4 weeks, then strain, squeezing all the berries through the fine cloth. Add the sugar syrup and mature 4-6 weeks.
For Crème de Framboise, use all brandy and add 2 cups of sugar syrup.
*Good over poultry.

****

RASPBERRY RHUBARB SAUCE

| 10-oz. frozen raspberries | 3 cups vanilla yogurt | 2 ½ cups rhubarb |
| ½ pt. fresh raspberries | 3 cups lemon yogurt | ½ cup sugar |

Mix the 2 yogurts together in a large bowl. Place the yogurts in a strainer with a double layer damp cheesecloth in it. Tie the ends of the cheesecloth together so that the yogurt is completely encased. Place in the refrigerator to drain for at least 6 hours or overnight. Mix the rhubarb with sugar in a heavy saucepan; bring to a boil and simmer 4 minutes, stirring occasionally until rhubarb is softened. Add the frozen raspberries; stir to incorporate red berry and cool. Unwrap the yogurt; scoop into dishes and top with sauce.
*Good over desserts.

****

RASPBERRY SAUCE I

| 2 tbsp. raspberry puree | Custard Sauce |

Make Custard Sauce in a saucepan; remove from heat; stir in at least 2 tablespoons sieved raspberry puree, whisking constantly, until well blended.
*Good over desserts or ice cream.

****

RASPBERRY SAUCE II

| 1 cup raspberry preserves | 1 tsp. almond extract | ½ cup almonds |

Coarsely chop unbalanced almonds. Melt preserves in heavy small saucepan over low heat, stirring occasionally. Mix in almond extract. Sprinkle with almonds.
*Good over desserts or ice cream.

RASPBERRY SAUCE III

10-oz. pkg. raspberries   ¼ cup powdered sugar   1 tbsp. framboise

Process raspberries and powdered sugar, in a food processor, until completely smooth, about 2 minutes. Strain raspberry mixture through fine-mesh strainer. Stir in framboise. Chill well before using.
*Good over desserts or ice cream.

****

RASPBERRY SAUCE IV

10-oz. pkg. raspberries   ½ cup currant jelly   1 tbsp. cornstarch

Combine raspberries and cornstarch in a saucepan. Cook and stir until thickened and bubbly. Add jelly; cook and stir 1 minute more. Strain and cool.
*Good over desserts or ice cream.

****

RASPBERRY VINAIGRETTE SAUCE

1 tbsp. raspberry vinegar   1 tbsp. cider vinegar   3 tbsp. water
¼ tsp. Dijon mustard   1 minced garlic clove   ¼ tsp. salt
2 tbsp. vegetable oil   2 tbsp. olive oil   Pepper

In a small bowl or jar with a cover, combine vinegars, water, garlic, mustard, salt and pepper. Whisk in the oils. Cover and refrigerate until ready to use. Before serving, shake well.
*Good over salads.

****

RASPBERRY-SESAME SAUCE I

¼ cup lime juice   ⅓ cup sesame seeds   10 oz. raspberry jelly
Peach slices and raspberries
In a saucepan, combine all ingredients. Heat, stir about 3 minutes, until well blended.
*Good over poultry or pork.

RASPBERRY-SESAME SAUCE II

¼ cup lime juice
10 oz. raspberry jelly

⅛ tsp. white pepper
⅓ cup sesame seeds, toasted

2 tbsp. butter

Heat butter in a saucepan, adding toasted sesame seeds, lime juice, white pepper and jelly and simmer for 10 minutes.
*Good over chicken.

****

RED BELL PEPPER SAUCE

1 lg. red bell pepper
3 tbsp. fresh oregano

1 cup olive oil
Dry white wine

Juice of 2 lemons
Salt and pepper

Stem, seed and dice red pepper. Mix all ingredients together in a saucepan, until well blended. Then heat 3 minutes.
*Good over steak.

****

RED BERRY SAUCE

1 pt. strawberries
1 pkg. raspberries or strawberries

1 tbsp. sugar

1 tbsp. Kirsch

Let berries barely defrost. Puree in a blender or processor. If using raspberries, strain puree through a sieve to get rid of seeds. Stir in sugar and Kirsch. Stir in berries. Chill.
*Good over ice cream or desserts.

****

RED CHILI SAUCE

8 dried red chilies
8 sliced mushrooms
2 tbsp. cilantro, chopped
½ tsp. dried oregano

1 sm. onion, chopped
2 tbsp. cornstarch
1 tsp. ground cumin
1 ½ cups chicken broth

½ cups water
1 tbsp. olive oil
1 tsp. salt

Seed red peppers and break into pieces; place in water with salt. Let stand for 1 hour. Drain and transfer to blender; add cornstarch and puree. Heat oil in a saucepan, over medium-low heat. Add onion and cook until softened, stirring occasionally, about 5 minutes. Add mushrooms and cook until tender, stirring occasionally, about 5 minutes. Stir in cilantro, cumin and oregano. Add chili puree and broth and bring to boil. Reduce heat and simmer gently 30 minutes to thicken.
*Good over pasta.

RED CURRANT SAUCE

¾ cup red currant jelly
½ cup fresh mint, finely chopped

⅓ cup orange juice
Strips of orange peel, to garnish

Melt jelly over low heat in a small saucepan. Remove from heat and stir in orange juice and mint. Garnish with strips of orange peel. Or microwave jelly in a bowl, covered with plastic wrap, on high for 1 ½ minutes, until melted. Stir in orange juice and mint.
*Good over hot dogs or fresh pork.

****

RED PEPPER SAUCE I

2 tbsp. peanut oil
1 garlic clove
1 cup chicken stock

2 sm. red bell peppers
1 Serrano chili

2 shallots
Salt and pepper

Heat oil in medium skillet over medium heat. Add chopped peppers, shallots, garlic and chili; cook until softened, stirring frequently, about 5 minutes. Add stock or broth and boil until reduced by half. Transfer to blender and puree. Strain into bowl and season with salt and pepper.
*Good over pasta or rice.

****

RED PEPPER SAUCE II

1 tbsp. wine vinegar
¼ cup lemon juice
1 ½ cups water

1 jalapeno pepper
2 tbsp. butter
Salt and pepper

4 lg. red peppers
2 tbsp. sugar

Stem, seed and chop peppers. Combine peppers, vinegar, sugar and water in a saucepan. Bring to a boil and simmer, loosely covered, until all but 5 to 6 tablespoons of the liquid has evaporated. Puree mixture in blender or food processor. Pass through a fine strainer, back into the saucepan. Whisk in the lemon juice and butter. Season with salt and pepper. *Good with grilled meats, steamed vegetables or poached fish.

RED PEPPER SAUCE III

2 lg. red peppers	1 Spanish onion	¼ cup olive oil
1 tbsp. Balsamic vinegar	3 cloves garlic	12 oz. tomato paste
⅓ cup parsley, chopped	1 tsp. oregano	1 tsp. basil
¼ tsp. red pepper flakes	salt and pepper	⅔ cup water

Chop red peppers, onion, and garlic. Heat onions in oil for 3 minutes. Add peppers and cook 15 minutes. Add remaining ingredients and cook 15 minutes more. Place ingredients in a food processor and pulse.
*Good over pasta or poultry.

****

RED PEPPER SAUCE IV

1 cup chicken broth	2 red bell peppers	2 tbsp. butter
1 garlic clove, crushed	Salt and pepper	1 sm. onion

Melt butter in a small saucepan, add onion and cook until soft. Add red bell peppers and garlic and continue to cook over medium heat 5 minutes. Pour in broth and simmer 10 minutes or until peppers are tender. Pour sauce through a sieve into a second saucepan. Season with salt and pepper and reheat.
*Good over sausage.

****

RED PEPPER SAUCE V

1 tbsp. olive oil	4 tbsp. onion, chopped	Salt and pepper
2 red bell peppers	1 tbsp. garlic, chopped	1 bay leaf
½ tsp. cumin powder	2 tbsp. lemon juice	2 tbsp. butter
1 cup chicken broth	2 tbsp. fresh coriander	Salt and pepper

Heat oil in skillet and add onions and red peppers. Cook, stirring, until peppers are wilted, about 5 minutes. Add garlic continue cooking for a few minutes. Add broth, cumin, bay leaf, salt and pepper. Cover and simmer 5 minutes. Remove and discard bay leaf. Place mixture in a food processor or blender. Add butter and lemon juice and pulse to blend to a fine texture. Return mixture to skillet and add cooked pork slices with their drippings. Bring to a simmer and serve immediately. Sprinkle with coriander.
*Good over pork.

RED-PEPPER SALSA SAUCE

½ cup shallots, chopped
½ tsp. crushed red pepper

½ tsp. ground cumin
6 med. red bell peppers

3 tbsp. olive oil

Peel and finely chop bell peppers. Cook shallots and crushed pepper in oil in small skillet over medium-low heat 5 minutes, stirring occasionally, until shallots are tender, but not browned. Add bell peppers, stirring often, cook 5 to 7 minutes until juices have evaporated. Remove from heat; stir in cumin and cool to room temperature before serving.
*Good over rice.

****

REMOULADE SAUCE I

½ tsp. Worcestershire sauce
2 tbsp. granulated sugar
2 tbsp. cider vinegar

2 cups mayonnaise
1 cup sour cream
2 tbsp. lemon juice

1 dill pickle
2 tbsp. capers
½ tsp. Tabasco

Mix all ingredients together in a bowl, until well blended. Chill 1 hour.
*Good over poultry or fish.

****

REMOULADE SAUCE II

2 tbsp. capers, chopped
2 tsp. Dijon mustard
¾ tsp. anchovy paste

1 tbsp. lemon juice
1 tsp. parsley

1 cup mayonnaise
2 tsp. chives

Mix all ingredients together in a bowl, until well blended. Cover and refrigerate.
*Good over pasta, fish or poultry.

****

RHUBARB-STRAWBERRY DESSERT SAUCE

3 cups fresh rhubarb
1 cup fresh strawberries

1 tbsp. cornstarch
2 tbsp. water

1 cup sugar

Combine rhubarb, sugar, and ⅓ cup water in saucepan; bring to boil. Reduce heat; cover and simmer 5 minutes. Add strawberries; cook until strawberries are tender, 2 to 3 minutes. Blend together cornstarch and 2 tablespoons water; add to rhubarb mixture. Cook, stirring constantly, until mixture thickens and boils; remove from heat. Chill in refrigerator until serving time.
*Good over desserts or ice cream.

RIB-TICKLING BARBECUE SAUCE

¼ cup prepared mustard	¼ cup Worchestershire	½ cup ketchup
¼ cup cider vinegar	½ cup corn syrup	½ cup onion

Finely chop onion. Stir together all ingredients in a saucepan. Bring to boil, stirring frequently; reduce heat and boil gently until thickened. About 15 minutes.
*Good over all meats and poultry.

****

RICH BUTTERSCOTCH SAUCE

1 ½ cups dark brown sugar	⅓ cup cream	⅛ tsp. salt
¾ cup light corn syrup	1 cup light cream	

Cook sugar, butter, corn syrup and salt together in a saucepan, over low heat. Stir frequently until sugar melts. Add cream very slowly, stirring constantly.
*Good over desserts.

****

RICH CHOCOLATE CARAMELS SAUCE

1 cup granulated sugar	1 cup brown sugar	2 tbsp. butter
½ cup half and half	½ cup corn syrup	1 tsp. vanilla
2-oz. unsweetened chocolate		

Place sugars, corn syrup, half and half and chocolate in large saucepan. Bring to boil, stirring to melt chocolate and dissolve sugar. Reduce heat to moderate and continue cooking, stirring occasionally. Remove from heat. Quickly stir in butter and vanilla just until blended and butter melts.
*Good over desserts and ice cream.

****

RICOTTA SAUCE

5 oz. gorgonzola cheese	1 ¼ cups milk	7 tbsp. butter
10 oz. ricotta cheese	Salt and black pepper	1 sm. onion

Heat the butter and add the chopped onion. Cook gently without letting them turn color. In a blender or food processor, puree together the milk, Gorgonzola, ricotta and cooked onions. Place in a saucepan and leave to heat through gently, stirring occasionally. Add salt and pepper to taste.
*Good over pasta.

****

ROASTED PEPPERS AND WALNUTS SAUCE

1 jar roasted peppers	½ cup virgin olive oil	Salt and pepper
1 minced garlic clove	¼ cup walnut pieces	2 tbsp. Parmesan

Mix the peppers with oil, garlic and season to taste with salt and pepper. Set aside for at least 10 minutes. Toss in walnut pieces and freshly grated parmesan cheese.
*Good over pasta.

****

ROASTED TOMATO SAUCE

6 lbs. plum tomatoes	1 ½ cups celery	1 ½ tsp. salt
9 minced cloves garlic	1 ½ cups carrots	9 shallots
6 tbsp. balsamic vinegar	1 ½ tbsp. oregano	1 bay leaf
1 ½ tbsp. parsley	1 ½ tbsp. thyme	1 ½ tbsp. basil
1 tbsp. black pepper	1 ½ cups onions	

Put all ingredients in a pan and roast for about 45 minutes, or until soft in a 400-degree oven. When soft, remove bay leaf, transfer remaining ingredients to food processor or blender, and puree until slightly chunky.
*Good over pasta.

****

ROBERT SAUCE

2 med. chopped, onions	½ cup dry white wine	2 tbsp. butter
1 cup Brown Stock Sauce	½ tsp. red wine vinegar	1 sm. dill pickle
2 tbsp. all purpose flour	1 tsp. Dijon mustard	

Melt butter in a medium saucepan; add onions and sauté until soft and golden brown. Remove onions with slotted spoon and set aside. Add flour and stir to make a roux, cooking 3 to 4 minutes, until bubbly. Return onions to pan. Add wine and stock. Bring just to a boil over medium heat, stirring constantly. Reduce heat and simmer for 20 minutes. Add vinegar, mustard and finely chopped pickle, brown sauce and cook 1 minute. Serve hot.
*Good over pork.

****

ROMESCO SAUCE

½ cup blanched almonds	1 tbsp. tomato paste	1 cup mayonnaise
1 ½ tbsp. red wine vinegar	2 tsp. minced garlic	3 plum tomatoes
¼ tsp. cayenne pepper	Salt and pepper	

Peel, seed and chop tomatoes. Spread almonds on baking sheet and bake 5 to 7 minutes in 350 degree oven, or until lightly browned. Set aside to cool. In a medium bowl, combine the tomato paste and 1 tablespoon of water; stir until smooth. Add the mayonnaise, garlic, tomatoes, vinegar and almonds; heat for 5 minutes.
*Good over pasta.

ROSE SAUCE

2 tsp. instant beef broth	2 tbsp. cornstarch	½ cup water
1 cup Rose wine	¼ cup butter	2 tbsp. ketchup
½ cup green onions	1 clove garlic	1 tsp. thyme

Combine cornstarch and instant beef broth in a small saucepan; stir in water until smooth. Add butter, wine, ketchup, thyme and garlic. Cook, stirring constantly, until sauce thickens and bubbles; lower heat; simmer 10 minutes. Add green onions and simmer 5 minutes longer.
*Good over pasta.

****

ROSEMARY LIQUEUR SAUCE

1 ½ tsp. rosemary leaves	¼ tsp. coriander	1 mint leaf
½ cup sugar syrup	Peel of ½ lemon	1 ½ cups vodka

Gently crush the rosemary leaves and mint with the back of a spoon on a breadboard so the aroma and oils are released. Add the lemon and herbs to the vodka and soak for 10 days. Strain; add the sugar syrup. Pour into a jar with a cover and mature for 2-4 weeks.
*Good over poultry.

****

ROSY PLUM SAUCE

¼ cup sugar	1 tsp. cornstarch	2 tbsp. water
5 or 6 fresh plums		

In a medium saucepan combine the sugar and cornstarch. Stir in the sliced plums and water. Bring to a boil, stirring occasionally. Reduce heat and simmer sauce, covered, for 6 to 8 minutes or until desired consistency. Cool the sauce slightly. Serve warm.
*Good over ice cream or desserts.

ROUILLE SAUCE

½ cup white bread crumbs
¼ tsp. red pepper flakes
2 2-oz. sliced pimentos

¼ cup olive oil
3 tbsp. clam juice
3 garlic cloves

¼ cup milk
Salt

Combine breadcrumbs and milk (or water), in a bowl; let stand 5 minutes. Squeeze crumbs dry; discard liquid. In a blender or food processor, process the drained pimentos, hot pepper flakes, garlic and soaked breadcrumbs until smooth. Gradually add oil until thoroughly blended. When ready to serve, stir in broth and salt to taste.
*Good over pasta.

****

ROYAL SAUCE

½ tsp. dry mustard
2 tbsp. vinegar

1 tbsp. brown sugar
6 tbsp. margarine

1 cup ketchup

Mix all ingredients together in a saucepan, until well blended; cook 4 to 5 minutes, stirring constantly.
*Good over ham or fresh pork.

****

RUBY BEET SAUCE

1 cup unsweetened apple juice
2 tbsp. cider vinegar

1 lb. fresh beets

¼ tsp. salt

Place fresh beets in a 3-quart casserole. Cover and microwave on high for 10 to 12 minutes or until beets are tender. Add cold water to cover beets; drain and let cool. Trim off beet stems and roots; rub off skins. Place beets and remaining ingredients in container of a blender; process until smooth.
*Good over chicken or pork.

****

RUBY RASPBERRY SAUCE

2 tbsp. orange-flavored liqueur

10-oz. raspberries

2 tbsp. sugar

Use frozen raspberries with syrup, thawed. Combine raspberries, sugar and liqueur in a blender or food processor. Blend until smooth. Strain to remove seeds. Refrigerate.
*Good over desserts or ice cream.

RUM SAUCE I

| ⅓ cup packed brown sugar | 4 med. oranges | 1 tbsp. cornstarch |
| ¼ cup pineapple juice | ¼ cup dark rum | 2 tbsp. butter |

Grate the peel from one of the oranges, then squeeze the juice from all of them. Put cornstarch in a small saucepan, add pineapple juice and brown sugar, blend together. Pour in orange juice. Bring to a boil, stirring constantly, and simmer 2 minutes. Beat in butter, orange peel and rum; serve hot.
*Good over fruit, desserts or ice cream.

****

RUM SAUCE II

| ¾ cups unsalted butter | 1 ½ cups sugar | 2 oz. white rum |

Whip the butter in a mixer, until light and gradually add the sugar until the mixture is fluffy. Add rum and beat for two minutes. Refrigerate for 1 hour.
*Good over warm pudding or other desserts.

****

RUM SAUCE III

| 2 tbsp. cornstarch | ½ tsp. vanilla | ½ cup sugar |
| ¼ cup dark rum | 1 ⅔ cups milk | |

Mix sugar and cornstarch in a glass bowl, whisk in milk and microwave, uncovered, on high 5 to 5 ½ minutes, whisking every 2 minutes, until sauce thickens. Mix in rum and vanilla and serve warm.
*Good over fruit, desserts or ice cream.

****

RUM WALNUT FUDGE SAUCE

½ cup light corn syrup	½ cup sour cream	2 cups sugar
2 tsp. rum extract	2 tbsp. butter	Dash of salt
1 cup walnuts, chopped		

Combine sugar, sour cream, corn syrup, butter and salt in a heavy saucepan. Bring to a boil, stirring constantly, until sugar dissolves. Remove from heat and let cool, then stir in rum extract. Beat vigorously until mixture thickens, stir in walnuts.

Optional: Use ½ cup peanut butter, ½ cup milk and 1 tsp. vanilla in place of sour cream, rum extract and walnuts.
*Good over desserts or ice cream.

RUM-APRICOT SAUCE

1 cup apricot preserves	2 tbsp. sugar	3 tbsp. water
1 ½ tsp. dark rum		

Combine ingredients in a small saucepan; simmer, stirring occasionally, for 5 minutes. Stir in 1 ½ teaspoons dark rum.
*Good over ice cream.

****

RUM-RAISIN-PEACH SUNDAES SAUCE

2 tbsp. orange juice	2 tbsp. brown sugar	2 tbsp. raisins
8-oz. can peach slices	2 tbsp. butter	2 tbsp. rum
2 tbsp. walnuts, chopped		

In a small saucepan stir in raisins, brown sugar, orange juice and butter. Cook and stir 5 minutes or until hot. Stir in peach slices and rum. Heat through. Add walnuts.
*Good over ice cream or desserts.

****

RUSSIAN RED BEANS AND PLUM SAUCE

½ tsp. red pepper flakes	2 tsp. fresh basil	2 garlic cloves
⅓ cup damson plum jelly	20 oz. red kidney beans	Salt and pepper

Combine all ingredients except beans in a food processor and pulse until garlic is pulverized and mixture is well combined. Add to beans, stir well and allow flavors to develop for 2 to 3 hours at room temperature.
*Good over duck.

****

RUSTIC SAUCE

14 oz. plum tomatoes	3 tbsp. butter	1 sm. onion
7 oz. lg. pork sausages	1 cup white wine	1 clove garlic
1 cup peas	Salt and pepper	

Melt the butter and add the finely chopped onion and garlic. When the onion begins to turn color add the tomatoes with their juice. Add salt and pepper to taste. Cook for 20 minutes. In a separate covered pan, cook the sausages gently in the wine. When cooked, strain the liquid into the tomatoes. Skin the sausage and slice.
*Good over pasta or rice.

SAFFRON SAUCE

2 tbsp. wine vinegar
½ tbsp. salt
cayenne or white pepper

7 garlic cloves
6 egg yolks

pinch of saffron
2 cups olive oil

Puree garlic cloves in a blender, then place in a bowl with wine vinegar, saffron and salt. Add two egg yolks and blend carefully. Add remaining egg yolks, one at a time and oil slowly until sauce is thick and heavy. To make thinner, add drops of vinegar and oil. Season to taste.
*Good for pasta.

****

SAGE SAUCE I

1 cup white wine

1 tbsp. butter

1 tsp. sage

Heat all ingredients in a saucepan, for about 5 minutes.
*Good over pasta, fish or any meat.

****

SAGE SAUCE II

½ cup half and half
1 ¼ cups parmesan cheese

1 stick butter
½ tsp. sage

Fresh pepper
½ cup peas

Heat half and half and sage, in a saucepan, over low heat about 5 minutes to reduce slightly and release flavor of sage. Add butter, when melted, add remaining ingredients. Keep warm.
*Good over pasta.

****

SAGE SAUCE III

4-8 lg. sage leaves
Parmesan cheese

1 cup chicken broth
¼ cup cream

4 tbsp. butter

Melt butter in a saucepan; add sage leaves and heat 3 minutes in bubbling butter, then remove. Add chicken stock. Turn heat on high and reduce to ½ to ¾ cups. Stir in heavy cream, bring to a boil for 3 minutes; add cheese.
*Good over pasta or ravioli.

SALSA SAUCE I

2 cups fresh tomatoes
2 tbsp. fresh cilantro
Juice of 1 fresh lime

1 ripe avocado
1 lg. clove garlic
1 tbsp. olive oil

1 med. onion
1 fresh jalapeno

Seed and chop tomatoes in small pieces, dice avocado and finely chop cilantro, onion and garlic. Seed and derib jalapeno and finely dice. Combine all ingredients in stainless steel bowl. Allow to steep for at least ½ hour.
*Good over chicken, fish, hamburger or salad.

****

SALSA SAUCE II

3 cups tomato, diced
¼ cup tomato juice
½ cup cilantro, chopped

2-3 jalapeno peppers
3 tbsp. lime juice

⅓ cup onion, diced
½ tsp. salt

Puree half the tomatoes, jalapenos and half the onion, tomato juice, lime juice and salt in the food processor. Transfer to a bowl and add remaining tomatoes and onion. Refrigerate before serving, add the cilantro.
*Good over chicken.

****

SATAY SAUCE I

1 lg. onion, quartered
6 sm. dried red chilies
1 tbsp. grated lemon peel
¾ cup crunchy peanut butter

2 cups boiling water
2 tbsp. peanut oil
1 tbsp. pine nuts
¼ cup shredded unsweetened coconut

2 garlic cloves
1 tsp. sugar
Salt

In a medium bowl, pour boiling water over coconut. Let stand about 30 minutes until cool. Squeeze through fine cheesecloth to make coconut milk. Set aside; discard coconut. Place onion, garlic, chilies, pine nuts and lemon peel in a food processor or blender and puree. Heat oil in a saucepan and add the blender mixture. Transfer to a saucepan and cook over low heat for 3 to 4 minutes, stirring. Add coconut milk to saucepan and bring to a boil, stirring constantly. Reduce heat and add peanut butter, sugar and salt. Simmer for about 3 minutes.
*Serve hot over skewer of broiled marinated beef or chicken cubes.
*Cool, it makes a good dip for crisp vegetables.

SATAY SAUCE II

1 clove garlic	1 tbsp. peanut oil	2-3 cups coconut milk
2 dried chilies	2 tsp. lemon juice	2 tbsp. sugar
1 cup unsalted peanut butter		

Sauté sliced garlic in oil, in a saucepan, until lightly browned. Remove garlic slices and discard. Cool slightly, then add 1 cup of coconut milk, dried chilies, lemon juice and sugar. Bring to a simmer and add peanut butter. Simmer over low heat for 20 minutes, thinning as needed with additional coconut milk. Sauce should be slightly soupy.
*Good over pasta.

****

SAUERKRAUT CHAMPAGNE SAUCE

1 cup sauerkraut (drained)	¼ cup white wine	¼ cup chicken stock
½ cup onion, chopped	¼ cup cooked bacon	6 oz. champagne

Heat sauerkraut in a saucepan, with the white wine, chicken stock, onion and champagne until reduced by half. Add bacon and continue to simmer for another minute.
*Good over veal or meat.

****

SAUERKRAUT CREAM SAUCE

1 cup sauerkraut	½ cup chicken stock	1 tbsp. butter
½ cup cream	1 egg yolk	1 tsp. paprika

Mix the cream and eggs together, in a bowl. Heat sauerkraut, chicken stock, butter and paprika, in a saucepan, for a few minutes. Remove from heat and blend it into the cream mixture.
*Good over veal.

****

SAUERKRAUT DUTCH SAUCE

1 cup sauerkraut	½ cup white wine	¼ cup chicken stock
¼ cup sliced apples	1 tbsp. flour	1 tbsp. butter

Heat white wine, thin apple slices, chicken stock and sauerkraut in a saucepan, for 35 minutes. To thicken the sauce add melted butter with flour.
*Good over ham.

SAUERKRAUT FRENCH SAUCE

1 cup sauerkraut	½ cup white wine	1 tbsp. butter
¼ cup cooked carrots	¼ cup juniper berries	

Cook sauerkraut with the white wine in a saucepan; add butter, carrots and juniper berries for about 5 minutes.
*Good over ham.

****

SAUERKRAUT HUNGARIAN SAUCE

1 cup sauerkraut	½ cup onion	1 tbsp. butter
½ cup tomato puree	¼ cup shredded red pepper	½ cup white wine
½ cup cooked bacon		

Sauté onion in butter, in a skillet, until lightly brown. Add sauerkraut, tomato puree, red pepper and cook for 5 minutes. Add white wine and cook an additional 5 minutes. Add cooked bacon.
*Good over chicken.

****

SAUERKRAUT RUSSIAN SAUCE

1 cup sauerkraut	½ cup onion	1 cup white wine
½ cup sour cream	1 tbsp. butter	

Lightly brown onion in butter, in a saucepan; add sauerkraut and white wine. Continue to simmer for 10 minutes; add sour cream.
*Good over pork chops.

****

SAUSAGE AND MUSHROOM SAUCE

1 lb. Italian sausage	¼ cup onions, chopped	½ cup white wine
2 cups tomato sauce	8 sliced mushrooms	Salt and pepper

In a large skillet, sauté loose sausage until it loses its raw look. Add onion and garlic. Continue cooking until the sausage is lightly browned. Add mushrooms and sauté until the mushrooms lose their white color. Add wine and reduce liquid until pan is almost dry. Add tomato sauce and season to taste with salt and pepper. Bring to a boil.
*Good over pasta.

SAUTERNE SAUCE

¼ cup green onion
1 ½ cups milk
1 tsp. leaf thyme

¼ cup all purpose flour
½ cup Sauterne wine
¼ tsp. white pepper

¼ cup butter
1 tsp. salt

Melt butter in a small metal saucepan; sauté green onion until soft. Stir in flour and cook, stirring constantly, until mixture bubbles; stir in milk, wine, salt, thyme and pepper. Cook, stirring constantly, until sauce thickens and bubbles 3 minutes; lower heat and simmer 10 minutes. Serve warm.
*Good over turkey or lamb.

****

SAVORY APPLE SAUCE

10 med. apples
Rind of 2 limes
1 tsp. curry powder

1 tbsp. water
4 tbsp. honey

1 tsp. nutmeg
1 tsp. ginger

Peel, core and quarter the apples. Place in a large heavy saucepan with the water, apple juice or lemon juice and nutmeg. Cover and simmer about 30 minutes, until the apples are tender. Puree in blender or food processor and stir in the seasonings.
*Good over pork.
*Optional: Replace lime rind, ginger and curry powder with 4 tbsp. brandy.
*Good over duck or goose.

****

SAVORY SPAGHETTI SAUCE

½ cup onion, chopped
½ cup carrots, chopped
2 8-oz. can tomato sauce
14 ½ oz. can stewed tomatoes

2 garlic cloves, minced
¼ cup celery, chopped
1 tsp. crushed basil

2 tbsp. olive oil
1 tsp. oregano
¼ tsp. pepper

Sauté onion and garlic in oil, in a skillet, until onion is soft. Add carrot, celery, oregano, basil and pepper. Sauté 5 minutes. Add tomato sauce and stewed tomatoes, breaking tomatoes with a spoon. Simmer, uncovered, 30 minutes.
*Good over pasta.

SAXON SAUCE

2 tbsp. butter
1 cup white wine
1 tbsp. lemon juice

¼ cup shallots, chopped
½ cup fish stock

1 tbsp. flour
1 tbsp. mustard

Heat all ingredients in a saucepan; boil until mixture is reduced by half.
*Good over fish.

****

SCALLOPS AND HERBED CHEESE SAUCE

1 tbsp. onion, chopped
4 oz. herbed cream cheese
2 tbsp. parsley, chopped

1 tbsp. peanut oil
¾ lb. bay scallops
Salt and white pepper

1 cup white wine
1 tbsp. lemon juice

Sauté finely chopped onion in peanut oil, in a saucepan, until soft. Add wine and lemon juice; reduce by half. Add scallops and poach until firm, about a minute. Remove from heat and stir in cream cheese until smooth. Season to taste with salt and white pepper; add parsley.
*Good over pasta.

****

SCAMPI CREAM SAUCE

2 tbsp. olive oil
1 cup heavy cream

12 unshelled shrimp
salt and pepper

6 oz. white wine

Sauté shrimp in oil, in a saucepan, for 2 minutes, adding wine and cook for another 1 minute. Add cream and continue to cook another 2 minutes. Add seasoning to taste.
*Good over pasta.

****

SCANDINAVIAN MUSTARD SAUCE

2 ½ tbsp. prepared mustard
¼ tsp. white pepper
9 tbsp. olive oil

3 tbsp. white vinegar
⅛ tsp. cardamom

¾ tsp. salt
¼ cup sugar

Place all ingredients in a blender and blend thoroughly. Make 2 hours before serving.
*Good over poultry.

SEAFOOD DIABLO SAUCE

½ lb. shrimp
½ cup (jar) mussels
28 oz. crushed tomatoes
½ cup chicken broth

½ lb. calamari
½ tsp. crushed pepper
2 tbsp. olive oil
½ tsp. oregano

½ doz. clams
2 cloves garlic
½ cup red dry wine
salt and pepper

Clean calamari and cut into pieces, peel and devain shrimp. Sauté garlic in olive oil in a saucepan, over medium heat. Add crushed tomatoes, chicken broth, red wine, oregano, crushed pepper, salt and pepper to taste. Place calamari into tomato sauce and simmer for 25 minutes. Add the shrimp and clams and continue to cook for 10 minutes. Add muscles and continue to cook for 2 minutes.
*Good over pasta.

****

SEAFOOD SAUCE I

1 cup mayonnaise
1 tbsp. onion, minced

1 bunch watercress
1 tsp. Worcestershire sauce

1 tbsp. lemon juice

Chop watercress; add all ingredients in a bowl; mix well. Chill to allow flavors to blend.
*Good over cold pasta, salad or seafood.

****

SEAFOOD SAUCE II

1 cup mayonnaise
2 tbsp. chili sauce

2 tbsp. anchovy paste
¼ cup tomato ketchup

2 tbsp. tarragon
Lemon juice

Mix all ingredients together, in a glass bowl, until well blended. Add pepper if needed. Chill and serve.
*Good over shrimp.

****

SHELLFISH IN A FOIL SAUCE

½ lb. cleaned mussels
6 shrimp
4 oz. white wine

½ lb. clams
8 oz. plum tomatoes
basil

2 oz. squid
2 tbsp. olive oil
oregano

Place all ingredients into a large double layer of foil, season to taste. Place in a 450 degree over for 8 minutes.
*Good over pasta.

SHREDDED CHICKEN SPICY PEANUT SAUCE

1 tsp. dried hot pepper
3 tbsp. scallions, chopped
1 cup chunky peanut butter
1 cup defatted chicken stock
½ shredded Boston lettuce
2 cups shredded cooked chicken

1 tsp. sesame oil
2 tbsp. brown sugar
4 tbsp. rice vinegar
1 bunch watercress
8 Chinese pea pods

2 tsp. corn oil
2 scallions
2 tbsp. soy sauce
8 cherry tomatoes
1 cup bean sprouts

Heat the vegetable oil in a small pan, over low heat. Add the dried pepper and cook 1 minute. Add chopped scallions and remove from heat. Stir in sesame oil, brown sugar, vinegar and soy sauce; mix well. Place pan over low heat again, slowly adding peanut butter, then chicken stock. Remove from heat and let stand for 10 minutes for flavor to blend.
*Good over poultry.

****

SHRIMP CANTONESE-STYLE SAUCE

1 tbsp. Chinese black beans
1 tsp. grated ginger root
1 cup chicken broth
3 grated garlic cloves
Scallion leaves, sliced

¼ cup minced pork
2 tbsp. dry sherry
1 lb. cooked shrimp
2 tbsp. vegetable oil
1 tbsp. cornstarch

1 tsp. soy sauce
1 tbsp. sugar
1 tsp. salt
1 egg, beaten
2 tbsp. cold water

Mix cornstarch, in a cup, with 2 tablespoons cold water. Stir-fry pork in oil, in a skillet or a wok, until well done. Add shrimp, ginger, garlic, and beans; stir-fry briefly. Combine broth, soy sauce, salt, sugar, sherry and cornstarch mixture; stir. Add to wok or skillet; heat until thickened. Remove from heat; pour egg in slowly, stirring with fork and add scallion.
*Good on rice, with lobster, shrimp, fish dishes.

****

SHRIMP COCKTAIL SAUCE

6 drops Tabasco sauce
½ tsp. Worcestershire sauce

¾ cup Chili sauce
¼ cup green pepper

1 tbsp. lemon juice
⅓ cup celery

Blend Worcestershire sauce, chili sauce, Tabasco sauce, lemon juice; then add peppers and celery, in a glass bowl. Blend until pepper is thoroughly chopped, about 2 seconds. Refrigerate.
*Good with shrimp.

SICILIAN SWEET AND SOUR SAUCE

2 tbsp. vegetable oil
¼ cup parsley, chopped
1 tbsp. wine vinegar
1" cinnamon stick

¼ cup onion, minced
2 tbsp. chopped basil
2 cups tomato puree

Salt to taste
1 tsp. sugar
Ground pepper

Sauté onion, parsley, and basil until soft in oil in saucepan. Add tomato, salt, pepper, and cinnamon. Stirring until slightly thickened over low heat; add dissolved sugar in vinegar. Simmer 5 minutes. Remove cinnamon stick and serve.
*Good over poultry or fish.

****

SICILIAN-STYLE TOMATO SAUCE

2 garlic cloves, minced
2 ½ lbs. fresh tomatoes
½ cup golden raisins

2 tbsp. olive oil
1 tsp. sugar
1 tsp. tomato paste

1 lg. sliced onion
½ tsp. allspice
½ cup pine nuts

In a large skillet, heat oil and sauté onion and garlic about 5 minutes. Do not burn onion. Chop tomatoes in food processor using on/off motion. Add tomatoes, salt, sugar, allspice and paste to onions. Simmer, about 15 minutes, until sauce thickens, stirring occasionally. Stir in raisins and pine nuts. Cook 2 minutes.
*Good over pasta.

****

SIMPLE RED SAUCE

7 cups crushed tomatoes
Juice from 1 lemon
1 tbsp. oregano

5 red bell peppers
1 tbsp. rosemary
Ground black pepper

1 tbsp. thyme
1 tsp. salt

Broil peppers for 20 minutes then remove skin and seeds. Place in a food processor and puree until smooth. Add herbs, salt and pepper, in a large saucepan and simmer over low heat for 1 hour. Add the lemon juice.
*Good over pasta.

****

SIMPLE TOMATO SAUCE

½ stick butter
16 oz. can plum tomatoes

5 tbsp. flour
¼ cup dry white wine

1 tsp. oregano

Melt butter in skillet; stir in flour. Cook, stirring for 2-3 minutes over low flame, without browning. Stir in tomatoes, with their juice, oregano and white wine. Bring to a boil, lower heat and simmer 3 minutes. Add white wine, if needed. *Good over pasta.

SIMPLE WHITE SAUCE

½ stick butter
2 cups hot milk

1 tbsp. Dijon mustard
1 tsp. sweet Hungarian paprika

5 tbsp. flour

Melt butter in a skillet and stir in flour. Cook, stirring constantly, for 2-3 minutes over a very low flame. Flour should not brown. Whisk in 2 cups hot milk, mustard and paprika and continue stirring until thick, another 2 minutes. Lower heat and cook 5 minutes more.

OPTIONAL: Add a 6-8 ounce can of fish. Mix well with sauce.
*Good over pasta.

****

SLOPPY JOES SAUCE

8 oz. can no-salt tomato sauce
1 ½ tbsp. Worchestershire sauce
¼ tsp. grated orange peel
1 tsp. prepared yellow mustard

Hot pepper sauce
½ tsp. dry mustard
Pinch ground cloves
1 lb. ground sirloin

½ cup ketchup
1 tsp. molasses
1 clove garlic
½ sm. onion

In a saucepan, over low heat, combine tomato sauce, ketchup, Worchestershire sauce, mustards, molasses, minced garlic, orange peel, cloves, and pepper sauce; mix well and simmer. Place the meat in a non-stick skillet, over medium-high heat, stirring occasionally, 4 to 5 minutes, or until meat is no longer pink. Pour meat into a strainer lined with paper towels. Allow fat to drain out. Add onion to pan and sauté, stirring frequently, about 5 minutes, or until translucent. Return meat to pan and add sauce. Heat 3 minutes, stirring occasionally. Add additional hot pepper sauce, if desired.
*Good over hamburger buns.

****

SMOKED SALMON, CUCUMBER AND DILL SAUCE

1 cup white wine
Bunch of scallions
1 tbsp. chopped dill

¼ lb. salmon
4 tbsp. unsalted butter
1 cup light cream

1 clove garlic
1 cucumber
1 tsp. salt

Peel, seed and dice cucumber place in a mixing bowl with salt, let sit for 15 minutes. Turn into a towel and squeeze out as much water as possible. Wash and drain. Set aside. Sauté garlic and finely chopped scallions in butter in a skillet, until barely softened. Add wine and reduce to ⅓; add chopped dill and cream. Simmer until slightly thickened. Add the cucumbers and julienned smoked salmon. Season to taste with salt and pepper.
*Good over pasta.

SMOKED SALMON, PEAS AND CAVIAR SAUCE

¼ lb. smoked salmon
Salt and white pepper

½ cup heavy cream
4 tbsp. salmon caviar

1 cup sour cream
1 cup green peas

Slice salmon into strips. Combine heavy cream and sour cream together in a bowl. Cook peas until tender in a saucepan. Add salmon, peas, salt and pepper. Add cream mixture. Garnish with salmon caviar.
*Good over pasta.

****

SMOKED SALMON SAUCE

4 oz. smoked salmon
6 oz. cream

½ sm. onion
black pepper

1 oz. butter

Melt butter in a saucepan; cook chopped onions until soft and tender. Add half the chopped salmon and cream, warm, stirring gently. Add the rest of the salmon in strips and blend.
*Use over pasta.

****

SMOKED TURKEY, PIN NUTS AND ROSEMARY SAUCE

4 tbsp. peanut oil
1 tbsp. orange zest
1 tsp. minced garlic

3 tbsp. olive oil
1 tsp. rosemary
1 cup smoked turkey breast, diced

½ cup pine nuts
Salt and pepper

Heat peanut oil and olive oil in a skillet. Add pine nuts, turkey and crumbled dried rosemary leaves. Heat gently until the pine nuts are toasted lightly. Season to taste with salt and pepper. Add orange zest, and minced garlic.
*Good over pasta.

****

SNAIL BUTTER SAUCE

1 lb. soft sweet butter
7 crushed garlic cloves
2 tbsp. dry white wine

¼ cup parsley
1 ½ tsp. salt
1 tbsp. Pernod

1 tbsp. shallots
1 slice white bread
Ground white pepper

Two tablespoons of finely chopped chives may be substituted for shallots. Ricard or other anise aperitif may be used in place of Pernod. Peel, crush and chop the garlic cloves very fine. Finely chop the fresh parsley, and trim and blend the white bread. Combine all ingredients, in a large bowl, except the bread and wine and mix carefully. Then add the bread and wine and mix just enough to add it to the butter.
*Good over snails or fish.

SORREL SAUCE

4 tbsp. unsalted butter	1 cup unsalted fish stock	1 cup heavy cream
3 tbsp. all-purpose flour	1 cup sorrel leaves	Salt and pepper

Wash leaves, remove stems and cut into fine ribbons. Place the cream in a small saucepan and bring to a boil. Reduce the heat and simmer for 10 minutes or until reduced by half. Place the stock in another saucepan and heat over medium heat. Melt 3 tablespoons of butter, over medium heat, in another saucepan. When the foam subsides, remove the pan from the heat and whisk in the flour. Return to the heat and whisk for another minute and gradually add the stock. Raise the heat and bring to a simmer, whisking constantly. Add the cream and season with salt and pepper to taste; continue to cook for 10 minutes. Melt the remaining butter in a small pan over medium heat. Toss in the sorrel and stir into the sauce mixture.
*Good over pasta.

****

SOUR CREAM SAUCE

1 tsp. prepared mustard	1 cup sour cream	¼ tsp. sugar
2 hard-cooked eggs	⅛ tsp. pepper	¼ tsp. salt

Press eggs through a sieve, into a mixing bowl. Add sour cream and beat with a mixer at medium speed for 3 minutes. Add mustard, sugar, salt, and pepper. Beat 1 minute at high speed.
*Good with ham or veal.

****

SOUR CREAM GRAPE SAUCE

¼ cup onion, chopped	2 tbsp. white wine	1 tbsp. butter
½ cup sour cream	10 grapes	1 tbsp. sherry

In a saucepan, sauté onion in butter, until lightly brown; adding white wine, boil down to half. Add sour cream, grapes and sherry. Mix together until well blended and heat for another minute or two.
*Good pasta or baked potato.

****

SOUTH-OF-THE-BORDER SAUCE

4-oz. green chilies, diced	1 lg. onion, diced	1 tsp. salt
2 cloves garlic, crushed	16-oz. tomatoes	

Bring all ingredients to a boil in a saucepan. Reduce heat and simmer until the onion is tender, about 30 minutes.
*Good hot over vegetables, cold over salads.

SPEEDY RAISIN SAUCE

¼ tsp. ground ginger	½ cup brown sugar	2 tbsp. lemon juice
22-oz. can raisin pie filling	½ tsp. dry mustard	2 tbsp. water

In a saucepan, blend sugar, mustard, and ginger. Stir in pie filling, lemon juice, and water. Bring to a boil; simmer, covered, for 5 minutes.
*Good over ham.

****

SPICED GOOSEBERRY RELISH SAUCE

2 cups gooseberries	1 cup brown sugar	¼ cup vinegar
2 tbsp. sweet Marsala	⅛ tsp. allspice	⅛ tsp. cloves
1 tsp. orange peel	¼ tsp. cinnamon	⅛ tsp. nutmeg

Remove tops and stems from gooseberries, rinse and drain. Stir together berries, brown sugar, vinegar, wine and finely shredded orange peel in a saucepan. Bring to a boil and reduce heat. Simmer, uncovered, for 5 minutes. Stir cloves, cinnamon, allspice and nutmeg into the hot berry mixture. Simmer, uncovered, for 5 minutes more, stirring often.
*Good over ham, pork, or chicken.

****

SPICED PLUM PUREE SAUCE

1 ½ lbs. red plums	1 ¼ cups water	½ cup sugar
½ tsp. ground cinnamon	4 tsp. cornstarch	2 tbsp. ginger wine

Cut plums in half, discard pits, place in a saucepan, with sugar, cinnamon and water. Cover and simmer 15 minutes. In a small bowl, blend cornstarch with wine. Stir into plum puree and cook over medium heat until thickened.
*Good over desserts.

****

SPICY BLACK-EYED PEA SAUCE

1 cup black-eyed peas	1 med. onion, chopped	¼ cup butter
1 tsp. curry paste	1 garlic clove	½ tsp. salt
A few sprigs parsley	⅔ cup plain low-fat yogurt	

Soak black-eyed peas, in a bowl of water overnight. Drain peas and place in a medium saucepan. Add enough water to cover the peas, add garlic clove and parsley. Simmer 1 hour or until peas are tender. Stir salt into beans and cook 5 minutes; drain and remove parsley. In a small saucepan, melt butter and cook onion until tender. Put beans and onion in a blender or food processor and puree. Pour bean puree into the saucepan, stir in curry paste and yogurt and reheat.
*Good over rice.

SPICY BUTTERMILK SAUCE

2 tsp. peanut oil
1 tsp. chili paste
2 tsp. ground ginger
1 minced garlic clove

4 tbsp. onion, chopped
2 tsp. light soy sauce
½ tsp. coriander
¼ cup crunchy peanut butter

2 scallions
1 cup buttermilk
½ tsp. cumin

In a nonstick skillet heat oil; add onion and garlic and cook over a moderate heat until slightly softened. Add the scallions, chili paste, soy sauce, ginger, cumin and coriander. Cook for 2 minutes. Stir in and melt the peanut butter; over very low heat stir in the buttermilk. Do not allow to boil.
*Good over rice or noodles.

****

SPICY CRANBERRY SAUCE

2 cups cranberries
1 cup sugar

⅛ tsp. salt
1 3" stick cinnamon

1 cup water

Combine sugar, water, cinnamon stick, and salt in a 1-quart saucepan and stir over low heat until sugar is dissolved. Bring to a boil, for 5 minutes. Add the cranberries. Continue to boil uncovered without stirring, about 5 minutes, or until skins pop. Cool and remove cinnamon stick.
*Good with meat or poultry.

****

SPICY FRUIT SAUCE

¼ cup golden raisins
¼ cup strawberry spread
1 ¼ cups unsweetened pineapple juice

½ tsp. red pepper
Green onion strips

2 cloves garlic
¼ tsp. cornstarch

Combine pineapple juice, raisins, crushed red pepper, and sliced garlic in a large non aluminum skillet; bring to a boil. Cook 7 minutes or until reduced to ¾ cup, stirring occasionally. Combine strawberry spread and cornstarch; stir into cooking liquid, and cook 1 minute or until syrupy.
*Good over poultry.

SPICY GEORGIAN PEACH VINEGAR SAUCE

| 10 oz. rice-wine vinegar | 2 med. peaches | 1 lime |
| 2 nickel-size ginger slices | | |

Smash ginger flat with a glass. Peel and slice peaches and place in a 16 ounce glass bottle or jar. Carefully peel half of the zest off the lime in one long strip, being sure not to cut off the bitter pith. Add to the bottle. In a saucepan, over low heat, warm the vinegar until hot but not boiling. Immediately pour, through funnel, into bottle, leaving just enough room for the stopper or cork. Close and store in a cool, dark place. Marinate chicken or fish 1 hour.
*Good for marinating.

****

SPICY HORSERADISH SAUCE

| ½ cup chill sauce | 3 tbsp. lemon juice | 1 sm. garlic clove |
| 2 tsp. Worcestershire | 1 tbsp. horseradish | Dash red pepper |

Mix all ingredients together, until well blended. Cover bowl with plastic wrap and chill at least 1 hour to blend flavors. *Good over beef burgers.

****

SPICY ORANGE SAUCE

3 tbsp. vegetable oil	4 lg. garlic cloves	2 cups tomato puree
¾ cup orange marmalade	Juice of ½ lemon	Salt to taste
1 tbsp. fresh ginger root, chopped		

Heat oil in saucepan and add garlic. Cook over medium heat for 10 minutes until golden, turning frequently. Do not burn. Add tomato puree and cook for 10 minutes. Stir in all remaining ingredients and cook for 15-20 minutes, until slightly thickened.
*Good over pasta or vegetables.

****

SPICY PEANUT SAUCE I

| 6 oz. unsalted tomato sauce | 1 ½ tsp. chili power | 2 cups water |
| ½ cup unsalted peanuts | 1 slice white bread | 1 ½ tbsp. Mrs. Dash |

Put ingredient into blender or small mixing bowl. Blend or mix well. Transfer to 1 quart saucepan; heat to boiling, stirring frequently. Reduce heat and simmer 5 minutes, stirring often.
*Good over chicken.

SPICY PEANUT SAUCE II

2 tbsp. soy sauce
2 tbsp. peanut oil
1 tbsp. wine vinegar
⅓ cup peanut butter

½ cup onion, minced
1 tbsp. lemon juice
1 tbsp. brown sugar
½ tsp. coriander

2 tbsp. minced ginger
2 tbsp. minced garlic
Dash hot sauce
2 tbsp. ketchup

Sauté onion, garlic and ginger in oil, in a small saucepan, over low heat, until onion is soft. Add vinegar and brown sugar, cook until sugar dissolves. Remove from heat and stir in remaining ingredients, until smooth, about 2 minutes.
*Good over fish.

****

SPICY SAUCE

1 med. onion, chopped
½ cup Southern Comfort
½ tsp. chili powder

4 tbsp. bacon grease
⅓ cup brown sugar
Juice 1 lemon

1 pt. ketchup
1 tsp. salt

Substitute 3 slices chopped bacon for bacon grease. Lightly brown onion in bacon grease or chopped bacon, in a skillet. Remove from heat. Add ketchup and Southern Comfort; stir. Add remaining ingredients; simmer slowly for 10 minutes.
*Good for chicken wings.

****

SPICY SPECIAL SAUCE

1 tbsp. Worcestershire sauce
16 oz. can tomato puree
2 tbsp. Dijon mustard
⅓ cup cider vinegar

2 cloves garlic
1 tsp. chili powder
½ tsp. oregano
½ tsp. paprika

3 tbsp. oil
½ tsp. ginger
1 lg. onion
Salt and pepper

Chop a large onion and 2 garlic cloves. Place in a skillet; sauté in oil until limp and transparent. Stir in remaining ingredients and simmer gently for 10 minutes.
*Good for beef, lamb, chicken, veal and ribs.

****

SPICY THAI SAUCE I

½ tsp. red pepper
2 tbsp. currant jelly
1 tbsp. green chili peppers

8 oz. can tomatoes
1 clove garlic
2 tsp. vinegar

¼ cup raisins
Dash salt

Place all ingredients in blender or food processor, and blend until smooth. Transfer to a small saucepan and heat to a boil. Reduce heat and simmer 10 minutes or until mixture reaches brushing consistency.
*Good over chicken.

SPICY THAI SAUCE II

2 tbsp. currant jelly
½ tsp. crushed red pepper
1 tbsp. crushed chile peppers

8 oz. can tomatoes
1 clove garlic

¼ cup raisins
2 tsp. vinegar

Blend all ingredients until smooth in a saucepan. Heat to boiling, then reduce heat and cook for 10 minutes.
*Good over pasta.

****

SPICY TOMATO SAUCE I

9 tbsp. vegetable oil
6 med. cloves garlic
1 tsp. fennel seeds
¼ tsp. cayenne pepper

1 lg. eggplant
1 tsp. cumin seed
1 tbsp. coriander
¼ tsp. turmeric

1 piece ginger
3 med. tomatoes
1 tsp. salt

Preheat broiler. Cut eggplant lengthwise and then crosswise into slices. Brush slices on both sides with about 3 tablespoons of oil and arrange in a single layer on large broiling tray. Broil 3 inches from the heat for about 7 minutes on each side, or until browned. Puree ginger, garlic and 3 tablespoons of water in food processor or blender. Set aside. In a large skillet, heat the remaining 6 tablespoon of oil over medium heat. When hot, add fennel and cumin seeds; let sizzle 30 seconds, or until seeds start to darken. Add ginger-garlic puree and cook, stirring, 1 minute. Stir in chopped tomatoes, coriander, salt, turmeric and cayenne pepper, and bring to a simmer. Cook over medium heat 2 to 3 minutes, stirring often. Cover, turn heat to low, and cook 5 minutes. Fold the browned eggplant slices into the tomato sauce and bring to a simmer. Cover and cook over low heat another 3 to 5 minutes.
*Good over poultry or pasta.

****

SPICY TOMATO SAUCE II

16-oz. can tomato puree
1 tsp. jalapeno pepper
2 tbsp. red wine vinegar

⅓ cup green onions
¼ cup golden raisins
1 tbsp. lime juice

1 tbsp. brown sugar
¼ tsp. salt
1 sm. clove garlic

Combine all ingredients in a blender; Process until smooth. Pour into a bowl; cover and chill.
*Good over salad greens.

SPICY TOMATO SAUCE III

2 cups tomato puree
1 stick cinnamon
Salt and ground pepper

2 tsp. whole cloves
2 cups sugar

½ orange
1 lemon

Slice thin and seed the orange and lemon. Place cinnamon and cloves in cheesecloth bag. Put tomato puree, spices, sugar, orange and lemon slices, into large deep saucepan. Boil over medium heat, stirring frequently, until thick, about an hour, stirring occasionally.
*Good over poultry.

****

SPICY-FLAVOR OIL SAUCE

⅓ cup curry powder

1 cup olive or vegetable oil

¼ cup water

Chili powder may be used as a substitute for curry powder. Combine curry powder and water in a cup. Heat oil with spice mixture over very low heat, in a saucepan, until just warm. Remove from heat and pour into a small glass bowl. Cover, and let stand at room temperature for one week. Strain into a bottle; discard spices. Refrigerate.
*Good over pork or poultry.

****

SPINACH AND MASCARPONE SAUCE

1 ½ tbsp. butter
⅔ cup heavy cream
salt and pepper

1 clove garlic
⅔ cup mascarpone cheese

10 oz. of spinach
¼ cup chicken stock

Melt butter in a saucepan and sauté garlic until brown. Chop spinach and cook on a low heat for 5 minutes. Drain and add to saucepan with garlic, continue to cook a few minutes. Mix in cream, chicken stock and cheese; simmer a few more minutes.
*Good over pasta.

****

SPINACH SAUCE

1 lb. fresh spinach
16 oz. milk
½ cup grated parmesan cheese

4 tbsp. butter
salt and pepper

¼ cup flour
grated nutmeg

Wash spinach leaves and cook for 5 minutes in a covered saucepan. Mix butter and flour until well blended; add milk and nutmeg, simmer for 5 minutes in another saucepan. Drain spinach and add to mixture. Add cheese, salt and pepper to taste.
*Good over pasta.

STAR ANISE SAUCE

⅔ tbsp. star anise crushed   ½ cup sugar syrup   1 ½ cups vodka

Place vodka in a glass bottle; add the herb and let soak about 2 weeks. Strain and add sugar syrup (boil equal parts water and sugar until it becomes sugar syrup); add liqueur.

Optional spices: a pinch of mace, cinnamon.
*Good over desserts or ice cream.

****

STRAWBERRY GLAZE SAUCE

1 tbsp. corn starch   ⅓ cup light corn syrup   ¼ cup water
1 tsp. lemon juice   ¼ cup fresh strawberries   red food coloring

Mix corn starch, water and corn syrup in a saucepan, until smooth, add crushed fresh strawberries. Boil and strain. Add lemon juice and red food coloring.
*Good over desserts or ice cream.

****

STRAWBERRY SAUCE I

3 cups fresh strawberries   3 tbsp. powdered sugar   3 cups vodka
1 cup sugar syrup

Remove stems from berries, sprinkle them with powdered sugar and let dissolve; then add to alcohol. Let stand 2 weeks. Crush the berries through a strainer. Add syrup and mature one week. (Boil down equal parts of water and sugar for sugar syrup)
For Crème de Fraises, add 2 cups sugar syrup.
*Good over desserts or ice cream.

****

STRAWBERRY SAUCE II

2 cups strawberry puree   2 cups sugar   1 cup butter
2 egg whites

Cream together, in a mixing bowl, the butter and sugar until very light. Beat in egg whites and strawberry puree. Chill.
*Good over desserts and ice cream.

STROGANOFF SAUCE

2 tbsp. butter
½ tsp. thyme

1 cup sour cream
salt and pepper

¼ cup sherry

Mix sour cream and butter together in a saucepan; add remaining ingredients, and heat for about 10 minutes.
*Good over chicken or beef.

****

SUN-DRIED TOMATO CREAM SAUCE

⅔ cup sun-dried tomatoes
8-oz. soft cream cheese
2 tbsp. parsley, chopped

3-4 garlic cloves
¼ cup sour cream
¼ cup olive oil

¼ cup margarine
½ tsp. oregano
Salt and pepper

Cover tomatoes in boiling water; let stand 10 minutes. Drain. Place tomatoes, oil and garlic in food processor or blender, process until coarsely chopped. Add cream cheese and oregano; process until blended. Melt margarine in medium saucepan; stir in cream cheese mixture and sour cream. Cook until thoroughly heated. Season to taste. Sprinkle with chopped parsley. Serve immediately.
*Good for pasta.

****

SUN-DRIED TOMATOES, OLIVE AND BASIL SAUCE

8 oz. sun-dried tomatoes
¼ cup oil, from tomatoes
¾ lb. Brie cheese

½ cup lemon zest
2 cloves of garlic
½ cup olive oil

1 cup olives
1 cup basil
2 tsp. pepper

Combine all ingredients together in a large bowl. Cover and let stand at room temperature for 4 hours.
*Good over pasta.

****

SUPREME SAUCE

1 cup chicken stock or water
1 ½ cups Chicken Veloute Sauce

¾ cup whipping cream

½ cup mushrooms

Place stock and mushrooms in a saucepan and bring to a boil. Boil until liquid is reduced to ½ cup. Remove from heat and keep hot. In a separate saucepan, heat Chicken Veloute Sauce, about 10 minutes until reduced to 1 cup. Strain mushrooms and their liquid over sauce; discard mushrooms or use with meal. Stir mushroom flavored stock into sauce. Slowly add cream, stirring constantly.
*Serve hot with roast chicken, poached fish or over hard cooked eggs.

SWEDISH SAUCE

1 cup apple puree
¼ cup grated horseradish

1 cup white wine

2 tbsp. mayonnaise

Cook all ingredients in a saucepan, until well blended, about 5 minutes.
*Good over chicken or beef.

****

SWEET 'N SOUR CARROT SAUCE

1 clove garlic, minced
1 cup carrot strips
¼ cup soy sauce
1 cup pineapple juice

1 cup green pepper strips
1 ¼ cups chicken bouillon
3 tbsp. brown sugar
⅓ cup teriyaki sauce

1 tbsp. oil
2 tbsp. honey
2 tbsp. vinegar
½ tsp. ginger

Heat oil in a skillet and sauté garlic, add the remaining ingredients. Bring to a full boil, about 5 minutes.
*Good over steak.

****

SWEET AND SOUR ONION SAUCE

2 lbs. pearl onions
½ cup red wine vinegar
1 ¼ cups water
Salt and pepper

3 tbsp. olive oil
1 tbsp. tomato paste
⅓ cup raisins

1 oz. prosciutto
1 tbsp. sugar
1 bay leaf

Cook onions in pot of boiling water for 1 minute, drain. Refresh in bowl of ice water, drain and peel. Heat oil in skillet over medium heat. Mix in prosciutto and onions, then remaining ingredients; bring to boil. Reduce heat; simmer until onions are tender and almost no liquid remains in pan, about 1 hour 15 minutes, stir frequently during last 15 minutes.
*Good over hamburger or steak.

****

SWEET AND SOUR SAUCE

½ cup pineapple juice
1 tsp. Worcestershire sauce
¼ cup vinegar

1 cup brown sugar
1 tsp. cornstarch
2 tbsp. water

½ cup water
1 tbsp. soy sauce

Place sugar in ½ cup water in saucepan; bring to a boil. Cook until reduced by half; add vinegar, pineapple juice, soy sauce and Worcestershire sauce; bring to a boil. Reduce heat, simmer 15 minutes. Mix cornstarch with remaining water; add to sauce to thicken. Bring to a boil again; remove from heat.
*Good over pork.

SWEET AND ZESTY BRUSH-ON SAUCE

¾ cup cider vinegar
1 tsp. prepared mustard
⅛ pimento olives

⅓ cup brown sugar
1 tbsp. soy sauce
12 oz. can unsweetened pineapple juice

¾ cup ketchup
salt

In a saucepan, combine juice, sugar, vinegar, soy sauce, mustard and salt. Bring to a boil, then reduce heat and cook 30 minutes. Add olives.
*Good over poultry.

****

SWEET APPLE SAUCE

1 lb. Red Delicious apples
2 cups vodka or brandy

1 cup sugar syrup
Pinch of cinnamon

2 cloves

Cut apples in halves or quarters and remove the cores but do not peel. Place apples, cloves, cinnamon, and alcohol in a bottle and let stand for 2 weeks. Strain, add sugar syrup. Mature 2-3 weeks.
*Good over pork or desserts.

****

SWEET CHERRY SAUCE

2 16-oz. cans red cherries
3 tbsp. cherry brandy

2 tbsp. cornstarch

⅓ cup sugar

Drain cherries, remove pits and reserve juice. In a saucepan, blend cornstarch with a portion of the cherry juice, then add remaining juice with sugar. Cook over medium heat until sauce thickens. Stir in cherries and brandy and reheat.
*Good over ice cream.

****

SWEET ONION SAUCE

1 sm. Spanish onion
2 garlic cloves, minced
2 med. red bell peppers
½ cup sweet red wine

1 sm. Vidalia onion
1 med. red onion
½ cup tomato sauce
½ tsp. sugar

4 tbsp. butter
2 med. leeks
Salt and pepper
Cornstarch

Heat 2 tablespoons of butter in a skillet over low heat. Add peeled and sliced onions, cover, and cook until translucent. Add garlic and sliced leeks, sauté until tender. Heat 2 tablespoons butter in a skillet, add bell peppers and sugar. Sauté until tender. Add peppers, tomato sauce and red wine to onion mixture. Cook 10 minutes. If liquid needs to be thickened, use cornstarch dissolved in a small amount of water. Salt and pepper to taste.
*Good over fish.

****

SWEET PEPPER SAUCE

1 lbs. sweet red & yellow peppers
parsley

4 tbsp. olive oil
salt

4 cloves garlic

Remove seeds and fibers from peppers and cut into strips. Heat garlic in oil, in a saucepan, for 2 minutes; add peppers and cook 10 minutes. Add seasoning to taste.
*Good over all meats or pasta.

****

SYRACUSE SAUCE

2 sweet pepper, yellow
14 oz. can plum tomatoes
12 pitted black olives
1 ½ oz. grated cheese

1 lg. eggplant
4 anchovy fillets
3 cloves garlic
6 basil leaves

salt and pepper
2 tbsp. capers
2 tbsp. oil

Cut eggplant into slices and cube, roast peppers in oven, remove seeds. Cut in small strips, chop tomatoes, anchovies, eggplant and tomatoes. Cook 15 minutes, in a saucepan. Add peppers and cheese.
*Good over pasta.

****

TANGERINE SAUCE

4-5 whole tangerines　　　　　4 whole cloves　　　　　3 cups vodka
1 cup sugar syrup

Pierce tangerine skin with a fork, or skewer. Insert cloves into the indentations. Steep in vodka, in a jar, for ten days using enough vodka to cover the fruit. Strain and add sugar syrup. Mature. Mix well in blender before using.
*Good over ice cream and desserts.

****

TANGERINE BRANDY SAUCE

4 medium tangerines　　　　　3 cups brandy

Cut the tangerines in quarters, place in a tightly closed jar; let stand in brandy for 5 weeks, then strain. Sweetener may not be needed with brandy. Mature 6 months, at room temperature, before serving. Mix in blender before using.
*Good over ice cream and desserts.

****

TAO BARBECUE VINEGAR SAUCE

5 lg. cloves garlic　　　　　5 pearl onions　　　　　3 sprigs cilantro
2 tbsp. green peppercorns　　5 cherry tomatoes　　　6 jalapeno peppers
40 oz. apple cider vinegar

Place garlic cloves and onions onto small bamboo skewers. Place in a 42-ounce wide-mouth glass jar. Add cilantro and peppercorns. Place tomatoes and peppers onto skewers; roast over a medium flame until skin blackens; frequently tuning, add to jar. In a saucepan, over medium heat, warm vinegar until hot but not boiling. Pour into bottle leaving enough room for the cork or stopper. Close and store in a cool dark place. After two days remove and discard garlic.
*Good over poultry or pork.

****

TARRAGON WINE SAUCE

1 shallot, finely chopped　　¼ cup half and half　　2 tbsp. butter
2 tsp. chopped tarragon　　　⅔ cup dry white wine　　Salt & pepper

Melt butter in a saucepan, add shallot; cook until soft. Add wine, tarragon, salt and pepper; simmer 5 minutes. Puree sauce in a blender or food processor until smooth; return to saucepan. Stir in half and half and reheat before serving.
*Good over fish and poultry.

TARRAGON-CREAM SAUCE

2 tbsp. shallots, chopped
2 tbsp. lemon juice
1 tsp. fresh tarragon, chopped

½ cup heavy cream
2 tbsp. butter

8 cups water
Salt and pepper

Place shallots, cream, salt and pepper in a saucepan and bring to a boil. Add the lemon juice and cook about 2 minutes. Simmer and swirl in the butter and tarragon.
*Good over pasta.

****

TART APPLE SAUCE

1 lb. tart ripe apples
Peel of lemon or lime

2 cups sugar
2 cups vodka or brandy

2 cloves
Pinch of nutmeg

Cut apples into 8 pieces and remove the cores but do not peel. Place all the ingredients in a tightly closed jar and set in the sun for several days or until all the sugar has dissolved and been absorbed. Strain and let mature for 2-3 months.
*Good over ice cream, fruit or desserts.

****

TARTAR SAUCE I

2 tbsp. mushrooms, chopped
2 tsp. prepared mustard
2 tsp. pickle liquid
¼ cup dill pickles, chopped

2 hard-cooked eggs
½ cup mayonnaise
½ cup sour cream

2 tbsp. salad oil
¼ tsp. salt
¼ tsp. sugar

Mash cooked egg yolks and chop whites separately. Sauté mushrooms in oil, in a saucepan. Blend in mashed egg yolks, mustard, pickle liquid, salt, and sugar. Blend mayonnaise into sour cream. Add chopped egg whites, egg yolk mixture, and pickles; mix well.
*Good over shrimp.

****

TARTAR SAUCE II

¼ cup dill pickle
1 cup mayonnaise
¼ tsp. Worcestershire

1 tbsp. lemon juice
1 tbsp. pimento

2 tbsp. parsley
½ tsp. onion

Chop pickles, parsley, onion and pimento. Mix all ingredients together in a bowl, until well blended. Refrigerate.
*Good over fish.

TARTAR SAUCE III

¾ cup peanut oil
1 tbsp. white vinegar
2 tbsp. sour gherkins
1 tbsp. imported mustard

1 egg yolk
1 tbsp. parsley
1 tbsp. capers

Tabasco sauce
Salt and pepper
1 tbsp. onion

Finely chop gherkins, capers, onions and parsley. Put the yolk, mustard, Tabasco and vinegar in a bowl and start beating with a wire whisk. Gradually add the oil, stirring vigorously with the whisk. When thickened, add salt, pepper, gherkins, capers, onion and parsley. Blend well.
*Good over fish.

****

TEA LEAVES SAUCE

1 ½ cups vodka or brandy

2 tsp. tea leaves

½ cup sugar syrup

Black tea leaves or any other type of tea leaves may be used. Soak the tea leaves in a covered glass bowl or jar of brandy or vodka for 24 hours. No longer. Strain, and add sweetener to taste. Mature 1 week.
*Good over ice cream.

****

TEQUILA ORANGE SAUCE

3 tbsp. liquid from shrimp
3 tbsp. white-wine vinegar
2 sticks unsalted butter
Pinch cayenne pepper

¼ cup white wine
1 cup orange juice
3 tbsp. heavy cream

1 tbsp. orange zest
1 tbsp. orange juice
Salt to taste

Mix all ingredients together, in a medium saucepan, until well blended. Heat in a saucepan, for 5 minutes.
*Good over pasta.

****

TEQUILA SAUCE

¼ cup butter, softened
1 tsp. tequila or brandy

¾ cup heavy cream
Salt and white pepper

1 garlic clove
4 egg yolks

Put garlic through press and combine with the butter; place in a medium saucepan, over a very low flame. Beat cream with egg yolks and tequila in a bowl; season with salt and pepper. Stirring constantly, add mixture to the garlic and butter. Keep warm until ready to use.
*Good over pasta.

TERIYAKI SAUCE I

3 sm. garlic cloves, minced
¼ cup light brown sugar
2 lbs. chicken or fish pieces

1 tbsp. grated onion
½ cup Japanese sake
1 tsp. fresh gingerroot

1 cup soy sauce
1 tsp. sesame oil
Salt

Dry sherry may be used in place of sake. Grate the gingerroot. Place all ingredients in a small saucepan and warm gently over medium heat, stirring until sugar has dissolved. Strain, through fine cheesecloth, if desired.
*Good over all meats.

```
**************************************************
```

TERIYAKI SAUCE II

1 tbsp. brown sugar
1 tsp. ground ginger

½ cup soy sauce
2 garlic cloves, crushed

6 tbsp. dry sherry

Put 1 teaspoon brown sugar and 2 tablespoons soy sauce in a small bowl and set aside. In a large bowl combine remaining brown sugar and soy sauce with sherry, garlic and ginger; add meat and marinate 1 hour.
*Good over fish or meats.

```
**************************************************
```

TERIYAKI GLAZE SAUCE

¼ cup soy sauce
2 tbsp. gingerroot
¼ cup unsweetened pineapple juice

¼ cup dry sherry
1 tbsp. cornstarch

2 tbsp. brown sugar
1 clove garlic

In a small saucepan combine pineapple juice, soy sauce, sherry, sugar, cornstarch, grated fresh gingerroot (or ½ tsp. ground ginger), and garlic. Cook and stir until thickened and bubbly. Cook and stir 2 minutes more.
*Good for ribs.

```
**************************************************
```

TERIYAKI JAPANESE SAUCE

½ tsp. orange peel
¼ cup dry sherry
1 tsp. sesame seed
4 tsp. cornstarch

⅓ cup orange juice
2 tbsp. green onion
2 cloves garlic

¼ cup soy sauce
2 tbsp. gingerroot
¾ cup cold water

Combine finely shredded orange peel, juice, soy sauce, sherry, sliced green onion, grated fresh gingerroot, toasted sesame seed and minced garlic in a bowl. Add chicken to marinade, cover and let stand 30 minutes at room temperature. In a small saucepan blend water, ½ cup of the marinade, and cornstarch. Cook and stir until bubbly.
*Good with poultry, pork or rice.

THERMIDOR SAUCE

¼ cup Madeira wine
½ cup sliced mushrooms
1 tbsp. Parmesan cheese

1 cup cream
¼ cup butter
¼ tsp. black pepper

3 egg yolks
½ tsp. salt
1 lb. lobster pieces

Melt butter on top of double broiler, add mushrooms and sauté 2 or 3 minutes. Add lobster pieces, salt, pepper and wine. Cook for 2 minutes; add cream and beaten yolks. Stir constantly until slightly thickened. Sprinkle with cheese.
*Good over pasta.

****

THIMBLES AND BEANS SAUCE

3 garlic cloves, minced
2 cans cannelloni beans
Ground black pepper

¼ cup olive oil
¼ lb. prosciutto
½ can plum tomatoes

1 celery stalk
8 cups water

Heat oil in a saucepan; simmer minced garlic, diced celery and cubed prosciutto until celery is soft. Stir in tomatoes and simmer for a minute or two. Blend in undrained beans, water and seasonings. Cover and simmer until mixture thickens.
*Good over pasta.

****

THREE CHEESE SAUCE

2 tbsp. unsalted butter
½ cup parmesan cheese

¼ lb. gorgonzola
¼ lb. bel paese

1 cup heavy cream

Melt butter in large skillet until foamy. Add heavy cream that has been whipped to a semi stiff consistency. When the cream and butter are hot, add the Gorgonzola and bel paese and stir them into the mixture until smooth. Add freshly grated Parmesan cheese and bring the mixture just to the point of simmering, about 2 minutes.
*Good for pasta or dipping vegetables.

THREE MUSHROOMS SAUCE

¼ cup onion, minced
¾ cup white mushrooms
¾ shiitake mushrooms
Grated Parmesan

1 tsp. garlic, minced
¾ cup wild mushrooms
2 cups plum tomatoes

2 tbsp. butter
½ cup white wine
Salt and pepper

Sauté onion and garlic in butter until soft, in a skillet. Add mushrooms and cook until fully softened. Add wine and bring to a boil. Add plum tomatoes and heat thoroughly. Season with salt and pepper. Add grated parmesan before serving.
*Good over pasta.

****

TOMATO AND SWEET PEPPER SAUCE

½ cup chicken broth
1 lb. cherry tomatoes
½ cup garlic, minced
Pinch cayenne pepper

¼ tsp. dried thyme
½ cup heavy cream
1 sweet pepper
Salt and pepper

2 tbsp. butter
½ cup onion
½ bay leaf
1 tbsp. flour

Melt butter in a saucepan and add the chopped onion and minced garlic. Cook, stirring, until wilted. Sprinkle with flour and stir. Add the coarsely chopped sweet pepper. Cut the cherry tomatoes in half and add with thyme, bay leaf, broth, salt and pepper. Let simmer 15 minutes and add the cream and cayenne. Bring to a boil and remove from the heat. Pour the sauce into a food processor and blend thoroughly. Put the sauce through a fine sieve and reheat.
*Good over pasta.

****

TOMATO, BACON AND CAPERS SAUCE

1 tsp. garlic, minced
3 tbsp. capers and liquid

½ cup onion, chopped
3 cups ripe tomatoes

4 slices bacon
Salt and pepper

Cook the bacon in a skillet, over moderate heat, until crisp. Drain on paper towel and pour off all but 2 tablespoons of fat from the skillet. Cook chopped onions and minced garlic in hot fat over moderate heat until soft. Add capers and their liquid; simmer 30 seconds more. Add peeled and seeded tomatoes and cook 2 to 3 minutes until the tomatoes start to release their juices. Season to taste with salt and pepper. Crumble the bacon and swirl into the sauce.
*Good over pasta.

TOMATO CILANTRO SAUCE

28-oz. can plum tomatoes
1 cup chicken stock
½ cup whipping cream

½ cup shallot
¼ tsp. pepper
1 tbsp. fresh cilantro

3 tbsp. olive oil
Salt
Sugar

Heat oil in large skillet over medium heat. Add finely chopped shallots and sauté until softened, about 3 minutes. Mix drained and chopped tomatoes, chicken stock (or canned broth), pepper and sugar. Simmer until tomatoes are very soft, stirring occasionally, about 20 minutes. Puree tomatoes in processor until smooth. Pour puree into a small saucepan, add cream and cook over medium heat until sauce thickens.
*Good over pasta.

****

TOMATO COULIS SAUCE

2 cups tomatoes, chopped
¼ cup chives, chopped
¼ tsp. ground pepper

⅛ tsp. thyme
1 garlic clove
2 tbsp. olive oil

⅛ tsp. tarragon
1 ½ tsp. salt

Combine all ingredients except olive oil in 1 ½ quart saucepan; simmer until tomatoes are tender. Place in a blender and puree. Return to pan; add oil. Simmer 3 minutes.
*Good over pasta.

****

TOMATO CREAM SAUCE

3 cups whipping cream
Pinch salt and cayenne pepper

¼ cup tomato paste

3 garlic cloves

Combine all ingredients in a saucepan and bring to a boil for 10 minutes.
*Good over pasta.

****

TOMATO CREOLE SAUCE

⅓ cup peanut oil
6 Italian plum tomatoes
Salt and pepper

½ cup beef stock
1 garlic clove

2 med. onion
3 drops Tabasco

Heat oil in a saucepan, add onion, and cook over low heat until translucent but not browned. Add tomato, stock, and seasonings; stir until tomatoes are cooked to a fine puree, about 5 minutes.
*Good over pasta.

TOMATO FONDUE SAUCE

2 tbsp. onion, minced	½ tsp. sugar	1 tbsp. butter
¼ cup grated Romano cheese	1 cup tomato puree	Salt to taste
¼ tsp. garlic puree	½ tsp. oregano	1 egg
Freshly ground pepper	½ cup finely chopped prosciutto ham	

Heat butter in a saucepan and sauté onion for 2-3 minutes. Stir in ham, tomato puree, garlic puree, oregano, salt, pepper, and sugar. Cook over medium heat for 5 minutes until well blended. Stir in egg and Romano cheese and cook 5 minutes longer, stirring, until thickened. Serve hot.
*Good over pasta.

****

TOMATO, HOT PEPPER AND CREAM SAUCE

½ tsp. crushed red pepper	2 tbsp. olive oil	2 cloves garlic
3 cups ripe tomatoes	½ cup heavy cream	Salt and pepper

Heat oil in a large skillet, over moderate heat and cook the garlic until its aroma is released. Add the crushed pepper and stir briskly. Add the peeled and seeded tomatoes and cook 2 minutes. Add the cream and simmer for a minute, until the sauce lightly thickens. Season to taste with salt and pepper.
*Good over pasta, fish, shellfish, chicken or veal.

****

TOMATO JAM SAUCE

2 tsp. balsamic vinegar	1 tbsp. olive oil	2 lbs. tomatoes
1 tbsp. fresh gingerroot	1 cinnamon stick	⅓ cup honey
1 sweet red pepper	1 tbsp. orange rind	½ tsp. salt
⅛ tsp. hot red pepper	½ tsp. cardamom	¼ tsp. ginger

Sauté finely diced red pepper in oil in large skillet over medium-low heat until softened, about 7 minutes. Stir in ground gingerroot; sauté 1 minute. Add peeled, seeded, chopped tomatoes with juices, honey, cinnamon, slivered orange rind, ground cardamom, salt, ground ginger and ground red pepper. Cook over medium heat, stirring occasionally, until mixture is thick and glossy and reduced to 2 ¾ cups, 40 to 50 minutes. Stir in the vinegar; continue cooking 2 minutes.
*Good over salads or vegetables.

TOMATO KETCHUP SAUCE I

8 quarts tomatoes
¾ cup brown sugar
1 tbsp. peppercorns
2 inch stick cinnamon
1 ½ bay leaves

8 med. onions, sliced
1 tbsp. whole allspice
1 tbsp. celery seed
½ tsp. dry mustard
2 cups cider vinegar

2 red peppers
1 tbsp. clove
1 tbsp. mace
½ garlic clove
cayenne and salt

Cut up tomatoes; add sliced onion and red peppers without seeds or membrane. Simmer in a saucepan, until soft and blend in food processor. Place back in saucepan and add ¾ cup brown sugar. Place spices, mustard garlic and bay leaves in a bag and tie. Boil quickly, stirring often. Continue to stir until reduced by half. Remove the spice bag and add vinegar, cayenne and salt. Simmer the ketchup for 10 minutes longer.
*Good over poultry.

****

TOMATO KETCHUP SAUCE II

3 lbs. tomatoes
½ tsp. allspice
⅔ cup brown sugar
¼ tsp. cayenne pepper

½ tsp. ginger
½ tsp. cinnamon
½ tsp. cloves
1 cup vinegar

½ tsp. mace
1 tsp. pepper
1 tbsp. salt

Wash, chop and cook the tomatoes for 10 minutes. Press through a sieve. Dissolve the seasonings in the vinegar, and add to tomatoes. Place in saucepan and blend in the sugar and bring to a boil, reduce heat and simmer for 1 to 1 ½ hours. Pour into hot jars, seat and place in a hot water bath for 30 minutes.
*Good over beef, ham or pork.

****

TOMATO MEAT SAUCE

¼ cup olive oil
½ lb. beef chuck
7 cups canned tomatoes

½ cup onion, chopped
½ lb. pork shoulder
6 oz. tomato paste

1 tsp. salt
1 bay leaf

Heat oil in large saucepan; add onion and cook until lightly browned. Add the meat and brown on all sides. Stir in tomatoes, salt and bay leaf. Cover and simmer about 2 ½ hours. Stir tomato paste into sauce. Simmer, uncovered, stirring occasionally, about 2 hours, or until thickened. If sauce becomes too thick, add ½ cup water. Remove meat and bay leaf from sauce.

Option: Sauté ½ pound sliced mushrooms in 3 tablespoons melted butter until golden brown, add to sauce and simmer 10 minutes.

Option: Use ½ pound Italian sausage in place of, or with beef and pork.
*Good over pasta.

TOMATO MUSTARD SAUCE

1 cup mayonnaise ¼ cup Dijon mustard	1 lg. tomato	3 tbsp. capers

Mix all ingredients together in a mixing bowl, until well blended. Cover and chill.
*Good with chicken or vegetables.

****

TOMATO NICOISE FONDUE SAUCE

1 ½ lbs. tomatoes, quartered 1 6-oz. can pimentos, drained	1 garlic clove 2 tbsp. mayonnaise	¼ cup butter

Melt butter in a medium size saucepan; add tomatoes, crushed garlic and chopped pimentos and onions. Cook over medium heat 10 to 15 minutes or until soft. Press mixture through a sieve into a bowl, season with salt, pepper and a dash of sugar and allow to cool. Blend in mayonnaise.
*Good over poultry.

****

TOMATO SALSA SAUCE I

½ cup shallots, chopped 2 pickled jalapeno peppers	3 tbsp. olive oil 2 tbsp. chopped cilantro leaves	1 ½ lbs. ripe tomatoes

Peel and chop the tomatoes. Cook shallots in oil in small saucepan over medium heat, stirring occasionally, until shallots are tender but not browned. Transfer to severing bowl and stir in remaining ingredients.
*Good over pasta, fish or salad.

****

TOMATO SALSA SAUCE II

½ tsp. red wine vinegar 2 tbsp. green chili peppers ¼ tsp. hot pepper flakes 1 garlic clove, minced	½ cup plum tomatoes 1 cup tomato sauce 1 tsp. Worcestershire	1 med. onion 1 tsp. lemon juice Salt and pepper

Seed and dice tomatoes, finely dice onion, seed and finely chop chili peppers. Mix all ingredients together in a bowl and chill.
*Good over poultry.

TOMATO SAUCE I

1 lg. garlic clove
1 med. green bell pepper
1 cup chicken stock

1 tsp. Olive oil
1 Serrano chili
½ cup cilantro leaves

1 sm. onion
4 tomatillos

Mince onion and garlic in a food processor. Husk the tomatillos, quarter 1 and coarsely chop 3. Heat oil in 1 quart non-aluminum saucepan over medium-low heat. Mix in the minced onion and garlic. Mince the green pepper, 3 tomatillos and chili in a food processor. Add to saucepan, adding 1 cup stock. Cook over medium-high heat until vegetables are very soft, stirring occasionally, about 15 minutes. Mince cilantro and quartered tomatillo in the food processor. Add vegetable mixture and continue to puree.
*Good over pasta.

****

TOMATO SAUCE II

⅔ cup Brown Stock Sauce
8 fresh basil leaves

2 lbs. ripe tomatoes
Sugar (optional)

Salt and pepper

1 teaspoon dried basil can substitute fresh basil leaves. Cut tomatoes into quarters, add stock and basil, in a large saucepan; cook until tomatoes are reduced to a pulp, about 35 to 45 minutes. Strain through a sieve. Discard skins. Puree in a food processor or blender. Add salt and pepper and a little sugar. Serve hot.
*Good over pasta.

****

TOMATO SAUCE III

¼ med. green pepper
¼ med. red pepper
1 med. garlic clove
⅓ cup tomato puree
2 cups canned tomatoes

1 med. stalk celery
2 tbsp. olive oil
½ tsp. oregano
½ tsp. sugar
2 tbsp. dry red wine

1 sm. carrot
1 sm. onion
½ tsp. basil
⅛ tsp. thyme

Finely chop vegetables in food processor. In a large saucepan, sauté vegetables in olive oil with garlic, basil, oregano and thyme until tender. Add remaining ingredients. Simmer 20 minutes. Transfer to food processor or blender and process until smooth.
*Good over crepes.

TOMATO SAUCE IV

2 lbs. ripe tomatoes
½ cup onions, chopped
2 tbsp. tomato paste
6 fresh basil leaves, or 1 tsp. dried leaf basil

1 ½ tbsp. olive oil
1 celery stalk, chopped
1 tsp. salt

1 bay leaf
1 tsp. sugar
pepper

Dip tomatoes in boiling water to split the skin, then spear with a fork and peel. Quarter tomatoes and set aside. Sauté onions and celery in oil over a low heat in a medium saucepan, until onions are golden. Add tomatoes and tomato paste, bay leaf, basil, sugar, salt and pepper. Bring to a boil. Reduce heat and simmer gently for 45 minutes, stirring occasionally. Remove bay leaf and discard.
*Good over pasta.

****

TOMATO SAUCE V

3 med. ripe tomatoes
½ cup chicken stock
½ tsp. tomato paste

½ sm. onion
1 tbsp. butter
¼ tsp. rosemary

1 bay leaf
1 tbsp. flour
1 tbsp. sugar

Simmer tomatoes, onion, bay leaf, and stock 20 minutes. Put into blender 10 seconds; pass through sieve, removing tomato skins. Melt butter in a saucepan; add flour. Add 1 cup strained tomato juices gradually; stir with wire whisk until thickened. Add sugar and herbs; simmer 5 minutes. Add salt and pepper to taste.
*Good over pasta.

****

TOMATO SAUCE VI

¾ lb. ripe tomatoes
1 sm. garlic clove

2 tsp. vegetable oil
Salt and pepper

1 lemon juice

Dip tomatoes in boiling water to split the skin, then spear with a fork and peel. Chop and puree in a blender or food processor, then pass through a sieve to remove seeds. Place in a bowl and stir in oil and lemon juice. Squeeze garlic through a garlic press into mixture. Add salt and pepper, stirring thoroughly to combine all ingredients. Cover and refrigerate until ready to use.
*Good over pasta.

TOMATO SAUCE VII

3 tbsp. butter	1 lg. onion	2 lbs. ripe tomatoes
2 tsp. sugar	2 whole cloves	1 bay leaf
1 garlic clove	1 tsp. vinegar	Salt and pepper

Melt butter in a saucepan; add onion and cook until translucent. Add peeled, chopped tomatoes and remaining ingredients. Simmer uncovered 20 minutes.
*Good over pasta.

****

TOMATO SAUCE VIII

1 clove garlic, pressed	2 tbsp. olive oil	2 tbsp. butter
1 lg. green onion, minced	5 cups ripe tomatoes	1 tsp. basil
⅛ tsp. ground pepper	1 tsp. chives, chopped	1 tsp. oregano
½ tsp. sugar	1 tsp. salt	

Heat oil and butter in saucepan; until butter is melted. Add garlic and onion; cook over medium heat 5 minutes. Stir in skinned, chopped tomatoes and remaining ingredients; cook, stirring, several minutes, until tomatoes are soft.
*Good over pasta.

****

TOMATO SAUCE WITH TEQUILA AND CREAM

2 garlic cloves, minced	2 tbsp. olive oil	½ tsp. black pepper
12 lg. plum tomatoes	½ cup heavy cream	2 tbsp. tequila
Salt and pepper		

In a large skillet, cook 2 minced cloves of garlic over medium heat in 2 tablespoons olive oil for a few minutes. Add ½ teaspoon black pepper and stir briskly. Add skinned, seeded and chopped tomatoes; cook until they begin to release their liquid. Add heavy cream and simmer until the sauce thickens slightly, about 1 minute. Remove from the heat and stir in 2 tablespoons tequila. Season to taste with salt and pepper.
*Good over pasta.

****

TOMATO-FLAVORED BÉARNAISE SAUCE

1 lg. ripe tomato	2-3 tbsp. butter	1 tbsp. tomato paste
Béarnaise sauce		

Peel and seed tomato, then chop coarsely. Melt butter in a small skillet, and sauté tomato for about 5 minutes over a moderate heat. Stir in tomato paste and bring to a boil, then mix into the Béarnaise Sauce.
*Good over pasta.

TOMATO-HORSERADISH SAUCE

1 cup onions, chopped	4 tbsp. horseradish	1 bay leaves
1 tsp. garlic, chopped	Salt and pepper	1 tbsp. butter
1 ½ cups canned tomatoes		

Heat butter in a small saucepan; add chopped garlic and onions. Cook briefly, stirring, until wilted. Do not brown. Add crushed tomatoes, horseradish, bay leaf, salt and pepper; bring to a boil then simmer, covered, for 20 minutes. Transfer the mixture to a food processor. Blend until it is medium coarse. Serve hot.
*Good with sliced tongue.

****

TOMATO-VEGETABLE SAUCE

1 tsp. sweet paprika	6 cloves garlic	2 ribs celery (strung)
1 med. red bell pepper	3 sprigs parsley	¼ lb. onion
1 tbsp. sweet paprika	¼ cup olive oil	1 ½ tsp. salt
½ cup heavy cream	14 ½ oz. can whole tomatoes	

In a food processor, finely chop garlic, celery, onion, red pepper and parsley. In a 2-quart soufflé dish, combine chopped vegetables with olive oil. Cook, uncovered, in a 650 to 700 watt microwave oven at 100 percent power for 4 minutes, stirring once. Coarsely chop tomatoes in liquid in food processor. Add to chopped vegetables along with seasonings. Cook, at 10 percent power for 7 minutes, stirring twice. Stir in heavy cream and season to taste.
*Good over pasta.

****

TOMATO-VODKA COULIS SAUCE

4 beefsteak tomatoes	¼ cup white wine	1 tsp. salt
¼ cup minced shallots	½ tsp. oregano	pepper
2 tbsp. olive oil	2 tbsp. vodka	1 clove garlic
Pinch dried rosemary		

One can Italian plum tomatoes, drained may be substituted for the beefsteak tomatoes. Simmer the peeled and seeded tomatoes, wine, shallots, oregano, salt and pepper for 20 minutes in a saucepan. Pour the mixture into a blender and process; then set aside.
*Good over pasta.

TRY ME SAUCE

3 oz. Skitche mushrooms
1 oz. sun-dried tomatoes
½ oz. shallots, chopped
1 oz. Balsamic vinegar

1 oz. pignole nuts
6 oz. veal stock
1 oz. olive oil

1 oz. capers
1 oz. Brandy
2 tbsp. butter

Place sliced mushroom, capers, shallot, chopped tomatoes and pignole nuts into a medium saucepan; heat mixture together until translucent, about 2 minutes. Add brandy and vinegar, cook additional 2 minutes, then add stock and continue to cook 3 minutes longer.
*Use over chicken or veal.

****

TUNA AND TOMATO SAUCE

14 oz. plum tomatoes
6 ½ oz. can tuna fish
Salt and black pepper

2 tbsp. olive oil
¼ tbsp. parsley, chopped
½ tbsp. capers, chopped (optional)

2 cloves garlic
1 med. onion

Heat oil in a medium saucepan and sauté chopped onion and garlic until softened. Add tomatoes with their juice, salt and pepper to taste and cook on a high flame for 10 minutes, stirring occasionally. Puree in a blender or food process and return to the pan. Add the drained, flaked tuna fish and capers; cook for another 10 minutes.
*Good over pasta.

****

TUNA SAUCE

3 ⅓ oz. tuna in oil
14 ½ oz. can tomatoes

¼ cup olive oil
¼ tsp. black pepper

½ tsp. salt
1 sm. red onion

Cook onion in hot oil over low heat, in a small saucepan about 10 minutes, until golden brown. Add tomatoes; break up with fork and cook about 10 minutes until liquid is evaporated. Add tuna, stir with a fork to break up chunks; mix well. Add salt and pepper; simmer 8 to 10 minutes.
*Good over pasta.

TUSCAN PASTA SAUCE

⅓ oz. dried mushrooms
¾ cup dry red wine
1 cup chicken stock
⅛ tsp. fresh nutmeg
8 oz. can tomato sauce
⅛ tsp. fresh allspice

2 oz. pancetta
1 sm. onion
1 tbsp. parsley
1 tsp. fresh thyme
3 tbsp. olive oil
Zest of ½ lemon

4 oz. round steak
4 garlic cloves
1 tbsp. celery
1 tsp. rosemary
3 chicken livers
1 tsp. fresh sage

Place mushrooms in a bowl of hot water. Set aside to soak. Chop the pancetta, beef, livers, onion and garlic. Sauté mixture in olive oil over medium heat, in a large saucepan, stirring frequently, until the meats are browned. Drain mushrooms, reserve the water. Coarsely chop and add to meat mixture. Strain mushroom water through a sieve lined with a paper towel, add to the saucepan. Stir in parsley, celery and herbs. Add tomato sauce and chicken. Increase heat until sauce begins to bubble; then lower to a gentle simmer. Stir to prevent sticking and, as sauce reduces, add wine to maintain a dense but fluid consistency. The sauce should be done, the meats softened and almost disappearing, in 30 to 45 minutes. Just before serving, add the allspice, nutmeg and grated lemon zest. Mix well.
*Good over pasta.

****

TUSCAN VINEGAR SAUCE

15 oz. red-wine vinegar
1 tbsp. black peppercorn

4 sprigs rosemary
4 sprigs thyme

4 sprigs oregano
1 stalk basil

Insert fresh herbs, cut end first, into a 16 ounce glass jar or bottle. Add peppercorns. In a small saucepan over low heat warm vinegar until hot but not boiling. Pour immediately through funnel into bottle, leaving just enough room for a cork or stopper. Close and store in a cool, dark place.
*Good over poultry.

****

VANILLA BEAN SAUCE

2 whole vanilla beans   ½ cup sugar syrup   1 ½ cups vodka

Soak the vanilla beans in vodka in a glass jar or bottle; be sure they are immersed. Shake well and soak 2-3 weeks. Remove the beans and strain if necessary. Add the sugar syrup. Mature about 1 month.
*Good over ice cream.

****

VANILLA EXTRACT SAUCE

1 ½ tsp. vanilla extract   ½ cup sugar syrup   1 pinch cinnamon
1 ½ cups vodka or brandy

Dried or ground vanilla may be substituted for vanilla extract. Mix the vanilla and alcohol and shake well in a glass jar or bottle. Soak 1 week. Add the sugar syrup to the solution with the vanilla extract; no straining will be required. The dried or ground vanilla should be strained before adding the sugar syrup. Mature at least 1 week.
*Good over desserts or ice cream.

****

VANILLA SAUCE

2 cups milk   1 vanilla pod   3 eggs
4 tbsp. sugar   ¾ cup whipping cream

One-teaspoon vanilla extract can be substituted for vanilla pod. Whip cream until stiff peaks form. Pour milk in small saucepan; add vanilla pod; heat to just under boiling point. Remove vanilla pod; wipe dry; store. Beat eggs until lemon-colored. Pour small amount hot milk over eggs; stir constantly. Return to remaining hot milk in saucepan; cook, stirring constantly, over low heat about 20 minutes, until thick. Remove from heat; stir in sugar. Let cool; fold in whipped cream gradually. Add vanilla pod after removing from heat.
*Good over desserts or ice cream.

****

VANILLA VINEGAR SAUCE

2 cups champagne   4 vanilla beans   ¼ stick butter

¼ cup vanilla extract may substitute for vanilla beans. White wine vinegar can be used instead of champagne. Split beans lengthwise and add to the champagne, in a jar. Let stand at room temperature for 4 days. Heat butter and 1 cup of mixture, in a saucepan, for 2 minutes.
*Good over ice cream or dessert.

VELOUTE SAUCE I

3 cups White Stock   ⅓ cup butter   White pepper and salt
⅓ cup all-purpose flour

Warm the stock in saucepan. Melt butter in another saucepan; stir in flour and cook about 3 minutes, until bubbly. Gradually add warmed stock, whisking constantly. Cook, uncovered, at a slow simmer 50 minutes to an hour, stirring occasionally, until reduced by one-third. Skim any foam during cooking, then strain through a fine sieve. Keep hot in top of a double boiler until ready to use. Season to taste.
*Good over pasta.

****

VELOUTE SAUCE II

¼ cup onion, chopped   Pinch of mace   1 carrot, chopped
1 rib celery, chopped   4 sprigs parsley   pinch of thyme
½ cup dry white wine   ¼ tsp. salt   1 ½ tbsp. flour
1 cup heavy cream   1 ½ tbsp. butter   1 cup water
2 egg yolks, beaten   Salt and Cayenne   Flounder trimmings

Put the peeled, chopped carrot, onion, celery, parsley, thyme, mace, trimmings from flounder filets, water, and wine into a saucepan and simmer covered, for 10 minutes. Strain; discard solids. Melt butter in saucepan, stir in flour, cook briefly, add broth and whisk rapidly until thickened and smooth. Add cream and boil again. Pour some of the sauce over egg yolks, whisking constantly. Return egg-yolk mixture to saucepan and whisk to blend thoroughly. Do not allow to boil. Season with salt and cayenne pepper.
*Good over pasta.

****

VELOUTE SAUCE III

1 cup chicken stock or broth   1 tbsp. butter   1 egg yolk
2 tbsp. whipping cream   1 tbsp. flour

Melt butter in small saucepan; remove from heat. Add flour; stir with wire whisk. Add stock gradually; stir constantly over moderate heat. Add about 3 tablespoons hot sauce to combined egg yolk and cream; stir together. Return to remaining hot sauce. Do not let sauce boil after egg yolk and cream have been added.
*Good over pasta.

VELVET FUDGE SAUCE

2 cups powdered sugar	½ cup margarine	1 tbsp. corn syrup
1 cup evaporated milk	6-oz. pkg. chocolate chips	1 tsp. vanilla

Use semi-sweet chocolate. In a medium saucepan, combine powdered sugar, milk, margarine, corn syrup and chocolate chips. Cook over medium heat until mixture boils, stirring constantly. Reduce heat to low; cook 8 minutes, stirring constantly. Remove from heat; stir in vanilla. Serve warm.
*Good over desserts or ice cream.

****

VELVET LEMON SAUCE

½ cup butter, softened	2 tbsp. lemon juice	2 eggs
½ cup hot water	½ onion, sliced	½ tsp. salt
Few grains white pepper		

Put eggs, salt, lemon juice, butter, pepper, and onions into a blender and blend until smooth. Add hot water, a little at a time, while blending. Pour into top of double boiler. Cook over simmering water, stirring constantly until thickened; about 10 minutes.
*Good over pasta.

****

VENETIAN SAUCE

¼ tbsp. tarragon chervil	1 cup beef stock	sweet basil

Boil all ingredients together, in a saucepan, until reduced to ½ cup.
*Good over pasta.

****

VERONIQUE SAUCE

¼ cup dry white wine	2 tbsp. butter	1 tsp. cornstarch
1 tbsp. green onion, chopped	½ cup whipping cream	2 tbsp. cold water
16 seedless green grapes	Salt and white pepper	1 tbsp. brandy
1 cup fish poaching liquid, or Fish Stock Sauce		

Boil poaching liquid, wine, brandy and finely chopped green onion together in a medium saucepan until the liquid is reduced to about ½ cup. Strain through a sieve and return to pan. Blend cornstarch with water, then add to saucepan cook over medium heat until bubbly. Stir in cream and cook until sauce reaches a boil. Add salt and pepper to taste. Add grapes and soon as they are warmed through, add butter. Blend thoroughly but gently.
*Good over fish or poultry.

VIENNESE APRICOT SAUCE

1 cup apricot preserves   1 cup water   2 tbsp. sugar
¼ cup orange juice liqueur

Simmer preserve, water and sugar, in a saucepan, 10 minutes, then add liqueur.
*Good over desserts, ice cream or poultry.

****

VIETNAMESE DIPPING SAUCE

½ cup fresh peanuts   2 green chili peppers   1 cup peanut oil
2 tsp. dark soy sauce   2 tbsp. minced ginger   4 garlic cloves
4 tsp. Vietnamese fish sauce   ⅓ cup coconut milk   1 tsp. sugar
1 tsp. fresh lime juice   ½ cup coriander   ¼ tsp. salt

Warm 3 tablespoons of peanut oil in a skillet, until nearly smoking. Add peanuts and stir. Remove from heat; continue stirring until the peanuts are toasted. Cool and place peanuts in a food processor and puree to a rough paste. Add chili peppers, ginger, garlic, coconut milk, soy sauce, fish sauce, sugar, lime juice and salt. Puree until almost smooth. Place mixture into a bowl, stir in the remaining peanut oil until the sauce has a nice sheen. Stir in the minced coriander.
*Good over grilled meat or over cold noodle salad.

****

VINAIGRETTE DRESSING SAUCE

1 tbsp. fresh lemon juice   1 tbsp. olive oil   ⅛ tsp. salt
¼ cup Chicken stock   1 sm. garlic clove   1 tsp. basil
1 tsp. Dijon mustard   2 tsp. parsley   White pepper
2 tsp. distilled white vinegar

Snip parsley and basil; mince garlic clove. Place all ingredients into a jar with a tight cover: shake vigorously. Refrigerate until chilled. Shake before serving.
*Good over salad.

****

VINAIGRETTE SAUCE

¼ tsp. fresh pepper   ½ tsp. Dijon mustard   ½ cup oil
¼ cup red or white wine vinegar ¼ tsp. salt

Use a whisk to blend all the ingredients, except the oil, together in a bowl. Add the oil slowly, whisking continuously. If the taste is too oily, adjust with vinegar, salt or pepper.
*Good over salads.

VINEGAR AND OIL TOMATO SAUCE

2 tbsp. red wine vinegar
1 tbsp. Dijon mustard
1 tbsp. capers, chopped

2 whole scallions
½ cup olive oil
2 tbsp. parsley

1 lg. tomato
1 tsp. dill

Put mustard and vinegar into a small bowl. Add olive oil while stirring with a whisk. Add remaining ingredients; mix well. Refrigerate sever hours before serving.
*Good over pasta.

****

VINEGAR FIERY SAUCE

2 cloves garlic, slivered
1 qt. red wine vinegar

1 sprig tarragon
1 oz. pepper vodka

1 sprig mint
1 slice lemon

Put the tarragon, mint and garlic into a quart bottle. Pour the pepper vodka over the seasonings. Squeeze the lemon into the bottle; pour the vinegar into the bottle, cover and shake contents. Shake daily for about one week. Strain contents if desired.
*Good over veal or beef.

****

VINEGAR HORSERADISH SAUCE

1 tsp. powdered mustard
1 sm. diced onion

1 tbsp. horseradish
1 qt. white distilled vinegar

1 bay leaf

Bring all ingredients to a simmer, in a saucepan. Let simmer for 3 minutes. Remove from heat, and let cool. Strain and bottle.
*Good over poultry or fish.

****

VINEGAR MINT SAUCE

1 pt. distilled white vinegar

2 sprigs fresh mint

Wash the mint, and place it in a pint bottle or jar. Fill with the vinegar, cap and store in a cool place. After 10 days, strain, and use.
*Good with lamb.

VINEGAR TEX-MEX SAUCE

2 long hot peppers
1 clove garlic, silvered

1 sprig cilantro
1 pt. white wine vinegar

1 slice lime

Remove stems and seeds from peppers. Place peppers, cilantro and garlic into a pint jar. Squeeze the juice from lime into the jar; insert the slice itself. Add the vinegar, cover, and store in cool place. Shake bottle every day for 10 days.
*Good over salads or poultry.

****

VINEGAR-BALSAMIC AND BASIL MARINADE SAUCE

2 tbsp. balsamic vinegar
1 tbsp. minced shallot

⅓ cup olive oil
1 tbsp. fresh parsley

2 tbsp. fresh basil
Salt and pepper

Mix all ingredients in a mixing bowl, until well blended. Marinade fish for about 30 minutes.
*Good to marinate fish.

****

VODKA SAUCE

½ tbsp. butter
Parmesan cheese

2 cup heavy cream

1 cup Vodka

Heat butter with vodka, in a saucepan; slowly add cream and cook for 5 minutes. Remove from heat, then and cheese.
*Good over pasta or vegetables.

****

VODKA CREAM AND GREEN PEPPERCORNS SAUCE

2 tbsp. green peppercorns
1 ½ cups whipping cream
3 tbsp. fresh lemon juice

4 tbsp. unsalted butter
Salt and pepper

½ cup vodka
¼ cup chives

Drain and crush peppercorns. Snip fresh chives. Heat oil in large skillet over high heat. Add cream and vodka and boil until slightly thickened, about 4 minutes. Add peppercorns and 4 tablespoons of butter and stir until butter just melts. Mix in lime juice; season with salt and pepper.
*Good over pasta.

VODKA CREAM SAUCE

4 tbsp. olive oil	8 tbsp. butter	4 onions
1 cup heavy cream	2 lbs. tomatoes	Salt and pepper
4 tbsp. dried red pepper	1 cup vodka	Parmesan cheese

Place 4 tablespoons dried red pepper in a cup of vodka overnight. Dip tomatoes in boiling water to split the skin, then spear with a fork and peel. Slice tomatoes in half horizontally and squeeze out seeds. Chop into small cubes. Heat oil and butter in skillet, add onions and soften without browning. Add tomatoes and cook for about 4 minutes. If tomatoes seem very watery, cook a little longer to evaporate excess liquid. Add cream and cook another minute. Add vodka and simmer for an additional 3 minutes.
*Good over pasta.

****

VODKA ORANGES SAUCE

3 cups vodka	2 whole cloves	½ lemon
1 cup sugar syrup	3 whole sweet oranges, cut into wedges	

Place the oranges, lemon, cloves, and vodka in a jar and store 10 days. Strain and add sugar syrup. Mature 3-4 weeks.
*Good over desserts.

****

VODKA, TOMATOES AND CREAM SAUCE

1 tbsp. virgin olive oil	10 plum tomatoes	2 shallots
1 tsp. red pepper flakes	½ cup heavy cream	3 tbsp. vodka
Salt and fresh pepper		

In a large skillet, cook the minced shallots in oil until softened. Add the crushed pepper and cook for another minute. Add chopped plum tomatoes and cook until they start to release their liquid. Add the vodka. Bring to a boil and add the cream. Boil briskly for a few minutes, until the sauce just coats a spoon. It will be fairly light and thin. Season to taste with salt and pepper.
*Good for pasta.

****

VODKA TOMATOES CREAM SAUCE

6 plum tomatoes, chopped   2 cloves garlic, minced   ¼ cup vodka
½ tsp. crushed red pepper   2 tsp. olive oil   ½ cup cream

Heat oil, garlic and tomatoes, in a saucepan, for 2 minutes. Add the remaining ingredients and heat 3 more minutes.
*Good over pasta.

****

VODKA-SOUTHWESTERN SAUCE

¼ sm. Serrano chili   ¼ sm. red jalapeno chili   2 cups vodka
¼ sm. hot yellow chili   ¼ sm. green jalapeno chili   ½ cup oil

Mix all ingredients together in a jar, until well blended. Cover with lid and let stand 3 days at room temperature. Strain into large bottle; add oil.
*Good over pasta or vegetables.

****

WALNUT SAUCE I

¼ cup all purpose flour
¾ cup fresh orange juice
1 tbsp. shredded orange peel

½ cup walnuts, chopped
1 cup chicken stock

1 tbsp. lemon juice
3 tbsp. butter

In a medium saucepan, melt butter over medium heat. Sprinkle flour into the hot saucepan, stirring 3 minutes to cook the flour without browning. In a measuring cup, mix orange and lemon juice, and slowly add to flour mixture. Stir vigorously to avoid lumps. Add chicken stock all at once, stirring over low heat until sauce is smooth and thickened. Stir in orange peel and walnuts. Cook 1 to 2 minutes.
*Good over poultry or pork.

****

WALNUT SAUCE II

2 ½ cups chicken bouillon
2 cups ground walnuts

1 tbsp. paprika
3 slices bread

Salt to taste

Remove crusts from bread, then soak in ½ cup of the chicken bouillon and squeeze dry. Put bread and nuts in blender or food processor and blend until just mixed together. Place into a bowl and add salt and 1 tablespoon paprika. Beat in remaining bouillon, adding liquid gradually until sauce is consistency of a thin mayonnaise.
*Good over pasta.

****

WALNUT SAUCE III

½ cup unsalted butter
4 oz. toasted walnuts
½ tsp. lemon juice
¼ tsp. freshly grated nutmeg

½ tsp. garlic
2 cups heavy cream
¼ tsp. fresh pepper

2 tbsp. parsley
2 tsp. basil
½ tsp. salt

In a saucepan, melt butter over low heat. Add minced garlic, parsley, and fresh minced basil. Cook, stirring, until garlic is softened, but not colored, 3 to 5 minutes. Stir in nuts, cream and lemon juice. Slowly bring to a boil, stirring constantly. Then simmer, stirring often, until thickened, about 15 minutes. Add salt, pepper, and nutmeg.
*Good over pasta.

WALNUT AND POMEGRANATE SAUCE

⅓ cup pomegranate juice
¾ tsp. sweet paprika
½ cup Chicken stock
Pinch hot Hungarian paprika

½ tsp. lemon juice
1 med. garlic clove
½ tsp. coriander

¼ tsp. salt
White pepper
1 cup walnuts

Combine walnuts, garlic, salt, sweet and hot paprika and coriander in a food processor. Process until an oily paste forms. Place in a medium bowl; stir in the pomegranate juice and stock, blend to a thin, smooth sauce. Add lemon juice to taste. Cover and refrigerate until serving. Season with ground white pepper and additional salt to taste.
*Good over pasta.

****

WALNUT CREAM SAUCE

2 cups whipping cream
2 celery stalks

⅓ cup walnuts
½ tsp. salt

2 carrots
Fresh pepper

Remove strings from celery, finely dice; peel and finely dice carrots; coarsely chop walnuts. Boil cream in large saucepan until reduced to 1 ½ cups. Add carrots, celery, walnuts and salt, boil 2 minutes; season with pepper. Serve warm.
*Good over pasta.

****

WALNUT GEORGIAN SPICES SAUCE

1 sm. garlic clove
¾ cup Chicken stock
3 tsp. rice vinegar

1 cup walnuts
¼ tsp. hot paprika
¼ tsp. fenugreek

¼ tsp. salt
1 tsp. coriander
⅛ tsp. turmeric

In a food processor, combine the walnuts, salt, garlic, coriander, fenugreek, turmeric and paprika; puree until smooth. Pour into a medium bowl and stir in the vinegar and enough chicken stock to make a light, smooth sauce. Place in a small glass bowl, cover and refrigerate to blend the flavors, at least 1 hour.
*Good over poultry.

****

WALNUT RAISIN SAUCE

½ cup brown sugar
1 tsp. Worcestershire sauce
½ cup walnuts, chopped

¼ cup vinegar
½ tbsp. mustard
½ cups raisins

1 ¾ cups water
½ tbsp. flour
1 tbsp. butter

Heat the vinegar, water, and sugar together in a medium saucepan. Cook until sugar is dissolved. Combine mustard and flour. Slowly stir into hot liquid over medium heat. Add butter and Worcestershire and cook until syrupy. Stir in raisins and walnuts.
*Good over poultry.

WALNUT VINAIGRETTE SAUCE

½ cup walnut oil
1 tbsp. Dijon mustard

¼ cup white wine vinegar
1 tbsp. snipped fresh chives

2 tbsp. water
¼ tsp. pepper

Mix all ingredients together in a jar; shake until well blended. Chill.
*Good over salads.

****

WALNUT-RAISIN SAUCE

1 cup maple-flavor syrup
1 cup walnut pieces

1 cup raisins

1 cup hot water

Molasses or dark corn syrup may be used as substitute for maple syrup. Soak raisins in a bowl of hot water for 5 minutes, then drain. Stir in maple syrup and walnut pieces.
*Good over banana or vanilla ice cream.

****

WATERCRESS PUREE SAUCE

2 bunches watercress
1 clove garlic

2 tbsp. unsalted butter
1 sm. shallot

2 scallions
Salt and pepper

Remove stems from watercress and blanch in boiling water for 30 to 45 seconds. Press out all moisture and set aside. In a skillet, heat butter and sauté coarsely chopped shallot, scallions and garlic until softened but not browned, about 3 to 5 minutes. Add watercress and cook, stirring, until well wilted, about 5 minutes. Puree in blender or food processor. Season with salt and pepper.
*Good over pasta.

****

WELSH SAUCE

2 tbsp. all purpose flour
2 ½ cups Caerphilly cheese

½ lb. leeks
1 cup beer

2 tbsp. butter
Pepper

Melt butter in a large saucepan, over low heat. Add trimmed and finely chopped leeks, cover pan and cook 10 minutes or until tender. Stir in flour and cook 1 minute. Add beer and heat, stirring constantly, until thickened. Gradually add cheese and continue to cook, stirring until cheese melts. Season with pepper.
*Good over fish or chicken.

WESTERN SAUCE

⅛ tsp. ground pepper   1 tbsp. paprika   1 tsp. salt
½ garlic clove   1 tbsp. sugar   1 med. onion
¼ cup butter   3 tbsp. white vinegar   1 cup ketchup
⅓ cup water   1 tbsp. Worcestershire sauce   ⅛ tsp. pepper

Place all ingredients in a saucepan and bring to a boil, then simmer for 20 minutes.
*Good over poultry or pork.

****

WHIPPED HONEY BUTTER SAUCE

2 tbsp. honey   ⅛ tsp. ground cinnamon   1 cup butter

At medium speed, beat butter with honey and cinnamon, in a small bowl, until well blended. Cover and refrigerate.
*Good over biscuits, muffins or pancakes.

****

WHISKEY SAUCE I

½ tsp. cornstarch   1 cup heavy cream   4 tbsp. unsalted butter
¼ cup sugar   1 tbsp. bourbon   Pinch of cinnamon

In a small bowl, dissolve the cornstarch in ¼ cup of water. Combine the cream, sugar, cinnamon and butter in a saucepan. Bring to a boil over high heat and cook, stirring frequently to dissolve the sugar, about 3 minutes. Stir in the cornstarch mixture and cook until the sauce thickens slightly, about 3 minutes. Remove from the heat and stir in the bourbon.
*Good over pasta.

****

WHISKEY SAUCE II

1 lb. light brown sugar   ½ lb. sweet butter   3 ½ oz. bourbon
1 cup heavy cream   ½ tsp. salt

Place all ingredients in a saucepan; bring to a boil. Cook until thickened, about an hour, whisking regularly. Serve hot.
*Good over pudding or desserts.

WHITE BEANS, TUNA AND OLIVE OIL SAUCE

2 tbsp. onion, minced
1 tsp. garlic, minced
1 tbsp. parsley, chopped

6 ½ oz. can tuna in oil
Salt and pepper
1 cup cooked cannelloni beans

¼ cup olive oil
1 tsp. rosemary

Sauté crumbled rosemary in olive oil, in a saucepan for 10 seconds. Add onion and garlic; cook another 30 seconds. Add tuna and tuna oil and mix well; cook another minute. Add cooked cannelloni bean; season with salt, pepper and chopped parsley.
*Good over pasta.

****

WHITE CHOCOLATE SAUCE

1 ½ cups whipping cream
4 oz. white chocolate

¼ cup powdered sugar

2 tbsp. rum

Heat cream and powdered sugar in a saucepan, over medium heat until mixture boils, stirring constantly. Reduce heat and simmer 3 to 4 minutes. Add white chocolate and rum, stirring until chocolate is melted and smooth. Serve warm or cold. Store in refrigerator.
*Good over desserts or ice cream.

****

WHITE CLAM SAUCE

1 ¾ cups bottled clam juice
4 doz. Little Neck clams
1 ½ tsp. oregano

¾ cup olive oil
½ cup parsley
¼ cup Worcestershire sauce

6 cloves garlic
Salt and pepper

Four cups of canned clams can substitute the raw clams. Shuck and coarsely chop clams. Reserve the liquid. Heat oil in a deep casserole. Add peeled and very thinly sliced garlic and cook over low heat until just golden, about 3 minutes. Combine reserved clam liquid, clam juice and white wine, Worcestershire sauce to make 3 cups. Add to the casserole along with chopped parsley, oregano, salt and pepper. Simmer, partially covered for 10 minutes.
*Good over pasta.

****

WHITE HERB SAUCE

1 tbsp. mint, chopped
3 tbsp. butter
salt and pepper

1 ½ cups hot milk
½ tsp. thyme

3 tbsp. flour
Dash nutmeg

Heat milk in a saucepan, mix butter and flour, and add to milk. Add remaining ingredients; cook for about 2 minutes.
*Good over pasta.

WHITE SANGRIA SAUCE

4 cups dry white wine	10-oz. bottle carbonated water	2 lemons
1 tbsp. honey	¼ cup brandy	3 oranges

Cut orange and lemon in half. Slice one half of each to use as garnish; wrap and chill. Squeeze juice from remaining oranges and lemons. Combine juices, dry white wine, brandy, and honey in a bowl; cover and chill. Just before serving, pour chilled mixture into a large pitcher. Slowly add carbonated water. Add the reserved fruit slices.
*Good over poultry.

****

WHITE SAUCE

¼ cup all purpose flour	2 cups milk	Salt and white pepper
¼ cup butter		

Warm milk in a saucepan, over low heat. In a separate saucepan, melt butter; add flour all at once and cook until bubbly. Whisking constantly, gradually add milk. Continue whisking until sauce thickens, cook 2 to 3 minutes over low heat until the consistency is rich and creamy. Season and serve hot.
*Good over poultry or pasta.

****

WHITE STOCK SAUCE

1 ½ lbs. veal or chicken bones	2 onions, halved	3 qts. water
2 sm. carrots, chopped	2 leeks, chopped	4 whole cloves
1 celery stalk, sliced	8 black peppercorns	bouquet garni

Place bones in a covered pot with water and let stand for 1 hour. Bring water to a boil, skim off foam and fat. Simmer until liquid is clear. Place cloves in onion halves, add onions and remaining ingredients. Bring to a boil; cover, reduce heat and simmer 3 hours, skimming as necessary. Remove bouquet garni and strain through a fine sieve; refrigerate until cool. Spoon off any fat that solidifies on surface. Cover tightly and store in the refrigerator up to 2 weeks.
*Good over rice.

****

WHITE TUNA SAUCE

1 cup tuna in oil	½ cup olive oil	2 tbsp. butter
¼ cup parsley	¼ cup hot chicken stock	

Heat butter and oil in a saucepan, add broken up tuna and chopped parsley and simmer until tuna is smoothly blended into sauce. Add chicken stock and serve hot.
*Good over pasta.

WHITE WINE SAUCE

3 oz. all-purpose flour
4 oz. dry white wine
6 oz. heavy cream

3 oz. unsalted butter
Salt and white pepper

½ oz. shallot
16-oz. white fish stock

Heat butter in a casserole; sauté peeled and chopped shallot for a few seconds. Add flour, and continue to sauté for a half a minute. Add fish stock and wine, stirring with a whisk. Bring to boil and simmer for 20 minutes. Strain through cheesecloth into a saucepan. Bring to a boil. Stir in the heavy cream and salt and pepper.
*Good over pasta or vegetables.

****

WILD BLUEBERRY SAUCE

2 tbsp. shallots, chopped
1 tsp. lemon peel, grated
2 tbsp. lemon juice

2 tbsp. butter
1 tbsp. cornstarch
2 15-oz. cans wild blueberries

½ cup Marsala wine
2 tbsp. sugar

In a large skillet, over medium heat, melt butter; add shallots and sauté 1 minute. Add the remaining ingredients and continue to simmer for 3 to 4 minutes.
*Good over desserts or ice cream.

****

WINE & CHERRY SAUCE

1 tbsp. sugar
1 16 oz. can black pitted cherries, drained

⅓ cup red wine

Pinch allspice

Simmer sugar, cherries, wine and allspice in a small saucepan for 15 minutes. Press through a sieve; serve sauce warm.
*Good over pork.

****

WINE SAUCE

3 tbsp. clarified butter
1 garlic clove, minced
1 chili pepper, chopped

2 cups onions, minced
1 cup dry white wine
Pinch of salt

½ tsp. oregano
½ cup parsley
½ cup beef stock

Heat the butter in a small saucepan; sauté onions and garlic until they are soft. Add oregano and wine and cook uncovered on high heat for 5 minutes. Mix in the chili, chopped parsley and stock and cook over high heat for 10 minutes more. Season and serve hot.
*Good over poultry or pork.

****

YOGURT SAUCE

½ cup instant nonfat dry milk   3 tbsp. prepared yogurt   1 qt. milk

Allow yogurt to reach room temperature. Scald milk, then cool. Add dry milk and mix. Dilute yogurt with ½ cup of milk; slowly add remaining milk. Pour into a bowl; cover. Wrap with large towel. Set in a warm place 6 to 8 hours (an oven with a pilot light is a good place). When thickened, store in refrigerator.
*Good over vegetables or fish.

****

YOGURT AND GREEN-ONION SAUCE

2 tbsp. green onion, minced   1 cup yogurt   Salt and pepper
2 tsp. curry powder

Mix all ingredients together, in a mixing bowl, until well blended. Chill well before serving.
*Good over rice.

****

ZABAGLIONE SAUCE I

8 egg yolks   ½ cup sugar   1 cup Marsala wine

Simmering water in bottom half of double boiler. In top half of the boiler, beat egg yolks and sugar until thick and frothy. Add Marsala wine and beat. Make sure the water from the bottom half of the double boiler, does not touch the top half of pan. Cook, beating constantly with an electric beater on medium speed, until mixture thickens and doubles in volume. It should have a fluffy texture. Serve hot.
*Good over desserts or fresh cut fruit.

****

ZABAGLIONE SAUCE II

¾ cup heavy cream   1 cup confectioners sugar   4 lg. egg yolks
½ cup almond-liqueur

In top of double boiler, combine egg yolks, sugar and ¼ cup liqueur. Beat with electric mixer for 10 minutes, until tripled in volume. Fold chilled whipped cream into egg yolk mixture.
*Good over desserts, ice cream, fruit or pound cake.

****

ZESTY TOMATO SAUCE

½ cup apricot preserves   1 cup chili sauce   3 tbsp. brown sugar
4 tbsp. red wine vinegar   ¼ cup white wine   Salt and pepper
1 tsp. Worcestershire sauce   ½ tsp. Tabasco sauce   ½ onion

Blend chili sauce, sugar, apricot preserves in a saucepan, until melted. Add vinegar, Worcestershire sauce, Tabasco sauce, grated onion, salt and pepper to taste. Bring to a boil, lower heat and simmer 10 minutes.
*Good for ribs, chicken, pork chops, or frankfurters.

****

ZIPPY GREEN BEAN SAUCE

2 tbsp. toasted sesame seeds   2 cups green beans   Fresh pepper
1 mild green chile pepper   1 garlic clove   Salt

Mince the green chile pepper, puree green beans and mash garlic clove. Combine all ingredients in a mixing bowl, and let stand for 2 hours.
*Good over poultry or as a dip.

ZUCCHINI SAUCE I

2 cups sliced zucchini	2 cups tomato sauce	¼ tsp. oregano
½ cup black olives	¼ tsp. basil	

Slice black olives; mix all ingredients together in a covered saucepan and steam for about 10 minutes.
*Good over angel-hair pasta.

****

ZUCCHINI SAUCE II

2 cups zucchini puree	2 tbsp. butter	2 tbsp. flour
Freshly ground pepper	1 cup milk	Salt to taste

Heat butter in saucepan and add flour. Cook, stirring, for 2 minutes. Add milk and cook, stirring until thick. Season. Stir in zucchini. Continue to cook a few more minutes.
*Good over pasta.

****

ZUCCHINI SAUCE III

¼ cup vegetable oil	½ cup onion, minced	¼ cup butter
1 mashed garlic clove	½ cup green pepper	Salt to taste
1 ½ lbs. sliced zucchini	3 cups tomato puree	Ground pepper

Heat oil and butter in saucepan; sauté onions and garlic for 2 minutes. Add remaining ingredients. Cook over low heat, stirring frequently, for 30 minutes.
*Good over large lettuce leaves or pasta.

****

INDEX

DIPS

	PAGE
ALLSPICE LIQUEUR SAUCE	3
APRICOT-YOGURT DIP SAUCE	12
CHEESE DIP SAUCE	61
CHEESE FONDUE SAUCE	61
CRANBERRY DIP SAUCE	83
GINGER LIME SAUCE	112
GUACAMOLE SAUCE	118
HOT ARTICHOKE SAUCE	123
HOT BUTTER DIPPING SAUCE	123
HOT CRAB SAUCE	124
JAPANESE DIPPING SAUCE	130
JIFFY CHIVES DIPPING SAUCE	148
JIFFY GREEN ONION SAUCE	163
JIFFY KAHLUA DIPPING SAUCE	170
JIFFY MASCARPONE DIPPING SAUCE	175
JIFFY PESTO SAUCE III	185
JIFFY SHRIMP SAUCE	196
JIFFY TEMPURA DIPPING SAUCE	207
LOW-CAL BLUE CHEESE SAUCE	224
LOW-CAL RAIFORT SAUCE	229
LOW-CAL VEGETARIAN SAUCE	230
MARINADE DARK SAUCE	236
ORIENTAL CRANBERRY SAUCE	262
SATAY SAUCE I	297
THREE CHEESE SAUCE	323
VIETNAMESE DIPPING SAUCE	338
ZIPPY GREEN BEAN SAUCE	351

SALADS (HOT & COLD) / VEGETABLES

	PAGE
AIOLI SAUCE	2
AVOCADO SAUCE I, III	13,4
BALSAMIC VINAIGRETTE SAUCE	17
BEARNAISE SAUCE II, III	25,6
BERNAISE SAUCE	29
BERNAUSE SAUCE	29
BLUE CHEESE SAUCE I	34
BROCCOLI SAUCE I	42
CAESAR NO-YOLK SAUCE	48
CAESAR SAUCE	49
CELEBRATION CHAMPAGNE SAUCE	58
CHAMPAGNE-HERB DRESSING SAUCE	59
CHEESE SAUCE I	61
CHILE OIL SAUCE	66
CHILI MAYONNAISE SAUCE	68
CREAMY CURRY SAUCE II	86
FRENCH GREEN SAUCE	105
FRESH HERB AND TOMATO VINAIGRETTE SAUCE	107
GARLIC SAUCE I, III	109
GARLIC SAUTED SHIITAKE MUSHROOMS SAUCE	110
GERMAN CHEESE SAUCE	111
GINGER LIQUEUR SAUCE	112
GUACAMOLE SAUCE	118
HOMEMADE WALNUT OIL SAUCE	121
HONEY-LEMON DRESSING SAUCE	122
HOT ARTICHOKE SAUCE	122
HOT CHEDDAR BEAN SAUCE	123
HOT CIDER SAUCE	123
HOT FISH SAUCE	124
INDIAN CURRY SAUCE	127
ITALIAN GREEN SAUCE	128
IVORY SAUCE	129
JIFFY ANCHOVY FRENCH SAUCE	133
JIFFY APPLE-SHERRY WINE VINEGAR SAUCE	135
JIFFY AVOCADO SAUCE	137
JIFFY BAGNIET SAUCE	138
JIFFY BLUE CHEESE VINAIGRETTE SAUCE	142
JIFFY CALIFORNIAN SAUCE	144
JIFFY CHIFFONADE FRENCH SAUCE	148
JIFFY CHIVES DIPPING SAUCE	148
JIFFY COOL AVOCADO SAUCE	151
JIFFY CREAMY FRENCH SAUCE	152
JIFFY CREAMY ROQUEFORT DRESSING SAUCE	153
JIFFY CREAMY VINAIGRETTE SAUCE I, II	154
JIFFY CREOLE DOG SAUCE	155
JIFFY DIJON VINAIGRETTE SAUCE	157
JIFFY ESCABECHE SAUCE	157
JIFFY FRENCH MARINADE SAUCE	158
JIFFY FRENCH SAUCE	159
JIFFY GARLIC-VINAIGRETTE SAUCE	161
JIFFY GIN SAUCE	161
JIFFY GUACAMOLE VINAIGRETTE SAUCE	163
JIFFY HAZELNUT SAUCE	164
JIFFY HONEY FRENCH SAUCE	165
JIFFY INDIAN TURMERIC SAUCE	168
JIFFY INDONESIAN SAUCE	169
JIFFY ITALIAN SAUCE	169
JIFFY LEMON VINAIGRETTE SAUCE	171
JIFFY LIME-THYME SAUCE	173
JIFFY MAYONNAISE LIGHT SAUCE	176
JIFFY MAYONNAISE RED-WINE VINEGAR SAUCE	176
JIFFY MINT MAYONNAISE SAUCE	177
JIFFY MIXED OIL SAUCE	177
JIFFY MUSTARD CREAM SAUCE	178
JIFFY MUSTARD VINAIGRETTE SAUCE	179
JIFFY NO-CALORIE SALAD SAUCE	180
JIFFY OIL AND EGG SAUCE	180
JIFFY OLIVE FRENCH SAUCE	180
JIFFY ONION-HORSERADISH SAUCE	181
JIFFY PESTO SAUCE II	184
JIFFY PESTO VINAIGRETTE SAUCE	185
JIFFY RASPBERRY VINAIGRETTE SAUCE	188
JIFFY ROQUEFORT FRENCH SAUCE	191
JIFFY RUSSIAN DRESSING SAUCE	191
JIFFY RUSSIAN SAUCE	192
JIFFY SOUR CREAM SAUCE	198
JIFFY STRAWBERRY SAUCE	200
JIFFY SUPREME SAUCE	202
JIFFY SZECHUAN PEANUT SAUCE	203
JIFFY TARRAGON FRENCH SAUCE	206
JIFFY THICK WHITE SAUCE	209
JIFFY THOUSAND ISLAND SAUCE I, II	209,10
JIFFY TRIPLE SEC GLAZING SAUCE	211
JIFFY VINAIGRETTE FRENCH SAUCE	212
JIFFY WALNUT SAUCE I, II	214
JIFFY YOGURT SAUCE I	218
LEMON MUSTARD SAUCE	221
LEMONY-CHEESE SAUCE	222
LORD CHESTERFIELD SAUCE	223
LOW-CAL BLUE CHEESE SAUCE	224
LOW-CAL BUTTERMILK SAUCE	225
LOW-CAL GORGONZOLA SAUCE	227
LOW-CAL HONEY SAUCE	227
LOW-CAL LEMON SAUCE	227
LOW-CAL LEMON-CURRY SAUCE	228
LOW-CAL MICHEL SAUCE	228
LOW-CAL NO-OIL ROQUEFORT SAUCE	229
LOW-CAL POPPY-SEED SAUCE	229
LOW-CAL RASPBERRY SAUCE I	230
LOW-CAL SAUCE	224
LOW-CAL TOMATO PIMENTO SAUCE	230
LOW-CAL VEGETARIAN SAUCE	230
LOW-FAT YOGURT SAUCE	231
MAGIC MARINADE SAUCE	233
MANGO VINAIGRETTE SAUCE	235
MARINATED ROASTED PEPPER SAUCE	237
MAYONNAISE SAUCE IV	239
MINT YOGURT SAUCE	245
MOCK MAYONNAISE SAUCE	248
MORNAY SAUCE I, II, III	249,50
NEWBURG SAUCE	256
ONION CREAM SAUCE	257
ORIENTAL VINAIGRETTE SAUCE	262
PANG PANG SAUCE	263
RASPBERRY VINAIGRETTE SAUCE	285
RED PEPPER SAUCE II	287
SALSA SAUCE I	297
SATAY SAUCE I	297
SEAFOOD SAUCE I	302
SOUTH-OF-THE-BORDER SAUCE	307
SPICY TOMATO SAUCE II	312
THREE CHEESE SAUCE	323
TOMATO JAM SAUCE	326
TOMATO MUSTARD SAUCE	328
TOMATO SALSA SAUCE I	328
VIETNAMESE DIPPING SAUCE	338
VINAIGRETTE DRESSING SAUCE	338
VINAIGRETTE SAUCE	338
VINEGAR TEX-MEX SAUCE	340
VODKA SAUCE	340
VODKA-SOUTHWESTERN SAUCE	342
WALNUT VINAIGRETTE SAUCE	345
WHITE WINE SAUCE	249
YOGURT SAUCE	350
ZUCCHINI SAUCE III	352

MARINADE

	PAGE
ACAPULCO SAUCE	1
ADOBO SAUCE	1

AMERICAN-STYLE LIGHT MARINADE SAUCE	6
BEEF MARINADE SAUCE	27
BLACK OLIVE SAUCE	32
BOMBAY SAUCE	38
BRAZILIAN BARBECUE SAUCE	40
CEBOLLITA (PICKLED ONIONS) SAUCE	57
CHILE OIL SAUCE	66
CHINESE MARINADE SAUCE I, II	70
CRAB SAUCE	82
FLAMBE SAUCE	103
FRENCH MUSHROOM MARINADE SAUCE	105
GARLIC SAUCE II	109
GLAZED CRANBERRY SAUCE	112
GREEK MARINADE SAUCE	115
GREEN SAUCE I	116
GRILLING MARINADE SAUCE	118
HOT PEPPER AND LIME-JUICE SAUCE	126
ITALIAN MARINADE SAUCE	128
JERK-STYLE JAMAICAN BARBECUE SAUCE	131
JIFFY AMARETTO MARINATE SAUCE	132
JIFFY APPLE MARINADE SAUCE	134
JIFFY APPLE-SOY SAUCE	135
JIFFY AU VIN ROUGE SAUCE	137
JIFFY AVOCADO COCKTAIL SAUCE	138
JIFFY BARBECUED GINGER SAUCE	139
JIFFY BEEF-BEER MARINADE SAUCE	140
JIFFY CHARCOAL BROILED MARINATE SAUCE	147
JIFFY COUNTRY HOT SAUCE	151
JIFFY FRENCH MARINADE SAUCE	158
JIFFY GAME MARINADE SAUCE	160
JIFFY LEMON SORBET SAUCE	171
JIFFY LIME MARINADE SAUCE	172
JIFFY MARINADE SAUCE	175
JIFFY MINTED MARINADE SAUCE	177
JIFFY ONION MARINADE SAUCE	180
JIFFY PEACHY MARINADE SAUCE	182
JIFFY PINEAPPLE GINGER SAUCE	186
JIFFY SESAME MAPLE SAUCE	195
JIFFY TANDOORI MARINADE SAUCE I, II	204,05
JIFFY TERIYAKI MARINADE SAUCE	208
JIFFY WINE MARINADE SAUCE I, II	215,16
JIFFY YOGURT SPICY MARINADE SAUCE	218
MAGIC MARINADE SAUCE	233
MARINADE DARK SAUCE	236
MARINADE SAUCE	236
MARINATED ROASTED PEPPER SAUCE	237
MEXICAN MARINADE SAUCE	243
ORIENTAL BARBECUE GLAZE SAUCE	261
PAPAYA-GLACE LIME MARINADE SAUCE	264
PEANUT SAUCE MARINADE	268
PICKLED CUCUMBER SAUCE	271
POLYNESIAN SAUCE	276
SPICY GEORGIAN PEACH VINEGAR SAUCE	310
TERIYAKI SAUCE II	322
TERIYAKI JAPANESE SAUCE	322
VINEGAR-BALSAMIC AND BASIL MARINADE SAUCE	340

MEAT
(ALL MEAT)

	PAGE
ALSTATIAN ONION SAUCE	5
AMARETTO BAR SAUCE	5
AZTEC CHILI SAUCE	14
BARBECUE MUSTARD SAUCE	18
BARBECUE SAUCE I, II, III, IV	18,9
BARBECUE SAUCE VII, VIII, X, XI	20,1
BASIC FRESCA SAUCE	23
BASIC GRAVY SAUCE	23
BLENDER BEARNAISE SAUCE	34
CEBOLLITA (PICKLED ONIONS) SAUCE	57
CREAMY PAPRIKA SAUCE	60
CREOLE BARBECUE SAUCE	90
CREOLE SAUCE I	90
CUCUMBER SAUCE II	91
CUMBERLAND SAUCE I, II	91
ESPAGNOLE SAUCE	101
FRESH HERB/TOMATO VINAIGRETTE SAUCE	107
GARLIC SAUCE II, III	109
JAPANESE DIPPING SAUCE	130
JIFFY BANKER'S SAUCE	139
JIFFY BASTING SAUCE	140
JIFFY BLACKBERRY BRANDY BROWN GRAY SAUCE	141
JIFFY BUTTER PARISIAN SAUCE	144
JIFFY COLD HORSERADISH SAUCE	150
JIFFY HOT MIXER SAUCE	168
JIFFY MAYONNAISE AND CHILI SAUCE	176

JIFFY MINTED MARINADE SAUCE	177
JIFFY PEACH SAUCE I	182
JIFFY SAVORY ONION TOPER SAUCE	193
JIFFY SCOTCH SAUCEUCE	194
JIFFY SHERRY SAUCE	196
JIFFY TANGY BUTTER SAUCE	205
JIFFY TERIYAKI MARINADE SAUCE	208
JIFFY TEXAS GARLIC SAUCE	208
JIFFY THAI GREEN CURRY SAUCE	209
JIFFY WINE MARINADE SAUCE I	215
JIFFY YOGURT SAUCE I	218
KETCHUP MUSHROOM SAUCE	220
KETCHUP NO-SUGAR, LOW-SODIUM SAUCE	220
KETCHUP TOMATO SAUCE	220
LOW-CAL MOCK BEARNAISE SAUCE	228
MADEIRA SAUCE IV	233
MEXICAN SAUCE	243
MUSHROOM SAUCE I, II	251
ONION SAUCE	258
PEACH SAUCE	266
PLUM JAM SAUCE	274
POLPETTI SAUCE	275
PROVENCAL SAUCE	278
QUICK BROWN SAUCE	281
QUICK CHILI SAUCE	281
RED PEPPER SAUCE II	287
RIB-TICKLING BARBECUE SAUCE	289
SAGE SAUCE I	296
SAUERKRAUT CHAMPAGNE SAUCE	298
SPICY CRANBERRY SAUCE	309
SWEET PEPPER SAUCE	318
TERIYAKI SAUCE I, II	322
VIETNAMESE DIPPING SAUCE	338

BEEF

	PAGE
AMERICAN-STYLE LIGHT MARINADE SAUCE	6
BARBECUE SAUCE V, VI,	19,20
BARBECUE SAUCE XIII, XIV	21,2
BEARNAISE SAUCE II, III	25,6
BEEF-BURGUNDY SAUCE	27
BERNAISE SAUCE	29
BERNAISE SAUCE	29
BROWN SAUCE II, III	43
CUCUMBER SAUCE I	91
DELUXE SOUR CREAM SAUCE	97
DEVILED CHEESE SAUCE	97
GREEN PEPPERCORN SAUCE II	116
GRIBICHE SAUCE I	117
GRILLING MARINADE SAUCE	118
HIGHLAND WHISKEY SAUCE	120
JAPANESE-STYLE SAUCE	130
JERK-STYLE JAMAICAN BARBECUE SAUCE	131
JIFFY AMARETTO APRICOT SAUCE	132
JIFFY ANCHOVY SAUCE	132
JIFFY APPLE MARINADE SAUCE	134
JIFFY APRICOT GLAZE SAUCE	136
JIFFY APRICOT SAUCE	135
JIFFY ASPIC SAUCE	137
JIFFY BARBECUED GINGER SAUCE	139
JIFFY BLACKBERRY JAM SAUCE	142
JIFFY BUTTER SAUCE	143
JIFFY CHILE BUTTER SAUCE	148
JIFFY COCONUT RUM BAR-B-Q SAUCE	150
JIFFY CORIANDER AND MINT CHUTNEY SAUCE	151
JIFFY COUNTRY HOT SAUCE	151
JIFFY CURRY MAYONNAISE SAUCE	156
JIFFY FRUIT GLAZE SAUCE	159
JIFFY GIN SAUCE	161
JIFFY GINGER SAUCE	162
JIFFY GINGER-GARLIC SAUCE	162
JIFFY HAM BUTTER SAUCE	164
JIFFY HOISIN SAUCE	165
JIFFY HONEY YOGURT SAUCE	166
JIFFY HOT MIXER SAUCE	168
JIFFY INDONESIAN SAUCE	169
JIFFY INDONESIAN SYRUP SAUCE	169
JIFFY JAMAICAN DELIGHT JERK SAUCE	170
JIFFY KEY WEST RUM AND LIME SAUCE	170
JIFFY LEMON BUTTER SAUCE	171
JIFFY LEMON VERONIQUE SAUCE	171
JIFFY LEMON VINAIGRETTE SAUCE	171
JIFFY LEMON-APPLE SAUCE	172
JIFFY LEMON-SESAME SAUCE	172
JIFFY LIME MARINADE SAUCE	172
JIFFY MINTED MARINADE SAUCE	177

JIFFY MUSTARD VINAIGRETTE SAUCE	179
JIFFY NIPPY PINEAPPLE SAUCE	179
JIFFY ONION MARINADE SAUCE	180
JIFFY ORANGE GLAZE SAUCE	181
JIFFY PALERMA SAUCE	181
JIFFY PAPRIKA MAYONNAISE SAUCE	181
JIFFY PECAN BUTTER SAUCE	183
JIFFY PIMENTO BUTTER SAUCE	185
JIFFY PINEAPPLE CHILI SAUCE	186
JIFFY PLUM SAUCE	186
JIFFY PLUM SWEET AND SPICY SAUCE	187
JIFFY RASPBERRY VINAIGRETTE SAUCE	188
JIFFY RATTLESNAKE CLUB BARBECUE SAUCE	188
JIFFY REMOULADE SAUCE I, II, III, IV	189,90
JIFFY SESAME DRESSING SAUCE	195
JIFFY SHERRY SAUCE	196
JIFFY SMOKED TOMATO SAUCE	197
JIFFY SOUR CREAM APRICOT SAUCE	198
JIFFY SOY SAUCE	198
JIFFY SPICY COLD SESAME SAUCE	199
JIFFY SPICY HONEY SAUCE	199
JIFFY SPICY ORIENTAL SAUCE	200
JIFFY SUBSTITUTE SOY SAUCE	201
JIFFY SWEET MUSTARD SAUCE	203
JIFFY TAHINI SAUCE	204
JIFFY TANDOORI MARINADE SAUCE I	204
JIFFY TANGY BUTTER SAUCE	205
JIFFY TARRAGON FRENCH SAUCE	206
JIFFY TEMPURA DIPPING SAUCE	207
JIFFY TEXAS BARBEQUED SAUCE	208
JIFFY TEXAS GARLIC SAUCE	208
JIFFY THANKSGIVING SAUCE	209
JIFFY VINAIGRETTE-MUSTARD SAUCE	213
JIFFY WINE MARINADE SAUCE II	216
KOREAN STEAK TARTAR (YUK KWE) SAUCE	220
MARCHAND DE VIN BUTTER SAUCE	236
MARINADE SAUCE	236
MEUNIERE SAUCE	243
ONION CREAM SAUCE	257
ORIENTAL BARBECUE GLAZE SAUCE	261
PANG PANG SAUCE	263
PHILADELPHIA PEPPERPOT SAUCE	270
PICKLE SAUCE	270
PICKLED CUCUMBER SAUCE	271
PIZZA SAUCE	274
RED BELL PEPPER SAUCE	285
SPICY HORSERADISH SAUCE	310
SPICY SPECIAL SAUCE	311
STROGANOFF SAUCE	315
SWEDISH SAUCE	316
SWEET 'N SOUR CARROT SAUCE	316
SWEET AND SOUR ONION SAUCE	316
TOMATO KETCHUP SAUCE II	327
VINEGAR FIERY SAUCE	339

CHICKEN/POULTRY

	PAGE
A LA KING SAUCE	1
ACAPULCO SAUCE	1
ADOBO SAUCE	1
AIOLI SAUCE	2
ALFREDO SAUCE I, II	2,3
ALLSPICE LIQUEUR SAUCE	3
ALMOND LIQUEUR SAUCE I, II	4
ALMOND SAUCE	4
AMARETTO BAR SAUCE	5
AMARETTO DUCK SAUCE	5
ANDALOUSE SAUCE	7
APRICOT GLAZED SAUCE	11
APRICOT SAUCE II	10
AZTEC CHILI SAUCE	14
BABY BACK RIB SAUCE	15
BACON AND HONEY MUSTARD SAUCE	15
BANANA KETCHUP SAUCE	17
BARBECUE CREAM OF COCONUT SAUCE	18
BARBECUE MUSTARD SAUCE	18
BARBECUE SAUCE I, II, III, IV, V, VI	18,9
BARBECUE SAUCE VII, VIII, IX, X, XII, XIII, XV	20,1,2
BARBECUED WALNUT SAUCE	22
BASIC BARBECUE SAUCE	22
BASIC FRESCA SAUCE	23
BASIC MOLASSES BARBECUE SAUCE	23
BEER CHEESE SAUCE	27
BEER SAUCE II	28
BERRY WONDERFUL SAUCE	29
BIGARADE SAUCE	30

BLACK PEPPER SAUCE	32
BLACKBERRY SAUCE	33
BLACKCURRANT CASSIS FONDUE SAUCE	33
BLENDER MAYONNAISE SAUCE	34
BLUEBERRY HONEY AND LIME SAUCE	36
BOURBON BARBECUE SAUCE	39
BOURBON JELLY SAUCE	39
BRANDY CREAM SAUCE	40
BREAD SAUCE I, II	41
BROCCOLI SAUCE I, II	42
BROWN SAUCE I, II	43
BROWN STOCK SAUCE III	43
BUN SPICY PEANUT SAUCE	44
BURGUNDY SAUCE	44
BUTTER GARLIC SAUCE	45
BUTTERMILK-HERB SAUCE	46
CACCIATORE SAUCE I, II	48
CAFE MARIMBA TOMATILLO SAUCE	49
CAJUN MIX SAUCE	49
CAJUN SAUCE	50
CANDIED CARROTS SAUCE	51
CARAWAY SAUCE	54
CHEESE DIP SAUCE	61
CHEESE SAUCE II	61
CHESTNUT PUREE SAUCE I, II	64,5
CHILE PEPPER SAUCE	66
CHILI COCKTAIL SAUCE	67
CHILI POWDER SAUCE	68
CHILI SAUCE I, II	68
CHINESE SWEET 'N' SOUR SAUCE	70
CHINESE-STYLE MUSTARD SAUCE	71
CHIVE AND CINNAMON SAUCE	71
CILANTRO SAUCE	75
CLASSIC CHEESE FONDUE SAUCE	77
CLASSIC SWISS FONDUE SAUCE	78
COCA-COLA BARBECUE SAUCE	78
CRANBERRY KETCHUP SAUCE	82
CRANBERRY DIP SAUCE	83
CRANBERRY SAUCE I, II, III	83
CRANBERRY-RAISIN SAUCE	84
CREAMY CURRY SAUCE I	86
CREAMY MUSTARD SAUCE I, II	87,8
CREAMY PAPRIKA SAUCE	60
CREOLE SAUCE I	90
CURRIED CHEESE FONDUE SAUCE	93
CURRY SAUCE I	94
DARK BEER SAUCE	93
DELUXE SOUR CREAM SAUCE	97
DILLY CHEESE SAUCE	99
FEISTY APRICOT SAUCE	102
FIVE-WAY CHILI SAUCE	103
FLAMBE SAUCE	103
FRENCH-STYLE MUSTARD SAUCE	106
FRESH APRICOT SAUCE	106
FRESH CORIANDER SAUCE	107
GARLIC MAYONNAISE SAUCE I	109
GARLIC SAUTED SHIITAKE MUSHROOMS SAUCE	110
GERMAN CHEESE SAUCE	111
GERMAN-STYLE MUSTARD SAUCE	111
GINGER LIQUEUR SAUCE	112
GLAZED CRANBERRY SAUCE	112
GOULASH SAUCE	113
GOOSEBERRY & WINE SAUCE	113
HAZELNUT OIL SAUCE	119
HONEY BAKED APPLES WITH WALNUT SAUCE	121
HOT STUFF BARBECUE SAUCE	126
ITALIAN MARINADE SAUCE	128
ITALIAN MOZZARELLA CHEESE SAUCE	128
JAPANESE DIPPING SAUCE	130
JAPANESE-STYLE SAUCE	130
JERK-STYLE JAMAICAN BARBECUE SAUCE	131
JIFFY AMARETTO MARINATE SAUCE	132
JIFFY APFELKEN SAUCE	134
JIFFY APRICOT BRANDY SAUCE	135
JIFFY ASPIC SAUCE	137
JIFFY BANKER'S SAUCE	139
JIFFY BARBECUE SAUCE	139
JIFFY BLACK BUTTER SAUCE	141
JIFFY BLACKENED RUBBING SAUCE	142
JIFFY BUTTER PARISIAN SAUCE	144
JIFFY CARAMELIZED GARLIC SAUCE	146
JIFFY CHARCOAL BROILED MARINATE SAUCE	147
JIFFY CHOCOLATE SORBET SAUCE	149
JIFFY COCONUT RUM BAR-B-Q SAUCE	150
JIFFY COUNTRY HOT SAUCE	151
JIFFY CREOLE DOG SAUCE	155
JIFFY EVER-GREEN SAUCE	158

JIFFY GARLIC FRENCH SAUCE	160
JIFFY GINGER TERIYAKI SAUCE	162
JIFFY HOISIN ORANGE SAUCE	165
JIFFY HONEY-LIME FRENCH SAUCE	166
JIFFY LEMON SORBET SAUCE	171
JIFFY PALERMA SAUCE	181
JIFFY PEANUT BUTTER SAUCE	182
JIFFY PEANUT-BUTTER BARBECUE SAUCE	183
JIFFY SESAME SAUCE	195
JIFFY SWEET 'N SASSY SAUCE	202
JIFFY TAMPA TINGLER SAUCE	204
JIFFY TANDOORI MARINADE SAUCE II	205
JIFFY TOMATILLO, TOMATO AND AVOCADO SALSA SAUCE	210
JIFFY TOMATO SALSA SAUCE	210
JIFFY WINE MARINADE SAUCE I	215
LEMON MUSTARD SAUCE	221
LEMON-HAZELNUT BUTTER SAUCE	222
LOW-CAL EGGPLANT SAUCE	226
LOW-CAL GORGONZOLA SAUCE	227
LOW-CAL MICHEL SAUCE	228
LOW-CAL POPPY-SEED SAUCE	229
MADEIRA SAUCE I, II, IV	232
MAGIC MARINADE SAUCE	233
MANDARIN SAUCE	234
MAPLE CRANBERRY SAUCE	235
MAPLE MUSTARD SAUCE	235
MARINADE SAUCE	236
MAYONNAISE SAUCE VI	240
MEXICAN MARINADE SAUCE	243
MOLASSES BARBECUE SAUCE	248
MORNAY CHEESE SAUCE	249
MORNAY SAUCE I, II	249,50
MUSHROOM AND HAZELNUT SAUCE	250
MUSHROOM PUREE SAUCE	251
MUSHROOM SAUCE III, IV	251,2
MUSTARD SAUCE VI	253
NAPA NO TSUKEMONO SAUCE	255
NEW ORLEANS BERNAISE SAUCE	255
ORANGE CRANBERRY SAUCE	259
ORANGE SAUCE	260
ORANGE TOMATO SAUCE	260
ORIENT PEANUT SAUCE	261
ORIENTAL APRICOT SAUCE	261
ORIENTAL CRANBERRY SAUCE	262
ORIENTAL PLUM SAUCE	262
ORIENTAL SAUCE	262
ORIENTAL VINAIGRETTE SAUCE	262
PANG PANG SAUCE	263
PAPAYA-GLACE LIME MARINADE SAUCE	264
PEANUT BUTTER SAUCE	266
PEANUT CHILI SAUCE	267
PEANUT LIQUEUR SAUCE	267
PEANUT ORIENTAL SAUCE	267
PEANUT SAUCE	267
PEANUT SAUCE MARINADE	268
PEARS BURGUNDY SAUCE	269
PHILADELPHIA PEPPERPOT SAUCE	270
PIQUANT SAUCE II	273
PISTACHIO AND WALNUT SAUCE	273
PIZZA SAUCE	274
PLUM SAUCE I, II, III	274,5
POLPETTI SAUCE	275
POLYNESIAN SAUCE	276
POOR MAN'S SAUCE	276
PORT & RASPBERRY SAUCE	277
PROVENCAL SAUCE	278
PRUNE SAUCE I, II	278,9
QUICK CURRY SAUCE	281
RAISIN AND CRANBERRY SAUCE	283
RAISIN SAUCE	283
RASPBERRY AND GIN SAUCE	283
RASPBERRY BRANDY SAUCE	284
RASPBERRY-SESAME SAUCE I, II	285,6
RED PEPPER SAUCE III	288
REMOULADE SAUCE I, II	289
RIB-TICKLING BARBECUE SAUCE	289
ROSEMARY LIQUEUR SAUCE	291
RUBY BEET SAUCE	292
RUSSIAN RED BEANS AND PLUM SAUCE	295
SALSA SAUCE I, II	297
SAUERKRAUT HUNGARIAN SAUCE	299
SAUTERNE SAUCE	300
SAVORY APPLE SAUCE	300
SCANDINAVIAN MUSTARD SAUCE	301
SHREDDED CHICKEN SPICY PEANUT SAUCE	303
SICILIAN SWEET AND SOUR SAUCE	304
SPICED GOOSEBERRY RELISH SAUCE	308

SPICY CRANBERRY SAUCE	309
SPICY FRUIT SAUCE	309
SPICY GEORGIAN PEACH VINEGAR SAUCE	310
SPICY PEANUT SAUCE I	310
SPICY SAUCE	311
SPICY SPECIAL SAUCE	311
SPICY THAI SAUCE I	311
SPICY TOMATO SAUCE I, III	312,3
SPICY-FLAVOR OIL SAUCE	313
STROGANOFF SAUCE	315
SWEET AND ZESTY BRUSH-ON SAUCE	317
TAO BARBECUE VINEGAR SAUCE	319
TARRAGON WINE SAUCE	319
TERIYAKI JAPANESE SAUCE	322
TOMATO, HOT PEPPER AND CREAM SAUCE	326
TOMATO KETCHUP SAUCE I	327
TOMATO MUSTARD SAUCE	328
TOMATO NICOISE FONDUE SAUCE	328
TOMATO SALSA SAUCE II	328
TRY ME SAUCE	333
TUSCAN VINEGAR SAUCE	334
VERONIQUE SAUCE	337
VIENNESE APRICOT SAUCE	338
VINEGAR HORSERADISH SAUCE	339
VINEGAR TEX-MEX SAUCE	340
WALNUT GEORGIAN SPICES SAUCE	344
WALNUT RAISIN SAUCE	344
WALNUT SAUCE I	343
WELSH SAUCE	345
WESTERN SAUCE	346
WHITE SANGRIA SAUCE	348
WHITE SAUCE	348
WINE SAUCE	249
ZESTY TOMATO SAUCE	351
ZIPPY GREEN BEAN SAUCE	351

FISH/SEAFOOD   PAGE

A LA KING SAUCE	1
ALBERT SAUCE	2
APRICOT-GINGER SAUCE	12
BACON AND HONEY MUSTARD SAUCE	15
BASIC FRESCA SAUCE	23
BASIL CREAM BALSAMIC VINEGAR SAUCE	24
BASIL TARTAR SAUCE	24
BEARNAISE SAUCE II	25
BERCY SAUCE	28
BERNAISE SAUCE	29
BERNAUSE SAUCE	29
BLACK BEAN CLAMS SAUCE	30
BLACK BEAN SAUCE III	31
BLENDER MAYONNAISE SAUCE	34
BOMBAY SAUCE	38
BOUILLABAISSE SAUCE	39
BREAD SAUCE II	41
BREAM BEER SAUCE	41
BUTTER GARLIC SAUCE	45
BUTTER SAUCE	45
CAFE MARIMBA TOMATILLO SAUCE	49
CAJUN MAYONNAISE SAUCE	49
CAJUN SAUCE	50
CAPER SAUCE I	52
CHILE OIL SAUCE	66
CHILI SAUCE I	68
CHILI-HORSERADISH SAUCE	70
CILANTRO, ORANGE AND TOMATO SAUCE	75
CLARIFIED LEMON BUTTER SAUCE	77
COCKTAIL SAUCE	79
CREAM SAUCE	85
CREAMY BLUE CHEESE SAUCE I	86
CREAMY CURRY SAUCE II	86
CREAMY HORSERADISH SAUCE	87
CREAMY MUSTARD SAUCE II	88
CREME DE DIJON SAUCE	89
CREOLE SAUCE I, II	90
CREOLE STYLE SAUCE	90
CUCUMBER-DILL SAUCE II	91
DILL SAUCE I, II	98
FIG SAUCE	102
FISH MARINADE SAUCE	102
FOOD PROCESSOR MAYONNAISE SAUCE	104
FRENCH GREEN SAUCE	105
FRENCH HERB SAUCE	105
FRENCH MUSHROOM MARINADE SAUCE	105
FRESH CORIANDER SAUCE	107
FRESH HERB AND TOMATO VINAIGRETTE SAUCE	107

GREEN SAUCE I, II	116
GRIBICHE SAUCE II	118
HERB OIL SAUCE	119
HOLLANDAISE SAUCE	120
HORSERADISH SAUCE	122
HOT BUTTER DIPPING SAUCE	123
HOT DILL SAUCE	124
HOT FISH SAUCE	124
HOT PEPPER AND LIME-JUICE SAUCE	126
ISRAELI SOUR CREAM SAUCE	127
ITALIAN GREEN SAUCE	128
JIFFY BALTIMORE SAUCE	138
JIFFY BEARNAISE SAUCE	140
JIFFY BLACKENED RUBBING SAUCE	142
JIFFY BUTTER HERB SAUCE	144
JIFFY BUTTER PARISIAN SAUCE	144
JIFFY BUTTER SAUCE	144
JIFFY CAPER SAUCE I, II, III	145,6
JIFFY CASINO SAUCE I, II	146
JIFFY CHARCOAL BROILED MARINATE SAUCE	147
JIFFY COCKTAIL SAUCE	149
JIFFY COLD HORSERADISH SAUCE	150
JIFFY CORIANDER AND MINT CHUTNEY SAUCE	151
JIFFY CREAMY BLUE CHEESE SAUCE II	152
JIFFY CREAMY DILL SAUCE	152
JIFFY CREAMY ONION SAUCE	153
JIFFY CREOLE DOG SAUCE	155
JIFFY CUCUMBER & YOGURT SAUCE	155
JIFFY CUCUMBER-DILL YOGURT SAUCE	155
JIFFY CURRIED MAYONNAISE SAUCE	156
JIFFY FIGARO SAUCE	158
JIFFY FRUITY SHRIMP SAUCE	160
JIFFY GINGER TERIYAKI SAUCE	162
JIFFY GLOUCESTER SAUCE	162
JIFFY GREEN GODDESS SAUCE	163
JIFFY GREEN ONION SAUCE	163
JIFFY GREEN SAUCE	163
JIFFY HERB BUTTER SAUCE	164
JIFFY HOISIN ORANGE SAUCE	165
JIFFY HOLLANDAISE ANISE SAUCE	165
JIFFY HORSERADISH CREAM SAUCE	166
JIFFY HORSERADISH MAYONNAISE SAUCE I, II	167
JIFFY HORSERADISH SAUCE	167
JIFFY JAPANESE SAUCE	170
JIFFY KEY WEST RUM AND LIME SAUCE	170
JIFFY LEMON BUTTER SAUCE	171
JIFFY LEMON-SESAME SAUCE	172
JIFFY LIME MARINADE SAUCE	172
JIFFY LIME SEASONING SAUCE	172
JIFFY LORENZO FRENCH SAUCE	173
JIFFY MANHATTAN SAUCE	174
JIFFY ONION MARINADE SAUCE	180
JIFFY PALERMA SAUCE	181
JIFFY POLISH SAUCE	187
JIFFY RAW TOMATO SAUCE	188
JIFFY RED SAUCE	189
JIFFY REMOULADE SAUCE I, II, III, IV	189,90
JIFFY ROCKEFELLER SAUCE	190
JIFFY SALSA AL PRADO SAUCE	193
JIFFY SALSA SAUCE I	192
JIFFY SCAMPI SAUCE	194
JIFFY SEAFOOD COCKTAIL SAUCE	194
JIFFY SEAFOOD SAUCE	194
JIFFY SOLE ANGELICA SAUCE	197
JIFFY SPANISH-STYLE HOT SAUCE	199
JIFFY SUPREME MUSTARD CREAM SAUCE	202
JIFFY TANGY COCKTAIL SAUCE	205
JIFFY TARTAR SAUCE I, II, III	207
JIFFY TEMPURA DIPPING SAUCE	207
JIFFY TERIYAKI SAUCE	208
JIFFY TOMATILLO, TOMATO AND AVOCADO SALSA SAUCE	210
JIFFY TOMATO SALSA SAUCE	210
JIFFY TOMATO VINAIGRETTE SAUCE	211
JIFFY WARM HERBED VINAIGRETTE SAUCE	214
JIFFY WINE MARINADE SAUCE I	215
JIFFY YAKITORI SAUCE	217
JIFFY YOGURT DILL SAUCE	218
JIFFY YOGURT SAUCE II	218
JIFFY YOGURT SPICY MARINADE SAUCE	218
JALAPENO CORN SAUCE	130
JERK-STYLE JAMAICAN BARBECUE SAUCE	131
KETCHUP LEMON SAUCE	220
LEMON PARSLEY SAUCE	221
LIGHT TARTAR SAUCE	223
LOW-CAL BUTTERMILK SAUCE	225
LOW-CAL CREAMY CHILI SAUCE	226
LOW-CAL ISLAND SAUCE	227

LOW-CAL MADRAS SAUCE	228
LOW-CAL MICHEL SAUCE	228
LOW-CAL MOCK BEARNAISE SAUCE	228
LOW-CAL RAIFORT SAUCE	229
LOW-CAL SAUCE	224
LOW-CAL TOMATO PIMENTO SAUCE	230
LOW-CAL VINCENT SAUCE	231
MAGIC MARINADE SAUCE	233
MANGO SAUCE II	234
MAYONNAISE SAUCE I	239
MEDITERRANEAN SAUCE	241
MEXICAN MARINADE SAUCE	243
MEXICAN STYLE SAUCE I	244
MOBILE SAUCE	246
MOLHO DE PIMENTA SAUCE	249
MORNAY CHEESE SAUCE	249
MUSTARD SAUCE I, II, III, IV, V	252,3
MUSTARD-DILL SAUCE	254
NORMANDY SAUCE	256
ORANGE & GRAPEFRUIT SAUCE	258
PIQUANT SAUCE I	273
PIRAO SAUCE	273
PLUM SAUCE I	274
POLYNESIAN SAUCE	276
POULETTE SAUCE	277
PROVENCAL OLIVE PASTE SAUCE	277
SAXON SAUCE	301
SHRIMP COCKTAIL SAUCE	303
SNAIL BUTTER SAUCE	306
SPICY GEORGIAN PEACH VINEGAR SAUCE	310
SPICY PEANUT SAUCE II	311
SWEET ONION SAUCE	317
TARRAGON WINE SAUCE	319
TARTAR SAUCE I, II, III	320,1
TERIYAKI SAUCE II	322
TOMATO, HOT PEPPER AND CREAM SAUCE	326
TOMATO SALSA SAUCE I	328
VERONIQUE SAUCE	337
VINEGAR HORSERADISH SAUCE	339
VINEGAR-BALSAMIC AND BASIL MARINADE SAUCE	340
WELSH SAUCE	345
YOGURT SAUCE	350

LAMB — PAGE

APPLE-ROSEMARY SAUCE	9
CAPER SAUCE I	52
CUMIN SAUCE	92
ENGLISH-STYLE MINT SAUCE	101
GREEK MARINADE SAUCE	115
JALAPENO CORN SAUCE	130
JIFFY CREME DE MENTHE SAUCE	154
JIFFY MINT JULEP SAUCE	176
JIFFY TANDOORI MARINADE SAUCE I	204
JIFFY WINE MARINADE SAUCE I	215
MINT SAUCE	245
SAUTERNE SAUCE	300
SPICY SPECIAL SAUCE	311
VINEGAR MINT SAUCE	339

PORK/HAM — PAGE

ADOBO SAUCE	1
AMERICAN CREOLE SAUCE	6
APPLE CIDER CHEESE SAUCE	8
APPLE GLAZE SAUCE	8
APPLE RAISIN SAUCE	8
APPLE SAUCE	9
APPLESAUCE-MAYONNAISE-MINT SAUCE	10
APRICOT & COGNAC SAUCE	11
BABY BACK RIB SAUCE	15
BACON AND HONEY MUSTARD SAUCE	15
BANANA KETCHUP SAUCE	17
BARBECUE SAUCE IX	20
BASIC MOLASSES BARBECUE SAUCE	23
BEARNAISE SAUCE III	26
BEER SAUCE I	28
BOUILLABAISSE SAUCE	39
BOURBON BARBECUE SAUCE	39
BOURBON JELLY SAUCE	39
BRAZILIAN BARBECUE SAUCE	40
BUN SPICY PEANUT SAUCE	44
CAJUN MAYONNAISE SAUCE	49
CAPER SAUCE I	52
CARAMELIZED ONIONS SAUCE	54
CARAWAY SAUCE	54

CHILI SAUCE I	68	SWEET APPLE SAUCE		317
CRANBERRY SAUCE III	83	TAO BARBECUE VINEGAR SAUCE		319
DARK BEER SAUCE	96	TERIYAKI JAPANESE SAUCE		322
DELUXE SOUR CREAM SAUCE	97	TOMATO KETCHUP SAUCE II		327
DUTCH CHEESE SAUCE	99	WALNUT SAUCE I		343
FEISTY APRICOT SAUCE	102	WESTERN SAUCE		346
GINGER PEAR SAUCE	112	WINE & CHERRY SAUCE		249
GRILLING MARINADE SAUCE	118	WINE SAUCE		249
HOMEMADE HOT MUSTARD SAUCE	120	ZESTY TOMATO SAUCE		351
HONEY BAKED APPLES WITH WALNUT SAUCE	121			
HOT MUSTARD SAUCE	125			
JERK-STYLE JAMAICAN BARBECUE SAUCE	131	**VEAL**		**PAGE**
JIFFY ANCHOVY MAYONNAISE SAUCE	133			
JIFFY APFELKEN SAUCE	134	ALSTATIAN ONION SAUCE		5
JIFFY APPLE MARINADE SAUCE	134	ANCHOVY SAUCE I		6
JIFFY APPLE SAUCE	134	BROWN SAUCE II		43
JIFFY APPLE-MINT SAUCE	134	BROWN STOCK SAUCE III		43
JIFFY APRICOT COCONUT GLAZING SAUCE	136	CHESTNUT DEVILED SAUCE		64
JIFFY APRICOT GLAZE SAUCE	136	CHESTNUT GLAZING SAUCE		64
JIFFY APRICOT GLAZING SAUCE	136	CHESTNUT PUREE SAUCE I, II		64,5
JIFFY BARBECUE SAUCE	139	JIFFY BLACK BUTTER SAUCE		141
JIFFY BEEF-BEER MARINADE SAUCE	140	JIFFY SOUR CREAM BEET SAUCE		197
JIFFY BLACKBERRY JAM SAUCE	142	LYONNAISE SAUCE		231
JIFFY BROWN SUGAR SAUCE	143	MUSHROOM PUREE SAUCE		251
JIFFY CALYPSO SAUCE	145	PIZZA SAUCE		274
JIFFY CAULIFLOWER SAUCE	147	PUREE MUSHROOM SAUCE		280
JIFFY COCONUT RUM BAR-B-Q SAUCE	150	SAUERKRAUT CHAMPAGNE SAUCE		298
JIFFY COUNTRY HOT SAUCE	151	SAUERKRAUT CREAM SAUCE		298
JIFFY FRUIT AND MIXED MUSTARDS SAUCE	159	SOUR CREAM SAUCE		307
JIFFY FRUIT JUICE FRENCH SAUCE	160	SPICY SPECIAL SAUCE		311
JIFFY GINGER SAUCE	162	TOMATO, HOT PEPPER AND CREAM SAUCE		326
JIFFY HORSERADISH APPLESAUCE SAUCE	166	TRY ME SAUCE		333
JIFFY JAM SAUCE	169	VINEGAR FIERY SAUCE		339
JIFFY LEMON-APPLE SAUCE	172			
JIFFY LEMON-SESAME SAUCE	172			
JIFFY MAPLE APPLESAUCE SAUCE	174	**PASTA/RICE/POTATO**		**PAGE**
JIFFY MUSTARD GLAZE SAUCE	179			
JIFFY PEACHY MARINADE SAUCE	182	ADRUZZESE SAUCE		1
JIFFY PLUM SAUCE	186	ALL DAY ALL NIGHT CHILI SAUCE		3
JIFFY PLUM SWEET AND SPICY SAUCE	187	ANCHOVY SAUCE II		6
JIFFY SOUR CREAM APRICOT SAUCE	198	ANCHOVY TOMATO SAUCE		7
JIFFY STIR FRIED ORANGE SAUCE	200	ANDALOUSE SAUCE		7
JIFFY SUEDOISE SAUCE	20	ANDALUSIAN SAUCE		7
JIFFY SWEET MUSTARD SAUCE	203	APPLE RAISIN SAUCE		8
JIFFY TANGY COCONUT SAUCE	206	APPLEJACK CREAM SAUCE		10
JIFFY TEXAS BARBEQUED SAUCE	208	ARTICHOKE PARMESAN SAUCE		12
JIFFY VINAIGRETTE DE MENTHE SAUCE	212	ASPARAGUS CHEESE SAUCE		13
JIFFY WARM YELLOW SAUCE	215	ASPARAGUS TIPS SAUCE		13
JIFFY WEST INDIAN HOT SAUCE	215	AVIGNON SAUCE		13
JIFFY WINE GLAZE SAUCE	217	AVOCADO SAUCE II		14
LEMON-HAZELNUT BUTTER SAUCE	222	AZTEC CHILI SAUCE		14
MADEIRA SAUCE III	232	BACON HORSERADISH SAUCE		15
MANGO GLAZING SAUCE	235	BACON SAUCE		16
MARINADE DARK SAUCE	236	BACON, TOMATO AND CHEESE SAUCE		16
MARINADE SAUCE	236	BAGNA CAUDA SAUCE I, II		16
MINT JELLY SAUCE	245	BASIL AND PROSCIUTTO SAUCE		24
MINT LIQUEURS SAUCE	245	BASIL AND SUNDRIED TOMATO SAUCE		24
MOCK HOLLANDAISE SAUCE	248	BEAN NEAPOLITAN SAUCE		25
MUSHROOM PUREE SAUCE	251	BEAN SAUCE		25
ORIENTAL APRICOT SAUCE	261	BECHAMEL SAUCE I, II		26
ORIENTAL PLUM SAUCE	262	BEEF AND MOZZARELLA SAUCE		26
PAPAYA RELISH SAUCE	264	BEER AND TOMATOES CASSEROLE SAUCE		27
PEACH BRANDY SAUCE	265	BLACK BEAN SAUCE I, II		31
PICKLED BEETS SAUCE	270	BLACK FRIAR'S SAUCE		32
PICKLED CUCUMBER SAUCE	271	BLACK OLIVE AND TOMATO SAUCE		32
PLUM SAUCE I, II, III	274,5	BLACK OLIVE SAUCE		32
POPPY SEED SAUCE	276	BLUE CHEESE SAUCE II, III, IV		34,5
PRUNE SAUCE II	279	BOLOGNA SAUCE		37
PRUNES AND BRANDY SAUCE	279	BOLOGNESE SAUCE I, II, III, IV		37,8
RAISIN AND CRANBERRY SAUCE	283	BREADCRUMB SAUCE		41
RAISIN SAUCE	283	BROAD BEAN SAUCE		42
RAISINS AND PINE NUTS SAUCE	283	BROCCOLI AND TOMATO SAUCE		42
RASPBERRY-SESAME SAUCE I	285	BROCCOLI SAUCE I, II		42
RED CURRANT SAUCE	287	BUN SPICY PEANUT SAUCE		44
RED PEPPER SAUCE IV	288	BUTTER GARLIC SAUCE		45
ROBERT SAUCE	290	CACCIATORE SAUCE I, II		48
ROYAL SAUCE	292	CAESAR SAUCE		49
RUBY BEET SAUCE	292	CALABANESE SAUCE		50
SAUERKRAUT DUTCH SAUCE	298	CALAMERI SAUCE		50
SAUERKRAUT FRENCH SAUCE	299	CARBONARA SAUCE I, II		54,5
SAUERKRAUT RUSSIAN SAUCE	299	CARIBBEAN CREOLE SAUCE		55
SAVORY APPLE SAUCE	300	CARROT SAUCE		56
SOUR CREAM SAUCE	307	CAULIFLOWER SAUCE		57
SPEEDY RAISIN SAUCE	308	CAVIAR SAUCE III		57
SPICED GOOSEBERRY RELISH SAUCE	308	CELEBRATION CHAMPAGNE SAUCE		58
SPICY-FLAVOR OIL SAUCE	313			
SWEET AND SOUR SAUCE	316			

CELERY SAUCE I, III	58	JIFFY PECAN MUSTARD SAUCE	184
CHARCUTERIE SAUCE	59	JIFFY PESTO SAUCE I, II, III	184,5
CHASSEM SAUCE	59	JIFFY PINE NUT SAUCE	185
CHEDDAR SAUCE	60	JIFFY PUTTANESCA SAUCE	187
CHEESE AND CREAM SAUCE	60	JIFFY REMOULADE SAUCE II, IV	189,90
CHEESE FONDUE SAUCE	61	JIFFY RICOTTA AND ROASTED PEPPERS SAUCE	190
CHICK PEAS SAUCE	65	JIFFY RICOTTA SAUCE	190
CHICKEN A LA KING SAUCE	65	JIFFY ROSEMARY SAUCE	191
CHICKEN AND OLIVE SAUCE	65	JIFFY RUSSIAN SAUCE	192
CHICKEN LIVER SAUCE I, II	66	JIFFY SALSA SAUCE II	193
CHILE POWDER SAUCE	67	JIFFY SAVVY SAUCE	193
CHILI CON CARNE SAUCE	67	JIFFY SCAMPI SAUCE	194
CHOCOLATE FONDUE SAUCE	73	JIFFY SHRIMP SAUCE	196
CHOCOLATE WHITE SAUCE	74	JIFFY SKORDALIA SAUCE	196
CHORON SAUCE	74	JIFFY SORRENTO SAUCE	197
CHUNKY-CREAMY BLUE CHEESE SAUCE	74	JIFFY SOUR CREAM SAUCE	198
CLAM SAUCE I, II, III, IV	76	JIFFY SPINACH HERBED SAUCE	200
CLASSIC CHEESE FONDUE SAUCE	77	JIFFY SUN-DRIED TOMATO ROUILLE SAUCE	201
CLASSIC WHITE BUTTER SAUCE	78	JIFFY SZECHUAN PEANUT SAUCE	203
COAMOISIER SAUCE	78	JIFFY TAPENADE SAUCE	206
COURT BOUILLON SAUCE	82	JIFFY TEXAS GARLIC SAUCE	208
CRAB SAUCE	82	JIFFY THAI GREEN CURRY SAUCE	209
CREAM AND SALMON SAUCE	85	JIFFY THICK WHITE SAUCE	209
CREAM OF CAULIFLOWER SAUCE	85	JIFFY TOMATO MAYONNAISE SAUCE	210
CREAM OF TOMATO SAUCE	85	JIFFY TOMATO SOUP FRENCH SAUCE	211
CREAMY GARLIC SAUCE	87	JIFFY TUNA, CAPERS AND TOMATO SAUCE	212
CREAMY LOBSTER SAUCE	87	JIFFY UNCOOKED FRESH TOMATO SAUCE	216
CREAMY PARMESAN CHEESE SAUCE	88	JIFFY UNCOOKED TOMATO SAUCE	216
CREAMY ROASTED-GARLIC SAUCE	88	JIFFY UNCOOKED TUNA SAUCE	217
CREAMY TOMATO SAUCE	88	JIFFY VIRGIN MARY SAUCE	213
CURRY, GINGER, TOMATO SAUCE	94	JIFFY VOLCANIC HORSERADISH SAUCE	213
DANISH CHEESE SAUCE	96	JIFFY WALNUT CREAM SAUCE	214
DEVILLED SAUCE	98	JIFFY WALNUT SAUCE I	214
EGG SAUCE II	100	JIFFY YELLOW BEAN SAUCE	217
EGGPLANT WALNUT SAUCE	100	LAMB SAUCE	221
FAZIO'S TOMATO SAUCE	102	LEEK PUREE SAUCE	221
FIST STOCK SAUCE	103	LIGHT MARINARA SAUCE	223
FOOD PROCESSOR MAYONNAISE SAUCE	104	LORD CHESTERFIELD SAUCE	243
FOUR CHEESE SAUCE	104	LOW-CAL BOLOGNESE SAUCE	224
FRENCH MUSHROOM MARINADE SAUCE	105	LOW-CAL CHINESE SAUCE	225
FRENCH-STYLE MUSTARD SAUCE	106	LOW-CAL CLAM SAUCE	226
GARLIC SAUCE I	109	LOW-CAL EGGPLANT SAUCE	226
GENOA SAUCE	110	LOW-FAT YOGURT SAUCE	231
GÉNOISE SAUCE	110	MAMA MIA TOMATO SAUCE	234
GENOVESE SAUCE	111	MARINARA SAUCE I, II	237
GERMAN CHEESE SAUCE	111	MASCARPONE SAUCE	238
GOLDEN VEGETABLE PUREE SAUCE	113	MATELOTE SAUCE	238
GORGONZOLA SAUCE	113	MAYONNAISE SAUCE II, III, IV, V	239,40
GREEK TOMATO SAUCE	115	MEAT SAUCE I, II	240,1
GREEN PARSLEY SAUCE	115	MEDIUM WHITE SAUCE	241
GREEN SAUCE II	116	MEXICAN STYLE SAUCE II	244
GREEN TOMATO CHUTNEY SAUCE	117	MIREPOIX BROWN SAUCE	246
GREEN TOMATO SAUCE	117	MIZUTAKI SAUCE	246
HARE SAUCE	119	MOCK BEARNAISE SAUCE	247
HERBS, TOMATO AND CREAM SAUCE	120	MOCK CABANARA SAUCE	247
HOMEMADE WALNUT OIL SAUCE	121	MOCK SOUR CREAM SAUCE	248
HORSERADISH CHEDDAR CHEESE SAUCE	122	MOREL SAUCE	249
HOT ARTICHOKE SAUCE	123	MUSHROOM FONDUE SAUCE	250
HOT CRAB SAUCE	124	MUSTARD CREAM SAUCE	252
HUNGARIAN SAUCE	126	NASU NO KARASKI SAUCE	255
ITALIAN SAUCE	127	NEAPOLITAN CLAM SAUCE	255
ITALIAN SAUSAGE SAUCE	129	NEWBURG SAUCE	256
ITALIAN SEAFOOD SAUCE	129	NORCIA SAUCE	256
IVORY SAUCE	129	OLIVE SAUCE	257
JARLSBERG VEGETABLE BISQUE SAUCE	131	ONION CREAM SAUCE	257
JIFFY ALIOLI SUN-DRIED SAUCE	132	ORANGE TEQUILA SAUCE	260
JIFFY ANCHOVY-CHEESE (LOW CAL) SAUCE	133	PAPAL SAUCE	263
JIFFY CAULIFLOWER SAUCE	147	PAPRIKA SAUCE	264
JIFFY CILANTRO PESTO SAUCE	149	PARMESAN CREAM SAUCE	265
JIFFY CLAM AND DILL SAUCE	149	PEAS AND PROSCIUTTO SAUCE	269
JIFFY COURGETTE FLOWERS SAUCE	152	PEAS SAUCE	269
JIFFY CREAMY FRENCH SAUCE	152	PEPERONATA SAUCE	269
JIFFY CREAMY FRUIT MAYONNAISE SAUCE	153	PICO DE GALLO SAUCE	271
JIFFY CREAMY TOMATO VINAIGRETTE SAUCE	153	PORK SAUCE	276
JIFFY CREME FRAICHE LOW FAT SAUCE	154	PROVENCALE OLIVE OIL SAUCE	278
JIFFY CURRIED FRENCH SAUCE	156	PROVENCE OIL SAUCE	278
JIFFY CURRY SAUCE	156	PULP SAUCE	279
JIFFY FRESH TOMATO SAUCE	159	PUMPKIN SAUCE	279
JIFFY GEORGINA SAUCE	161	PUMPKIN SEED SAUCE	280
JIFFY HOT BLOODY MARY SAUCE	167	PUTTANESCA SAUCE	280
JIFFY INDIAN TURMERIC SAUCE	168	QUICK BROWN SAUCE	281
JIFFY INDONESIAN SAUCE	169	QUICK TOMATO SAUCE AND RED BEANS	282
JIFFY INDONESIAN SYRUP SAUCE	169	RED CHILI SAUCE	286
JIFFY MACADAMIA NUT PESTO SAUCE	173	RED PEPPER SAUCE I, III	287,8
JIFFY PAPRIKA MAYONNAISE SAUCE	181	RED-PEPPER SALSA SAUCE	288
JIFFY PEANUT BUTTER DELIGHT SAUCE	183	REMOULADE SAUCE II	289
JIFFY PEANUTTY PESTO-SAUCE	183	RICOTTA SAUCE	289

ROASTED PEPPERS AND WALNUTS SAUCE	290
ROASTED TOMATO SAUCE	291
ROMESCO SAUCE	291
ROSE SAUCE	292
ROUILLE SAUCE	293
RUSTIC SAUCE	295
SAFFROM SAUCE	296
SAGE SAUCE I, II, III	296
SATAY SAUCE II	298
SAUSAGE AND MUSHROOM SAUCE	299
SAVORY SPAGHETTI SAUCE	300
SCALLOPS AND HERBED CHEESE SAUCE	301
SCAMPI CREAM SAUCE	301
SEAFOOD DIABLO SAUCE	302
SHELLFISH IN A FOIL SAUCE	302
SHRIMP CANTONESE-STYLE SAUCE	303
SICILIAN-STYLE TOMATO SAUCE	304
SIMPLE RED SAUCE	304
SIMPLE TOMATO SAUCE	304
SIMPLE WHITE SAUCE	305
SMOKED SALMON, CUCUMBER AND DILL SAUCE	305
SMOKED SALMON, PEAS AND CAVIAR SAUCE	306
SMOKED TURKEY, PIN NUTS AND ROSEMARY SAUCE	306
SORREL SAUCE	307
SOUR CREAM GRAPE SAUCE	307
SPICY BLACK-EYED PEA SAUCE	308
SPICY BUTTERMILK SAUCE	309
SPICY ORANGE SAUCE	310
SPICY THAI SAUCE II	312
SPICY TOMATO SAUCE I	312
SPINACH AND MASCARPONE SAUCE	313
SPINACH SAUCE	313
SUN-DRIED TOMATO CREAM SAUCE	315
SUN-DRIED TOMATOES, OLIVE AND BASIL SAUCE	315
SWEET PEPPER SAUCE	318
SYRACUSE SAUCE	318
TARRAGON-CREAM SAUCE	320
TEQUILA ORANGE SAUCE	321
TEQUILA SAUCE	321
THERMIDOR SAUCE	323
THIMBLES AND BEANS SAUCE	323
THREE CHEESE SAUCE	323
THREE MUSHROOMS SAUCE	324
TOMATO AND SWEET PEPPER SAUCE	324
TOMATO, BACON AND CAPERS SAUCE	324
TOMATO CILANTRO SAUCE	325
TOMATO COULIS SAUCE	325
TOMATO CREAM SAUCE	325
TOMATO CREOLE SAUCE	325
TOMATO FONDUE SAUCE	326
TOMATO, HOT PEPPER AND CREAM SAUCE	326
TOMATO MEAT SAUCE	327
TOMATO SALSA SAUCE I	328
TOMATO SAUCE I, II, IV, V, VI, VII, VII	329,30,1
TOMATO SAUCE WITH TEQUILA AND CREAM	331
TOMATO-FLAVORED BEARNAISE SAUCE	331
TOMATO-VEGETABLE SAUCE	332
TOMATO-VODKA COULIS SAUCE	332
TUNA AND TOMATO SAUCE	333
TUNA SAUCE	333
TUSCAN PASTA SAUCE	334
VELOUTE SAUCE I, II, III	336
VELVET LEMON SAUCE	337
VENETIAN SAUCE	337
VINEGAR AND OIL TOMATO SAUCE	339
VODKA CREAM AND GREEN PEPPERCORNS SAUCE	340
VODKA CREAM SAUCE	341
VODKA SAUCE	340
VODKA, TOMATOES AND CREAM SAUCE	341
VODKA TOMATOES CREAM SAUCE	341
VODKA-SOUTHWESTERN SAUCE	342
WALNUT AND POMEGRANATE SAUCE	344
WALNUT CREAM SAUCE	344
WALNUT SAUCE II, III	343
WATERCRESS PUREE SAUCE	345
WHISKEY SAUCE I	346
WHITE BEANS, TUNA AND OLIVE OIL SAUCE	347
WHITE CLAM SAUCE	347
WHITE HERB SAUCE	347
WHITE SAUCE	348
WHITE TUNA SAUCE	348
WHITE WINE SAUCE	249
YOGURT AND GREEN-ONION SAUCE	350
ZUCCHINI SAUCE I, II, III	352

DESSERTS/FRUIT/ICE CREAM · PAGE

ALMOND CHOCOLATE BAR SAUCE	3
ALMOND LIQUEUR SAUCE I, II	4
ALMOND-RUM FUDGE SAUCE	4
ANGELICA SAUCE	7
ANISE SEED SAUCE	8
APPLE SCOTCH SAUCE	9
APRICOT SAUCE II	10
APRICOT-YOGURT DIP SAUCE	12
BABA RUM SAUCE	15
BAKLAVA SAUCE	17
BANANA LIQUEUR SAUCE	17
BANANA SAUCE	18
BASIC CHANTILLY CREAM SAUCE	23
BERRY SAUCE	29
BLACKBERRY BRANDY SAUCE	33
BLACKBERRY CARAMEL CUSTARD SAUCE	33
BLUEBERRY CINNAMON SAUCE	35
BLUEBERRY SAUCE I, II	36
BLUEBERRY WINE SAUCE	36
BOOTHBAY BLUEBERRY SAUCE	38
BRANDY CHOCOLATE SAUCE	40
BROWN SUGAR-CINNAMON SAUCE	44
BUTTER WALNUT SAUCE	45
BUTTERED APPLESAUCE	45
BUTTERSCOTCH ALMOND SAUCE	46
BUTTERSCOTCH FONDUE SAUCE	46
BUTTERSCOTCH SAUCE I, II	46,7
CANNED APRICOTS SAUCE	51
CARAMEL BRANDY SAUCE	52
CARAMEL SAUCE I, II, III, IV	52,3
CARAMEL TOPPING SAUCE	53
CARAMEL-MOCHA SAUCE	54
CATALONIAN CREAM SAUCE	56
CHERRY CRANBERRY SAUCE	63
CHERRY JUBILEE SAUCE	63
CHERRY MINT LIQUEUR SAUCE	63
CHERRY SAUCE	63
CHOCOLATE BRANDIED SAUCE	72
CHOCOLATE BUTTER SAUCE	73
CHOCOLATE FONDUE SAUCE	73
CHOCOLATE KAHLUA SAUCE	73
CHOCOLATE MARSHMALLOW FUDGE SAUCE	73
CHOCOLATE MIGNONS A LA RITZ SAUCE	74
CHOCOLATE SAUCE I, II, III, IV, V	71,2
CHOCOLATE WHITE SAUCE	74
CINNAMON PLUM NUT SAUCE	75
CINNAMON-CORIANDER SAUCE	75
COCONUT HOLIDAY EGGNOG SAUCE	79
COCONUT HOT FUDGE SAUCE	79
COCONUT SAUCE I, II	80
COFFEE & RUM SAUCE	80
COFFEE LIQUEUR SAUCE I, II	81
COFFEE-VODKA SAUCE	81
CRANBERRY-APPLE SAUCE	84
CREAM 'N' BERRIES SAUCE	84
CREME ANGLAISE SAUCE	89
CREME de BANANA SAUCE	89
CREME FRAICHE SAUCE	89
CUMBERLAND SAUCE I	92
CURRANT AND RAISIN SAUCE	92
CUSTARD SAUCE I, II	95
CUSTARD SAUCE WITH ALMONDS	95
DAIQUIRI SAUCE	96
DARK CHERRY SAUCE	96
DARK CHOCOLATE SAUCE	97
DELUXE PINEAPPLE-RUM SAUCE	97
DRIED APRICOTS SAUCE	99
EGG SAUCE I	100
EGGS AND MARSALA WINE SAUCE	101
FLOWER PETALS SAUCE	104
FRENCH CHOCOLATE SAUCE	104
FRESH APRICOT SAUCE	106
FRESH BERRY SAUCE	106
FRESH MELON SAUCE	107
FRESH RASPBERRY SAUCE	107
FROZEN BERRY LIQUEURS SAUCE	108
FRUIT SAUCE	108
GINGER CREAM SAUCE	111
GINGER LIME SAUCE	112
GRAND MARNIER SAUCE	114
GRAPEFRUIT SAUCE I, II	114
GRAPES-BUTTERSCOTCH SAUCE	114
HARD SAUCE	119
HONEY BAKED APPLES WITH WALNUT SAUCE	121

HONEY VANILLA SAUCE	121
HONEY-ANISE SAUCE	121
HOT CARAMEL SAUCE	123
HOT FUDGE SAUCE I, II, III, IV	124,5
HOT PEACH SAUCE	126
IRISH MIST SAUCE	127
JIFFY BAILEYS IRISH CREAM SAUCE	138
JIFFY BANANA SAUCE	139
JIFFY BLACKBERRY CASSIS SAUCE	141
JIFFY BLUEBERRY MALLOW SAUCE	142
JIFFY BOURBON FUDGE SAUCE	143
JIFFY BOURBON SAUCE	143
JIFFY BROWN SUGAR SAUCE	143
JIFFY BUTTER SAUCE	143
JIFFY CHOCOLATE SORBET SAUCE	149
JIFFY COCONUT CHOCOLATE SAUCE	150
JIFFY COCONUT CREAM SAUCE	150
JIFFY CONFECTIONERS' GLAZE SAUCE	151
JIFFY FOAMY CREAM SAUCE	158
JIFFY HARD SAUCE	164
JIFFY HOT BUTTERED MAPLE SYRUP SAUCE	168
JIFFY HOT FUDGE SAUCE	168
JIFFY LIQUEUR DELIGHT SAUCE	173
JIFFY MAPLE BUTTER SAUCE	174
JIFFY MAPLE SYRUP SAUCE	175
JIFFY MARSHMALLOW CREME FUDGE SAUCE	175
JIFFY MASCARPONE DIPPING SAUCE	175
JIFFY MINTED MELON SAUCE	177
JIFFY MOCHA SAUCE I, II	178
JIFFY PEACH SAUCE I	182
JIFFY PEPPERMINT CREAM SAUCE	184
JIFFY PINEAPPLE GRAPEFRUIT SAUCE	186
JIFFY RASPBERRY GRAND MARNIER SAUCE	187
JIFFY RASPBERRY SAUCE	188
JIFFY RUM GLAZE SAUCE	191
JIFFY S'MORES SAUCE	192
JIFFY SEMI-SWEET CHOCOLATE GLAZE SAUCE	195
JIFFY SIMPLE SYRUP SAUCE	196
JIFFY SOUR CREAM SAUCE	198
JIFFY STRAWBERRY-LIME SAUCE	201
JIFFY SUZETTE SAUCE	202
JIFFY SWEET CREAM CHEESE SAUCE	203
JIFFY TANGERINE SAUCE	205
JIFFY TANGY BUTTER SAUCE	205
LEMON SAUCE	222
LEMON-LIME SAUCE	222
LICORICE ROOT SAUCE	223
LOW-CAL CHOCOLATE FRUIT SAUCE	226
LOW-CAL HONEY SAUCE	227
LOW-CAL RASPBERRY SAUCE I, II	229
MALTAISE SAUCE	233
MANGO SAUCE I	234
MAPLE QUICK SAUCE	236
MARMALADE LIQUEUR SAUCE	237
MARMALADE SAUCE	238
MARSHMALLOW CREAM SAUCE	238
MELBA SAUCE I, II	242
MELISSA BRANDY SAUCE	242
MELISSA VODKA SAUCE	242
MELONS MARINES SAUCE	243
MIMOSA SAUCE	244
MINT GRAPEFRUIT SAUCE	244
MIXED FRUIT FLAVORS SAUCE	246
MOCHA CREAM SAUCE	247
MOCK CREME FRAICHE SAUCE	247
ORANGE EXTRACT SAUCE	259
ORANGE JUICE SAUCE	259
ORANGE SAUCE	259
ORANGE TEQUILA SAUCE	260
ORANGE-PEACH SAUCE	261
PAPAYA, MANGO, AND MELON SAUCE	263
PARFAIT AMOUR SAUCE	264
PEACH BRANDY SAUCE	265
PEACH PRESERVES SAUCE	265
PEACH SALSA SAUCE	265
PEACH SAUCE	266
PEANUT BUTTER FUDGE SAUCE	266
PEANUT LIQUEUR SAUCE	267
PEAR BRANDY SAUCE	268
PEAR SAUCE	268
PEPPERMINT FONDUE SAUCE	270
PINEAPPLE AND BRANDY SAUCE	271
PINEAPPLE AND RUM SAUCE	271
PINEAPPLE AND VODKA SAUCE	272
PINEAPPLE LIQUEUR SAUCE	272
PINEAPPLE PLUM SAUCE	272
PINEAPPLE SAUCE	272

PLUM SAUCE II	275
PLUMS WITH SOFT CUSTARD SAUCE	275
PRALINE SAUCE	277
PUREE FRUIT SAUCE	280
RASPBERRY AND GIN SAUCE	282
RASPBERRY RHUBARB SAUCE	284
RASPBERRY SAUCE I, II, III, IV	284,5
RED BERRY SAUCE	286
RHUBARB-STRAWBERRY DESSERT SAUCE	288
RICH BUTTERSCOTCH SAUCE	290
RICH CHOCOLATE CARAMELS SAUCE	289
ROSY PLUM SAUCE	292
RUBY RASPBERRY SAUCE	293
RUM SAUCE I, II, III	294
RUM WALNUT FUDGE SAUCE	294
RUM-APRICOT SAUCE	295
RUM-RAISIN-PEACH SUNDAES SAUCE	295
SPICED PLUM PUREE SAUCE	308
STAR ANISE SAUCE	314
STRAWBERRY GLAZE SAUCE	314
STRAWBERRY SAUCE I, II	314
SWEET APPLE SAUCE	317
SWEET CHERRY SAUCE	317
TANGERINE BRANDY SAUCE	319
TANGERINE SAUCE	319
TART APPLE SAUCE	320
TEA LEAVES SAUCE	321
VANILLA BEAN SAUCE	335
VANILLA EXTRACT SAUCE	335
VANILLA SAUCE	335
VANILLA VINEGAR SAUCE	335
VELVET FUDGE SAUCE	337
VIENNESE APRICOT SAUCE	338
VODKA ORANGES SAUCE	341
WALNUT-RAISIN SAUCE	345
WHISKEY SAUCE II	346
WHITE CHOCOLATE SAUCE	347
WILD BLUEBERRY SAUCE	249
ZABAGLIONE SAUCE I, II	351

MISCELLANEOUS

	PAGE
APRICOT BUTTER SAUCE	11
APRICOT PRESERVE SAUCE	11
BROWN SUGAR SAUCE	44
BUTTERY SAUCE	47
CARAMEL SAUCE III	52
CHEESE & ONION SAUCE	60
CHEESE FONDUE SAUCE	61
CHERRY-LIME SAUCE	64
CHILE OIL SAUCE	66
CLASSIC HOLLANDAISE SAUCE	77
CONEY ISLAND SAUCE	81
CRANBERRY-ORANGE SAUCE	84
CRANBERRY-RAISIN SAUCE	84
CUMBERLAND SAUCE I	92
FRESH HERB AND TOMATO VINAIGRETTE SAUCE	107
HONEY-ANISE SAUCE	121
HOT CIDER SAUCE	124
JIFFY BROWN SUGAR SAUCE	143
JIFFY BUTTER SAUCE	143
JIFFY CHANTILLY SAUCE	147
JIFFY COLD HORSERADISH SAUCE	150
JIFFY CREOLE DOG SAUCE	155
JIFFY CRIMSON GLAZE SAUCE	155
JIFFY FRENCH MARINADE SAUCE	158
JIFFY GAME MARINADE SAUCE	160
JIFFY GARLIC MAYONNAISE SAUCE	161
JIFFY HORSERADISH CREAM SAUCE	166
JIFFY MALTAISE SAUCE I	174
JIFFY MAYONNAISE AND CHILI SAUCE	176
JIFFY MOLASSES GLAZE SAUCE	178
JIFFY MUSTARD CREAM SAUCE	178
JIFFY PLUM SAUCE	186
JIFFY PLUM SWEET AND SPICY SAUCE	187
JIFFY RATTLESNAKE CLUB BARBECUE SAUCE	188
JIFFY SAVORY ONION TOPER SAUCE	193
JIFFY TAMARIND SAUCE	204
LOW-CAL SAUCE	224
LOW-CAL CREAMY CHILI SAUCE	226
LOW-CAL GORGONZOLA SAUCE	227
LOW-CAL HONEY SAUCE	227
MOCK MAYONNAISE SAUCE	248
ONION-CHILI SAUCES	257
ORANGE BUTTER SAUCE	258
PALOISE SAUCE	263

PIZZA SAUCE 274
PLUM DESSERT SAUCE 274
RED CURRANT SAUCE 287
RED PEPPER SAUCE II 287
SALSA SAUCE I 297
SLOPPY JOES SAUCE 305
SUPREME SAUCE 315
SWEET AND SOUR ONION SAUCE 316
TOMATO SAUCE III 329
TOMATO-HORSERADISH SAUCE 332
VIETNAMESE DIPPING SAUCE 338
WHIPPED HONEY BUTTER SAUCE 346
ZESTY TOMATO SAUCE 351